A Quest for Life

A Quest for Life

AN AUTOBIOGRAPHY

Ian L. McHarg

John Wiley & Sons, Inc,

New York • Chichester • Brisbane • Toronto • Singapore

This book was developed and brought to publication by the Center for
American Places, Harrisonburg, Virginia, George F. Thompson, founder
and president, and by the School of Planning and Landscape Architecture
of Arizona State University, Frederick Steiner, professor and director.
Initial funding for this project was provided by the National Endowment for
the Arts.

This text is printed on acid-free paper.

Published by John Wiley & Sons, Inc.

This publication is designed to provide accurate and
authoritative information in regard to the subject
matter covered. It is sold with the understanding that
the publisher is not engaged in rendering legal, accounting,
or other professional services. If legal advice or other
expert assistance is required, the services of a competent
professional person should be sought.

Library of Congress Cataloging-in-Publication Data

McHarg, Ian L.
    A quest for life: an autobiography / Ian L. McHarg
       p. cm. —The Wiley series in sustainable design)
    Includes bibliographical references (p.   ) and index.
    ISBN 0-471-08628-2 (cloth: alk. paper)
    1. McHarg, Ian L. 2. Landscape architects—United States–
–Biography. 3. Regional planners—United States. 5. Regional planning–
–United States. I. Title. II. Series.
    SB470.M33A3 1996
    712'.092—dc20
    [B]   95-50489
                                                 CIP

Printed in the United States of America

10 9 8 7 6 5 4 3 2 1

Show me any civilization that believes that reality exists only because man can perceive it, that the cosmos was erected to support man on its pinnacle, that man is exclusively divine, and then I will predict the nature of his cities and its landscapes, the hot dog stands, the neon shill, the ticky-tacky houses, the sterile core, the mined and ravaged countryside. This is the image of anthropocentric man. He seeks not unity with nature but conquest, yet unity he finds, when his arrogance and ignorance are stilled and he lies dead under the greensward.

Ian L. McHarg, in *Multiply and Subdue the Earth*, 1969

Contents

Foreword

This book is a personal testament to the power and importance of sun, moon, stars, the changing seasons, seed time and harvest, clouds, rain and rivers, the oceans and the forests, the creatures and the herbs . . . essential partners to survival and with us now involved in the creation of the future.

> Excerpt from Ian McHarg's
> *Design with Nature* (1969)

This volume is also a testament. In his introduction, with the colorful candor that is one of his trademarks, Ian McHarg informs his readers straightaway that his obsession is the environment and that in his lifetime he has seen his obsession "come from oblivion to dominate the world stage." Indeed, no living American has done more to usher the gentle science of ecology into mainstream thought than the author of this autobiography. Between these covers is an account of a journey—a journey by a teacher, philosopher, designer, and activist who changed the way we view, and shape, our environment.

For over four decades the American people were mesmerized by assurances that a group of physicists, universally hailed as supermen, had "changed the world" by unlocking the secrets of the atom. In 1955, as a fledgling member of Congress, I was present at a briefing in which Dr. John von Neumann, one of the many "fathers" of the atomic bomb, declared that in the foreseeable future atomic electricity would be produced so inexpensively that it would no longer be necessary to meter it.

Implicit in this prophecy was the idea that limitless "free" energy would, in due course, eliminate the resource shortages that had long hindered human advancement. Later, when I was learning the ropes as President Kennedy's secretary of the Interior, I was taken aback by one prominent scientist's prediction that with the advent of new technologies produced by "the new science," conservation of the earth's resources would diminish as an issue of national importance.

An unstated premise of the blue-sky promises advanced by seers of the atomic and space ages was that the work of biologists, landscape architects, and designers of rural and urban environments would be consigned to peripheral roles in human affairs. Yet as this turbulent century draws to a close, some fascinating ironies command our attention. One is that many of the overblown balloons of the atomic wizards have been punctured. Another is that ecologists and students of earth stewardship have emerged from the shadows to claim center stage as practitioners of a science that provides guidelines to communities and regions concerned with creating life-giving environments.

A few years ago, I used these words to describe this turnabout: "I began to see in the 1970s that the rise of environmentalism and the faltering of Big Technology were part of a single, interacting episode of history. I also began viewing this whole matter as a competition in which ecology, a tenacious earthbound tortoise, outran a hare that called itself Big Science."

I can identify three individuals who provided the philosophical foundation for this revolution. The first prophetic figure was the father of the science of wildlife biology, Aldo Leopold. Leopold died in 1948, just as he finished a slender book, *A Sand County Almanac,* in which he set forth a land ethic for the human community. By 1960 this book was reaching a worldwide audience, and it ranks today as a work of biblical influence.

Another pioneer was the biologist Rachel Carson. With the publication of *Silent Spring* in 1962, she initiated a reorientation of scientific thought. One of her aims was to proclaim an "ecology for man" that would counterbalance the excesses spawned by atomic-age arrogance. Dr. Carson's global bestseller dramatized the adverse environmental impacts of some new technologies, and made ecological concepts part of mainstream thought, and elevated humanity's awareness of earth's laws.

Readers for this autobiography will readily see why Ian McHarg belongs in this illustrious company. He developed a holistic method of ecological planning that has made possible a crucial change in the way environmental decisions are made. McHarg's *Design with Nature* is one of the most influential books of the ecological era. And his gifts as a master teacher enabled him to "reproduce himself" by creating a small army of devoted professors and planners who are busy here and abroad carrying their own "McHarg approach" innovations to new levels of creativity.

But by what unusual metamorphosis did a Scottish youth who grew up in the countryside just beyond the "satanic mills" of Glasgow, and who then somehow survived seven brutalizing years as a paratrooper in the British army, become one of the world's leading ecologists? What were the talents that made him an exceptional teacher? How did his ideas as an ecological planner evolve? What was the source of the verve that, as a planner, turned all of his projects into memorable, challenging endeavors?

As a planner, what caused Ian to refuse to do the same type of job the same way twice, and to insist that "every project had to advance the state of the art"? Indeed, what infused him with the audacity to denounce bad developers to their faces as "Vandals"—and to once warn a Japanese official that if he didn't produce a suitable environmental plan for national development, "the only thing to do is to pull the plug and let the whole archipelago sink beneath the waves"?

This book contains answers to these questions, and more. It also provides access to the mind and faith of a remarkable human being.

STEWART L. UDALL

Santa Fe
October 1995

Acknowledgments

I wish to thank Deirdre Stevenson and Clara Lewis, who typed the main body of the manuscript. Chris Duplissa typed the many drafts of the bibliography, figure legends, and chronology, and I am most grateful for her attention to detail.

Ed Deegan of the University of Pennsylvania Library provided valuable information about specific citations in the bibliography and the inventory of projects. Graduate students Paul Langdon and Michael Skinner of Arizona State University School of Planning and Landscape Architecture assisted with checking the accuracy of several citations and identified additional works. Bill Roberts was extremely helpful providing details for the Wallace, McHarg, Roberts and Todd projects. Dennis C. McGlade, Leslie Sauer, Anne W. Spirn, Ann L. Strong, Michael G. Clarke, John Keene, Anthony Walmsley, Danilo Palazzo, E. Bruce MacDougall, Richard Westmacott, and James Bischoff also helped with specific information for several of the citations.

I also appreciate the cooperation of Wallace Roberts and Todd, in particular Bill Roberts for the use of illustrations. Others who generously contributed illustrations, permitted me to use illustrations, or executed the original illustrations include: William R. Moore of Amelia Island Plantation, Sir Peter Shepheard, A. E. Bye, Lawrence Halprin, Becky Young, Deborah Dalton, Marcel Gautheret, Conrad Hammerman, Michael Clarke, Andropogon Associates, Ltd., Hanna/Olin, Ltd., Frank Garnier, Austan S. Librach, Anthony Walmsley, Colin Franklin, Narendra Juneja, Jorge G. Sanchez-Flores, Dorothy Wurman, Lisa Carol Hardaway, Paul Hester, Felice Frankel, Michael Laurie, Carolus Hanikian, Melanie Simo, John Dixon Hunt, Kim Douglas, Ken Keltai, Lisa Miles, Jeanne Thompson, Rob Staudt, Michael Van Valkenburgh, Julia Moore Converse, Dan Cogan, Catherine Brown, Tom Hammerberg, Gina Bonsignore, Jan Price, the Frances Loeb Library of the Harvard Graduate School of Design, the Thomas Church office, *The Herald* and *Evening Times*, Scotsman Publications, Diana Webster and Margaret Wilkes of the National Library of Scotland, Minneapolis *Star Tribune*, the Bush Presidential Materials Project, and the U. S. Department of State, Bureau of Public Affairs. Jon

Berger provided a helpful review of the section on the Three Mile Island Public Health Fund.

The National Endowment for the Arts provided support for the writing of the initial manuscript for this autobiography, for which I am grateful. I also continue to have office space at the University of Pennsylvania, as a professor emeritus, which I appreciate. My administrative assistant, Lenore Sagan, was an invaluable aid for thirty years at the Penn Department of Landscape Architecture and Regional Planning. She was helpful in numerous ways, including in the writing of this book.

It also is important to recognize Dan Sayre, senior editor, Professional, Reference and Trade Group, John Wiley & Sons. Dan's abiding faith in this book means much to me. I thank Dan as well as the many talented individuals at Wiley who have assisted in the book's editing, production, promotion, and sales. In addition, I am grateful to George Thompson of the Center for American Places for his valuable editorial assistance.

Finally, I wish to acknowledge the enormous contributions made by Frederick Steiner. Fritz helped through the entire process of publishing this book—from critically reviewing the original manuscript and helping to negotiate the publishing contract to coordinating the collection of the illustrations, writing the illustration captions, compiling the bibliography, editing the chronology, and preparing the index. Fritz made fundamental and significant contributions to this book, for which I am profoundly indebted.

A Quest for Life

Introduction

Could there possibly be a more enthralling subject than nature? Consider—a cosmos so immense as to exceed language or understanding; a time scale that is an abstraction beyond imagination; origins more improbable than the most bizarre exercises of fantasy; the earth a planet so fortuitously located; a temperature range so felicitous; water, carbon, oxygen, hydrogen, and nitrogen so exquisitely opportune; the animation of matter from the ashes of stars and the emergence of life; the extraordinary, inordinately protracted process that led to the cell and thence to the multistemmed adventitious elaboration of life-forms proceeding through evolution. The beginning revealed a violent earth, a hostile atmosphere, an uninhabitable land bathed in ultraviolet light, racked by volcanism, which was slowly transformed by life to make it more habitable; first the atmosphere, reconstituted by the breaths of ancient life, then the oceans, and last the land. Then terrestrial evolution began to include, among others, the tree shrew, the tarsier, the lemur, australopithecus, and, finally, people.

Massive extinctions have occurred in times past, yet there are more species today than ever in history. It appears that the most recent threat of extinction, the atomic cataclysm, has just been averted, or at least, delayed. Now is a time to pause, to reflect, to resolve, and to act—to treasure the earth, to green the earth, to restore the earth, to heal the earth and humankind.

It may well be that future historians will view this time as a threshold in the history of the planet. Certainly the unilateral efforts of Mikhail Gorbachev, which diminished the threat of nuclear war, will be significant. The discovery of global warming, which will likely be thought of as salutary, brought the subject of our planet's environment into prominence. And perhaps as important, although this is harder to predict, the emergence of the Gaia hypothesis by James Lovelock and Lynn Margulis, the conception of the earth as a single interacting superorganism that has been actively developing and maintaining the environment, may be most significant of all. Should it be so, and should people discover a role as a benign enzyme in the biosphere, our time will be a signal threshold indeed.

One subject follows inevitably, the matter of divinity. I write this with hesitation and trepidation. I wish to make clear that my observations do not apply to any ultimate God but to lesser yet probably palpable manifestations. The Greeks had a hierarchy of greater and lesser gods; Gaia was one of these, goddess of the earth. Many of us pray, we kneel and close the eyes and appeal to a distant god. We hear our own thoughts; perhaps prayer is simply a resolve. We cannot know if the prayers are heard or answered. Perhaps, instead of turning to the skies, we should address the earth, Gaia. Indeed, if the hypothesis is true, many of the prayers we invoke involve systems apparently mediated by the earth, its processes and creatures, notably microbacteria.

For humans and all earth's creatures alike, health has to do with pathogens and aging. Flood, drought, volcanism, earthquakes, and fire are natural processes, but the most awesome are the majestic motions of the great tectonic plates. As they sunder and merge into subduction zones, volcanism results. As they move, earthquakes occur, tending toward a new equilibrium. Water heated by the sun produces vapor, which rises, cools, condenses, and precipitates, and thus—the magic cycle of water. Sunlight falls upon the leaf, the chloroplast uses this with carbon dioxide and water to fix carbon and make glucose and, so, feeds the world. Flowers are pollinated, seeds form and fall to the ground, and the rhythm of plant life continues. In the winter forest leaves cover the soil, but they are slowly ingested by microorganisms and fungi and their nutrients are returned for another manifestation. Yet these are the things that provide seed time and harvest, flowers and fruit, sunshine and rain, mountain and plain, ice caps and oceans, life and death.

These forces affect our destiny. Should we turn our backs to the sky, turn our eyes downward, sense the ground below us, view the creatures, hold the soil in the hand, raise the head, feel rain in the face, and pray? Probably not. All of these phenomena are real, tangible, palpable, and identifiable, but mute. Of course, volcanoes, great waves, and wind all produce sound but, if a language, not one we understand. Yet there clearly is a language, or languages. Plant and animal parts obviously communicate; their activities are not random but highly organized and purposeful. There must be communication. Given the extraordinary interactions between organisms in ecosystems, there must be communication at work here too. But it is mute. I suppose all language is chemical-electrical, but only animals process meaning through sound. Can we learn the mute languages of creatures? Should we be able to do so, we need not pray but communicate. Does communication make the interchange secular rather than mystical or religious? Perhaps not. Loren Eiseley once wrote a beautiful little book, *Mind as Nature*. I lunched with him soon after its publication.

I said, "Loren, you realize you have identified the sequel."

"What will it be?"

"When God became Natural."

Why not? Nature exceeds any description of the supernatural. We are made from the ashes of stars; any cell from any creature includes all of the information necessary for its replication, including the probability for mutation and evolution; and ice, improbably, floats. Were it not so there would be no life. The natural world is more magical than any scripture. I recommend we consider that godliness is natural and that the earth and its creatures are the most accessible aspects of divinity available to us. While I urge the pursuit of the matter of language between creatures and things, we need not wait for this discovery. Better act than pray. Make prayers into acts; to do this we have much to learn. We are the bullies of the earth: strong, foul, coarse, greedy, careless, indifferent to others, laying waste as we proceed, leaving wounds, welts, lesions, suppuration's on the earth body, increasingly engulfed by our own ordure, and, finally, abysmally ignorant of the way the world works, crowing our superiority over all life.

This book is a testament to one man's experience. It spans seventy years. I remember well when it began, on a trip to the countryside, Craigallion Loch. Whereas the city was dangerous and a young boy needed an adult companion, the countryside was safe, with no dangerous animals, no poisonous plants, and benign people. Nature was rich and various and to me represented freedom as it has ever since. But such richness! To realize that every event that has occurred on this planet has left its mark and is awaiting to be read, that every creature alive devolved from the same origin, is kin and contains within its genes the entire history of life, that the sounds of the Big Bang, which signaled the creation of the cosmos, are perceptible today as a celestial static, is to sense its grandeur. There is no question that can be asked that cannot be answered by the phenomenal world.

What more can be asked of the world? Loren Eiseley titled one of his works *The Unexpected Universe*. I prefer *improbable* and *miraculous*. What better concern can there be than nature? What better role than to be a modest steward? "The land is mine," saith the Lord.

There are innumerable personages, famous, notorious, extraordinary, whose lives deserve record. Not mine. I have had more than my share of ovations and awards, more acclaim than I ever expected. And there are surprises. This year I received a calendar from the University of Arizona, College of Architecture, in which the luminaries of art and architecture were depicted on their birthdays: Picasso, Cezanne, Monet, Matisse, Frank Lloyd Wright, Louis Kahn, Le Corbusier, Mies van der Rohe, and I! However, this cannot vault me into the ranks of those whose lives justify autobiography. But my subject can.

There need be no reservation about the subject of my obsession—the environment. In my lifetime it has come from oblivion to dominate the world stage. I have been a participant for two generations, and that is the reason for this work.

It has been an evolutionary process, dramatic changes over time, and now a climax and threshold. So time is crucial; chronology is the essence of autobiography, from little boy to old man.

Autobiography is a difficult discipline. The necessary repetition of "I" groans with immodesty. It is necessary to be self-effacing, self-deprecatory, at least interesting and humorous. The strictures of the implacable calendar are also constraining. The brain, however, is under no such limitation. It can fly through time, backward and forward, and savor events. I employ it continuously. There never need be a dull moment with a lively memory. In autobiography time is continuous, moving from left to right, inexorable, irreversible. Yet in the process of retrieving past events, the mustache darkens, the bald patch shrinks, wrinkles disappear.

Is life a narrative? Autobiography seeks to make it so, yet, of necessity, it is uneven, possibly untrue. It selects great peaks and chasms of events; small perturbations do not show in the long cycles. Events are smoothed and simplified in memory, footnotes and small print are expunged. Some stories may become more telling or humorous but less exact in the process.

As the narrative nears the present, there is a slowing, the cycle trembles irresolutely. Will there be more of the same, up or down, and for how long?

Despoliation of the environment is not new. Impoverishment of North Africa, the Mediterranean, and the Balkans has a long history; deforestation of Europe occurred centuries ago, in North America quite recently, and is happening in Brazil and Southeast Asia today. The capacity to destroy advanced with technology; indeed, it might be the most important generator of technological power. But our understanding has grown, as has an awareness of the implications of our actions. This is new.

As a young man, my concerns were local. I sought to ameliorate my immediate environs. Edinburgh forty miles away was distant, and England was a foreign country. The world was immense; a voyage to Australia was a lifetime commitment.

A decade later the earth shrank: the United States was but a week from Europe, there were faintly accessible continents and regions. But the environment had not been discovered as a subject of concern.

By the time I was thirty-five, the world had shrunk again. The week's voyage now took twelve hours on a Constellation, a tenfold reduction, but the environment had emerged as a subject.

Next, jet planes halved the earth's size again, but supersonic transports were halted because of their threat to the atmosphere. The environment experienced a meteoric rise in importance. Now there was an improved knowledge of natural systems, a wider understanding of the effects of human actions, and first a popular, then an institutional, response.

In the 1970s concern for the environment reached a new peak. In the 1980s a new concept emerged: not that the world is smaller or larger, but that the earth is a living being, Gaia, much more important than nuclear war, nuclear winter, world warming or cooling, inundation, desiccation, ozone attenuation, soil erosion, or the pollution of air and water. The world may be an ancient superorganism that has transformed the primeval earth and continuously made it more fit for life. It is no longer composed of people and the environment as separate entities. There is a new unity. Gaia apparently has developed self-regulating mechanisms by trial and error, which have created and maintained the oceans and the atmosphere, modified the lithosphere and the hydrosphere, in the continuous evolutionary quest for more fitting adaptation.

Moreover, the Gaia theory incorporates the quick and the dead, the live and the inert, as components of the living planet Earth—in contrast to Darwinism, in which organisms adapt to the environment, and apparently act reciprocally with it.

But the process is a circle. The mechanisms employed by Gaia apparently depend upon the activities of microorganisms. It is these that regulate and develop the macrosphere. So we can begin small and end large, or reverse, as long as we see the parts in the whole, and the whole as the product of the parts, which includes us.

Severed from the language of that genetic knowledge that has guided evolution, we must seek to equal or excel using the conscious brain. This tentative hypothesis, Gaia, can provide the basis for a new understanding of nature and ecology, a revised philosophy, an appropriate theology, a new economics based on the fundamental value of the earth's processes, workers and regulators, the costs of human interventions, and for me, a new approach to adaptation, planning, and design.

The earth and life are more than unexpected. They are improbable. No myth, no religious miracle, no human invention begins to compare with nature. Can we really accept that we and our world are made of the debris of space, that our substance existed as atmosphere, ocean, rocks, plants, animals, and other people before comprising us, and will take future forms? Do we really understand and acknowledge that life is transmitted only by life and that all creatures share the same origins, that we are kin? Do we sense that we live by the sun, that only its arrested energy fuels our system and ourselves? Do we fully appreciate the miracle of photosynthesis? Do we understand that life largely depends upon plants? The decomposers are ignored, yet they are the return stroke in the cycle of matter that ensures survival. Do we sufficiently appreciate the astonishing miracle of life, the transmutation of a few elements into responsive, self-replicating, perceptive, and self-conscious beings?

We must change our ways. The historical legacy is of people puny in the face of nature, suffering and offended by the vicissitudes of flood, drought, volcanoes, hurricanes, and pestilence, determined to bring nature to its knees and terminate these assaults. This view was and is based on ignorance; such events are not introduced to harm people. They are simply natural phenomena to which we must respond. Yet a human inferiority complex has evolved in Western man. Long oppressed, we would be merciless in victory—as we have been. Yet to pillage, mutilate, and destroy nature is only a pathway to suicide, genocide, and biocide.

"Do not kill the goose that lays the golden egg" provides a good metaphor for that spherical orb, the earth our home, richer than gold. It is here where life has evolved, where our antecedents have sought to fulfill their destinies, the arena in which we and our progeny must seek to fulfill ours. We must find another way. Our ancestors knew the path as simpler people do today, until they were corrupted by Western thought and empowered by its technology. We are of nature, we live in nature. The appropriate response is to understand its ways and behave accordingly—deferentially, perhaps better, reverentially. Once in pantheism and polytheism it was the pervasive metaphysical view; today we need a new metaphysic that employs scientific knowledge of how the world works from which appropriate, adaptive behavior becomes obvious.

My first concerns were local and small scale, next urban, then metropolitan, then for regions, nation-states, and continents. Here, now at age seventy-five, it is the entire improbable, unexpected planet that becomes the central issue for me, and for you.

My life history parallels the environmental revolution. It has been an enthralling journey. Now that the global environment has assumed primacy in the world's agenda, there is at once a triumphant conclusion and the onset of a challenging century. It has been a privilege to participate in this venture. I regret that the environment has assumed its rightful place in human concerns so late in my life, but better now than never.

This work describes my pursuit of an understanding of the environment and a search for a method of intelligent intervention. But, more, it involves sharing the evolutionary yearning of microorganisms, plants, animals, and the earth itself, a quest by and for life, a pursuit that engaged all creatures in time past and involves them all now. People alone, freed from ecological imperatives, inflict lesions on the world lifebody (and themselves) and inhibit their future. It was not always so and need not be today. We must find a better way, *a quest for life.*

Chapter 1

Growing Up in Scotland

McHarg is an odd name. I have never felt entirely comfortable with it. It requires repeated spellings for telephone operators; the difficult aspirate requires emphatic pronunciation. However, this problem is not pervasive, for there are very few of us: half a dozen in the Glasgow phone book, fewer in Edinburgh, a sprinkling in London, Toronto, Philadelphia, Dallas, Perth, Sydney, and Auckland. There are few unions, far fewer reunions. There is a psychiatrist of that name in Dundee who has traced us back to the early Middle Ages when a redheaded and recalcitrant McHarg became embroiled in English law. There was a Provost of Ayr who was an exciseman and smuggler, an Alistair who sang and another who played rugby, but we have generally evaded distinction.

The name itself is of clouded origin; books of Scottish clans fail to include it. Two apocryphal stories purport to explain the name. The first is that the Grahams split over the behavior of their lord. James Graham, duke of Montrose, espoused the Covenanter cause to rid the church of papal liturgy and hierarchy, to strengthen Parliament at the expense of royal power: the Presbyterian revolution. He was a brilliant soldier, nicknamed Bonnie Dundee. He later reversed his position, fought with Cromwell, became the scourge of the Scots and Covenanters, and earned the title of Bloody Claverhouse. He was hanged by the neck in the Mercat Cross in Edinburgh in May of 1650. The Grahams were divided in loyalty and rejection. The latter contingent, it is asserted, decided to reverse the name from Graham to Maharg and thereafter scottified it to McHarg. I have met some Mahargs, which adds substance to the legend.

The other story, my own, involves a fearsome and savage man living far from the tribe, known only by his identifiable noise—"Arg". A careless wench came within his grasp and was inseminated. What name to give the child? Well, Mac or Mc means "son of," so the child was properly called McArg—McHarg? Plausible.

Map of the United Kingdom. (U.S. Department of State, Bureau of Public Affairs, *Background Notes: United Kingdom,* October 1990.)

My lineage is from John Lennox McHarg and Harriet Bain. Her kin were weavers from Paisley and Kilbarchan; her mother's name was Love, from a family of Paisley weavers too. Her father, Baldy Bain, a powerful, redheaded man, was a carter. He drove great carts drawn by Clydesdales, transporting whiskey kegs from the distillery to bonded warehouses in Glasgow. My father's father was a carrier. He and his brother operated a business between Glasgow and Dundee. These grandfathers had nothing in common: Bain drank and fought, McHarg was a gentle abstainer. My father's mother was Mary Lennox, of a family with slightly noble connections, among them a lawyer of some note in Dublin and prosperous farmers in Ayrshire.

My father had a brilliant beginning. He achieved a prodigious record at Albert Road Academy, learned Pitman shorthand as a challenge, and quickly became the fastest shorthand writer in Scotland. He joined the Diesel Company and became a manager at twenty-three, on the basis of which he married, found a home in the suburbs outside Clydebank, and begat me. However, the Diesel Company foundered. My father then secured a similar position with the Edison Lamp Company, which duly contracted and made him superfluous. Thereafter he worked as a part-time reporter for the Associated Scottish Newspapers until he found a position as a traveling salesman for an American purveyor of business machines and equipment, Moore's Modern Methods of Buffalo, New York. This post provided no salary, only commissions, and in the Clydeside of the Depression the appetite for business machines, let alone modern business methods, could not have been discerned with a microscope. So the poor man systematically courted the businesses of Glasgow and its environs, investing his intelligence and passion into a myriad of enterprises in the hope that his vaunted equipment and machines could help his flock to survive the economic disaster. His success was such that we, as children, were forbidden to ask on his return each evening whether he had received an order. On those rare occasions when he was very successful, he brought flowers for my mother and "sweeties" for the children.

My father had planned to become a minister. Yet some circumstance in my mother's home life, never identified, caused my father to abandon this quest and marry, but he never lost his passion for the Presbyterian church. It remained his vocation throughout life. He viewed his business clients as parishioners and ministered to the family. There was always a parade of people seeking his advice and financial support. He had little to give but gave what he could. He spent his tithe on missionary causes, which provided the basis of a stamp collection for me.

From the present vantage of a world accessible by jet-powered aircraft, it is astonishing to recall the tiny dimensions of the common experience half a century ago. My parents' social world was a district of Glasgow with the Presbyterian church as its focus. In this small world my mother was a celebrated beauty, pursued by all the bright young men in her community. I met many of them later, and they acknowledged their quest with pride and congratulated John Lennox McHarg, to whom she had bestowed her hand.

Not only beautiful, my mother was beautifully dressed. She had been apprenticed to the leading couturier of Glasgow, W. R. Greive, as dress designer and dressmaker. This company imported high fashion from Paris; toiles, fabric patterns, were transmuted into dresses for rich Glaswegians by my mother, and some years later, for her daughters, Joyce and Moira, beautiful little girls, garbed to evoke astonishment and admiration.

She was gentle, warm, affectionate, and easy to laughter. The Depression was not friendly to these sentiments, but her smile, laughter, and warmth were undiminished.

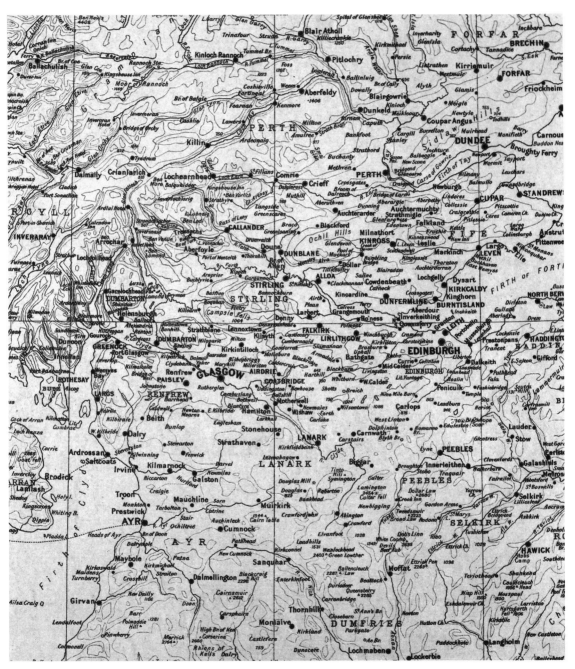

The Glasgow region, Scotland, early 1910s. (Detail from *Bartholomew's Survey Atlas of Scotland 1912*; reproduced by permission of the Trustees of the National Library of Scotland, Edinburgh.)

My mother, Harriet Bain McHarg,
and father, John Lennox McHarg,
after their marriage in 1919.

Painting, drawing, and design played an important role in my early career. Whatever talent I had was a bequest from my mother, as was my love of nature and gardening. My father never put foot to spade in his entire life. As soon as I was old enough, what gardening was done was done by me under my mother's tutelage.

Father and mother had been members of a Rambling Club. This involved a trip by tram, bus, or train to a certain destination and a hike through the countryside. It was my mother who exclaimed over the beauty of nature: bluebells in beechwood shadow, nodding foxgloves, or the prospect of a glorious landscape. This, too, I inherited from her.

The lifetime preoccupation with religious attitudes to nature within a widely religious inquiry was clearly a bequest from my father, as was an exuberant energy. I bless him for both.

At regular intervals of three years I was followed by a brother, Kenneth, and two sisters, Joyce and Moira. Immediately I acquired a sense of shared responsibility for the family. Of the many roles I performed, the most significant was to nurse my mother for a year when she suffered from rheumatic fever. I cleaned grates and set fires, went shopping and collected firewood, polished boots and shoes.

McHarg family, circa 1926.
Clockwise from left: Harriet Bain McHarg,
John Lennox McHarg, Ian, Kenneth.

McHarg family, circa 1929. *From left*: Harriet, Joyce, Kenneth, Ian, John.

The Depression hit the Clydeside hard. The great ships lay abandoned in the docks, most notably "the 534" in Brown's Shipyard, which would become the *Queen Mary.* When the shipyards closed, so did the steel mills, iron foundries, mines, and all related services. Long lines formed outside the Unemployment Bureau, the "Buroo," where the dole was dispensed. Proud men, third generation of the world's finest shipbuilders, were embarrassed to confront family or friends. The Depression was much deeper than economic. It tested the human spirit; dignity and decency were threatened. This was the world I inherited. By 1932 the Depression was complete, and it would remain so until 1938.

Life was grim, a total aura of despair and poverty. Silence seemed the only response to loss of dignity, the inability to provide. Yet our family was one of the few fortunate ones—my father was working. The living environment in the Clydeside was mean. Built almost instantaneously in the late nineteenth century, its pervasive housing type was the red sandstone four story walk-up tenement, grimy with soot, cold water in the sink, most often a toilet on the landing serving tenants above and below. Behind was a tiny plot with a washhouse and drying green poles

Urban Glasgow in the 1920s. (The Scotsman Publications, Ltd., North Bridge, Edinburgh.)

where the sodden washing hung. The hall or close was the entrance to the stairs and the boilerhouse. The corner of the block often had a pub and a tobacconist.

Block after block of tenements without street trees, or little parks, or any redemption. Children played football in the streets, headball in the close. Clumps of unemployed men hung around the street corners. In the poorest neighborhoods despair prevailed: there were children with rickets, bowlegged, in rags, dirty, seriously poor. Yet even in this pervasive urban squalor there were bright events, choir concerts, the Glasgow Art Gallery, theaters, ballet, restaurants, the circus at the Kelvin Hall, and international football matches.

The home where I was born and lived for eighteen years was a terrace house of no distinction whatsoever. The location, however, was very distinctive. It was on the threshold of town and country. Beyond the house the road petered into farm tracks, bordered by hedgerows, and entered continuous countryside. So, too, the views; looking south and east could be seen the cranes of the Clyde shipyards, great hulls of giants in the making, and more than ten miles away, smokestacks and

A Scottish landscape in the 1920s; Ben Lomond from a point near Inverbeg. I grew up close to nature, born with mountains just behind my home. They were very beautiful to me. (Picture courtesy of *The Herald* and *Evening Times*, Glasgow.)

Dixon's blazes, the night glow of steel mills. North and west were fields, the Old Kilpatrick Hills, and, beyond them, the Campsies. I was born and bred on a fulcrum with two poles, city and countryside.

Had I been born near Edinburgh, a handsome medieval and eighteenth-century city, my views might well have developed differently, but here, outside Glasgow, a beautiful and powerful landscape contrasted with a mean, ugly city, a testament to man's inhumanity to man. I found benison in nature, more repugnance and challenge than stimulus from the city. This point was reinforced by the fact that a trip to Glasgow required the accompaniment of an adult, but I had complete freedom to explore the countryside alone, even as a youngster. Nature was freedom.

I was ten when I was first permitted to go on a day walk. My friend Alistair McLean and I, each with a haversack containing lunch, each with tuppence to phone in an emergency, set off for Craigallion Loch, perhaps five miles away. Scotland had no law of trespass, so the countryside was fissured by rights-of-way. The stone walls and stiles that crossed the fields resolved the problems of travelers in gaining entry and avoiding livestock. The road to Craigallion was over Craigton Moor, bracken and heather underfoot. Blaeberries, a prostrate blueberry, were abundant; raspberries were found in the rough, blackberries in the hedgerows, and wild strawberries grew on the stone walls. An old road appeared from time to time, flanked by trees, reputedly taken by Rob Roy, the red-bearded patriot, brigand, and cattle thief. The path followed a burn, almost continuously in waterfall, where in the pools were small trout and red breasted minnows.

The loch was a surprise. I assume now that it is a glacial kettle, for it lay in a basin, its containment heightened by the encircling forest of beeches, mountain ash, and some pine and larch. Foxgloves nodded along the margin, flag iris grew by the lake, waterlilies colonized the water, dragonflies and damselflies flew, and fish jumped. It was quite silent.

In the Scotland of the Depression a number of young men decided to forgo the dole, a payment to the unemployed. Instead they walked around the country and frequently traveled abroad, offering their services whenever possible, living off the land when it was not. That meant trapping rabbits, catching trout and salmon, taking a few potatoes, cabbages, kale, and turnips, and maybe finding an egg or two.

This behavior became institutionalized. Firepots were constructed; that is, fireplaces were built, generally near a spring, with two basins—one for drinking, the other for washing pots and pans. They were adjacent to firewood and to bracken, which was used to sleep in. The other institution was the bothy, a small building used by shepherds during lambing and sometimes by farm laborers. Such structures were left open and available to hikers.

McHarg children at the beach, circa 1931. *From left*: Kenneth, Joyce, Ian.

To reach Craigallion, five miles away, meant four miles per hour, one meal out from Glasgow, going and coming. It lay on the upland route to Loch Lomond and beyond. Travelers beginning a trip and those returning would converge on Craigallion at midday. We two boys, starting later and traveling slower, succumbed to many diversions, and when we came to a firepot we found half a dozen people there. We listened enthralled to men who had traveled Scotland far and wide, picked grapes in France, but even more wondrous, had fought with the Scottish Brigade in the Spanish Civil War. They had light aluminium Bergen carriers, a primus stove, a blanket and ground sheet, a tin can and cup hanging from the pack, and big tackety boots. They were notably well spoken and, it transpired, spent much time during the inclement winters in the public libraries. One of them became quite distinguished—Sir Robert Grieve, mountain climber, nature photographer, and ultimately professor of city planning at Glasgow University.

What was a destination for a ten-year-old became a point of departure thereafter. Every year the radius extended, generally west and north. We could walk thirty miles a day comfortably, which meant sixty miles on a weekend and more during school holidays. There were fascinating destinations: the Devil's Pulpit, a long descent down a sandstone face to a turbulent river in a deep gorge, Dumgoyne, a great round hill with a cairn on top and a marvelous panoramic view. Strathblane and Blanefield, charming villages; the Pots of Gartness, where the salmon leapt. I recall catching my first salmon, standing under the waterfall, in my underpants, salmon jumping around me. As one fell, I caught it in a sandbag. The salmon was boiled in a pot with pebbles on the bottom to ensure that the skin would not stick, cooled in the Enrick, and eaten with potatoes, gooseberries, and rhubarb for dessert. A feast.

Twelve was a crucial age in Scotland, for then one takes the qualifying examination for high school and that performance determines the future. The top one or two percent from all primary schools were admitted into the A stream of the high school, which included two ancient languages or one ancient and one modern. One step down offered one modern language and science, followed by the commercial course and, finally, woodworking. A poor performance in that exam, even when caused by the flu, mumps, or measles, could not be overcome. There was no return from woodworking or commercial to Latin and Greek.

The A stream led to the ministry, law, medicine, and the civil service. Success therein was a passport to the university. At the next level were technical colleges, lower still teacher colleges, and the bottom level terminated with a Lower Leaving Certificate and entry into the labor force at fourteen or fifteen. Fortunately, I had neither flu, mumps, scarlet fever, nor any other impediment, and so entered the A stream of Clydebank High School.

School never posed a serious problem. I enjoyed learning, teachers and subjects were interesting, the system seemed just. Performance was rewarded and education was essential for growth and development. I never questioned whether this type of instruction, absorption, and examination might inhibit exploration, discovery, or originality. No, my attention was never drawn to any necessary improvement in education but to other more obvious problems. The first of these was pervasive poverty. All the men in the area were idle. What an inappropriate word—no men could have been more anxious to work. They were atrophied by the shame of unemployment. Had they not built the greatest ships in the world? Were they not the finest shipbuilders in the world? But there was no work to be had. This was a great theft of pride and self-respect. There was little left to be proud of.

The church held a very powerful role in this society. Each community focused on its church, the leader of religious life but also the center of most social activities. My father saw this church role as the center of his life. It was a matter of pride when, as quite a young man, he was made an elder. The ministers came to confer with my father, and I got to know them well.

The minister who baptized me, the Reverend William Orr Brown, was a saintly man with a white tonsure, flat hat, and pockets in his gown with sweeties for children. But it was his successor who had a profound impact on my life. In his early thirties, John M. Graham, M.A., was selected as the minister of Radnor Park Church. He was a handsome, strong, vital, energetic man, a superb speaker and married to a beautiful wife. He was much engaged by the social issues of the time, spoke forcibly as a liberal, then joined the Labour party, an extraordinary act. He subsequently became professor of systematic theology at Aberdeen University, thereafter a Labour lord provost of Aberdeen, and later still lieutenant governor of Aberdeenshire.

Through him I entered into contemporary issues—economic theory and Keynes, pacifism, the League of Nations, communism and fascism. Because of him I gave my first speech, on Kagawa, a Japanese aristocrat who became a missionary. Because of him I joined the school Literary and Debating Society and became a spokesman for the League of Nations, an opponent of fascism, and a critic of capitalism. I was ardently wooed by members of the Young Communist League, who left tracts on my doorstep daily. I rejected their overtures.

I was much preoccupied by the necessity of acquiring that degree of faith which would make it possible to be confirmed and take communion. I watched carefully whether there was growing in me a greater surety about Christ and God. I sought what I would then have described as a religious experience. I pressed to find this in church. I read the Bible, learned great lumps by heart, listened carefully to sermons. These appealed to my brain. I had no doubt of the merits of the ethics taught; the congregation, young and old, were admirable people, distinctively so. In general, they were exemplary. But what of spirituality? And that I found, but not in church, not in the company of men or women, but in the mountains and by the sea. Again and again in lovely landscapes, great hovering clouds, shafts of sunlight falling on the land, granite outcrops, headlands pointing into the sea, violent waves crashing on rocky cliffs, I felt such exaltation, a sublime experience. Here, indeed, was God's grandeur. Here God was immanent. So my predicament was clear. God's presence was palpable, or so it seemed, in nature, but elusive in church. Experiencing this paradox at sixteen, I sought to find support in the Bible. "The lilies of the field, how they grow," "the feather on the wings of a sparrow," and other passages were little help but the first chapter of Genesis was a mortal blow. I felt as Gerard Manley Hopkins did about God's grandeur, but the Creation story in Genesis provided no support for this view; indeed, it was total rejection. I had, it appeared, embraced the heresy of pantheism.

"God made man in his own image, made he him." Did that mean that the acts of man to man had a moral content, were sacramental? But what then of the acts of man to nature; were these only secular? Next, I considered, "Ye shall have dominion . . . over all life." This was not my instinctive reaction. Did I wish to exert dominion over golden eagles, salmon, trout, deer, hedgehogs? No indeed. But worse was to come. "Ye shall multiply and subdue the earth." *Multiply.* To reproduce seemed reasonable, but to subjugate was surely only a terrible magnification of dominion, murder, rape, and pillage. I rejected this categorically.

So there I was, now sixteen, looking for a career, troubled by the poverty and meanness of Glasgow and its surroundings and the failure of society represented by the Depression, alert to the problems of the city and to the threats of fascism and communism, pathetically hopeful for the League of Nations—a committed Christian who had discovered that the most powerful emotions were invoked by wild nature and rejected by his faith.

I decided to accept Christian injunctions for moral behavior toward humans but to reserve my opinion on the appropriate attitude to nature. For the moment I would conclude that nature was God's creation and that deference and gratitude would be an appropriate posture.

At sixteen, I was six foot, two and a half inches, as tall as I would get, and I was irked by being a dependent. I was doing well at high school. I liked academic courses, but I also liked drawing and painting. I won prizes for my drawings. I was the only student in my class aspiring to a Higher Leaving Certificate in Latin and art. I had for years won children's painting competitions and from the age of fourteen had spent my Saturday mornings in the Glasgow Art Gallery, where I would rent a stool and a board, buy sheets of drawing paper, and draw pencil sketches of the Head of a Faun, Laocoon, and the like. I also climbed from the sculpture gallery to the salons above and gazed painfully at Rubens and Renoir and their acres of breasts.

Each day I traveled by train and by bus from Radnor Park to Glasgow. The single story tram I chose to take was a rarity in the British world of double decker tramcars (this was designed to pass over a canal and under a low railway bridge). It stopped in Clydebank near the public library. I would collect books en route and often returned them the same day. My favorite author in 1936 was Percy F. Westerman, a prolific author whose subject was constant: the adventures of boys— merchant marine cadets—serving on tramp steamers, traversing the globe and visiting marvelous faraway places. I would refer to those places in a book I owned, a birthday present, *The Book of the British Empire.* I was enthralled by these stories and dreamed of fulfilling my own life in such a way. I decided to act.

McHarg children, 1936. *From left*:
Moira, Kenneth, Ian (age 16), Joyce.

I learned that the Cunard Line was to hold examinations for prospective cadets. I applied and was selected for interview and examination. I passed both and was given information on the clothes I would need for the role: work clothes, dress clothes, tropical dress, sou'westers, and more. I was also advised of tailors who made such uniforms. I then went to see my father's insurance agent, who administered an annuity in my name designed to pay for my university education. He agreed that this money might well be used for the education of a merchant marine cadet. He telephoned the tailor to authorize my purchase of uniforms, and I took to my father the document that would authorize my assumption of the role of Cunard Line cadet officer. He refused categorically. "You will complete high school. You will thereafter enter Glasgow University." He canceled the tailor's order. I cannot remember the punishment. It certainly involved pocket money and mobility. I would not go down to sea in ships.

So I returned to my high school studies but remained irked by dependence. My father was exhausted by his efforts, and here was I, able-bodied, a mere dependent. What could I do? The City of Glasgow had established a "Careers Council," where young people could obtain advice on prospective careers. I made an appointment. The official was John Mitchell. I well remember his name because I owe him so much. He reviewed my school report cards and observed my record in drawing competitions. He drew from me descriptions of the walking trips in which I engaged every summer, farther and farther from Clydeside into the lochs and mountains of western Scotland. Then he said, "Have you ever considered landscape architecture?" I had never heard of it. "I have a friend who is a landscape architect," he said. "His name is Donald Wintersgill. I will arrange to have you meet him."

Donald Wintersgill, a Yorkshireman, was trained as an architect but had gravitated into landscape architecture. He had designed large and beautiful estates for the Rothschilds in France and Canada. He was an École des Beaux Arts designer. The Renaissance was his major repertoire but not his only one. He had been involved in some pecadillo in a great house and demoted to Scotland to run a landscape design and construction operation for the largest grain salesman and nurseryman in Scotland, Austin & McAslan Ltd., Glasgow.

He was small and round, with a red face and dimpled nose that spoke of whiskey. The owner of Austin & McAslan, one H. Stewart Patton, also owned Johnny Walker. He kept two full bottles in his office, and with his business associates, managed to empty them daily. Donald Wintersgill helped.

Mr. Wintersgill told me that the best introduction to the profession would be to accompany him on a trip to a job. Could I receive my parent's consent to travel with him to Glenlivet?

We drove to Perthshire where we met the client, Captain Grant, owner of the Glenlivet Distillery. He also owned an enormous tract of Perthshire, much of it barren, bracken and heather. He had a large labor force that worked sporadically in growing the grain and distilling the whiskey and spent much time drinking it. What he had in mind was employing this labor force more productively to improve his place. He needed a plan.

We proceeded to an eminence where we could see most of the property. Wintersgill was quite a sight. He wore an Inverness cape, a deerstalker hat, a bow tie and spats; around his neck hung a Rolleiflex camera and Zeiss-Ikon binoculars. He held a shooting stick.

He viewed the great panorama and, raising his stick, made a great arc of 180 degrees from west to east and pronounced: "This should be planted to forest . . . but these," pointing to the heather and russet bracken foothills, "should be left alone. Now the bottom of the valley should have a loch, so let us build a dam there. Your tenants are spread about; why don't you build a village, near the dam, overlooking the loch, protected by the high grounds and the forest from north winds, flat, facing due south? There is a good place, warmed by the sun, protected from the cold winds, a pretty view."

My mouth dropped open. Here was a man covering land in forests to the horizon, making dams, lakes, a village. "Could I do this for a living?" I asked.

"Indeed, yes, if you become my apprentice. I will direct your education, and in four or more years you will be a landscape architect."

That moment, that event crystallized my resolve. I would become a landscape architect.

I became an apprentice to Donald Wintersgill. I withdrew from Clydebank High School and was admitted as a special student to the Glasgow College of Art and the West of Scotland Agricultural College. I, therefore, never completed high school, but then I didn't complete college either. This, along with the fact that I do not possess a Ph.D., has provided many nightmares when I am required to complete the necessary academic hurdles.

Wintersgill designed a training schedule that alternated design and administration with realization and supervision. For the first, I dressed in my Sunday suit, took the train with stockbrokers to Glasgow, and worked in the head office. I plotted surveys, did designs and watercolor plans, developed estimates and discussed matters with clients. After three months the role changed. I traveled to the firm's nursery where I undertook surveys, dispatched materials and workmen to projects, and supervised construction. Each evening I studied at either the college of art or the agricultural college.

For symmetry, Wintersgill's training program needed another apprentice. He was George Ferguson, my senior, a wonderful but difficult colleague. George was of modest size, with a head of red hair and a volatile temperament. He was a paragon. He played First Division football for Queen Park, he was a Scottish diving champion, and a steward at Crosmyloof ice skating rink, played competition tennis and the piano, and performed a remarkable imitation of the Mills Brothers. I could do none of these things. I was tall, skinny, awkward, a hobbledehoy. The arrangement that ensured that I would not be where he was much diminished the embarrassment of comparison and, undistracted by the necessity of being famous, accomplished, and in demand, I was able to devote all of my passion, energy, and intelligence to the work at hand, which Wintersgill appreciated. I would have had it otherwise.

Wintersgill drove a little Ford 8. He smoked a pipe, but little tobacco, for his attempts to light his pipe while driving were almost totally ineffectual. But not his conversation. He had a wealth of information on the Scots aristocracy, their idiosyncracies, preferences, and the skills of their staff gardeners. He was also knowledgeable of geography, soils, plants, and construction materials and methods. He was thoughtful, informative, observant, kindly, and tolerant. He used these occasions to interrogate me on my studies. He also taught me to drive.

The design process involved a vernacular vocabulary. There were many set pieces: lawn, herbaceous border, rose garden, wildflower garden, tennis court, swimming pool. Within each there was a range in elaboration, from geometric panels in a lawn planted with hybrid tea or polyantha roses to sunken gardens with beds set in rectangular York sandstone paving surrounding a fountain, sundial, or birdbath. Lawns could be rough turf or sea-washed Solway agrostis maritima, and rock gardens ranged from modest banks using native stone to an elaborate system of outcrops, ledges with pools, and waterfalls using pitted and picturesque Westmorland limestone. Herbaceous borders could be one to three yards wide and infinitely long. And each had a price.

While most of the projects were gardens, many involved large estates, others large-scale sports facilities, and, later, camouflage of airports, notably Biggin Hill, famous during the Battle of Britain. But never during my apprenticeship did Wintersgill have as encompassing a challenge as that presented by Captain Grant at Glenlivet, which occasioned the event that persuaded me to become a landscape architect.

The one large benefit from the hours of travel each day was that I could read. Happily, my transfer from tram to bus occurred near the Clydebank Public Library, and so I could withdraw books easily. I often read two books a day. My choices were catholic, influenced in part by my father's subscription to *Bookman*, a splendid literary journal. I read Joyce, Huxley, Lawrence, and Waugh, Bernard Shaw, H.G. Wells, G. K. Chesterton, and Sacheverill Sitwell, but also Conan Doyle, Compton McKenzie, Eric Linklater, A. J. Cronin, Edgar Wallace, and Agatha Christie. Interspersed were texts on botany, horticulture and soils, and a good deal of political commentary.

In the last year before the war, the minister of our church, the Reverend John M. Graham, decided that members of the Young Men's Guild should give short talks at the morning service. I recall them as extraordinarily memorable. Most addressed contemporary problems—poverty, unemployment, nazism, fascism, communism, pacifism, and more. I found my own subject in a correspondence engendered by my father's contributions to foreign missions. I learned, from correspondence by Presbyterian missionaries requesting financial assistance, of a Japanese aristocrat, Kagawa, who had determined to be a Presbyterian missionary in the slums of Kobe. He was thoroughly unsuccessful. He resolved to study medicine and return as a medical missionary, at which he was a great success. In Scotland at that time both David Livingstone and Mary Slessor, medical missionary and nurse, were widely admired by the Scottish ministry. I found the story of Kagawa, another medical missionary, moving and resolved to present it. I have never since written a speech as carefully, nor rehearsed it as often. My mother tested me dozens of times until I was word perfect. I recall walking to the platform on which the choir was arrayed, below the pulpit, beside the organ. I placed my notes on the golden oak surface of the organ. The organist and choirmaster, an impressive man with the impressive name of H. Broughton Shatford, looked at me reassuringly, but over his head I could also see the apprehension on the faces of my mother and father. I began, faltered, pushed my shaking knee against the organ, and continued without error. There was, of course, no applause, but I could sense that there was general approval of the subject, the message, and the delivery. My speaking career had begun.

As a copy boy for Associated Scottish Newspapers, my Saturday afternoon work, I received a press badge. This authorized me to report incidents, mostly accidents, formalized my rate, which was one shilling and sixpence (roughly twenty cents) per printed line, and ensured payment. The first occasion I used my badge was when a window washer fell off his ladder and was injured. I reported the incident at length. One of the most successful of the many accidents I reported involved me as a subject. One summer, while passing along Ayr harbor, I heard a scream. A girl was drowning. There were Clyde steamers moored, and people thronging the dock; there were many witnesses. I dived in and swam to the girl's rescue, pulled her up an iron ladder, employed artificial respiration, and then retired to write my report. This included a description of the event, names and addresses of observers, their comments, time of day, weather, names of the steamers (one, I recall, was *The Marchioness of Bredalbane*). I wrote the story modestly but fully and was gratifyingly rewarded. From many such reports I came to note that an acute observation, a happy turn of phrase, an unlikely but appropriate metaphor, would escape the blue and parsimonious pencil of the editor. Being paid by the line, this mattered.

Those years, from sixteen to nineteen, cannot be revisited without consideration of the most compelling urge of all—sex. My physiological capability was evident quite early. I once sought to enhance my manliness by inducing the growth of my meager chest hair. The prevailing schoolboy wisdom was that this could be accelerated by an application of wagon grease, tallow, from the brake boxes of railway wagons. It had no effect save on underpants and singlet. But my instinct was strong.

I had a powerful romantic spirit. Young Lochinvar was my model. "Oh, young Lochinvar is come out of the West, through all the wide border his steed was the best." Rescuing beautiful maidens was gallant. My knowledge of love and romance was derived from novels. My direct experience was a father and mother who held hands, hugged, and kissed, and I speculated about babies. My father did not help. When I was fourteen he gave me a book that contained photographs of the Venus de Milo and a Greek god, from which the visible sexual organs could be discerned. I was struck by the modest equipment of the Greek male but obtained no useful instruction on the sex act. My French teacher for one year, a young Frenchman, Mr. Claude Mourmoutonet, brought copies of *La Vie Parisienne* to class, thereby employing our lascivious instincts to better learn French. There were "dirty" poems which passed hand to hand, but my knowledge was modest. The official line was clear: adultery was a massive sin, promiscuity was as bad, and even coveting a neighbor's wife was serious. Virgin marriage for both men and women was the moral requirement.

How to accommodate my persistent lust to these constraints? The answer was *don't* and the rationale was fear—fear of censure by a society in which children out of wedlock were extremely rare and deemed to be a total social disgrace. This view was held by boys and girls alike. In my high school one girl was assumed to have "done it." Her mother was a midwife who allegedly performed abortions. Presumably therein lay her protection. No girl during my time at high school became pregnant, nor did I hear of anyone who had. What continence! Still I dreamed of nymphomaniacs who had the power of moral absolution. But actual experience could not have been more distant.

At sixteen I went to my first high school dance. I had a new tailored suit with long trousers. There I met a girl in the parallel class for girls, Winnie Moffatt. She was of middle size, with straight brown hair, a comely figure, beautiful legs, and a fantastic smile with a dimple. Her father was a head clerk with John Brown's Shipyard. They lived several miles on the opposite side of the high school from my home. So the offer to walk her home was a five-mile commitment, which I gladly made.

For a year the closest encounter was to hold her hand. Then I decided to be bold. I had accumulated savings from my job as copy boy. I planned an adventure. We would skip Latin class for an afternoon, take the bus to Glasgow, see *A Midsummer Night's Dream* with James Cagney, and then go to what I at the time believed was the fanciest restaurant in Glasgow, Rogano's, and have a meal.

I confided my plan to my Uncle George, my father's younger brother, who was the most worldly of my relatives. He told me that I could be embarrassed by the mâitre d' hôtel but that, as I came under his supercilious gaze, I should imagine him in shirt-sleeves wearing braces (that is, suspenders), frying sausages over a gas ring in a Glasgow tenement. Thus seen, his power of humiliation would be dispelled. As indeed it was. We both had curried shrimp, a great novelty, and we held hands returning on the bus.

In reciprocity I was invited to her home, which was very grand in comparison to mine. Indeed, they had a greenhouse, to which I was invited, to see her moth cocoons. I realized that this was a serious gesture, held her in my arms, and kissed her. And that is as far as that romance went.

During World War II we communicated sporadically. I never really expected to survive the war, and that may well account for the weak pursuit. On my disembarkation leave in 1945, I met her and found that she had married a dentist.

My view was innocent, naive—perhaps I was a boy-man—but my view respected women and girls; sex was deemed to be a consummation between those who loved; marriage was believed to mean "until death do ye part"; babies were sought, welcomed, and cherished. I do not truly believe in a wonderful past, but in this one respect moral decisions were easier for me than for my sons.

From sex to jazz is but a step. It entered my life when I was sixteen or so. It began with a visit to Woolworth, where I heard a most extraordinary vital, wild, lyrical, exuberant music. It was Louis Armstrong playing "West End Blues." I bought the record, but I had to find a gramophone. My Uncle George owned one. He had joined the Cameronians in 1916 at the age of sixteen, and had been terribly wounded with sixteen bullets in his body, captured, whipped as a recalcitrant prisoner of war, and had salt rubbed in his wounds; he lost his mind. He returned to a troublesome future that included brief but terrifying eruptions of violent behavior. Sometimes only a few months, sometimes a decade, elapsed between these episodes. My father was his protector. Whenever my uncle felt an episode was imminent, he would phone my father who would have him admitted to Gartnavel Asylum. He would have his paroxysm in a padded cell and quickly return to normalcy. However, official practice required him to languish in the company of the permanently bereft. Clearly, he could only be self-employed, so my father initiated a number of ventures. One was a mobile lending library, another involved the sale of records, for which he had a gramophone.

Uncle George visited us weekly, bringing his gramophone. I bought more records and soon found that other boys were doing so too. We were confronting serious difficulties. What were vocalists saying? This was a new language. We needed a glossary of terms. What was a hot dog, jellyroll, a monkey woman, a barrel house, a bun (in the American sense), barbecue, and "viper mad"? What, indeed, was a flat-foot floogie with a floy floy? We also needed to learn the geography of jazz. Chicago, Memphis, and New Orleans presented no difficulty, but where were

Bourbon Street, Canal Street, Beale Street, 18th and 19th on Chestnut Street, and Summit Ridge Drive? As compelling was the identification of performers. Record labels initially identified only the melody and the bandleader. Red Nichols and His Five Pennies, Miff Mole and his Little Molers, Fletcher Henderson, Sidney Bechet. Who were these musicians? Some were easy—Armstrong's tone and delivery sounded like rending sailcloth, Sidney Bechet's lyrical vibrato on soprano was unique, the gravel voice of Bessie Smith, Red Norvo's xylophone, Johnny Hodges' gliding alto were all unmistakable. It took more work to distinguish Coleman Hawkins from Ben Webster and Lester Young or identify Frankie Newton, Frankie Trumbauer, Jimmie McPartland, and Jack Teagarden, but we persevered. Soon there were mimeographed glossaries, lists of personnel on records, record reviews, and we organized ourselves to create the Jazz Sociological Society of Scotland.

Jazz and alcohol have a historical affinity. In my boyhood jazz was not understood. It is incredible that lyrics of barrelhouses, drugs, and copulation sounded in my father's ears without his comment. But whiskey was well known.

Alcohol presented a powerful moral choice. Scots and whiskey were inextricably linked, and the union brought obvious pleasure to many and shame to others. The consequences of excess were most evident. When I was a boy, going to Glasgow Central Station on a Saturday night, returning home from grandparents, the problem was to negotiate recumbent drunks who had paused on their erratic path to the train. They had acceded to Harry Lauder's song, "When I get a couple of drinks on a Saturday, Glesca' belongs to me." My father would rebuke them, audibly, forcibly, censoriously: "You are a shame to Scotland and manhood. Look at yourself lying in the gutter!"

But for every drunk, for every modest imbiber, there was a Rechabite, a total abstainer, who fought alcohol with religious fervor. These enthusiasts gave slide shows of addled livers, hungry waifs, mistreated wives, poverty induced by drink. Such was my family, total abstainers all; the reprobate, my maternal grandfather, had succumbed reluctantly to virtue in his later years. He was the exception that proved the rule. Scotland was divided almost equally between those who drank too much and those who drank not at all.

Summer brought a most welcome release. Evening classes terminated, Saturday morning's drawing classes were suspended, and with the end of the football season the need for copy boys shrank, so I had evenings and, father and church permitting, weekends. This allowed for limitless exploration of the countryside, always north and west, toward the Highlands and the islands.

There was a particular annual summer event, the Highland Show. This involved exhibits and competitions of cattle, horses, sheep, and other farm animals, equipment, grains, and seeds. There was always a garden exhibit, and each year Austin & McAslan created the dominant entry, which consisted of a rock and water garden. The ground was raised at the back, on which were planted large conifers with an edge of flowering trees and shrubs. The ground fell in rough stony terraces made with Westmorland limestone. From a spring, water fell into a pool, over waterfalls into small streams, and thence to a large pool. The edges were framed with flowering trees and shrubs between rocks, and below these were planted alpine jewels—gentians, saxifrages, sedum, sempervivum, helianthenium, thrift, and many more. Around the pool were varieties of primula, iris, and myrtensia.

The first of these events in which I participated was in Alloa in 1937, the second in Dumfries, and the last in Edinburgh, opened by the duchess of Gloucester. My role escalated from observer to participant and, finally, designer. While the design was based on plans and perspectives, the actual realization was much affected by the particular forms of trees, shrubs, rocks, and plants. It was an exercise in composition—weight, color, texture, balance—and, it transpired, I had a gift, or so it was thought at the time. This occasion gave me the opportunity to leave home and was my first release from the chores of cleaning out fireplaces, making fires, polishing boots and shoes, going for messages, looking after brother and sisters, and the other required household tasks. It was a wonder of freedom.

The culminating experience of my prewar career was the design and execution of the Empire Exhibition in Bellahouston Park, Glasgow, in 1938. Wintersgill had been selected as the landscape architect to design and construct all landscape works. I was his staff. However, his task was enormous. He had to arrange for the planting of all the millions of flowering bedding plants, many forced, plus all of the other materials. He had to execute a myriad of subcontracts, which meant that I was entrusted with large responsibilities for which I was not adequately trained. I was too young and inexperienced for a project of such scale. Imagine the resources allocated to World Fairs today in comparison.

The site was an existing city park, built in the nineteenth century on the model of the eighteenth-century English landscape tradition. It consisted of wooded uplands, and valleys in lawn, with copses and free-standing trees, and a curvilinear system of walks.

On this site Wintersgill superimposed a Renaissance design, a bilaterally symmetrical axial system with a main and subsidiary axes. Flanking these were the major pavilions, all lined with Japanese flowering cherry trees. At axial intersections were fountains, statues, and large flower beds. The whole formal system was to be planted with seasonal bedding plants. For the opening, daffodils, narcissi, tulips, crocus, and myositis would dominate, with naturalistic plantings of daffodils in the lawns.

When the design was complete and tasks had been distributed to the work force, my next job was to prepare the press release, 5,000 words of the most purple prose I have ever penned. This done, I was pressed into the labor force. Bad weather had hindered the work; it was behind schedule. More employees were hired, then evening and weekend work added, time and a half and double time. Next, lights were installed so that work could proceed twenty-four hours a day. I laid turf, planted tulips, daffodils, crocus, flowering cherries, and made, in my terms, a fortune. Just when it appeared that all would be ready for their royal majesties, King George VI and Queen Elizabeth, there was a killing frost.

All the beautiful flowers crumpled and browned. Wintersgill was galvanized into a frantic search for their replacement from all over the kingdom. Railroad wagons and lorries converged and there was a frenzy of activity. No one went home, people slept where they fell, and the core of the exhibit was replanted for the opening, but king and queen had to be shepherded carefully lest they should see the chaos of incompletion.

There was a magnificent parade, perhaps the last great demonstration of the British Empire, with troops from New Zealand, Australia, Canada, Nigeria, Bechuanaland, British West Indies, India, South Africa, and Fiji, not to mention the proud Scots Regiments. When the royal entourage left there was music and dancing in the streets, a carefree and enchanting event not to occur in these lands until the Festival of Britain after the war, but then, of course, there was little Empire to celebrate, only a tattered island.

My career was beginning to take form, apprentice landscape architect, incipient speaker and writer, and professional liberal, resolved to manage and design the environment for human health and well-being. But, this career would be delayed. I had to embark on another—as a soldier.

This was a difficult decision. My Christian instruction had emphasized turning the other cheek (the meek shall inherit the earth), compassion, and forgiveness. The wars of the Old Testament, smiting the Philistines, had not evoked admiration; they seemed more territorial than moral. I had chosen in favor of faith, hope, and charity, the greatest of these, of course, being charity. There was also the contemporary example of Mahatma Gandhi and his exhortation to nonviolence. I read about the case of the then-prominent Episcopalian pacifist, the Reverend Shepard, and leaned to his cause.

But in the summer of 1938 I went to a Boys Brigade summer camp at Bridge of Weir in the Renfrewshire Hills, south of the Clyde. The issues of war, pacifism,

Sapper Ian L. McHarg, summer 1940.

and military action were crucial to most of the members. The majority were between sixteen and nineteen, ripe for service. The progeny following World War I were of age for another eruption. John Graham, the minister, decided that this issue required confrontation, and so he and an elder, John McPherson, attended the camp and led evening campfire discussions on pacifism versus military service. The barbarity of Mussolini's son bombing Ethiopian natives, the insolent arrogance of Hitler, and the futility of appeasement were discussed. My opinion was shifting.

I sought an interview with the Territorial Army, the reserves. I was advised that, as a landscape architect, I should apply to the Royal Engineers, which I did. I thus became 2079085 Sapper Ian L. McHarg, 243d Field Park Company, R.E., Fifty-second Scottish Lowland Division based in Rutherglen, Glasgow.

A year later on September 2, 1939, when war was declared, I was a "trained soldier"; that is, I had learned foot and arms drill and had passed the range test. I was eighteen years and nine months old when, on vacation in Douglas, the Isle of Man, I received a telegram intimating that war had been declared, mobilizing me into the regular army, and instructing me to report to barracks immediately.

Chapter 2

Soldier, 1939–1946

The decision to join the army was voluntary. I had anticipated the war and sought to be a trained soldier when it was declared. I also assumed that this would not be a short-term engagement and that I was embarking on a career. It then became necessary to learn to become a good soldier. When you join the services you concede freedom and autonomy and enter a despotic order. In times of emergency this loss of freedom is a necessary sacrifice. The person is submerged, numbered, and dressed in uniform. Yet even within a despotism there is an urge to express and develop. How to achieve this? Had I finished college I would have entered Officer Cadet Training, but I was now too young and unqualified. I must first serve in the ranks. Identification as a person and promotion was now much more difficult, particularly in my circumstance where I was the youngest in the company and more than half the troops had been regular soldiers and had at least seven years of service.

I decided on a strategy that included, first, learning the tools of the trade: next, volunteering for assignments; and, last and most important, fighting. The most admired accomplishments were superior military appearance and skill in foot and arm drill. It required strenuous work to polish and burnish buckles, buttons, badges, and boots. It was also necessary to apply a colored cake, blanco, to all equipment (to provide uniform color and texture), to have well-pressed tunic and trousers and a polished rifle. The key to distinction in arms drill lay in mastering the first move of "Slope Arms," wherein the rifle would appear to leap spontaneously from the ground to a vertical position ten inches above. I hired a veteran sergeant to teach me, practiced the move interminably, and mastered it. Now with beautiful equipment, accomplished in drill, I was selected for a ceremonial honor guard. I felt certain that if I could get out of the ruck, I could advance, but the first step, from obscurity to person, from sapper to lance corporal, would be the hardest.

The next stratagem was to volunteer. During morning inspections volunteers were always sought, and when none offered they were selected. Volunteering took me from the ranks of two hundred and fifty men and placed me in a smaller group, or, sometimes, in a solo position. One early assignment involved the medical officer, Colonel Gunn, a regular army doctor. I volunteered to be his assistant, and when I reported for duty, he described the task. It was the fashion at that time for working-class Scotsmen to wear blue serge suits with wide trouser bottoms and pointed patent leather shoes. The points caused the toes to overlap—the little toe on the second and so on. This condition must be cured; soldiers had to march long distances and carry heavy loads. The remedy involved large galvanized basins, set up in a gymnasium, filled with boiling water to which had been added salicylic acid (aspirin). The troops sat with their feet in the water for hours; boiling water was added constantly. As their callouses began to slough off, I had to treat each soldier. I had secateurs rather than nail scissors, spatulas, tape, and cotton wool. Callouses were removed, each corn extracted like a cork from a bottle, nails trimmed with special attention to ingrowing toenails, padded spatulas were inserted between toes, with cotton wool, and the whole foot taped. It worked.

The last stratagem involved survival. Fighting was common, anyone identified as weak would be victimized. I was a likely candidate, I was young, tall, skinny, had a distinctive accent, and, worst of all, was identified as an art student. I had been tested early. When mobilized, I had come from a vacation for which I had purchased blue silk, cossack-necked pajamas in hopes of a romantic encounter. It did not happen. When I reported I was assigned to a billet in Thistle Hall, the home of Rechabites (people devoted to temperance) in Rutherglen. I arrived late in the evening to find no one there.

Upon mobilization each soldier had received a bounty of five pounds, more than most had ever had in their hands at one time in their lives. They took to the pubs to drink it. So it was in the middle of the night that I awoke to see a dozen drunken soldiers looming above me, ridiculing the art student. They had pulled off my greatcoat and exposed my pajamas and they were planning to tear them off. There was a rifle rack in the room. I rose, grabbed a rifle, held it by the muzzle and swung it. Men went down like ninepins. Several needed medical attention. I had achieved a little regard, but vigilance was essential. I quickly learned that the best method of defense is attack. Encounters usually began with words, then pushing, shoving, and, finally, punching. I found that at the first abuse the most effective response was to punch immediately, kick, or, best of all, use the "heid"—grab the tunic neck, twist and butt the head toward the opponent's face. But this was not enough. The majority were older, tougher, and stronger than I was, so I needed an ally. Sam Forrest was a big man, a carpenter from Wick. He was a great fighter. Moreover, he needed me; he wanted tutoring, he was determined to be promoted. Sam wished to study the *Manual of Military Engineering, Volume II*. I consented to tutor him if we could have an agreement. Anyone who attacked either would have to deal with both. It worked very well. The only sour note was that Sam liked to drink, and when he drank too much he fought. I did not drink, but for two years, 1939 and 1940, I was summoned to pubs to engage in fights for Sam Forrest's survival.

In 1939 in Edinburgh there was an invitation tournament for the Scottish novice ballroom dancing championship. I enrolled. At that time dancing skill in young ladies produced a slightly steatopygous aspect, a conspicuous rear. So I regarded the dancers, selected one, appropriately endowed, and asked if she would be my partner. She was an evacuee from London, a poet; her name was Angela Black. Through foxtrot, slow foxtrot, tango, and waltz, the judges would move among the numbered dancers. A touch on the shoulder meant dismissal. We survived many rounds to reach the semifinal, at which time I was dispatched to Tregantle in the south of England for Army gas training, never to conclude the competition.

Army Gas School was my first encounter with the regular army. My unit was a workhorse; we were working engineers. My arrival at Tregantle was traumatic. I entered the guardroom and found it to be dominated by a regimental sergeant major from the Scots Guards. He was majestic and impeccable. I was rumpled and dirty after a twenty-seven-hour train journey. I presented my papers only to find that my company was in error. The course was for sergeants, and I was only a lance corporal. I could neither sleep nor eat with sergeants. I must live with the cooks. Moreover, my dress and bearing did not reach the standards of the regular army. I would have compulsory remedial drill each morning at six o'clock. In six weeks I would not only look like a guardsman, I would also be a gas instructor. "On the command, 'Gas', take the facepiece at the valve holder..."

When I returned to my unit I was viewed with astonishment. I had a new tunic, trousers, burnished boots, equipment, and Guards bearing and foot drill. I was immediately promoted to corporal and dispatched for more instruction to the Small Arms Schools at Hythe, near Reading. Here again was ceremony, discipline, and order, but not so on the Continent where British troops were in disarray. When I rejoined my unit it was in Somerset, near Crewkerne, where we mined an underground headquarters. This seemed ominous to us. Was the War Office contemplating warfare in Britain? From Somerset we traveled to Aldershot, where we became entangled with the evacuees from Dunkirk. Thence we entrained to Portsmouth to sail to St. Malo. The Fifty-second Lowland Scottish Division was the

Second British Expeditionary Force. We landed to ecstatic greetings, marched toward Paris, halted, waited, turned around, marched back to St. Malo, embarked, and returned to Portsmouth. At that time we were the only fully armed division in Britain, and so we were dispatched to guard the coast in East Anglia–King's Lynn, Thetford, Diss, and Massingham. Each man with a rifle, bayonet, and five bullets—the first line of defense against invasion!

Thank God no invasion occurred. We were withdrawn and sent to Inverary in Scotland, where a small contingent was assigned to Second Commando, the Green Berets. Here we participated in amphibious exercises. We would embark on HM Troopship *Ettrick*, go out to sea, then approach the simulated objective, generally on the shore of Loch Sunart. We climbed down nets to whalers and proceeded ashore. There were as yet no amphibious vessels. One day, I manned a Bangalore Torpedo, a ten-foot length of cast iron pipe stuffed with explosives. My task was to insert this into the enormous barbed wire fence, detonate the torpedo, and rush through the hole; my section would follow to make paths through minefields. The first exercise was a fiasco. People fell off the nets into the sea, whalers crashed on the rocks and sank. I was one of the few to arrive and accomplish my task. Beyond the shore on a dune stood Winston Churchill, Lord Louis Mountbatten, and a wealth of dignitaries looking at the disarray. Mountbatten addressed the staff: "Do it again." We did, again and again and again. But at least we were being assertive. Attacks were being performed. A small Commando group went to Vaagso, near the Lofoten Islands, and blew up an oil installation.

Shortly after Dunkirk I volunteered again. This time the objective was to become a parachutist. It seemed an appropriate response to the humiliation of Dunkirk and the fiasco in North Africa. But there was no response to my request.

The division was designated to become a mountain division and was dispatched to Scotland, where my task was to plan, survey, and mark foundations for a Nissen (Quonset) hut encampment, my first army role as a professional landscape architect. It was then that I received a communication, to report not for parachute training, but to the Officer Selection Board in Edinburgh.

The Board was housed in a mansion in the outskirts of Edinburgh. Each candidate took written examinations, and was required to assume a variety of roles, from drill and small arms instructor to various positions in tactical exercises. The culminating test was dinner with the commandant, a legitimate hero of the First World War. Clearly, our table manners and demeanor were being reviewed. Each candidate was asked a question. The one put to me was diabolically clever, a superb measure of class. "Does your mother ride, McHarg?" This separated sheep from goats. The only horses my mother had ever ridden were great Clydesdale cart horses. No, she

Second Lieutenant Ian McHarg, 1942.

did not ride. Goat I surely was. My sons would have been able to answer quite differently. However, in spite of my mother's inability and my transparent proletarian origins, I passed and was enrolled in the 142d Officer Cadet Training Unit, first
at Albahura Barracks in Aldershot, later in Newark, Nottinghamshire, where in
nine months I would be transformed into an officer and a gentleman.

This was excellent training. It included civil engineering, to which military
engineering was added. I was one of the few from the ranks, the majority having
been drawn from universities. I had more army experience than they, but much
less mathematics and science. While a cadet I learned that my application to
become a parachutist had been accepted, and on being commissioned I was post-
ed to the Second Parachute Squadron, Royal Engineers. I ordered my uniform and
a wonderful pair of mountain boots by Laurie of Nottingham, bootmaker for Sir
Edmund Hillary of Mount Everest fame.

Given weekend leave, I went home to discover a transformation. The Clydeside
had been badly bombed. The shipyards had been the target, but decoy lights lured
the German bombers north. They missed the shipyards but dropped bombs and
land mines on the houses of Clydebank and Radnor Park. Tens of thousands were
killed and injured. My mother, father, and sisters spent nights in the Anderson
shelter. Kenneth extinguished incendiary bombs. Land mines and bombs exploded nearby. Our house was not habitable, so my family moved in with relatives in

Paisley. My mother had suffered rheumatic fever as a young woman, and the trials of the bombing and accompanying hardships weakened her. But she recovered, so that when I returned, she seemed well. My weekend leave meant two days for travel, one for pleasure. I had planned to go to Glasgow on that day. When I reached the bus stop there was my mother with a bag of groceries. I offered to carry them and walk with her back home. "No, no," she said, "It's your only day of leave, take the bus, have a nice time." Which I did, for which I had never stopped reproaching myself. When I kissed her goodbye that day, it was for the last time.

My evolution from infantry division to parachute troops had involved a selection process. The Fifty-second Lowland Division that I first joined was largely composed of regular soldiers extending their military life in the reserves. For them, the army meant two weeks paid camp each summer away from home, job, children, and constraint and one drill night a week of relative freedom. These soldiers drank as much as they could afford. To get drunk was good, to have a drunken fight even better, and to round it off with copulation made for a great success.

For the smaller number of volunteers in the company the army was a sacrifice, willingly accepted. But they were not escapees from job, home, family. Their moral standards and behavior were much more admirable.

In the Commando, all troops were volunteers. They had also been subjected to a serious selection process that emphasized intelligence, skill, and initiative. And because parachute troops were initially selected from Commando, the standards were further escalated, so not only was I commissioned but I was admitted into the cream of the British Army. There was, at that time, in the winter of 1942, one brigade of perhaps a thousand men and the beginnings of a second. These would ultimately become the First Airborne Division.

North Africa and Italy

The *Nieuw Holland* had been provisioned in Australia, so when we embarked in Gourock, we entered a prewar world of fresh fruit, eggs, meat, poultry in abundance, cabins, beds with sheets and pillows, and a magnificent dining room; the minor hardship was saltwater showers and baths. The convoy made a wide sweep into the Atlantic, avoiding submarines and aircraft, passed Gibraltar at night, then Tangiers, a city of lights, and went on to Oran, the destination, where we disembarked and entrained inland to Tizi Ozou in Berber country, near to Sidi Bel Abbas, headquarters of the French Foreign Legion.

We had arrived too late to be of much use in the North African campaign, although the First Parachute Brigade did participate in a series of actions with the First Army. However, it soon became clear that there was another undertaking being contemplated—an invasion. Sicily looked probable. Troops engaged in strenuous exercises, sand models of the anticipated terrain were made, comparable sites were selected in the Ante Atlas mountains, parachute exercises were performed. We moved east to Algiers, then Constantine, Bône to Tunis where we encountered hordes of vanquished Germans building their own prisoner of war camps and marching into imprisonment. We met the raffish Eighth Army, sun-bleached and triumphant.

In Tunis I took a course on enemy weapons. I became an instructor and immediately applied my new skills in removing mines from the minefields that held tens of thousands of Italian antitank mines. They were not dangerous; they could not easily be detonated. The task was simply brute labor. I discovered that in each mine was a white metal cylinder through which passed the striker. This could be cut into dozens of rings, which the Arabs inscribed with scarabs to sell to British and American troops. I negotiated with an Arab chieftain; he could have all of the cylinders if he removed and piled the mines. Agreed. The rings were sold widely and at a good profit. My squadron received eggs, chickens, melons, peaches, and red wine.

The entire division assembled near Bizerta in July, where we were reviewed by General Montgomery. He announced that we would lead the invasion of Sicily, the objective of the Second Brigade was Augusta. But this was not to be. When our planes were short of Sicily; the order came to return. The Fifteenth Panzer Grenadier Division was ensconced on the dropping zone, denying it to the attacking British paratroops.

On September 8, the division assembled in Bizerta. As no aircraft were available, components of the division would be transported by the Royal Navy. The objective was Taranto.

I was assigned a special task, given instructions, and put aboard HMS *Abdiel* with a company of the Sixth Royal Welsh Parachute Regiment. This was a minelayer and the fastest ship in the British Navy. We set off with the Mediterranean fleet. Shortly thereafter we saw the Italian fleet and learned that it was en route to Malta to surrender. We also learned that General Badoglio had surrendered the Italian forces. The *Abdiel* circled the fleet at forty-five knots, with an enormous stern wave, the bow high in the water, and then shot off at a tangent for Taranto. We arrived in the outer harbor just before midnight.

I have never read an official account of the episode that followed, but later learned that the captain turned off the degaussing apparatus that protected the ship from magnetic mines. My batman and I were to be put ashore independently, and so we were on deck awaiting transportation. We were laden like pack mules. We carried Thompson submachine carbines, 34 and 42 grenades, and plastic high explosives and magazines in our pockets. We stood by the rail, waiting for the launch to take us ashore, when there was the most almighty bang, then more and more detonations. The mines in the hull were exploding. Flames engulfed the ship, jagged pieces of red hot metal erupted from the deck, and the ship listed to port. We could not go below to give help, we could not cross the deck; it was clear we had to jump. But first, we had to get rid of all the paraphernalia: the bandolier and belt, the smock and webbing equipment. Then the boots, my beautiful handmade mountain boots made by Laurie of Nottingham— I prized them, but they had to go. No time to loosen laces, I had to cut them. Engineer officers wear a jackknife over their right hip held by a lanyard that supports the trousers. I opened the knife, cut the lanyard, cut the laces, shed the boots, climbed on the rail, and jumped. My pants fell down. I landed above the Plimsoll line and slid on the hull. My bottom and back were lacerated with fine cuts by barnacles and other shells. My batman, Donnelly, and I hit water together. My pants were now inside out, held by buttons at the ankles. Some poor soul was trying to avoid drowning by holding onto my trousers. The sea was burning. I dived to escape the fire and to take off my trousers. Donnelly thought I was drowning and tried to pull me to the surface. But other hands were still pulling me down. I freed the buttons, rose to the surface, and left my trousers in some one else's hands. I told Donnelly to stay with me, and we made a course between the flames. Mines continued to explode, but suddenly there was silence and the *Abdiel* settled into sinking, stern first, bow raised high, then lowered in flames and smoke, gone.

Blackouts are never complete and it was possible to discover the hint of lights that suggested Taranto, so we swam, perhaps for about five hours. It was not yet first light when we saw a hulk ahead of us, a barge with a crane. We swam to it. Our appearances upon arrival were not prepossessing. My face was covered with lamp-black, my back and buttocks were naked and bleeding. As we climbed aboard the barge the occupant was lit by the flames of his boiler fire. He heard our noise, turned, saw us, fell on his knees, the whites of his eyes showing, and prayed. Neither Donnelly nor I spoke Italian, but we moved into his warm boiler room and asked for cigarettes. He rolled and offered them. Then he observed my bleeding back and went to a store of clean cloths, used for polishing the engine. He found an undershirt and gestured for me to put it on. It came to my navel, but served well as a bandage. We sat, smoking together, for an hour or so, when we heard the sound of an engine and, soon, the call, "Survivors, ahoy." We acknowledged, and a launch came alongside with a midshipman and two sailors. It was from the battleship *Howe*, flagship of the British Mediterranean Fleet. There had been a crew of several hundred and a company of some two hundred men of the Royal Welch Fusiliers. Although a mere lieutenant, I was the senior surviving officer. I was advised that I should report on the event to Vice Admiral Lord Cunningham. We approached the *Howe*, which, from the vantage of the launch, looked like a hundred-story building. A shipsladder zigged and zagged from water to deck. Quite naked and bloody, I then climbed higher and higher until I reached the bridge, lit only by a small blue light. Inside I saw, shining on sleeves and skips, an aura of gold braid. Awed by this array of authority, I assumed the tremulous and rigid posture of attention designed by the British Army as a signal of respect, brought my right arm into the position of salute, and held this for six counts before bringing it smartly to my side.

Humor and tragedy are perilously close. I think my realization of the incongruous picture I presented, skinny, naked and bleeding, black faced and erect, overcame me and, at once, we all burst into the most raucous laughter. We laughed until the tears came.

The following day I was outfitted by the Royal Marines in boots, socks, trousers, tunic, belt (but no badges of rank), a black beret, and a long-barreled Smith and Wesson revolver with five bullets.

The Division disembarked on that day, and I was ordered to report to Lieutenant Colonel Henniker, Chief Royal Engineer, First Airborne Division. When I entered his presence he was in conversation with a young Intelligence Corps officer. It transpired that the officer had gone to Eton and Henniker to another famous, but not quite as famous, public school. They were discussing schools. I had gone to Clydebank High School, as public as theirs were private and as proletarian as theirs were noble. I did not engage in the conversation on school days and old boys. But apparently I had a role. Colonel Henniker had served in India where transportation consisted of horses for officers and mules for troops and baggage. Irked by his unit's immobility, he was determined to make it muleborne. I was charged with obtaining the mules and horses, and the intelligence officer was to be my interpreter.

We set off on a motorcycle, looking for farms with mules. We encountered very few. At one point my colleague observed that what we needed was a cavalry depot where there would be horses and mules. Moreover, he recalled that in the 1938 Olympiad in London an Italian prince had won some important equestrian event. And he recalled having met the Count—or was it Prince—Romanazzi. The Germans had very considerately not cut telephone lines, so it was perfectly simple to phone directory assistance to ascertain the listing for one Count Romanazzi. He was found through a relative and located in Bari, where he commanded a cavalry depot!

So we knew that we must go to Bari and discuss matters with him. Conditions were uncertain, Montgomery owned a tip of the heel of Italy, British parachute troops had landed in the instep at Taranto, but foot and upper boot were firmly in German hands. We proceeded cautiously, and at the outskirts of Bari came upon an Allied jeep with a 50-mm-caliber machine gun on the hood. The insignia said LRDG, the famed Long Range Desert Group, part of Popsky's Private Army, which had begun their audacious lives in the Eritrean campaign fighting against Mussolini and brought their desert skills to aid the British Eighth Army in North Africa. They had reconnoitered Bari; there were lots of Italian troops, no German units, but some officers and soldiers. So we proceeded to the conspicuous hotel overlooking the bay, the Grande Albergo Imperiale di Bari.

We were dirty, unshaven, crumpled, unpolished. We reserved rooms, had showers, sent for a barber and a tailor, had haircuts and shaves and had our clothes cleaned and pressed. My friend then phoned Count Romanazzi. They had met in London in 1938 and had friends in common. He told the count that he was in Bari and would like to visit. "Yes, indeed," was the reply. "Could you come to tea this afternoon?" "Of course." So we descended the elevator to the foyer, where the palm court orchestra softly played "God Save the King" and staff and guests clapped quietly.

We met Count Romanazzi, drank tea, ate small sandwiches, and then discussed the matter of horses and mules. He was only too anxious to cooperate. He was a soldier, never a fascist. He would be delighted to load a train with eight horses suitable for officers, eighty Italian alpini mules, the requisite number of grooms, farriers, carrezza, hay, grain, saddles, bridles, and more. He would consign the train to Taranto. So I proceeded by motorcycle to make preparations for their arrival while the intelligence officer accompanied the Italian officers and grooms, horses, and mules on the train.

I think Colonel Henniker was surprised to learn that he would soon be mounted and that he had enlarged his charges to include an Italian unit and Italian mules. He certainly managed to suppress any hint of pleasure or acknowledgment. He was nicknamed Honker, but not as a token of affection. He never elicited any from me.

I came upon the mules again early in the spring of 1944, following a ridiculous experience. On patrol near Lama del Peligni in the Gran Sasso d'Italia, I was shelled. Generally, individuals do not attract artillery. The shells burst about me and I was blasted over the edge of a quarry where I landed in some telephone wires, injuring my knee on a piece of rock. Another blast knocked me off the wires onto the ground, whereupon a flying rock fell upon my left index finger, laying it open to the bone. My troubles were slight but when I returned I could not walk, so I was consigned to the base area where my command became eight Italian chargers, eighty alpine mules, and an Italian mule company.

In the autumn of 1943, I was summoned to meet Lieutenant General Foley, chief engineer of the Eighth and First Armies. He told me that I had been selected for a particular role. It transpired that most, if not all, of southern Italy obtained its water from a single source, an aqueduct that began at Caposele in the Gran Sasso d'Italia in Abruzzo and continued south until debouching into the sea at Lecce. Foley stated that this supply would be crucial to the Allied advance and that every effort should be made to ensure available water. My task was to contact the director of the Acquedotto Pugliese, one dottore engineere, Pietro Celentani-Ungaro, and have him persuade the Italian Army to persuade the German Army not to blow up the aqueduct. "Failing that," he said without changing pace, "you must have the Italian directorate repair the aqueduct as fast as possible." The headquarters of the Acquedotto Pugliese was in Bari, but it was believed it had been moved temporarily to the village of Matera.

There were several problems. I did not speak Italian, I knew nothing about aqueducts, and I had no maps. Moreover, although the Italian government had officially surrendered, not all Italian troops subscribed to this decision. Montgomery had just crossed the Straits of Messina, the American landing at Salerno was still to come, and the Germans owned the country and were ubiquitous.

The first objective was transportation. The surrender had given pause to ordinary activities. I walked toward the town and came to a bridge across a waterway leading to the inner harbor. On it was a man with a motorcycle. I wrote a note identifying myself by name, rank, and number assuring the bearer that the British Army would (in due time) reimburse him for his motorcycle. I then took out my long barreled Smith and Wesson, poked it in his stomach, gave him the piece of paper, and drove off.

I spent a lot of time in ditches watching German columns pass on the roads. Signposts were very helpful and a questioning "Matera?" was sufficient in Apuglia to obtain graphic manual directions. I had little fear of being identified. After all, was I not disguised? I was unshaven, had no badges of rank, and was wearing my beret inside out.

In a day or so I reached Matera, and it took little time to find out the temporary headquarters of the Acquedotto Pugliese and thereafter to meet its extraordinary director, Pietro Celentani-Ungaro. He was a small, thin, handsome, and intense man who wore authority like a cloak. I introduced myself with the only Italian I knew, "Sono tenente McHarg, officiali di collegamento del Armate Alliate con

The Acquedotto Pugliese at the Tragino Viaduct, destroyed by German troops in September 1943 and reconstructed under my direction in October 1943. The aqueduct was vital for Allied water supplies.

Acquedotto Pugliese." He spoke no English, so we spoke bad French. Yes, he was prepared to cooperate, but he doubted that the Italian Army could stop the Germans from destroying the aqueduct. Yes, he knew where all of the demolition charges were, and he had persuaded the Germans to permit him to store materials for repairs. (This was ostensibly to repair damages by Allied bombers.) Yes, he was prepared to undertake repairs with all possible speed.

Almost immediately the Germans began demolitions. Most critical was the source at Caposele and the Tragino aqueduct on the main stem. This viaduct had earlier been cut by British parachutists in 1941. Repairs would follow the earlier solution—an inverted syphon. The entire directorate moved to Tragino to begin repairs. There were problems, however, with the work force, a certain irresolution among the population. The Italian forces had surrendered, but an Italian fascist government still held civil power. Only in a very few villages had communist partisans overthrown the government and executed fascist leaders. It looked as if the Allies would ultimately arrive and take over, but where were they? Where indeed. Then we learned that the Americans had landed in Salerno. I obtained a jeep and a driver from Taranto; his first name was Percy, his last name long forgotten. I decided to meet the Americans at Salerno and proceeded there, but cautiously. I recall on this trip coming down a hill and seeing a trio of German soldiers on a motorcycle and sidecar approaching me. With five bullets I was in a poor position to take on three *Schmeissers*. We turned around briskly, but so did the Germans.

By this time I had some useful Italian. "Sono stati soldati Tedesci qui?" Are there any German soldiers here? It worked well. "Dove Americani?" worked as well, and suddenly I saw an American weapons carrier. The men listened to my story doubtfully but informed their officer that a purported British parachutist wanted them to accompany him to some hill towns and show the flag, so that the Allies could be seen to have arrived, and the necessary thousands of artisans and laborers could be induced to join the Allied cause and work to repair the Acquedotto Pugliese.

They gave me candy bars, fruit juice, cigarettes, a lieutenant's bars, and underpants, and we set off. The routine was simple and effective. We drove into a town, fired off blasts of rounds into the air, whereupon the townspeople immediately found the fascist leaders, kicked them, beat them up, threw them in jail, and started a party. A representative of the Acquedotto quickly followed us, offering bonus wages and overtime, food and cigarettes, for immediate labor. The American soldiers loved it. In every village was someone who had a relative in the United States, and many seemed to have worked on the Brooklyn Bridge. They drank the wine and kissed the *bella ragazzae*.

And so it went. Celantani-Ungaro closed valves after every German demolition so that the aqueduct became, in fact, a series of independent reservoirs. Repairs were undertaken expeditiously, and the Allies never suffered for lack of water.

Celantani-Ungaro had been a *squadrista*. He had marched with Mussolini in the fascist takeover. He claimed he had done so in return for a promise from

Mussolini that the aqueduct would be much enlarged and improved to provide public drinking supplies and irrigation for Apulia and Calabria, and it had been. However, he was a *squadrista* and a fascist and he was tried in Rome, but his services in repairing the Apulian aqueduct exonerated him.

As for me, separated from antibrin and mepacrin, I contracted malignant malaria. I chose to sweat this out in a Celantani apartment in Bari, and during my recuperation the Allies moved through and came to a halt south of the Sangro River. I wrote my first literary work during convalescence, "The Destruction and Repairs to the Apulian Aqueduct." It was completed by the time I rejoined my unit.

There was a puzzling footnote to the sinking of the *Abdiel*. I had been out of contact with the army for several months; thus I received no mail, wrote no letters home. When I did contact the British Army in Bari, I had arrears of mail, for my father and mother wrote weekly. One letter was dumfounding. Understand, my father was not a man likely to believe in spiritualism, he was a granitic Presbyterian. Yet the letter clearly said, "At midnight on the 9th of September, your mother sat up in bed and screamed: 'Ian called for me, Ian called.' We worry that something has happened. We wait to hear from you." I remember well when I called: I was standing on the rail of the *Abdiel*, about to jump, and I called, "Dear Mother, Mother." I cannot explain it, but neither do I doubt it.

Sangro and Cassino

From November of 1943 until the following spring the Second Independent Parachute Brigade acted as a light infantry unit, attached to New Zealand, Indian, Canadian, and sundry British Divisions of the Thirtieth Corps. The Allies were stuck in the mud of the River Sangro and its valley, overlooked by a steep escarpment dominated by German positions in Orsogna and Guardiagrele. There were interminable small actions at platoon, company, and, sometimes, at battalion and brigade levels. There were no breakthroughs. The Allies sought to outflank along the coast, then outflank in the mountains, in neither case with more than limited gains. The strategic success was to embroil many German divisions, but Churchill's hope of a quick stab through Italy at the soft underbelly of Europe was an illusion. The merest knowledge of physiography revealed Italy as a defender's paradise, a nightmare for the attacking force. Although these battles received scant attention in the newspapers, they were miserable for the participants. We experienced a very cold and wet winter and little shelter as all towns, villages, and hamlets had been destroyed by bombing and shellfire. We encountered entrenched positions with artillery and the diabolical German *Nebelwerfers* (multiple-rocket launchers) and minefields galore, many unmapped. We built bridges, cleared minefields, reinforced positions, laid booby traps, participated in reconnaissance and offensive patrolling. We lived in sangars (little depressions with cairns of rocks) that were excavated with an entrenching tool, savored a rare hot meal, and a rarer shower.

Still there were laughs. On one occasion I was making my way to a forward company position, whence I would proceed on a reconnaissance. Suddenly I saw my brigadier, a tall, thin Welshman with a large handlebar moustache and a high-pitched voice, in the middle of a minefield. These were no ordinary mines but "S mines," cylinders filled with shrapnel, which, when detonated, sprang a foot or so in the air and exploded a rain of metal fragments. Moreover, they had impact fuses and pull-and-release detonators. "Get me out of here!" he called. The general had walked well into the minefield before he saw the yellow skull symbol. He had been lucky. Because of long experience with these mines, most sapper officers carried a ring with S mine safety pins. If you observed the mine, you could neutralize it by inserting a safety pin. But there were also trip wires. Some mines could be detonated by touching, others by cutting, trip wires. It was necessary to prod to find a mine, or, holding a piece of stiff wire over a finger, sense when it touched a trip wire. When discovered the wire could be followed to a mine or mines, which could be rendered safe. This process took me quite a while, during which, at regular intervals, the general shouted, "Get me out of here, damn it, get me out!"

The term *military intelligence* consists of two utterly contradictory words. Certainly, with Panzer Grenadiers sitting on the dropping zone in Augusta in Sicily and later at Arnhem, the intelligence of Salerno, Cassino, and Anzio all had to be questionable. I had a personal experience of "intelligence." On Christmas day, 1943, I was ordered to send out a reconnaissance patrol. The order came from General Freyberg V.C., commanding general of the New Zealand Corps. Intelligence had learned that the Germans had evacuated Orsogna. This should be investigated. So Lance Corporal Richardson and Sappers Walsh and Roby were selected, three of the men with whom I had undertaken parachute training. With a patrol of the Sixth Royal Welch Parachute Battalion they set off across the valley, through the minefields, overlooked by the German positions in Orsogna. Of course, the Germans let them approach the very edge of the escarpment and then fired everything they had: heavy, medium, and light artillery, MG 34 and 42, mortars galore. All three were wounded. Richardson was captured, Roby died of his wounds, and Walsh's grave was found a year later. Military intelligence, indeed.

Avoiding death or injury was paramount, but the most immediate problem was to keep clean, dry, and get a night's sleep. Bill Mauldin, the cartoonist of *Stars and Stripes,* established the image of the American infantryman, G.I. Joe: dirty, unshaven, muddy boots, unkempt uniform, skeptical, battle wise. The British Army insisted upon a clean shaven face and as prepossessing an appearance as circumstances permitted. Out of gunshot, this meant a shaven face, proper haircut, polished boots, and clean and tidy uniform. But this cleanliness was superficial. The Ghurkas solved the problem more fundamentally. In a Ghurka area could be seen steel helmets filled with snow melting over cans of sterno, and small naked Ghurkas clad only in loincloths, washing their entire bodies. And they were magnificent soldiers.

Occasionally we occupied abandoned and derelict farm buildings. These were sandbagged to protect walls and roofs from mortars and shells. Most of the time we lived in sangars.

Rough walls made of loose rocks and covered with branches and then with more rocks, completed a sangar. It permitted lying down in a sleeping bag, and the entrance offered observation toward the enemy. These structures were not waterproof and had no insulation worth mentioning. Yet during that winter, this was home. The sleeping bag had a big hood that could be raised by a small stick so that it did not hit the face. It was like a small tent for the head. It could also be zipped closed. Within, it was possible to smoke. A small candle could provide considerable heat, but, of course, light could not show. Socks wrapped in newspaper and stuffed into boots would dry, at least somewhat. Washing could be accomplished by melting snow with a sterno stove. Warm water for shaving employed the dregs of a cup of tea. Sleeping, however, was the greatest difficulty. It was necessary to be alert. There were frequent German patrols, and in the mountains the front had great gaps between defensive positions—it was porous.

During this time, I met some American engineers and watched in respectful admiration as they constructed a tank barrier. They wound cordtex, an explosive cord, several times around tree trunks and felled them across the road. I asked for and received a coil. I then proceeded to invent automatic sentries. These consisted of two short wooden pegs about six inches long, a length of trip wire, and a pull igniter detonator. The pegs were arrayed around a defensive position, the cordtex wound around one peg and connected to a pull igniter. The igniter was connected to the second peg with a trip wire, at just above ankle height. The intruder, kicking the wire, would trip the igniter; the cordtex exploded with a brilliant flash, temporarily blinding the intruders and awakening the defenders. It worked beautifully.

March of 1944 involved Monte Cassino, the redoubtable monastery, high on the hill, commanding the valleys. The only area of dead ground where one would not be seen by the Germans was the embankment of the high-speed railway line from Naples to Rome. But even this was bracketed with mortars and artillery. Following the abortive American attack, the brigade was ordered to Cassino under command of the Second New Zealand Corps, with the objectives of stabilizing the front, undertaking mine sweeping, and reconnaissance for bridge crossings. During the preceding months death and wounds had depleted the squadron's officers and senior noncommissioned officers. As one of the few unscathed, I was pressed into the breach at Arielli, Poggiofiorito, Pennapiedamonte, and Lama del Peligni, hill towns in the shadow of Monte Miella—all front-line positions. When the wounded returned to service, I was dispatched to Capua to learn advanced techniques in bridge construction, notably, timber trestle bridges built most successfully by American engineers. It was a reward, a vacation from Cassino. On my return the brigade's objective had largely been achieved. My role was small, but a little of Cassino was quite enough, a diabolical inferno consuming enormous numbers of brave men.

I received another reward for my services during the long and arduous winter of 1943–1944. After Cassino, I was awarded a week's leave by my commanding officer, one Major C.D.H. Vernon, a magnificent soldier, who was my idol. I sought hard to emulate his courage and kindness. Through my aqueduct friend Pietro Celentani-Ungaro, I arranged to spend my vacation on a promontory on the Sorrento Peninsula in Albergo Palumbo, Ravello.

Nothing in my history, before or since, has equaled the degree of contrast I then experienced: Cassino one day—dead and dying on the battlefield, a clamitous carnage, blood, mud, sorrow, despair, bombs, rockets, and mortars—and the next waking to silence, whispers, footsteps, church bells, peace. This tranquil peace, man to man, and later, man to nature, this psychic healing, lies at the heart of my dreams. Peace.

Invasion of the South of France

On August 15, 1944, the brigade was encamped outside Rome, and the weather was wonderful. My redoubtable colleague from the Acquedotto Pugliese, Celentani-Ungaro, had an apartment in Rome to which I was invited for a party. There I met a stunningly beautiful young woman, Piera Gandolfo, *atrice de poesia*, a distant relative of Celentani. I invited her to dinner at the Osteria del Orso, near the Tiber, overlooking the Ponte and Castel San Angelo. This was a magic event.

Until Rome I had not been in the company of any women even remotely attractive. In rural Algeria small ladies in gowns revealed only dark eyes and, often, venereal sores; in southern Italian hill towns beauties were sensibly hidden, women in view were as muscular and often as well mustached as I was. My sense of the powerful sin of fornication was such that I was not going to abandon virtue lightly. This would require someone such as Lana Turner, accompanied by Leopold Stokowski and a thousand violins.

Piera Gandolfo met these standards, and we could probably get Benjamino Gigli, the world famous tenor, for I had met him at the party. We danced on the terrace. In my heart I felt sure the earth would move that night. I hired a horse and carriage and we clattered toward her apartment. Inside, she put on a record and began to dance. We danced together, held each other, and kissed. Suddenly she broke into spasms of sobbing. What could be the matter? The matter was that she was married, her husband was a prisoner of war in Yugoslavia, and she had two little daughters in a convent in Civitaveccia. She could not be faithless. So it goes. I became a proxy uncle, transporting her and expensive basket lunches from the Osteria del Orso to Civitaveccia to meet her lovely little girls and play on the beaches.

In mid-August the brigade was informed that it would be the spearhead of the American invasion of the south of France. Our objective was near Frejus between Le Muy and La Motte, two villages some miles inland. The purpose was to hold ground to deny reinforcements to German troops lining the coast. This involved mining roads and bridges, taking and holding defensive positions.

After 1:00 A.M. on a clear night, we set off from Rome in one of the DC3s that circled as the formation organized Vs of three, comprising Vs of nine, leading north. The route was well marked. Below us, ships were aligned, the mast lights pointing to the south of France. Across Sardinia fires and lights illuminated the route; thereafter craft were smaller and fewer. The path was admirably marked, that is, until we reached the coast, when we encountered antiaircraft fire. The planes dived and turned, climbed and turned again. Where were we? The crew chief walked down the fuselage. "We're lost," he shouted. "Get back on course, we'll jump as arranged at 0500." Then it was necessary to disconnect all strops and safety pins, realign the troops, pin them up, and return to the door. We had seen air photographs and sand models and were familiar with the terrain, but nothing was recognizable, nor were there any other planes in view, only our V of three. At 5:00 A.M. first the red light came on, then the green. "Jump." The plans were for the first man to jump at 700 feet, the last, number 17, at 400 feet. To land from 700 feet takes about ten seconds. At that time I arranged myself to land, but found myself in a cloud, and then another. How high had we jumped? The consequences are simple: the greater the altitude from which troops jump, the more distant they are from each other on the ground. As was proved. I landed high on a pine tree; it took some time to divest myself of the parachute, but not long to fall from the tree. On the ground I first whispered, "Myahee," our troop call. No answer. Louder; still no answer. A shout; silence. Finally I yelled at the top of my voice and heard a faint reply. It took hours to converge on the containers that held antitank mines, weapons, and explosives. These were loaded on the Everest carriers. But where to go? We found a track and followed it. It widened and suddenly there was a house. We organized—point section, right flank, left flank, order group—and, in rotation, tiger-crawled to the house. When the lead section was within seconds of kicking in the door and tossing in grenades, it opened. Out walked a Frenchman. He took a few steps, opened his fly, and peed, at which point a dozen British parachutists stood up in front of him. "Anglais, Anglais, Allies!" He welcomed us, we drank in celebration, and he showed us where we were, miles from where we should have been. Our inability to find the mountain silhouettes we had been looking for was now explained: we were standing on them.

The operation was a great success. Surprise was achieved, reinforcements were denied to the enemy. The British contingent landed on D-Day, followed by the American paratroop division the next day, and glider-borne troops the day after. The major source of casualties may have been the gliders' crashing into stone walls. There was some resistance. My troop engaged with a company of Germans, perhaps 200 of them, in a farmhouse called Clastron. Their defense was desultory; then they surrendered. It was my task to march the prisoners to the dropping zone. The road was narrow. The Germans marched three abreast, and we, the captors, perforce, had to walk in the ditches. We were unshaven and in smocks, whereas the Germans were polished and handsome, particularly the *Hauptman* who led. He had magnificent polished boots and a hat with gold oak leaves. I found this incongruous. To an unknowing observer it would appear that the column of triumphant Germans was bordered by scruffy camp flowers. I stepped forward, halted the column, took off the *Hauptman's* hat, jumped on it several times, then put it back on his head. No longer the conquering hero, he looked more like a comic. Now justice prevailed. "Quick, march."

Greece

Evacuated from the south of France, the brigade was moved to Brindisi. It was clear that an operation was imminent, but where? The acquisition of a new officer, Major Mullen, of the South African Engineers, gave direction to this inquiry. He was an expert on the destruction and construction of airports. Where would air-

Behind enemy lines in Greece. *From left*: Sergeant Player, Lieutenant Henderson (interpreter), Sergeant Guyan, Captain McHarg, Sergeant Homersham, 1944.

ports be important? Could it be in Greece? We knew that the Germans were planning to evacuate Greece. Should the Allies cross the Po they might be able to isolate the German Army in the Balkans. The capture of Greek airports could facilitate our harassing the evacuating army. The plan emerged. The major objective was to capture Kalamaki airport in Athens. It would also be advantageous to secure Elevis airport; however, an earlier and easier objective would be to capture the small airfield at Megara, twenty miles from Athens.

We all preferred jumping at night, for the protection that darkness provided. There was no need to give defenders excellent illumination, the better to hit their targets. However, there was a contrary consideration. Navigators had demonstrated a deplorable inaccuracy at night—planes had left Bizerta and had been unable to find Sicily! Their skill in locating dropping zones was much in doubt. In this case, daylight was preferable. Even if pilot and navigator did not know the way, an officer looking out the door with a map in hand could advise them. So we set off from Foggia on October 12 in DC3s and flew to Greece, over the Peloponnesus to Megara. It was very identifiable: a large lump of a hill ending a bay, the airstrip, olive groves, the village and mountains behind. First came the red light, then the green. "Action stations, go." We jumped one, two, three, until eight then, container, container, container, container, nine, ten, to the last man at seventeen. Poor last man. Unlike Americans, with two parachutes, who had to jump from heights that permitted the second one to open, British parachutists, with only one parachute, started at 700 feet and the last man left at 400 feet. This gives him just enough time to make one oscillation and turn to face the ground before he hits it. But not this day. Instead of making large, gentle oscillations, parachutes scudded across the sky. There was a wind of forty-five knots. I prepared my release box; it was open before I hit the ground. I began to free myself from the harness, but not soon enough. I was immediately dragged, and the pull in the webbing made it impossible to shed the harness. Fortunately, I had a haversack on my chest with a metal water bottle and a mess kit. This saved my face from being pulverised. I also had a Bergen carrier filled with mines and explosives attached to my waist, which I had lowered as I dropped, and now this acted as a providential anchor. I was dragged over the runway, across a minefield, through a barbed wire fence, and up a hill until, finally, my anchor caught on some boulders and I was stilled. I had lost my four lower front teeth and a good deal of skin from my face and hands, but was operational. Others were not so lucky. Donald Marsh, an experienced pathfinder parachutist, was bumped to pulp. There were many casualties, not the least important of which was the entire paramedical team. As we assembled in an olive grove flanking the airfield, shelling began.

The runway had been extensively cratered and the holes were filled with aircraft bombs, engines, airframes, and more. However, it was possible to mark out a glider strip for Waco and Horsa gliders. And soon the procession was seen, the gliders were released and planed to land successfully. From these were unloaded little bulldozers, a grader, and jeeps. A large contingent of Greeks had arrived from Megara, and they immediately offered their services. Soon a large workforce was engaged in removing bombs and debris, filling craters, and repairing the runway. By 0600 the work was finished.

A contingent consisting of the Fourth Parachute Battalion—artillery, engineers, and medics—named "Pompforce" was assembled. Its purpose was to "cause alarm and despondency" to the Germans, whose evacuating troops constituted a column from Athens to the Monastir Gap in Yugoslavia. To comply, we had to harass the German column from end to end and, above all, to give the impression of being larger, more a significant force. Our problem was mobility. Parachute troops are designed for short-term operations; they land and accomplish their objective. They cannot keep up with the troops who relieve them and press forward; they have no transport, no heavy weapons, no support structure. But someone had found a dozen Chevrolet trucks. Had they been captured by the Germans in North Africa, brought to Greece, and then retrieved? I never learned, but suddenly I was responsible for undertaking the reconnaissance of the route to the north, finding bypasses for blown bridges, blowing bridges clear of the span to enable construction of temporary bridges, lifting minefields, defusing bombs, and above all, ensuring the passage of our little convoy, which had to transport the troops in leapfrogging shifts. There were several skirmishes, but the first major engagement was at Larissa. Here the main north-south route was engorged by the German column, some segments motorized, others horse drawn, still others yet afoot. Spaced between these segments were armored units with Mark V Tiger tanks, awesome powers for which we had no answer. Larissa sits at the confluence of the east-west road and the spinal route. Here was General Sarafis, leader of ELAS, ELAM, and KKE—Labor, Socialist and Communist partisans, with a mighty army. Lord Jellicoe and Colonel Coxen planned a major attack on the column. Our small British contingent would capture the high ground commanding the valley route. At daybreak we would open fire with mortars and artillery on the column below, and then the Greek partisans would fall upon the column with bugles blowing, pennants flying, some tens of thousands of them, cut the column, and cause massive despondency.

The British part began at dusk. Two companies set out, each to take a high point occupied by a German company. We achieved this objective without incident. An armored car and a small contingent were located on the Kozane-Larissa Road to protect against penetration that could isolate both positions. The light rose, the German column assembled and began to move north. Now was the time; three-inch mortars and twenty-five-pound guns opened fire. The column scattered. Suddenly, Tiger Tanks appeared and began to move forward. Where were the partisans? How long could we wait? The single armored car was no protection. Colonel Coxen decided that withdrawal could not be delayed, and when the ammunition was exhausted the troops withdrew. There would be no Sarafis. He had concluded that although he hated Germans, he had no affection for the British either. *Let them kill each other, a pox on them both* was a tactic he employed on other occasions as well. Troops piled into the Chevrolets and headed for the mountains, searching for slender bridges that could not support Tiger Tanks and for refuges in the mountains where they could plan the next sorties. There were several more encounters: a railway cut, a troop train severely damaged, and a skirmish at Florina. Finally the vanguard reached the Monastir pass where the road entered Yugoslavia. By this time the contingent was smaller; there were some forty-five men for the meeting with the Yugoslav partisans. Moreover, we were not prepossessing. Six weeks or more without baths, sleeping in our clothes, crabs, fleas, lice, scabies, and eczema had made our heroic group look more like bandits than conquering heroes. The partisans took one look at us and concluded they did not need our assistance. They could handle the Germans themselves—and they did.

Fighting in the streets of Athens, Greece, October 1944.

We returned to Athens, where we were deloused, painted blue for crabs, and anointed for other ailments. Our hair was shaved, our uniforms were cleaned, and pressed, and we became fit and handsome once again. I took over a villa in Kalamaki Bay that had previously housed German staff officers. Having been out of contact with the army for some months, each soldier had an accumulated store of entitlements: food, cigarettes, and, for officers, whiskey and gin. These were readily bartered for chickens, fish, and eggs. Hunger changed to plenty. We swam in the bay, drove to Athens, examined the Acropolis and other celestial ruins, ate at the Grand Bretagne Hotel, and recuperated. But not for long. The forces in Athens consisted of the Second Independent Parachute Brigade: more than three thousand men and a much larger contingent of doctors, nurses, military government officers, and those engaged in staffing hospitals, dispensing food, repairing municipal services (water, sewer, tram cars, trains) and more. Suddenly we learned that General Sarafis had mobilized his entire army of several hundred thousand and that they were en route to Athens.

Immediately mobilized, we traveled to Piraeus, where there was already sporadic firing on British soldiers by ELAS. Thence we drove to the Rouf barracks, midway between Piraeus and Omonia Square in Athens. Within hours partisans had concentrated on this route. It would be necessary to run the gauntlet from Rouf to join the remainder of the brigade installed in Academious Street, the main street of Athens. The convoy was led by a Covenantor armored car. A convoy of open trucks followed, bedrolls piled against the sides, the floor was covered with Brens, Thompsons, Smeizers, Berettas, grenades, and ammunition. The plan was simply to fire continuously from each side of the trucks at the partisans who occupied the windows of the houses on the route. A Covenantor brought up the rear. I was in the first truck. I well recall a rifle pointed at me from a window, perhaps thirty feet away. Without thought I fired my Colt .45 through the windscreen, shattering it. The driver stalled the truck. At that moment partisans threw German Teller antitank mines from buildings, which could well have destroyed us and the armored car and stalled the entire column, but they did not explode. The rain of fire continued; we moved on into Omonia Square.

The British Army held only the south side of Academious Street from the Grand Bretagne to Omonia Square. We controlled neither the back of the buildings we occupied nor the other side of the street. Moreover, Athens had a complex system of sewers, ancient and modern; these provided access for ELAS into the basements of the buildings. My squadron was quartered in the Agricultural Bank of Athens, squarely in the center of Academious. Expansion of the perimeter was accomplished by "mouseholing," expanding room by room. A hole would be blown in a wall, the room would be covered with fire, entered, occupied, and so onto the next room. Flanking movements were undertaken on side streets to command our rear. This worked slowly but effectively. The greatest menace lay, however, not in these small-scale skirmishes, but in the threat of a major attack by Sarafis's army. Yet because our perimeter was so small, he could not dispose his troops. He tried mouseholing, without success, and then changed tactics. At nighttime he collected large groups of civilians and marched them ahead of his troops down the avenues intersecting with Omonia and Academious. The Allied response was to fly Typhoons and Mosquitoes from Foggia with magnesium flares that turned night into day. Then the artillery fired mortars over the heads of the civilians at the partisans—a very effective action.

Meanwhile, high level negotiations were proceeding. General Alexander, GOC First Army, Lieutenant General Scobie, of the Middle East Forces, and Archbishop Damaskinos were to converge in Athens. Churchill would follow. General Sarafis was to be given an ultimatum. The Greek government in exile would be installed, and there would be amnesty and general elections.

Patrolling was the order of the day. Many Greeks had joined the cause. Each was given a forage cap, a greatcoat, a short Lee Enfield rifle, and an arm band and was allocated to a British unit. One of the patrol tasks was to check the sewers. My second in command, Lieutenant Dennis Bramwell Thomas, took a contingent of Greeks on a sewer patrol in a large sewer with headroom, generally running under Academious Street. Quite soon he saw footprints in the sludge and wires newly installed in the roof. He cut the wires, then, using his prismatic compass, he proceeded, following the wires, recording his progress. Finally he came to a sandbagged emplacement filled with explosives. He removed the detonators, then calculated the location of the proposed demolition. It was beneath the Grand Bretagne Hotel prepared for Churchill, Alexander, Scobie, and Damaskinos. I believe he never received a single note of thanks.

Sarafis conceded to the ultimatum. There was an amnesty and elections were held. Early in 1945 we left Greece and returned to Italy, there to end the war.

Postwar Prospect 1944–1946

By Christmas of 1944 there was a sense that victory would come, that the war would end and we would triumph. Instructions filtered down to units that Civil Affairs officers should be identified and assigned to bringing the civil issues of the time to the attention of troops. The officers in the squadron were all Tories; my

Cemetery in Athens, Greece, for British soldiers killed in action during the Second World War, which I designed as a result of competition in 1945. (Photographs by Carolus Hanikian, 1994.)

position was between the Liberal and Labour parties, leaning more to the left as the Liberals were ineffectual. Most of the troops tended toward a similar persuasion. Given the affinity between my views and the troops', I was chosen Civil Affairs officer. In this capacity I received two publications each month, which I assimilated and then presented for discussion.

The fate of postwar Britain was the paramount subject being discussed. Lord Beveridge, a notable Liberal, had produced a report outlining the nation's general social aspirations, including participation by the labor force in industrial management and profit sharing. There were three studies undertaken—the Scott, Uthwatt, and Barlow reports. These addressed the necessity of siphoning the population from the central city slums, building satellite towns, and exploiting the opportunities created by bomb damage to undertake central city redevelopment. The one original proposal was that, because development values are largely a product of public investment, the fruits of such actions should be recovered, a theory entitled "Compensation and Betterment."

Very soon thereafter I learned of a planning school in London led by Dr. A. L. Rowse and including Jacqueline Tyrwhitt, the London School for Reconstruction and Development. It offered a correspondence course, in which I immediately enrolled. Now I could combine two interests: a generalized concern for a new and better Britain, consisting of a more equitable distribution of wealth and the

elimination of class struggle, and the more specific goal of a new physical expression in cities, towns, and countrysides. We would replace the mean cities, the smear of low-grade urban issue, the dark satanic mills bequeathed by the nineteenth century.

But suddenly I had a more immediate opportunity to rediscover myself as a landscape architect. In December of 1944 I learned of a competition to design a British military cemetery in Athens. This presented no problems. It would be a plot facing Phaleron Bay on which would be superimposed a serried array of tombstones marking those who had died in Greece. My submission won.

Victory

The brigade returned to Naples in March 1945 and prepared for innumerable engagements in support of the attack on the German positions in the Po Valley. We lived through planned drop after drop, incessant briefings, and cancellations. Then, in May, came the jubilant news of surrender. Although a total abstainer, I relaxed on this occasion and toasted victory with the Martell Three Star Brandy I had captured in Taranto in 1943. But we were not excused, and our jubilation was short-lived. It transpired that the Yugoslavs planned to attack Trieste, and so for

Officers of the Second Parachute Squadron in civilian garb in Ramsbury, Wiltshire, 1945. I was a captain and am in the back center.

weeks we lived under the wings of DC3s, the last combatants in Europe, planning operation after operation, but none eventuated. We had survived.

In June the squadron embarked on HM Troopship *Almansera* at Naples and proceeded to Gourock. We arrived on a summer evening, in the gloaming, the luminous predusk, to a serene Clyde, a quiet, verdant, landscape. Gone were the sere, arid lands of the Mediterranean; here was a green and pleasant land.

The contrast between war and peace could not have been more dramatic than that provided by Ramsbury, the village in Wiltshire where the squadron was billeted after disembarkation. The place was a picture postcard with thatched cottages and an ancestral oak surrounded by a bench where sat the village elders. There were a legitimate grand seigneur and lady of the manor to whom locals touched their forelocks, curtsied, or doffed hats. We were immediately welcomed by the local society and pressed into social and church functions—garden parties, teas, bazaars, and more. Our accommodations subtended a magnificent garden with enormous deodar cedars, tall clipped yew hedges, and lawns. Bees buzzed on herbaceous borders, flowers gleamed, voices were rarely raised, a very gentle courtesy prevailed, and the weather was beautiful. You could feel the healing.

The war was over, it was proper and necessary to abandon violence, to enter into quiet discourse, to discover an unthreatening life and savor it. It was for this and the freedom from Hitler that we had fought.

This salubrity, the healing power of nature, came to be a major recurring and reinforcing theme in my life: Ravello after Cassino, Ramsbury at war's end, Leysin in Switzerland, recovering from tuberculosis, annual visits for decades to Lake Temagami, Ontario, and currently, residence in bucolic Chester County, Pennsylvania.

These living experiences have generated and maintained my conviction of nature's power; they have provided substance for a succession of sermons, generating principles for a sequence of projects. The purpose was always to advocate and apply the beneficence of nature, as benign and salubrious as these experiences have been for me.

Demobilization

As the war drew to a close, plans were made to organize demobilization. The magic number became Age and Service Group 27. Those who ranked above that number would remain in the armed forces and, presumably, engage in the campaign against Japan. Those with that number and below would be demobilized. I had joined the Territorial Army at the age of 17 in 1938; I served for more than seven years during the war and was to be demobilized in September of 1946. As the vast majority of my colleagues had served for the entire war, the staging of demobilization, in fact, related to age. I was the youngest major among all of the Royal Engineers of both the First and Sixth Divisions. Thus, because of my youth, I came to have my finest command: Residues, First and Sixth Airborne Divisions, Royal Engineers. Initially, the command was 1,500 strong, and we thought ourselves the cream of the British Army.

We were located in Bulford barracks in Salisbury Plain, in facilities that had been in continuous use during the entire war. The British Army at that time had a procedure entitled "Barrack Damages." Before a unit left a facility, all damages were identified and costs were levied upon all soldiers, which money accrued to a fund deemed sufficient to pay for repairs. I inherited the damaged Bulford barracks and the fund.

I had many problems to contend with, not the least of which was my youth. This command consisted of experienced veterans who had parachuted into Tragino, Bruneval, North Africa, Sicily, the south of France, Normandy, Greece, and Arnhem. For them the war was over; they were impatient to go home. Yet the army's scenario for a soldier's day was parades, training, foot drill, weapons drill, exercises, and more parades. This program I felt, would incite mutiny. I was not a grizzled senior officer who would maintain rigid discipline and enforce a continued army regimen until the bitter end. I was the youngest in the command. So I devised a stratagem. All officers and men who could be admitted to a university, college, technical training school or teacher's college would be sent to such establishments and would, at the appropriate time, present themselves to their regional demobilization centers and terminate their military careers. Exit one hundred.

Next, I contacted all the tradespeople in the region—builders, construction companies, carpenters, plumbers, masons, tinsmiths, riggers, others and—and complied a large list of such employers. I then made them a very generous offer. Soldiers having the appropriate skills would be made available to them. They would be delivered to the workplace in denims with a packed lunch and picked up at the close of the working day. The employers were free to pay such soldiers at rates mutually agreeable. My interest laying in seeing that the soldier-tradesmen and soldier-laborers had the opportunity to recover their skills and to be usefully employed. However, they could work only four days a week, because on the fifth day all troops were required to make repairs to the barracks. One other gratifying stratagem was that, with the exception of a standing guard and other essential personnel, all troops would have weekend leaves.

The plan worked. The troops retrieved their skills, were to all intents free from Army life during most of the week, made money, and had weekend leave. There was one requirement, which was well received: Before their departure each Saturday, there was to be a ceremonial parade and inspection. This was a proud crew. The majority had a row of medals, and it was a matter of pride to execute foot and arms drill to perfection. Each troop was inspected by the troop commander. All then reported. "Troops, ready for inspection, sir." After inspection, I proceeded to my platform to await the next command. "Troops will advance, in review order, by the center, quick march." This marvelous array, 1,500 strong in lines of three, marched sixteen paces and, without command, came to a thunderous halt. "Parade, present arms." Crash, crash, crash. The regimental band played the regimental march. I saluted, palpitating with pride and fear. My salute dropped. "Order arms." Rifles crashed on shoulders, and the adjutant advanced toward me. "March off, sir, please." "March off." "Parade, by the left, quick march." Each troop marched past at the salute, the First Parachute Squadron, the Second, the Seventh Field Company R.E. (Airborne), the Fourth (Middle East) Squadron, the 261st Field Park Company (Airborne). They marched off, halted, were dismissed, climbed on trucks, and drove to the station.

Slowly the ranks dwindled as did the necessity for barrack repairs, so that when my batman and I were the only remaining troops I was able to report a fully rehabilitated barracks and transmit keys and documents to the Base Area Command. But there remained one task. I had the Barrack Damage Fund. What to do with it? Easy. I sat down and wrote two checks, dividing the fund in half. One half, several thousand pounds, was consigned to the Royal Engineers Benevolent Fund, the other to the Airborne Forces Security Fund. I took the train to York, my regional demobilization center, collected a vile, ill-fitting pinstripe suit, and entrained to Glasgow and home, a civilian.

CSM Middlemass

When I enlisted in the Territorial Army in May of 1938, the dominant figure in the 243d Field Park Company, Royal Engineers, was a regular sergeant major with more than over 20 years of service. He was CSM Middlemass, almost a caricature, a martinet, of rigid bearing, unsmiling face, and a bellow that could be heard for miles. He would measure hair length in millimeters, could discern the requisite polish on boots and rifle barrels, as well as mute insolence by demeanor, at a distance, and he meted out punishments with relish. All to the good—the unit decidedly needed discipline. However, Middlemass was also a bully. He selected persons whom he considered unsuited to become Royal Engineers and allocated to them particularly dangerous, painful, and offensive duties. His model for an exemplary sapper was a rigger with military skills and deportment. Skill as a rigger involved ropes, tackle blocks, spars, derricks, gins, shears, scaffolding and, not least, levers. I know none of this.

I was a raw recruit. The majority of the unit had at least seven years regular service and were skilled in these matters. But it was my identification as an art student that distinguished me from the other recruits. CSM Middlemass held that artists were effete, weak, and far too delicate for the role of sapper. So I came to be identified as The Art Student. Each morning, after first parade, tasks were allocated. As sure as death, I would be singled out. "Art Student, report to...." The duty would assuredly be the most unwelcome of those to be allocated. I am certain that this selection did speed my learning process, unpleasant though it was, but far too often he assigned me to tasks that were very painful and, in a number of cases, downright dangerous. The inevitable selection for guard duty, weekend duty, latrine and kitchen duty was only a minor victimization. The painful tasks were more memorable, the dangerous ones stay with me to this day.

Among the painful experiences three remain vivid. The first involved steel wire rope. This kind of rope comes in the form of a coiled spring. If released carelessly, it will writhe violently, capable of removing arms, legs, or head. Moreover, if it is handled without gloves, small pieces of steel strands lacerate the hands. These splinters are difficult to remove and produce painful sores. I was always selected for this task and was refused gloves—the work would harden my soft hands, I was told. The same reasoning applied to unloading truckloads of bricks. One man on a truck was to throw throw six bricks to a person on the ground, who had to catch them before they fell. However, it was not only necessary to catch, but also to press the bricks together lest they separate. Within an hour the fingers were sensitized and the skin was abraded. After several hours the hands were bleeding and every clasp was excruciatingly painful, but there could be no escape until medical inspection on the following day. If there ever was a dangerous role, involving derricks, cranes, and levers, you can be sure that it was mine. Perhaps my increasing skill challenged the sergeant major's ingenuity. There was one occasion when he threatened my life.

The unit was engaged in constructing emplacements for naval guns and anti-aircraft artillery on the seawall of Leith Harbor. These were thirty-feet-high reinforced concrete structures. Concrete was barrowed up scaffolding to be poured into forms. The gangplank was narrow, slippery with spilled concrete. It was thirty feet to the ground and almost as much again from the riprap wall to the sea.

Without a doubt Middlemass ensured that my barrow load of concrete was very wet, which made stability more difficult. Of course, off the scaffolding I fell, concrete, barrow, and all. During the project I suffered many nasty tumbles. After the last of these, my sergeant, Jimmy Gold, remonstrated with Middlemass and had me taken to the medical officer who treated multiple lacerations with iodine and bandages, checked for broken ribs, examined me for concussion, and consigned me to bed rest.

Fortunately, I was transferred to the 241st Field Company, recruited from Motherwell miners and steel workers led by another regular, "Okeydoke" McDowell, who had an entirely different temperament. He was noisy, profane but jocular. His commentary was salacious, impugning father, mother, legitimacy, sanitary habits, and intelligence, but he never identified me as an art student. I was only one in two hundred and fifty, all thoroughly inadequate, who must be trained to become soldiers.

I saw Middlemass again after the war had ended. I was in Glasgow: I had completed a satisfactory dinner in an excellent restaurant. I stepped out the door, and there was Middlemass, now a regimental sergeant major. He had made one promotion in seven years. I had made eight. It was Major McHarg who confronted

CSM Middlemass. He gave me a parade ground salute. I addressed him, "Sergeant Major Middlemass, is it not?"

"Sir."

"Perhaps you remember me, we spent some time together in 1939."

"No Sir."

"But we did, indeed. We shared some memorable experiences together, you and I, in the 243d Field Park Company." "I do remember the officers in that unit, but I cannot recall you, Sir."

"But, Sergeant Major, I was not then an officer, but a sapper, a recruit." Now it was winter, with snow on the ground, an icy wind, and perhaps sleet. I was warmly clad in a greatcoat. I wore gloves. Middlemass was in his tunic, aiming for some cozy pub nearby, unprotected from the weather. "Let me tell you of some of our shared experiences." So I exhumed the bitter memories—hands lacerated by steel wire rope, bricks, concussion, further lacerations, cracked ribs, and more. I recounted these in detail as he stood there, blue with the cold, rigidly at attention, a drip on his nose. "And what have you been doing since we parted?"

He had served in military prisons, an exquisite allocation of resources. Finally, I released him: "March off, Middlemass." With a tremulous salute, he walked away. A small, but gratifying, revenge.

The Military Experience

My decision to join the Army in May of 1938 was quite an extraordinary one. No member of my high school or college classes made such a choice, nor did any member of my church, family, or friends. Why did I? Clearly, I had developed a strong repugnance for fascism and nazism, sufficiently strong to explain this quite independent act.

When I became a soldier in 1938 at 18, I was tall, thin, gangling, a hobbledehoy. My clothes looked too short, they often were. I had grown like a weed in adolescence.

In the Army, youth and weakness were magnets for bullies, so to increase my apparent age I grew a moustache. Spare and unconvincing it needed the black ends of burnt matches to have an effect, but in time it became a distinguishing feature: brown, bushy, bristly; now white, downy, and docile.

From 1938 to 1946, through the war, I changed from adolescent to young man. I became stronger, more muscular, better coordinated. As a measure of fitness I once engaged in walking-running for seventy-five miles in twenty-four hours, carrying full equipment and weapons. This was in preparation for parachute support of the Dieppe landing. The plan was to land behind the lines, deny movement to reinforcements, then walk-run to the coast to be evacuated by submarines. Bad weather canceled parachute participation.

I was quite parochial in 1938, having left Scotland only once for a trip to Belfast. The army, into which I was mobilized in 1939, changed that. My travels could hardly have been improved had they been designed for my education. I traversed North Africa, saw Muslim cities, the Roman ruins in Carthage and elsewhere, Paestum, Herculaneum, Pompei, and the *trulli* in Italy; Italian hill towns, Rome, Athens, the length of Greece, the Italian Alps; Udine, Cannes, Nice, Frejus; monasteries in Siatista and Grevena. I made visits to Albania, Yugoslavia, and Bulgaria, not to mention my extensive travels in that foreign neighbor England: Ely and York, Glastonbury and Salisbury, Diss, Thetford, Massingham, Little Chickering, and Bridport.

Rank increased with age as did responsibility. At eighteen a section of eight men was my command; as a corporal, at nineteen, I had two sections; as a second lieutenant in parachute troops, seventeen soldiers, the capacity of a DC3; as a lieutenant, two of these; as a captain, a "V" of three and fifty-one troops. As a major at twenty-four, my command was a squadron of 250 soldiers. My final command, residues of the First and Sixth Airborne Divisions, was 1,500 strong.

As acting chief royal engineer I had the staff car and pennant, so when I drove to meetings in London at the War Office soldiers in sight of my pennant had to turn toward me and salute. This is a severe test for a twenty-four-year-old. In addition to association with superb human beings and a wide aray of experiences, I suppose the single most identifiable product of my military service was the development of a strong sense of self-confidence that I have not relinquished.

The first letter of recommendation ever written for me was from my commanding officer, C.D.H. Vernon, who wrote, "Ian McHarg will do well whatever he chooses." Later, Lewis Mumford, another idol, wrote of my confidence. Both men contributed to that state, for which they have my eternal gratitude.

Chapter 3

Harvard
1946–1950

I well remember the joy of war's end. VE day had come and gone and I was alive. For almost seven years I had disciplined my mind to avoid the long term, to address the moment, to survive another night, to greet another morning, and here I was with all limbs intact and nothing more than a few trivial scars. Best of all, at last, I was able to predict a long future. There could be years, decades, wife, children and grandchildren, and a professional career.

At the age of sixteen I had resolved to become a landscape architect. I had become the properly bound apprentice to Donald A. Wintersgill, perhaps the only landscape architect in Scotland at that time. For five pounds a year he had undertaken responsibility for my education and would, after five years, certify to my accomplishments. I withdrew from high school and was admitted as a special student to three institutions: art school, agricultural college, and engineering school. While admitted to an engineering school, I did not undertake studies before the war. I studied military engineering as a cadet officer.

Here it was May of 1945, and I had to decide how to finish my education. Should I continue in my Scottish program or was there another way? There was a very distinguished officer from the First Parachute Squadron, Captain Steven George, who had graduated in architecture from Liverpool. He had a friend, William, later Sir William, later still Lord William Holford, who had taught at Liverpool and also at Harvard, where it so happened there was a curriculum in landscape architecture. It was possible to study all that I required in one place. So I wrote for a catalogue and an application for admission. I also applied for an Army Education Release Scheme Scholarship. But there was a serious problem: the Harvard curriculum was a graduate program in which a B.A. or B.S. was the least prerequisite for admission. I had neither, nor had I finished high school. All I had were documents attesting to my studies at sundry institutions as a part-time student.

The British Army had several mottoes; one was "Bullshit Baffles Brains," another, "When in Doubt, Charge." It seemed to be the time to employ both. Of course, I could have written. I could have assembled letters testifying to service and valor, but my academic credentials were meager. I would not have had a chance. I decided upon a different stratagem. I sent a telegram to the chairman of the department, one Bremer Whidden Pond, which read: "Dear Professor Pond, I propose to begin studies towards a Master in Landscape Architecture with effect from September 1946. Please make necessary arrangements. (Signed) Ian L. McHarg, Major."

I received a most generous reply that said, among other things, "Dear Major McHarg: We are so proud that you chose Harvard."

At that time crossing the Atlantic was not two-meals-and-a-snooze (or even less on the Concorde); it was still a major event. It took me two weeks on the *Manchester Shipper*, a small ship beleaguered by a pod of whales in the St. Lawrence. So a European arrivee at Harvard could not very well be summarily rejected and deported. No, the rules were simple. There were a number of prerequisite courses I must pass, and there were also required graduate courses I must pass. If, at the end of a year I had done so, I could stay. I did. But I learned a lesson: every year for more than thirty years I reviewed applications for admission to the University of Pennsylvania with a particularly sensitive eye for those who do not meet all prerequisites, who could not draw a line, who had had a calamitous college experience or had made a late career change. Many such candidates have been admitted, and many have done extraordinarily well.

I attended Harvard for four calendar years, from 1946 to 1950, including summer school throughout the period, so I actually compiled more than five years of study. I was very fortunate on several counts, not least of which was to have been admitted into a graduate program and to have joined what is still remembered as a prodigious class. The group that entered in 1946 drew from the wartime accumulation of deferred students and an enlarged body of candidates given access by the G.I. Bill. It was also a high point in Harvard's history.

Universities rise and wane; their reputations follow more slowly. At that time there were giants galore. The Graduate School of Design held certainly national, perhaps international, primacy in modern architecture and planning, dominated by the powerful presence of Walter Gropius.

Harvard was a new world. No longer were the criteria rank, regiment, campaigns, or medals. In their place was a new hierarchy of undergraduates, graduates, doctoral candidates, and ranks of professor. The common denominator was not valor, but intellect.

If parachute troops were thought to be the army's finest, Harvard was then considered to be the zenith of academia. My status had not changed, but the context had. Brain, not muscle, was critical.

There was one other change, relative age. During my service I had generally been younger than the troops I commanded; at Harvard I was among the older students. My service had been twice as long as theirs, and so I was their senior, as was my rank. There were no other majors among my colleagues, which may have explained my selection as student representative and, subsequently, chairman of the Student Council, in which capacity I met with Dean Hudnut and Walter Gropius each week, an impressive experience.

The fall of 1946 was a major threshold in my life. I had moved from soldier to civilian, with the wonder of new-found freedom. I had changed from being a son in a family to becoming an independent person. Of course, the army had robbed me of my adolescence, but then it appeared recoverable. There could be women and parties, I might even try alcohol, and America was the home of jazz and striptease. Above all, I was living in a charming town, learning in a great university, embroiled in an intellectual ferment, meeting new friends, young and enthusiastic. I was profoundly happy.

Pauline

At twenty-five I arrived at Harvard, still a major, as I had several months of accumulated leave, and "Major" I came to be called.

I had some money. In Scotland it was the custom for sons to transmit their salaries to their fathers, and that is what I had done with my military salary. My father deposited this into an account in my name. So I had a seven year accumulation of salary. In addition, I had been awarded an Army Education Release Scheme Scholarship, the British G.I. Bill. This included free tuition and a stipend. A committee at Harvard advised the Scottish Educational Office of the dollars required to support a British major. This was twice the G.I. Bill allotment. And I was well tailored. There was an excellent tailor in Glasgow at the time, William Shearer. He made me suits, hacking jackets, whipcord trousers, and an overcoat. I had handkerchiefs, shirts, shoes, and boots made, and even a soft hat and a cloth cap. I bought ties, socks, gloves, and scarves. I have never since been as well dressed. The overcoat and boots I still have to this day.

Although the authors of the legislation conceived of the army scholarships as payment for services rendered, I always viewed the award as a debt. So when I finished my education I did return to Scotland as a civil servant, but my repayment was fulfilled by training the majority of landscape architects, not only in Scotland, but in Britain, all at the University of Pennsylvania.

I was fit. Whatever else the Army did for me, it made me strong and healthy. So that September I was at a peak of animal health, fitness, energy, and enthusiasm. I was enchanted at being alive, aglow with the prospect that Harvard represented. This was the man who met that young lady who was to become my wife of thirty years, mother of my two older sons, Alistair and Malcolm.

Our meeting was dramatic. I knew no one at Harvard, but I learned that the Foreign Student Center in Cambridge was having an introductory reception and dance for new foreign students. I was invited. I entered a polyglot group: Indians with turbans, Nigerians in native dress, the majority in Western clothes but drawn from the entire world. Immediately I saw a tall, blonde, and powerfully beautiful woman. When the music started I asked her to dance. She was Dutch, from Amsterdam, and her name was Pauline Crena de Iongh. This was her second year at Radcliffe; she was studying English literature. We sat down to talk. She had served in the Dutch underground, a member of a group that had hidden Jewish children and transported Allied aviators. She had also been a courier. I knew nothing of the Netherlands; my only association had been vicarious and tragic. The First Airborne Division, in which I had served, had fallen at Oosterbeek and Arnhem, "A Bridge Too Far." But we shared astonishment at America's abundance of food, clothing, movement, and energy. She had lived through the "hunger winter" on a diet of tulip bulbs. She had obtained fuel for the stove by dismembering park benches and railroad ties. Yet here were eggs, butter, sugar, meat, fish, fresh fruit, vegetables—and clothes. Through the war she had lived with the same wardrobe. Here there were choices galore. We shared an exultation at this cornucopia and its strangeness of accent, behavior, and language.

I learned that her father was in the United States and that he had arranged for Pauline to come here and repair from the stress of the last war years, particularly the death of her fiance in a concentration camp. He had been a member of the same underground cell.

Her father, Dr. Daniel Crena de Iongh, was treasurer and director of both the International Bank for Reconstruction and Development and the International Monetary Fund. He had been president of the Handelmaschapij, the largest bank in the Netherlands; then, before the war, he had gone to the Dutch East Indies as a financial advisor, had been evacuated to Australia after the collapse there, and had subsequently gone to London with the Dutch government in exile. He had been the Dutch delegate to the Bretton Woods Conference. Now he lived in Washington, D.C.

Pauline had been to New York City, to Connecticut, Long Island, and Washington. She was full of observations about this fascinating region of the country. She had friends. There was a Dutch group at Harvard and MIT, and that night I was introduced to its members, including Nico de Iongh, now Nobel laureate physicist at Harvard, and others, not quite so well appreciated, but all charming. When the evening ended we arranged to meet the next day.

Now my reluctance to engage in casual encounters was vindicated. At last here was a fit object of adoration; she had warmth, intelligence, charm, and beauty. I immediately fell in love.

The relationship prospered. We held hands, we kissed goodnight. It's hard to believe this decorum when passion was raging. Those were different times.

I found myself in the company of a novel person. Nothing in my experience had prepared me for this. Pauline spoke Dutch, German, French, and English. She had a strong command of Latin and Greek. She had majored in history at Leiden and possessed a great knowledge of European history. She was knowledgeable about Dutch history, philosophy, and art, and about German literature. She was acquiring familiarity with English literature and philosophy at Radcliffe. She played the cello and was involved in music. I was quite ignorant of these realms.

The greatest contrast was our respective social lives. Mine, as you know, was modest and lower-middle class. Pauline's was quite different. Conversations disclosed servants, butlers, grooms, sojourns to many cities and locations in Europe, winters in the Alps, a home designed by M. J. Grandpré Molière (who had been an influence on and was influenced by Frank Lloyd Wright), encounters with Casals, the Dutch poet laureate as friend and neighbor, Maria Montessori, and others. But the distinction between social levels was most dramatically demonstrated by the revelation that Prince Bernhardt was a familiar in her family's house. It transpired that when the young German was chosen as consort, his introduction to the Dutch economy was entrusted to Crena de Iongh. As near as I ever got to royalty was when inspected by George VI. He had passed me by without acknowledgment. As for servants, the only one we ever had was Mrs. Campbell, the midwife, who would cook and clean for a few weeks after the birth of each child.

As Pauline's life and family were revealed, there emerged a very strong and dominant figure—her mother. Anne Elisabeth Gransberg was a *hogebusigezedelweib*, high-born aristocrat of ancient German lineage with castle, heraldic devices, and other accoutrements of rank. It had been a great success for young Crena de Iongh to capture this beautiful and rich young woman. Beauty she was indeed, but this distinction was equaled by her barbed tongue. She was censorious of husband, children, servants, and Prince Bernhardt, whose accent and manners she found barbarous. At one hundred years of age she is still a feisty lady, until quite recently collecting signatures for nuclear disarmament in Bergen, North Holland, and upbraiding those who do not cooperate.

I soon learned that I had become the subject of her attention. Who was this Scotsman who was courting her daughter? She wrote a peremptory letter to the Dutch consul general in Edinburgh. "Advise me of this young man, Ian McHarg, his family and circumstance." Later, in 1950, I was to see this correspondence. "John McHarg is a manager in Singer Sewing Machines, he is a pillar of the community and the church, widely respected. His children, including Ian, are well behaved and admirable. Major McHarg has an excellent military record." My father had never worked for Singer.

This was not what she wanted to hear but was all she got. When she learned that I was training to become a landscape architect, she said, "Oh dear, why even architects are not gentlemen." It may be that the highest praise I have ever achieved is the surprise and admiration of my original mother-in-law. It came slowly but ultimately.

The matter was now becoming serious. Pauline used some stratagem to bring her father to Cambridge. I joined them at dinner in the Continental Hotel, and it was clear that I was being interrogated and evaluated. I could not match his offers of connection. He was a member of the Reform Club in London, a familiar of Keynes, Dalton, and Beveridge, people whom I knew only from the press and books. He abandoned that line of inquiry and elicited my wartime impressions and future plans.

He was a magnificent gentleman whom I came to know very well: concerned, conscientious, and deeply involved with the World Bank's investments in Third World countries. I was never successful in my continued advocacy of ecological analysis and planning as a prerequisite to investments in large projects such as the Aswan Dam and massive structures in India and elsewhere. My only success was that when he was asked by UNO to advise on independence for Somalia, I persuaded him to retain the great South African ecologist, John V. Phillips, to accompany and advise him. He said that I seemed like an estimable young man. He approved and would so advise Pauline's mother.

Pauline's parents, I discovered, were separated. He had left the Netherlands before the war to take the position of financial advisor to the government of the Dutch East Indies. He was not to see his wife and family for eight years. When he returned he found that, although beauty might have waned somewhat, the censorious tongue was even more acerbic. Now his son and his twin daughters were married. Only his youngest daughter, Pauline, was at home. He determined to send her to the United States, and, this settled, initiated divorce proceedings.

I proposed marriage to Pauline at Christmas, and was accepted. We arranged to be married following the end of summer school in August.

An Education Reviewed

I have tried to describe my Harvard experience as it happened, a chronological recapitulation, but it is impossible to recover the innocence and experiences of discovery, for there has been an immense time lapse during which my learning has been reviewed, much discarded, and the remainder modified and synthesized in ways then unknown to me. Better to present it through retrospective criticism. Some years later I found myself immobilized as a patient in a hospital, unable to read, write, or listen to the radio, limited only to the mind. During this time, I reviewed my entire Harvard education and reorganized it as a hoard of valuable perceptions. This may be the most palatable form in which to relate the experience.

Although I had been admitted as a master's candidate in landscape architecture, I concluded within two weeks that this curriculum would not engage the mind, far less challenge it. The faculty were committed to the interwar tradition of gardens for the rich; their visions were small as was their scale; they were without distinction, an anomaly in a great university. Yet it need not have been. The faculty was a product of the great Olmsted tradition—among its founders was Charles Eliot, son of the Harvard president, a brilliant and innovative landscape architect. This marvelous origin, however, had been largely abandoned. Upon my appointment as chairman of the Student Council, a resolution of no confidence in the faculty of landscape architecture was passed and transmitted to President Conant.

For my part, I resolved to also enroll for a master's degree in city planning, and my application was approved. This program would, and did, challenge the mind. It was also consonant with my image of the professional life I sought and expanded the studies I had begun in the correspondence course with the London School of Reconstruction and Development. I viewed city planning and landscape architecture as a unity, and, indeed, instruction in the first semester reflected this view. Architects, landscape architects, and planners all participated in a common experience, a planning study of Cambridge.

I suppose the primary value of my education was the provision of a systematic view, which allowed me to see artifacts as products of time, process, culture, and environment. The histories of cities and landscape architecture were cases in point. I was, after all, a European. I had a familiarity with Edinburgh, Bath, and the London parks and squares. I had spent almost three years abroad with the army and had traveled extensively. I had seen Carthage, Tunis, and the elaborate Roman ruins in North Africa, had spent more than two years in Italy, had seen Pompeii, Herculaneum, and Paestum, indeed, had seen Vesuvius erupting, *trulli*, hill towns galore. I knew Rome quite well, and Athens too; indeed I had fought communists on the Acropolis, in

Thermopolae, Parnassus, Salonika, Siatista, and Grevena. Back in England, I knew Wells and Salisbury cathedrals. But all this experience was random. Dean Joseph Hudnut used chronology in his course, "The City in History," to present a pilgrimage through cities in time. A small man with a lisp, audible only as far as the second row, he savored the excesses of Caligula, Livia, and the de Medicis. He spoke of the Renaissance popes, whom he deemed great humanists but indifferent Christians. He proceeded from Egypt to Greece then to Rome, medieval Europe, the Renaissance in Italy and France, eighteenth-century England, nineteenth-century America, and ended with Daniel Burnham and the Chicago World's Fair of 1893. Ancient Athens, classical and Renaissance Rome, Haussmann's Paris, eighteenth-century Edinburgh, Bath, and London were his exclamation points. The course was comprehensive and well illustrated.

Bremer Whidden Pond covered the same paths, but viewed from the vantage of landscape architecture—peristyle and atrium, the monastic gardens, the evolving scale and symmetry of medieval gardens in France, the Renaissance efflorescence in Tivoli, d'Este, Lante, Aldobrandini, Mondragone, the transfer of leadership to France represented in Vaux-le-Vicomte and Versailles. The English eighteenth-century landscape movement was treated without sympathy, as a deflection, an aberration, impeding the march of the Renaissance. Of those in the United States, Frederick Law Olmsted, Sr., the giant, founder of the profession, was slighted and Eliot was ignored, as were the young turks, all from Harvard—Church, Eckbo, Halprin, Kiley, and Rose—who were then seeking the forms for a modern landscape architecture.

The intellectual basis for both inquiries—*The Culture of Cities* by Lewis Mumford—was resolutely excluded from reading lists, yet it was this great book, which employed culture as the measure of artifacts and read from these to interpret culture, that imbued these chronological exercises with significance and meaning.

The subject of cities was addressed from a quite different and more fundamental view by geographers Derwent Whittlesey and Edward Ullman, professors of location theory and economics, respectively. Their approach included defensible positions, significant routes and their conjunctions, fords, river crossings, the geometries of agricultural economies, farms, hamlets, villages and towns, and, later, resources and their locational powers—iron ore, coal, limestone, water, and markets, and, still later, technological effects, mechanized farming (including cotton picking), the movement of defense department installations sunward, and cheap power from the Tennessee Valley Authority (TVA).

These insights were given a different focus by sociologist Oscar Handlin and political scientist Arthur Maas. Handlin addressed the Boston community and proferred a historical analysis beginning with the Puritan origins and early history, followed by the influx of the Irish and the Italians, culminating with Mayor Curley in jail and winning reelection. The books of John Marquand were high on his reading list for the course. The conflicts of ethnic groups, their values, and their identification, I found novel and interesting. In contrast, Scotland was all but homogenous. The environment, however, received no mention, although the reclamation of the Back Bay was surely significant to the development of Boston. There was no linkage of ethnicity, religion, occupation, resources, environmental selection, attendant values, or institutions. Yet the course gave a complementary view to cities and gardens in regard to history, location theory, and economic geography.

Arthur Maas's subject was the region and his instrument the TVA, which he approached as a political scientist. He set forth the problem of the seven poorest states in the nation with one abundant latent resource, water power, and the history of its exploitation. This was my first encounter with the regional scale, and I found it enthralling. No course can satisfy criticisms assembled a half century later. Maas was excellent, lively, witty, and perceptive. Political science knew nothing of the environment—crucial to the TVA—nothing about people, not even at Handlin's level, but it did present the institution and powers of government in a most effective way. I received a serendipitous reward from this course. Sitting next to me in class was the wife of Bernard DeVoto, the famous writer, critic, historian, and conservationist, whom I subsequently met and from whom I first learned of the conservation movement. His many books remain classics today.

G. Holmes Perkins was chairman of city planning and my advisor. He recommended that I take an undergraduate course in government. My growing interest in planning made it clear that although I was quite familiar with the British experience, I needed to understand the entirely distinct American system. So I began with the Federalist papers and listened enthralled to information most schoolboys already knew. My Scottish education had not even mentioned the Revolutionary War, far less the Constitution. My attitude toward the United States changed from a simple view of an energetic and prosperous people to admiration for an entirely original and marvelous form of government.

I was led then to a modern application of this system, a study of the Boston metropolitan community by Maurice Lambie. It included for me the astonishing revelation that planning did not repose in central government, as in Britain where it was imposed upon minor subdivisions. The reverse was true in the United States. The power to plan and zone reposed in municipalities alone, and counties, states, even the federal government, retained no powers in this realm. However, Lambie's burden was that the process revealed redundancy, omissions, inefficiency, and most of all, that municipalities did not have the resources or the will to coordinate, plan, or manage.

Here again was a complementary perception, and the analysis made then holds substantially true for today. The problems of planning have expanded and become more intractable, but the consciousness of the environment is now a significant element.

Kenneth Galbraith and John T. Black offered a seminar, "The Economics of Agriculture." For me, it offered a most original experience, that of criticizing senior officials in government and their policies, none of whom elicited the admiration of either professor. Their low regard of politicians and senior government officials was a new view for a soldier imprinted by hierarchy. Their reviews of policy for agricultural practice were extensive and revelatory, addressing subsidies for western irrigation, grazing on public lands, timber forestry, the effect of mechanization

Kenneth Galbraith

In 1948 I enrolled in a course, "The Economics of Agriculture." The professor was Dr. John T. Black, an eminent figure from Wisconsin. His assistant was John Kenneth Galbraith, a very tall, cadaverous, and witty Canadian of Scots extraction. In effect, Galbraith ran the course. The class had fourteen students; thirteen were Ph.D. candidates, many from the Food and Agriculture Organization of the United Nations in Geneva. There were Australians, Canadians, Englishmen, and two Scotsmen. I was an anomaly, a master's candidate in city and regional planning.

The structure of the course involved examining the recent history of American agriculture with a review of the resulting policies and interrogation of the principle actors—the secretary, undersecretaries, and division chiefs from the United States Department of Agriculture. Success was measured by assimilation and criticism of these policies.

I well remember the occasion when the secretary of agriculture appeared before the class. We had reviewed the Agriculture Act and interrogated the secretary. We did quite well, I thought, mere graduate students examining a secretary. Galbraith was unimpressed. He decided to undertake the task himself. "Mr.

Secretary," he said, "you do not have any understanding of the profound and pernicious effects of your legislation. You will engender three very painful costs and deleterious consequences, all inadvertent. Your Act subsidizes large-scale mechanized agriculture, and, in particular, it subsidizes mechanized cotton picking. As the labor force consists of black tenant farmers, living in states without welfare, these will be rendered surplus and homeless, and, seeking employment and welfare, will migrate in massive numbers to northern states and cities for which they are unsuited. They will be forced into environments they would not choose, they will prove to be indigestible to these economies and will provide an enduring social problem. But more, by your subsidies to corporate mechanized agriculture you will kill the family farm, first in New England, then the South, and, finally, the Midwest. From this follows the final indictment. Studies after the First and Second World Wars revealed that the finest recruits to the services were farm boys. Thus you will also undermine the quality of the armed services of the United States. These are not trivial; your inadvertent effects will overwhelm the ostensible benefits of the Act."

on southern blacks, and the demise of the family farm. Strangely, however, there was no discussion of the environment.

On one field trip I visited Harvard Forest, saw the hurricane devastation of 1939, listened to arguments on whether white pine represented the forest climax, and met my first ecologist, Dr. Hugh Raup. He was in limbo and had no impact on either biology or landscape architecture. I regret that he had no effect on me either, and that almost a decade would pass before I came to realize that ecology provides the theoretical basis for all biological adaptations, and most important, for planning and landscape architecture.

The most demanding courses I took were in landscape engineering, taught by Walter Chambers. He was a bitter man, demanding, meticulous, and merciless, who could not tolerate errors in the second decimal of a foot. He failed students regularly and with relish, yet he was the only competent professor in the department. He was well organized, taught seriously, and gave weekly tests. His subjects were necessary but tedious: calculating earthworks, cut and fill, earth movement, highway design, horizontal and vertical alignment, highway capacities, municipal and highway engineering, water and sewage treatment facilities.

But he was a barbarous man. It so happened that "Municipal and Highway Engineering" was a required course for both landscape architecture and city planning. I took it and received an A$^+$, notably for a paper on soil stabilization, which employed my experience in making and repairing runways using this method during the war. I went to Chambers with a paper authorizing my exemption from the course within my curriculum in planning, having already taken it for landscape architecture.

"Not so," said Chambers, "You'll have to take it again. It cannot count twice."

"I have taken it and passed. Wouldn't it be better to take something else?"

"No way."

I stood up and closed the door to his office. I moved toward him. "Chambers, you are a barbarous bully and a fool to boot. How can you require me to repeat this course? If you don't sign that paper, I promise to punch your teeth down your throat."

"Sit down, McHarg. Look, I am involved in a painful divorce, and I suffer migraine headaches."

"If ever a man deserves to be divorced it's you, and you amply deserve migraine headaches."

"Give me the paper," he said. I did and he signed it. Years later he left Harvard to become chairman at the University of Michigan. He invited me to speak annually and always introduced me as the only student who had ever offered to punch him. "And he was right," he would conclude.

William Linus Cody Wheaton, a descendant of Buffalo Bill Cody, was an economist and political scientist. His realm of expertise was housing. He operated much as Galbraith and Black did, inviting key officials in the Urban Renewal Agency and the housing industry and subjecting them to criticism and analysis. The subject was entirely novel to me. In Britain housing was overwhelmingly undertaken by municipalities operating through a subsidy system controlled by central government. In the United States this was primarily performed by private enterprise. The new government offerings of federally guaranteed mortgages, equal payments, and the exemption of equity for veterans constituted the leverage that could be employed to guide policy. Wheaton examined housing market analysis, comparative resource allocation, and the role of business. He was particularly contemptuous of the efforts by architects to provide low-income housing by reducing standards for space and materials. Rather, he suggested, mortgages should be subsidized or the payoff time lengthened. Either or both, he said, would effect much larger economies.

The Federal Housing Administration (FHA) policies, which were central to this course, would, of course, become the primary agent for the suburbanization of the United States, and the decline of inner cities. They were also crucial to understanding the planning process. The FHA did not participate in planning, and the Urban Renewal Administration was ineffectual; their successor, HUD (the Department of Housing and Urban Development), proved even less effective and headed toward dissolution and corruption under the Reagan administration. Yet, unhappy as the story is, achieved with the prodigal use of resources and enormous environmental despoliation, the housing stock acquired in North America since World War II is the envy of the world. The expansion of American urban slums, in contrast, has no equal in Europe, and this is one of the greatest indictments of the United States. We have performed very well for the rich, the middle, and the working classes, but abominably for the poor, especially African Americans.

I audited many courses, some with benefit, but with the single exception of Black and Galbraith, I found no utility in economics. Courses in economics were totally abstract and made no contribution to my concerns with the human environment. Indeed, at best they were oblivious to the environment; at worst they were totally antithetical to the ecological view, as they still are.

The case study method was employed by all departments at the Graduate School of Design. This consisted of the selection of a planning-design topic and its investigation performed, as by professionals, under the supervision of an appropriate faculty. Initiation at Harvard at that time involved a joint studio including architects, landscape architects, and city planners. The subject was Cambridge, and its focus was

Harvard Square. The forty students were divided into small groups, and each of these investigated a single topic: historical development, current land use, population, economic indices, ethnicity, housing stock, commerce, industry, land and building values, property ownership, zoning. This effort was followed by an investigation of innovative ideas of development: garden cities, the linear city, Le Corbusier's plans for Paris, Ludwig Hilberseimer's plan for Chicago, and the British new towns. A particular focus was given to the emblems of modern architecture—high-rise slabs and towers. There followed design exercises of housing types and neighborhood institutions. I designed a bathhouse. The conclusion of the course was the preparation of a comprehensive plan for Cambridge. The faculty included Professors Frost and Burchard from architecture, Lester Collins from landscape architecture, and Holmes Perkins from city planning. It was a thrilling enterprise and a superb learning experience. This academic exercise was performed in 1946, but such integration is not yet a common experience in these professions. Reductionism still rules.

In planning, I participated in a study of the Boston metropolitan aviation system, from which the hub idea emerged. The Framingham studio was an investigation into the regional shopping center concept. A study of Gloucester, Massachusetts, included an examination of the fishing industry. It was interesting to learn that Gorton Pew had exploited the quick-freeze process to filet menhaden, a fish previously used for chicken feed and fertilizer, and sell it under various names, including white perch, to different regions of the country. We also saw how fish sticks were manufactured from the debris of the process.

These planning studios, conducted by practitioners from public agencies and private firms, were excellent examples of professional education. This cannot be said for landscape architecture, however, whose faculty had no distinction whatsoever. The contrast between the energy and idealism of planning and architecture, and the pusillanimity of landscape architecture, was marked.

The greatest concern in the Graduate School of Design was not with coursework or even with studios, but with the emergence of modern architecture. It was, in 1946, an aberration. Only a few independent and generally rich clients selected modernism for design of their projects. At Harvard it was believed that this was a crusade. Espousing modern architecture was a religion. We were saved; therefore, we must save the world. So every success was savored.

Meanwhile, we examined examples of this rare creation, the modern building. We stood in awe at the Gropius House, in Lincoln; visited a small subdivision called Six Moon Hills designed by the young faculty—Ben Thompson, Chip Harkness, and Louis McMillan—and a nearby companion project by Carl Koch. We ventured to New York City to examine Lever House, the Museum of Modern

Art, particularly the garden, and a town house conversion by Philip Johnson. The number of examples was small. The interest was fanned by visiting architects—Johnson, Johansen, Noyes, and Saarinen—and by the master's degree candidates, among them, I.M. Pei and Paul Rudolf. Magazines were scanned, and works depicted therein elicited intense study and criticism. Rumors abounded: Would Le Corbusier be permitted to design the United Nations Building? Would I.M. Pei build a circular tower on an island in the East River? It was a war, with every skirmish examined and every advance against or by the Philistines who opposed modern architecture carefully calculated.

Even then I had some doubt about the claims of the mission. The houses at Six Moon Hills by the young faculty, for example, were cinder-block shoe boxes with flat roofs and unexceptional spaces. There was no landscape. I was not impressed with cinder block, two-by-fours, and six-inch nails. I could admit economy, but the houses in Edinburgh New Town, the Grachtenhuisen in Amsterdam, and even Williamsburg and Savanna, had vastly superior qualities. Nor could I mobilize intense enthusiasm for the lesser technology being advocated: lally columns, space frames, escalators, elevators, and steel beams: these seemed improbable instruments to transform mean and satanic cities. I was not alone. Mumford had studied this matter extensively and had spoken and written about it. He convinced me, but I was a member of a small minority.

The most profound event of my American early experience, however, did not occur in Cambridge. Having studied for three years—fall, spring, and summer, nine semesters without surcease—my chairman, Holmes Perkins, requested the Department of Health for Scotland to permit me travel across the United States during my final summer, as an educational experience. There was no precedent for this action. The department consented. So I bought my first car, a 1942 Studebaker Commander. This purchase was not lightly made. It was the largest expenditure of my life. A classmate, distinguished by his ability to draw vintage cars on everyone's perspectives and thus deemed knowledgeable of automobiles, accompanied me for the purchase. Neither of us perceived that the engine had been steam cleaned to disguise the car's addiction to oil, which soon became apparent.

Armed with a large can of oil and many letters of introduction, my wife and I set off on our grand tour. Our first stop was Washington, D.C., where we could live in Crena de Iongh's suite at the Shoreham and from this luxurious vantage visit Greenbelt (the new town in Maryland), the Capitol, and the National Park Service. Next we proceeded south toward the TVA, examining en route the Blue Ridge Parkway and the Skyline Drive, an exemplary highway designed by landscape architects. Norris Dam first revealed the practice of segregation. A visit to a toilet was imperative. I found one: Blacks only. Needs must transcend etiquette and I entered. There was no black face to accept my apology for intrusion or to recognize my accent and perceive my Scottish innocence.

In 1949, the TVA consisted of dams and transmission lines. Its effects were still imperceptible, but the winds of change were revealed in the widespread hopes and expectations that were later realized. It was a great vision, democracy on the march.

Segregation, heat, and humidity deflected us from further southern excursions. We fled north. Our living accommodations contracted after the Shoreham. A pup tent, inflatable mattress, kerosene stove, groundsheet, blanket, and portable typewriter constituted our impedimenta. Our budget was five dollars per day, including gas. With an introduction to Hugh B. Lee, owner of the Maumee Mines, we investigated open-cast coal mining and land reclamation in Indiana and then shot westward. Kentucky, a limestone landscape, coal mining; Kansas, grain to the horizon; and then the Rockies came into view. We journeyed up the corridor of the Arkansas River to Salida where, one Sunday morning, the fuel pump succumbed. Its repair precipitated a crisis: our per diem budget was inadequate and a remedy was needed. I phoned a colleague, Robert Van Duesen. He had graduated in architecture the previous year, and we had acquired his apartment on Beacon Street. He and three others were practicing in Grand Junction. Could he find me a job, I inquired—pick, shovel, fruit picking, anything? "Dress in your best clothes," was his answer. "We will represent you as a distinguished British planner to the town manager. We will recommend that he hire you to do a comprehensive plan for Grand Junction. After all, it is the uranium capital of the world." I drove into town and met the town manager, a Gary Cooper with Stetson, riding boots, brown face, and white teeth. Would I undertake to prepare a comprehensive plan? No, I had appointments in Los Angeles; I could spend only three weeks. But could I plan a park? Yes, indeed. Van Duesen and his colleagues could find no work for modern architects. Their single commission was to build oaken pews for a church. So all of us participated in the design, produced working drawings and specifications. I accepted a munificent check that would finance our trip.

The visit to Grand Junction coincided with the first Aspen Festival, so we convened in Saarinen's orange tent, Maroon Bells Mountains visible under the awning, and heard Albert Schweitzer, José Ortega y Gasset, Dimitri Mitropoulos, Piatigorsky, and the Minneapolis Symphony Orchestra—a celestial experience at high altitude.

Westward we went to Yellowstone, to the Tetons in Wyoming, to Bryce and Zion in Utah, experiencing new and fantastic landscapes and realizing that the National Park Service administered a nation-state with unequaled civility. At the time it was the habit of the Park Service to employ college and university professors to perform during the summer season the role of "interpreters" of the parks. These temporary public servants were without compare in any civil service—for their commitment, knowledge, and courtesy. Unhappily the tradition of using academics in this way has been terminated.

We went on to Arizona and California, where I had an appointment in Los Angeles with Thomas Church, great landscape architect and human being. His taking time to give a day of his life and show his works to a foreign landscape architectural student was extraordinarily gracious. He took me to his office, showed me his current work, and then drove me to a dozen or so gardens—all little private paradises—at once powerful and modest, as was he.

Garrett Eckbo did the same for me, as did Lawrence Halprin later in San Francisco. In Los Angeles, then as now, the smog hid the Coastal Range and traffic was maniacal; the city was a cancerous wen, but it contained enclaves of great beauty. Its problems are now many times more intractable.

In 1949, Pauline and I drove across the United States. I spent a day with the great California landscape architect, Thomas Church. He showed me his office and his work. I was impressed by Church's revolutionary approach to landscape architecture.

The Sonoma garden designed by Thomas Church with Lawrence Halprin and George Rockrise. (Photograph, 1948, by Rondal Partridge; courtesy of the Thomas Church office.)

We found Monterey, Point Lobos, and then San Francisco, much more coherent and attractive: ocean and bay, Presidio, bridge, Sausalito, Alcatraz, Victoriana, painted buildings, and Berkeley. A Swiss painter, friend of Andreas Feininger, and his Dutch violinist wife were our hosts, and through them we met a succession of charming people, an experience delightful enough to establish San Francisco as my favorite city on earth.

Then we were traveling north on Route 101, avoiding massive trucks with massive logs barreling along beyond the power of brakes, through the coastal redwoods to Corbel, California. Here was a friend, a nurse from Boston who had married an Indian lumberjack. With his brother, one truck with a winch, and chainsaws he cut giant trees, lopped and discarded branches, each bigger than a mature Scottish tree, and wound wire round the trunks, rolled the winch and stripped the bark, cut logs and yanked them to the truck. Such waste it all was, such despoliation, such skill—all for garden furniture and tomato stakes.

Seattle was as rainy as Glasgow, so we turned east to the Columbia River, to the Grand Coulee Dam, and then to Wyoming, the Badlands, Dakota, Montana. The landscapes were beautiful, powerful, silent, unpopulated, moving. Since that time, these enclaves have become even more precious—pristine landscapes, emblems of what was, examples of what could be. Sacred.

Time was running short. School would start again soon, and so there ensued a breathless trip: Denver to Chicago to Boston. We arrived in Cambridge on a Sunday night, with no banks open, only twenty-nine cents in cash, a package of spaghetti and a can of tomato sauce. Best of the fruits of the trip, Pauline was pregnant. Our firstborn should arrive when it was time to return to Europe.

Looking back, the four years briefly encapsulated here were exciting. The participation in an important cause—the creation of new sunlit cities and towns, healthy landscapes populated by prosperous and happy people—was worthy of a life's work. My student colleagues were intelligent, passionate, industrious. There were giants in the school faculty and the university. My own private world was marvelous.

It was later, when I began my teaching career, that I perceived the omissions in my education. I have mentioned the total absence of natural science, the lack of integration of the subject matter. The degree of synthesis represented by this book took years to assemble. At that time they were independent perceptions, not visibly related or of consequence. The greatest failure lay in instruction in landscape tradition. The extraordinary contributions of Andrew Jackson Downing, Frederick Law Olmsted, H.W.S. Cleveland, Charles Eliot, Jens Jensen, and other designers which should have been the foundation for contemporary practice, were not presented. The aspirations of the young turks should have been employed explicitly.

Indeed, these young men and women should have been retained as visiting faculty. Landscape architecture had failed totally.

The omissions were serious. I realized this only later, when I was required to teach. The only instruction I ever received in natural science was at the West of Scotland Agriculture College in the late 1930s. Harvard required no natural science. This was a paradox then and later became a source of infuriation. I have been described as the inventor of ecological planning, the incorporation of natural science within the planning process. Yet Charles Eliot, son of Harvard's president, a landscape architect at Harvard, preceded me by half a century. He had associated with some of the most distinguished scientists of his day and employed environmental insights in the preparation of his "Emerald Necklace" plan for metropolitan Boston. This concept bequeathed two enduring benefits: the Boston Metropolitan Parks System and the Metropolitan Transportation Authority. He also conducted an excellent study of Mount Desert Island in Maine. He invented a new and vastly more comprehensive planning method than any preexisting, but it was not emulated. Unfortunately, he died in his thirties. Had he lived we might well have a different America today. Eliot was brilliant and powerful, with access to the great and influential. His ideas could have been widely applied and could have had pervasive effect. Yet no one at Harvard ever mentioned his name. So I, perforce, had to reinvent the wheel, ignorant of my illustrious predecessor whose achievements far outstripped my first exercises.

On my annual visits to Harvard for decades after, I continued to encounter the same disinterest in Eliot and ecological planning. These experiences ultimately bred a bitter comment. Usually introduced as the recipient of three degrees from Harvard, I would respond, "Yes, indeed, I do have three degrees from Harvard. They have conferred instant respectability upon me as on countless others, but they are no substitute for an education. I have been required to teach at Pennsylvania for over thirty years to complete the education that Harvard so expensively denied me."

Between 1940 and 1950 Harvard was the dominant influence in the development of modern architecture and planning. Walter Gropius had transplanted the Bauhaus from Dessau to Cambridge, Massachusetts. Modern architecture had a powerful idealistic component. It envisaged the rejection of traditional École des Beaux Arts formalism, a commitment to technology, and a new architecture. It identified itself with social revolution, decent housing for the poor, the replacement of dark, mean urban environments by gleaming sunlit cities. The students were in a state of high excitement, believing that under the leadership of Walter Gropius, they were the vanguard.

Naturally, there were degrees of commitment. The Department of Architecture was dominated by Gropius and his young graduates; Chip Harkness, Louis McMillan, Ben Thompson, Conrad Nagel, and Ming Pei formed an uncritical monolith, a multi-person Gropius.

The chairman of City and Regional Planning, G. Holmes Perkins, who later was to invite me to Pennsylvania, held the belief that planning is an applied social science and devised a curriculum that included anthropology with Carleton Coon, geography with Derwent Whittlesey and Edward Ullman, government with John Gaus, Maurice Lambie, and Arthur Maas, economics with John Black and Kenneth Galbraith, sociology with Oscar Handlin and Talcott Parsons, planning with Martin Wagner and Perkins, housing with Catherine Bauer and W.L.C. Wheaton, engineering with Walter Chambers, history of cities with Dean Hudnut, history of landscape architecture with Bremer Pond, and the dominant, powerful influence of Walter Gropius himself. While I undertook professional education in both landscape architecture and city planning, there was a very large component of social science that afforded me a belated general education.

Landscape architecture of the 1940s was an anachronism, still living in the days of private estates and small-scale landscape projects. It lacked theory and did not engage in criticism. It was *pusillanimous.*

As I review the Graduate School of Design forty some years later, it is clear that the instincts were splendid and the energy and commitment admirable, but there was a notable absence of wisdom. Yet this quality existed in the person of Lewis Mumford. He came each year, gave marvelously thoughtful lectures, diagnostic and prescriptive, but he was seen as aberrant. He would not give unqualified support to modern architecture. He warned of the dangers of deifying technology, the necessity of giving primacy to human values. Had he been dean, for which he had more than the necessary qualifications, things might have been different. As it was, Mumford was correct. He was later to state, and I paraphrase, "the tragedy of modern architecture is that it has achieved its objectives, and they are hollow."

It took years for my response to coalesce, and it drew from Mumford. I recall a fantasy in which I am falling asleep. I find myself in a room, filled with the founders of modern architecture: Bruno Taut, Berlage, Ludwig Mies van der Rohe, Walter Gropius, Le Corbusier, Rietveld, Brinkman, Van der Vlught, Theo van Doesberg, Marcel Breuer, Maxwell Fry, Jane Drew, and Lotte Stam Beese. They are discussing the proposal to rename modern architecture as the International Style. I listen, then feel impelled to intervene. "I am unknown, my comments bring no authority, but I beg you to listen. As you contemplate this motion, please ask yourselves: Is it your intention to expunge all of the regional architecture and city building of the world? Beware." But this, of course, did happen. Western forms were believed to endow the hallowed benefits of Western wealth, technology, and success. They inexorably replaced traditional architecture and planning so that today, with the exception of scale and some landmarks, it is difficult to distinguish much of New York City from much of Tokyo, Rio, Minneapolis, Rotterdam, Melbourne, or Auckland. All reveal the same fatuous, faceless prisms, equally inappropriate for all people, all places, and all times.

Hindsight is certainly easier than prediction, but review is valuable, particularly if learning occurs. The fallacies of modern architecture and its planning ideas are now clear.

The first error was, as Mumford observed, a deification of technology. It was in the use of new technologies and materials that modern architecture sought its form and distinction. Note that this was not a commitment to science but to its baser minion, engineering. Indeed, science was resolutely excluded. Looming near the Graduate School of Design was Gaylord Simpson, then founder of evolutionary biology. Neither Darwin, Henderson, nor Simpson was invoked, although evolution was then certainly the most powerful perception in biology. Nor was ecology, only recently powerful at Harvard, given any attention. There was one ecologist associated with Harvard Forest, Hugh Raup, who could have introduced students to the illuminating new views of nature in the writings of Paul Sears, Pierre Danserau, Howard T. and Eugene Odum, Frederic Clements, Frank Fraser Darling, Charles Elton, Wynne Edwards, Stanley Cain, and Aldo Leopold, then all alive and well. But ecology was never mentioned, far less invoked. No, technology was the god. Better that it had been seen as a tool, as it makes a better servant than master, for it was technology that gave modern architecture its characteristic form, the cube. Theo van Doesberg, friend of Piet Mondrian, may well have been the most influential force in this determination. Here these Germans and Dutchmen sat, in buildings waterproofed from rain and snow by slate and tile pitched roofs, insisting on the cube and flat roof as an emblem, the badge of modern architecture. I remember a sketch problem at Harvard for a cottage on Cape Cod. One student designed a traditional Cape Cod cottage. I recall Gropius's scorn. "This man is a traitor. A pitched roof, indeed. Shingles!" No, Breuer's wooden shoe box was the ideal form for Cape Cod!

Within the general commitment to technology was a morality—the structure must be expressed. I recall with wonder how Gropius stood before a slide of the Bauhaus, demonstrating the separation of columns from the glass wall. Now, this is hardly an adequate basis for a morality. It can be ridiculed with one malevolent image: Albert Speer, Hitler's architect, is receiving instruction from his führer. "We will initiate a massive social program to purify aryan blood. We will execute Slavs, Poles, gypsies, and Jews. I charge you to design the incinerators." Speer gathers his architects, delegates the commissions, and gives them parting advice: "This aspiration should be resolved functionally and symbolically. Ensure that the structure is lucidly expressed."

Now we can perceive the role of morality. This degenerate, inhuman policy reached dimensions of depravity never before achieved in civilized society. The measure of architecture is its ability to enhance human health and well-being. By that contention, human incineration must be anathema. Expression of the structure was and is a trivial contention, yet it dominated architectural criticism for decades.

Modern architecture had a deep antinatural content. There were contrary assertions. Le Corbusier wrote, "Le pacte est signé avec la nature," and under his Voisin Plan for Paris he wrote, "L'espace, soleil, verdure." But these assertions were honored only in the breach. Nature, if considered, was believed to provide the podium for the building and, perhaps, its backdrop. Natural science, particularly environmental science, was never considered. The earth was assumed to be an environmental uniformity without influence on people, place, architecture, or town building. Only because of this belief could the International Style be advocated for worldwide employment without consideration for the appropriateness and specificity of regional vernacular architecture and settlement.

However, modern architecture may be dead. There has been an extended wake presided over by Peter Blake, Vincent Scully, Robert Venturi and Tom Wolfe, the last bitter and hilarious. But what of its successor? Postmodernism (a corrupt term for the contemporary) is surely a new undisciplined eclecticism, borrowing past styles from any and all sources, a kind of architectural potpourri. It has denigrated architecture to a decorative art form, bringing it into severe competition with confectionery and millinery at best. At worst it is akin to the mortician cosmetician affixing a smile on a cadaver. It is trivial. A prominent architect, principal in a large office, said to me recently, "There is no way of avoiding this current obsession with style."

How poignant to remember that forty-five years ago this same eclecticism was identified with the École des Beaux Arts, the enemy of progress. Perhaps the baby was thrown out with the bathwater. There was much to learn, both from the high styles of architecture and from vernacular design. Had they been examined as adaptive responses to people and places, perhaps an inheritance could have been used as the basis for innovation. Certainly modern architecture, in the sense of modern physics, biology, or geology, has eluded us. Modern physical, biological, and, indeed, social science in general, still remain outside the domain of architecture, and there is no apparent interest in incorporating these modern perceptions.

Planning followed a different course. Architecture could and did evolve through private clients. Planning, perforce, depended mainly on public institutions. Immediately this posed a profound problem. While planning in the Department of Defense or in General Motors is thoroughly reasonable and impeccably capitalistic, planning in the public sector apparently savors of socialism, perhaps even communism. Laissez faire is not tolerable in large public or private undertakings such as the TVA or IBM, but is required for cities and towns. This hostility to planning has had profound effects, which probably reached a zenith in the Reagan and Bush administrations where planning, in general, and environmental planning, in particular, were actively discouraged and believed to be inimical to growth. Yet the great beauty of America is its complexity and diversity; whereas there may be a dominant theme, there are likely to be aberrant subdominant themes. In planning there have been a number of remarkable accomplishments, at the urban scale, in Philadelphia's Penn Center and Society Hill, Baltimore's Charles Center and Inner Harbor, Georgetown and Southwest Washington, at Faneuil Hall in Boston, and at Riverpark in Chattanooga. Does anyone seriously doubt the necessity of planning to send an astronaut to the moon? Surely not. Indeed, let us contemplate our own selves—how well-planned are we without help from the conscious brain?

While the national antipathy to planning was (and is) a major problem, it was not the only one. The decision to derive a theoretical basis for planning from the social sciences was reasonable. It was also, paradoxically, inadequate. Patrick Geddes, perhaps the founder of modern planning, was a biologist with a well-developed knowledge and interest in natural science. He was also a pioneer in sociologic thought, but his successors quickly abandoned his biological emphasis. The earliest planning in the United States on a national scale was done by landscape architects, notably of the City Beautiful Movement. They were joined by architects and, subsequently, engineers. Holmes Perkins, himself an architect, felt that planning should become an applied social science and so designed the planning curriculum for universities.

But the problem was fundamentally one of the institution of the universities and their processes of selection and promotion. Social sciences are defined in university departments as sociology, anthropology, geography, economics, statistics, demography, and like disciplines. Each has a hierarchy that sets standards. Now consider an applied scientist hired by a planning department. He or she will be deplored by the "pure" scientists. No matter that these people are addressing and perhaps solving social problems, no matter that their engagement with social problems may well enhance their perceptions and research, they are seen as lesser brethren. At the University of Pennsylvania there is a powerful department of economics with a Nobel laureate, Lawrence Klein; there is also a department of regional science, econometrics, long chaired by the father of that science, Walter Isard, and, at the bottom of the ladder, are the economists in the department of city and regional planning. These last are bedevilled. Of course, they should ally with architects, landscape architects, and urban designers in confronting and resolving urban problems, but to do so would alienate them from the high priesthood. Moreover, their promotion and preferment depends on publication in scientific journals. Inevitably, they are forced into theory and abstraction, into separating themselves from the practitioners and explicit problems. It is fair to say that they have tended to fail in both realms. They have not achieved respectability in the social sciences, and they have abandoned the utility of serving practitioners.

Thesis: Providence

The culminating requirement, for both landscape architecture and city planning, was a thesis. Selecting an appropriate topic was serious business. In my case, I sought to undertake a combined thesis incorporating both fields. My search was resolved by three friends: Robert Geddes, for long dean of architecture at Princeton, William Conklin, partner in the distinguished firm of Conklin, Rossant of New York City, and the late Marvin Sevely, who taught at the Pratt Institute. These were the brightest architects in my year. Geddes had formed a friendship with Lou Wetmore, then executive director of the Providence Redevelopment Agency. Wetmore was interested in having a group of Harvard students investigate the possibilities afforded by the New Housing Act which permitted center city redevelopment. We welcomed this opportunity and determined to undertake a collaborative thesis, the first of its kind at Harvard. The thesis essentially was that interdisciplinary cooperation among architects, planners, and landscape architects could benefit urban renewal. Our thesis was pursued in the form of a redevelopment plan for the downtown of Providence, Rhode Island. The program was enthusiastically supported by the three faculties.

The legislation permitted exercising the power of eminent domain, assembling parcels of land, identifying projects and appropriate purposes, writing down land costs to use value, and selling the land to developers who produced acceptable plans and had adequate financial resources. This authorization involved both the public and private domains. In the former were federal and state programs for highways and state and municipal expenditures for parking and amenities, including parks. The private domain included the market possibilities and, indeed, the prospects for the central business district.

I worked with three architectural students at Harvard on my thesis (William J. Conklin, Robert L. Geddes, and Marvin Sevely). In the first collaborative thesis in the school's history, we spent the better part of a year in research and design for the future of downtown Providence, Rhode Island. I lived several months in Providence conducting research.

This 1950 model of downtown Providence was a product of our work.

The program took form. Geddes, Conklin, and Sevely would investigate specific architectural problems—federal office buildings, a retail center, and a church. I would be responsible as both planner and landscape architect. The planning role emphasized economic feasibility and the opportunities afforded by the new legislation; the landscape role involved investigating the generating power of open space in enhancing the amenities and inducing development in the central business district.

Program development for all of the parts and the combined thesis were required in the fall of the final year. In the spring semester we would produce documenting evidence and develop plans, designs, and a model.

I cannot remember who the thesis supervisors were. Support and direction was received principally from Lou Wetmore, and Maurice Lambie and John Gaus of government, G. Holmes Perkins of planning, and the Federal Reserve Bank in Boston were all of great assistance to me. Sevely worked closely with Buckminster Fuller, Geddes with Konrad Waachsman, and Conklin, I believe, with Schweiker, a church architect then at MIT. There was much support from the younger faculty and senior students, Chip Harkness, Ben Thompson, I.M. Pei, and Paul Rudolf.

Today it is hard to believe that in the late 1940s the general assumption was that the decline in vitality of city centers would accelerate. Indeed, we had in the previous year engaged in a study that would successfully compete with the commercial core. A collaborative studio involving architects, landscape architects, and planners had developed plans for the first regional shopping center in the United States, on Route 128 at Framingham, Massachusetts. Many such facilities were soon to be developed, which would spread like a plague around the cities of America. These facilities, with abundant free parking, were the basis of the pessimistic prognosis for central business districts.

That such regional centers would be built and be successful was not in doubt. FHA and VA loans were creating a massive suburbanization, which, along with equally massive investment in highway programs, guaranteed success. But was there no hope for city centers?

I suppose that our thesis investigated many of the threshold ideas of the time. The office building complex owed much to Buckminster Fuller. The prototype was a cylinder with a central diaphragm from which beams were cantilevered. The extremities of these were supported by a network of steel members in tension. It satisfied Fuller's aspirations for lightness and economy of materials. God knows, towers erupted all over the world soon thereafter, but to the best of my knowledge no building of this type was ever built. The retail complex derived its structure from a Konrad Waachsman's space frame, providing enormous areas of column-free space, and the innovation of the escalator permitting retail sales to occur on more than one floor. Another invention, the Badwin-Auger parking system, consisting of six-story garages served by elevators, was also investigated. It was economical in space but questionable as to cost. The church involved a more modest technology, with battered soil walls and a garden, supporting a roof that was a garden too. Conklin had been a student at divinity school before transferring to architecture. He sought a new expression for church building. Note the technological emphasis of the architectural program.

The landscape component, however, involved no technology whatsoever. It addressed the degree to which open space, trees, and parks contributed to the

We presented our thesis for downtown Providence to a jury that included Walter Gropius. Here, I am standing and presenting, with Gropius located immediately in front of me. Walter Gropius summed up our presentation to the faculty with these words: "They have worked with their brains and with their hearts, but most of all they have worked as a team. The work of a team is greater than the sum of the work of individuals." (Photograph from *The Rhode Islander, Providence Sunday Journal Magazine*, 11 June 1950, by H. Raymond Ball and courtesy of Frances Loeb Library, Graduate School of Design, Harvard University.)

delight of London, Paris, Amsterdam, and Edinburgh; it sought to utilize this ameliorative power. The landscape was viewed as a major public investment for urban pleasure and an inducement to private investment.

Obviously, planning for the central business district was a consuming task that absorbed us all. But this was overshadowed by the economic analysis. Boston, New

York City, Philadelphia, and Baltimore were investigated to ascertain the trends in central business activity. The results were not reassuring. Decline was the retrospective conclusion; decline was the prediction. However, we decided to investigate the market that did exist, and to what extent reduced land values would affect the trend. What contribution could be expected from the provisions of parking, amenities, and improved traffic and transportation? This was the research question to be investigated.

It was an ambitious undertaking. It involved interminable discussions, incredible hours, miles of yellow tracing paper, and tons of type, but the greatest effort was needed for the model, the key product. A model of the entire central city center of Providence was constructed at a scale of one inch to forty feet (1" = 40'0"). I believe that every single student in the Graduate School of Design participated in making models of all existing buildings for this project. The presentation was also a schoolwide event, dominated by Walter Gropius. It was very well received, and we were given an ovation.

The plan was accepted as the Central Redevelopment Plan for Providence and elaborately presented in the rotogravure supplement to the Sunday paper. It was over, finished, ended, and we were totally exhausted. The thesis took a year to complete, and the entire project was a successful educational experience. It had posed a real problem, and the advisors, the actual functionaries engaged in seeking solutions, were of high caliber. They included sociologists, economists, political scientists, city planners, architects, engineers. In retrospect, it should be observed that geography and the environmental sciences were conspicuously absent. The largest component of the investigation consisted of economic analysis and predictions made in concert with the Federal Reserve Bank of Boston.

The chronic problem of adequate highways and parking was seriously addressed. A circumferential highway, linked to a parking system, was developed, and several intersections, intractable because of physiography or water courses, were resolved.

The opportunities afforded by new legislation for center city redevelopment were investigated and applied. The role of open space in cities was recognized as an appropriate instrument for providing amenity and inducing private development, as was the crucial role of public buildings, in this case, federal office buildings, in initiating redevelopment. Municipal parking garages and street closings could also make important contributions. The conclusions were positive; remedy was possible. It was not inevitable that cities must passively succumb to decentralization because of shopping centers or suburbanization.

Yet decentralization proceeded apace, in spite of dramatic rehabilitations such as Philadelphia's Penn Center and Society Hill, Baltimore's Charles Center and Inner Harbor, Southwest Washington and Georgetown, and Battery Park City in

New York. The rate of decay has accelerated; cities are no longer serious subjects of discussion. There are no remedies. Yet, fortunately, the concern for the environment has escalated prodigiously.

One event occurred during my last year at Harvard that introduced an entirely novel option, one I ultimately pursued but which was unimaginable then—teaching. I was invited to attend a dinner of the Society of Fellows, a very self-conscious and select group. My host was Professor Richard N. Frye, Aga Khan Professor; President Conant, Arthur Schlesinger, Jr., Kenneth Galbraith, and, I believe, George Wald were among the luminaries. Discourse was dominated by Schlesinger, who discussed the merits of generals as emperors or presidents, moving meticulously from Seneca to De Gaulle and Eisenhower, exhaustively but inconclusively.

I became aware that I was a candidate and began to appreciate that being a professor might be a future role. Indeed, it came to be, and by invitation from a Harvard graduate and professor, my future dean, G. Holmes Perkins.

Chapter 4

Scotland,
1950–1954

As graduation approached it became important to find employment. I planned to return to Britain, and my preference was for a post in Scotland. There, planning was invested in the Department of Health, an inspired location. Of course, planning should be directed to enhancing human health and well-being; it should be within a department of health. Disease, apart from aging, is a consequence of inadequate planning. Only failures should become the patients of medicine. I assume that this inspired unity of medicine and planning came from the brilliant mind of that Edinburgh biologist-turned-planner, Sir Patrick Geddes, founder of modern town planning. He was also the originator of sociology, one of the first, if not the first professor, in this field. Unfortunately, his successors quickly abandoned the biological and environmental content of this new science and focused on social problems in an exclusively social and increasingly aspatial world. Indeed, if anyone had maintained that the environment was a factor in the conduct of human affairs to Talcott Parsons or Oscar Handlin, dominant sociologists at Harvard during my studies there, he would have been scorned. Their colleagues, the anthropologists, then studying in Micronesia, had no such illusions. They accurately perceived that the natural environment was the basis of an economy and that it influenced language, religion, art, values, and cultural institutions. So today there are self-described ecological ethnographers and anthropologists, but ecological sociologists are very scarce. The idea of people and place as linked systematically has emerged in ethnography but is rare in sociology.

Robert Gardner-Medwin, chief architect and planner for Scotland, had contact with my chairman, C. Holmes Perkins, and wrote inviting me to consider a post with him. I also received an invitation from Donald Reay, chief architect for the new town of East Kilbride, and another to become a planner for Cambridgeshire in England.

The academic requirements for a planner in Britain at that time consisted of a one-year diploma following a first professional degree in architecture, surveying, or engineering. It was assumed by Gardner-Medwin that my four years of graduate study would more than meet the basic requirements. However, although he was chief architect and planning officer for Scotland, he could not make appointments. That power reposed in the Civil Service Board. Thus I was interviewed by one Mr. Auld, a sour individual with a pronounced aversion to foreign, particularly American, credentials. He started the interview offensively: "What is Harvard?" Now that is a question that should be raised frequently in Cambridge where the assumption prevails that all excellence in all fields exists at Harvard and nowhere else. Superiority complexes and superciliousness there have achieved peaks unmatched in the rest of the United States. Mr. Auld could have been a salutary influence in Cambridge. I merely responded that Harvard was a great university, where, more to the point, a master's degree in city and regional planning required three years of graduate (that is, postgraduate) study. "So," he replied, "But are you a member of the Town Planning Institute?" Now was my turn to be offensive. "Not yet," I said, "but if you require this I will send off five bottle tops and five guineas." He told me that the post paid 600 pounds per annum, or approximately $1,800, significantly less than my stipend as a student.

This encounter was typical of many. Some were, I suppose, motivated by envy. Britain had been impoverished by war, America had prospered. British power had declined as America's had grown. Rationing in Britain still persisted five years after the war's end; Americans worried about diets. General Marshall had outlined his plan at the Harvard commencement of 1947. I remember it well. Former enemies would be given massive economic support, but not allies.

Before accepting this invitation I was interviewed for a position in Cambridge, which I declined. To reject the opportunities and fleshpots of the United States in order to spend a life improving the lot of upper-class Englishmen did not appeal powerfully. Sacrifice for Scotland was patriotic and appropriate. I next went to the new town of East Kilbridge, a satellite of Glasgow. There I met the chief architect, Donald Reay, a Canadian, now emeritus professor at Berkeley, bathed in sunshine. On that September day he was clad in a sou'wester and gum boots. The rain drove horizontally across the sodden landscape. The few trees were permanently bent to the wind. This was "glauer," Scots for argillaceous mud. The trees and soil said "uninhabitable." I could not induce my Dutch wife to live in such an environment. No, Edinburgh was better. So I became assistant planning officer for the Department of Health for Scotland.

The first thing I learned was that the doctors were comfortably esconsed in Saint Andrew's House, the home of Scotland's puppet government. Planners and architects were in crumbling quarters some miles away. Unfortunately, planning had nothing whatsoever to do with health; certainly, it transpired, not with mine.

During a vacation in Holland, en route to Scotland, I had been tired and listless. In Scotland I developed a bad cough, and one day I spat blood. The following day I was X-rayed and my sputum examined. I was diagnosed as having active pulmonary tuberculosis, right apical cavity. This was a fearful blow. I had always believed myself to be unusually strong and healthy. With the exception of malaria, I had managed to avoid illness all my life.

Tuberculosis—Southfield

Who knows why some people catch a disease and others do not? In my case the circumstances were propitious. One drafting room in Robinson Hall at the Harvard Graduate School of Design was reserved for students on thesis. My neighbor was Nat Adler, a charming and brilliant architect with a poetess wife and a young daughter. Programs could be accelerated, as was mine. I had studied every fall, spring, and summer for four years. I was near the end; with completion of the thesis I would pick up my three degrees and return to Scotland. Whereas my Army days had been active, university life was sedentary. Moreover, work was conducted indoors and well into the night. Sleep was indulgence. Studying two curricula simultaneously was accomplished largely at the expense of sleep. I was tired and debilitated, and so was my neighbor. But he was not only tired and listless, he was despondent. He saw a psychiatrist; it was assumed that his malaise derived from the suicide of his parents. However, just before graduation he learned that his little child had shown a positive reaction to the tuberculin test. First the maid was X-rayed. Clear. Next, his wife. Also clear. Finally, Nat was examined and was discovered to have an advanced case of tuberculosis. He and I at that time had adjacent desks. We spent much of every day together, we even slept on our desktops when unable to go home to bed. He retired to Santa Fe, built a marvelous house, and began to write a book. I returned to Scotland.

Beds in Scottish sanatoria were full, for Scotland ranked only after Portugal in the incidence of tuberculosis. Yet I was living in a hotel and I was infectious. As a result of my status as a health menace and a civil servant I was admitted to the Southfield Colony for Consumptives in Corstorphine, Edinburgh. I wonder as to what fate would have befallen me had I been less favored, for Southfield was a dirty, lugubrious place staffed by doctors who, like medicine at large, were impotent to cure tuberculosis and had an appropriate lackluster attitude to the matter. The matron, sisters, and nurses seemed infected by the tedious process of maintaining hopeless patients on their way to death and brought no cheer, little care, and much indifference to their tasks. The place, an old Victorian house, was dirty, drafty, and cold. The food was transported from some distance to the ward. Whether it had ever been palatable we never knew. I had an operation, pneumolysis, to cut and cauterize adhesions between lung and chest wall. This produced massive pleural effusions and a persistent temperature of 104 degrees Fahrenheit. I became the object of interest for medical students and was regularly wheeled in and fluoro-scoped for their delectation. No one worried that I might be excessively irradiated. I came to know my own record. The diagnosis was not favorable. I was very ill and appeared to have little prospect of improving; it was clear that the doctors were not optimistic. These were the days when treatment consisted of rest and fresh air, and, clearly, these were not working well for me.

I was a patient at Southfield for six months. I had a high fever throughout. Thus, I could not wash, shave, or walk to the bathroom. I could not sit up, read, write, or even listen to the radio. I was consigned to lying down, dozing, and wait-ing. I had only my mind. I decided to set it to work. I would review my four years of graduate study at Harvard, day by day, lecture by lecture, and collect such grains of enduring perception into a hoard. Using every trick of memory I could muster—signposts of large events, places, faces, birthdays, major events—I slowly resurrected this pilgrimage, starting with my arrival in Cambridge. I began by recreating every detail, my room, the walk along Harvard Street, Robinson and Hunt Halls, offices, furniture, trees, and slowly began to reconstruct my classes. In my first semester were Derwent Whittlesey and Edward Ullman, the geographers; G. Holmes Perkins, then chairman of planning, later to be my dean at Pennsylvania; Dean Joseph Hudnut, and, later, Charles Maas; Oscar Handlin, John Gaus, John Kenneth Galbraith, John T. Black, Maurice Lambie, and many more. So my reconstruction proceeded; day by week by month by semester after semester, for four long exhila-rating and exhausting years. My mnemonic devices worked, and slowly the tapes became more detailed. Within the sad ward of Southfield the blue skies, the warm sunlight, and the luminosity of Cambridge springs and falls filled my mind. In a landscape populated by animation and discourse, a quest was constructed. In this exercise I was selective. I set aside only grains of perception and tools that could do work. This was the useful product of an education. However, it so happened that it was less than I had expected. I did produce a small set of first principles by which I have since lived, but, clearly, I had not selected very wisely; indeed, I had not been well advised. A man who wished to dedicate his life to managing, planning, and designing with nature might well have benefited from instruction in the natural sciences. This, I had managed to avoid.

Recollection and analysis of the past was a disciplined and tiring task. I needed a respite, an alternative, another subject for mental exercise. It was provided almost as soon as the need was perceived. There was a boy in the ward, fourteen or so, Wee Willie. He suffered spinal tuberculosis. The staff did not like Wee Willie. Above all, they valued tidy beds, smooth pillows, and neat coverlets. Keep tidy while you die. Wee Willie was messy. He tossed and turned, his covers were rumpled, his pillows were crumpled. They continually admonished him. A nurse decided to cure his condition. One winter night she left his window wide open. That would keep him under the covers. It snowed that night, and Willie woke to a blanket of snow for a cover. Sister Durie discovered him. She shook the snow off his coverlet and said, "Never mind, it doesn't matter. He'll be dead soon enough anyway."

"You heartless, miserable, misbegotten misanthrope, may you suffer eternal damnation," I said.

I was required to apologize. Professor Cameron, Dr. Horne, the matron, and Sister Durie stood awaiting my contrition. My response was slurred. Did I say, "I would never have spoken so to a lady"? Or was it, "I should never . . ."? They did not insist upon clarification. I never did recant.

So was provided my alternative mental exercise. I proceeded to develop a formal indictment of the Southfield Colony for Consumptives. Day by day I accrued instances of incompetence, indifference, and sloth, the impersonal objectivity, the sanctimony of the professor and his crocodile of assistants, the neglect of the martinet of a matron, the perfunctory performance of nurses, and the general air of dirt and decay—windows never washed, with veils of dirt containing subliminal obscenities, spiderwebs in corners controlled by bluetits who flew in and out of windows at will. I honed this speech. In my mind I took it first to the Department of Health, next to the secretary of state for Scotland, and then to Parliament. Each time the rhetoric improved, the speech blossomed.

Among the patients at that time was a man named Tom Rutherford. He had been subjected to thoracoplasty, a barbarous surgical technique long since abandoned. This involved removal of the tips of all the ribs and was designed to suppress lung movement and possibly enhance healing. It was a remedy of last resort: painful, crippling, and not efficacious. Rutherford engaged in physical therapy and so had greater mobility than the other recumbent figures in the ward, and thus access to more information than the rest of us. One day he came to me with startling news. It appeared that a Swiss sanatorium was treating British parachutists who had tuberculosis. Perhaps I was eligible. I had to escape from Southfield (abandon hope all ye who enter here).

I was too weak to write, so Rutherford did, and within a few days I received a wonderful reply from Brigadier Spafford of the Airborne Forces Security Fund.

Dear Major McHarg,

How wonderful to hear from you. How sorry to hear of your plight.
How well I remember your name which I first saw on a most generous and
memorable cheque. Be assured we will have you out of that colony, soon
you will be in the Alps, in sunshine with good food and excellent medical
care. In no time you will be as good as gold.

He was as good as his word, and within a week I was in the Hotel Belvedere, in
Leysin, Switzerland. But the miracle was that the person who left Scotland with dis-
astrous X-rays and prognosis was not recognizable as that person who was examined some thirty-six hours later in Leysin. Here the prognosis and treatment were
optimistic—sleep when you wish, eat well, take walks—and send for your wife. I
was transformed, no longer bedridden, free, able to wash, shave, dress, go to the
bathroom, walk outside, all of which I did and thus recovered at great speed.

I spend six enchanting months in Leysin; this was a time of recuperation, but
it was also an idyll. I typed the lecture courses from my Harvard notes, climbed the
Dents du Midi, traveled to Lausanne and St. Gingolph, and looked forward to
beginning my professional career.

Perhaps a month before my departure I learned that the sanatorium would be
visited by two distinguished Scotsmen, the secretary of state for Scotland, Hector
McNeil, and his chief medical officer, Sir Andrew Davidson. Because Scotland
had too few beds for tubercular patients, the government sought to rent space in
Switzerland. These gentlemen knew that I, an appointee to the Department of
Health, was a patient in Leysin and they planned to visit me. The hospital staff prepared for the occasion. My suite was bedecked with flowers, a table was sent for tea
on the balcony with a view of the village of Leysin, the Dents du Midi, and the
Swiss sky. They arrived. Hector McNeil had distinguished himself as the British
representative at the United Nations. He was a member of Parliament from
Greenock, a shipbuilding town on the south of the Clyde. He looked and sounded
like a working-class Scot. Sir Andrew was larger and more anglicized. I led them
through my bedroom to the living room and thence to the balcony. They sat down
and I locked the door. "Have some tea, gentlemen, I have a story to tell you." Then
proceeded the formal indictment, rehearsed a hundred times: names, dates, events,
incompetence, indifference, and sloth, a catalogue of uncaring. It took hours. The
sun sank and lights came on in the crepuscule of Leysin below as I ended. Hector

McNeil turned to Davidson and, "Andra, ya bastard, if it's true, I'll have your heid."
It was true, and he did.

A month or so later I received a letter from McNeil.

Dear Mr. McHarg:

How glad I am to learn that you will soon be returning home. You will
need medical attention in Edinburgh. It would be too painful to have you
attend Southfield. I have made arrangements for you to be treated at
Comleybank Hospital. I hope you will find this agreeable. And, by the by,
do take an opportunity to visit Southfield. I would be glad to have your
opinion of the changes made there.

Which I did. The place was barely recognizable. The building had been gutted
and rebuilt; it was spacious, clean, and attractive, with smiling nurses and smiling
patients. Of course, the discovery of streptomycin and para-aminosalicylic acid
gave more reason for smiles than the rehabilitation of the hospital. Yet I went
through the wards, exultant at the change and that I had helped to make it so, and
determined on a career to plan and design for human health and well-being.

The tuberculosis experience had profound effects on my life. Imprisonment in the
Southfield Colony for Consumptives was the Slough of Despond. Hopeless. Yet I had
employed my mind to accumulate and review the knowledge presented at Harvard, I
had engaged in an evaluation of a hospital's operation and achieved remedy, but by far
the most powerful resolve arose from the transformation achieved by the rediscovery
of freedom and dignity. When I escaped from Southfield, I was consigned to early
death. When I began my travels to London, Paris, and Leysin, I was an invalid. The
ability to dress, move, eat, travel, and the absence of a visible stigma improved by the
hour so that soon I was walking unaided. Thirty-six hours later, on examination, I had
become transformed. No longer destined to die, I was advised to walk at will, to do as
I wished, to recuperate, which I did. This experience hardened my recognition of the
importance of health, dignity, and freedom, of the power of nature to heal. It directed
my life's work.

Then came the day to go home—farewell to the bright sky, snowcapped Dents du
Midi, Yvorne, edelweiss, gentians, flower-lit meadows, soaring eagles, jangling cows—
down the funicular railway to Aigle, Paris, Calais, Dover, London, and Edinburgh. What
a transformation from the dying tubercular of six months previously, now bronzed, fit,
energetic. As I left someone said, "Ah, McHarg, comment vous êtes sportif!"

In Edinburgh, Pauline had found an apartment in the Dutch Consulate, 18-A
Abercromby Place, to be our home for the next three years.

Assistant Planning Officer 1951–1954

When I assumed my position as assistant planning officer, I was allocated to the staff of the dominant planner in the department, Robert, later Sir Robert, Grieve. He had trained as a surveyor, undertaken the diploma course in town planning, worked with Sir Patrick Abercromby on the Clyde Valley Plan, and thence come to the department. He was a passionate, intelligent, and effective man. While I was on his staff, however, I saw little of him. Mine was too junior a position. I was allocated to a failed sanitary engineer, a man of bad breath, spittle, and egg stains, Humphrey Edwards. He quickly determined to humble this American-trained upstart. My task would be to color maps of the Glasgow Comprehensive Plan. This document was the shame of the department. Because Glasgow refused to undertake its legal responsibility, this task was being performed by the department without the participation or consent of Glasgow. It was an exercise in coloring with no planning significance whatsoever.

I had a remedy. As I had had tuberculosis, I was considered a potential threat to health. There were two consequences. The first was that I could never become a permanent civil servant, which fostered a vigorous independence; the other was much better: I must have my own office. I would be insulated from continuous surveillance. Yet supervision was hardly stringent. Whatever passion had generated the powerful planning movement in Britain, it was barely visible in this department. People arrived late, took extended tea breaks, had long lunches, and made early departures. One senior official, Butler, responsible for the Western Isles, was reported only to come to the office to collect his checks.

Humphrey Edwards was no exception. I could develop and pursue my own agendum without fear. A number of planning ideas had not yet reached Scotland; in addition, American experience, particularly with automobiles, had produced some solutions to new problems. Surface mining, widely practiced in the United States, was beginning in Scotland, but the problem of land rehabilitation had not been considered. Hydroelectric power was being harnessed, but the Tennessee Valley Authority (TVA) had not been investigated as an exemplar. Finally, public housing, a massive public investment and sacrifice, was proceeding with no intelligence, as little skill, and, most regrettably, without any landscape architectural participation.

The most immediate and promising opportunity appeared to lie with the Scottish Hydroelectric Board. For Arthur Maas, professor of government at

Harvard, I had written a paper examining the applicability of the TVA initiative to Scotland. Surprisingly, the comparison was valid; Scotland was much smaller than the TVA region but had much more rainfall, steeper gradients, more head, and almost total runoff. The significant idea of the TVA was to use federal funds to build hydroelectric facilities, use the low electricity rates to lure industry, use the income to improve agriculture and forestry, and to provide higher levels of community services. The TVA was permitted to integrate the programs of all federal agencies operating within its region, the poorest seven states in the Union. Soil conservation, improved agriculture and forestry, community development, and health services were integrated by the region and the institution. Whereas new income was crucial, the success of the experiment included the integration of innumerable public programs, all toward a single end, the improvement of the quality of life for the population. The fact that TVA is now just a large public utility should not obscure these accomplishments. The seven poorest states are no longer so, and, indeed, there has been a massive improvement. I well remember an old crone in Tennessee with a jar of water on her head. She had carried it up the mountain daily, but would not need to much longer. Electricity was coming. The TVA would bring it.

In Scotland, the idea of cooperation between the departments of Forestry, Fisheries, Agriculture, Planning, Mines, and Commerce was total anathema. At the expense of the benefits, the decision was made to develop hydroelectric power without reference to improving the region. It was decided to sell it at postage stamp rates, so that the bus bar, point of generation, would have no locational value. The first battle was lost. Of course, I was too low on the totem pole. I could only offer ideas; I had no power. The idea was revolutionary, as it had been even in the United States, where it was not implemented for the Columbia River Basin either. It certainly was too revolutionary for Scotland at that time.

The second item on my agenda was rehabilitation of open-cast coal mining. I had undertaken a serious investigation of this subject in the United States. Having received an introduction to one Hugh B. Lee of Terre Haute, Indiana, a large open-cast operator in the Wabash River Valley, I visited him during the summer of 1949, heard his story, and saw his operation. He directed me to scientists at Purdue University who had long engaged in research in rehabilitation.

Lee's story was enchanting. He was a geologist mining gold in Timmins, northern Ontario, when he learned that the Panama Canal had been completed. It occurred to him that the mechanical equipment employed, much of it designed for the canal project, might be available and cheap. He knew that in the Wabash Valley was an extensive seam of good quality coal about seventeen feet below ground. This was too shallow to mine and produced too much overburden to remove with existing technology, but not with the canal steam shovels. He went to New York City, met some bankers, made a bid, and acquired the equipment. He bought land and mineral rights and began excavation. But before he started, and this is a most important point, he hired a Yale forester by the name of Doc Sawyer to plan the program of rehabilitation and afforestation.

Of course, the operation was quarrying, not mining; it avoided the problems attendant to shuttering, galleries, and pumps and the hazards of gas and explosives; it would have no problems with unions. The enterprise was economical, profitable, and, with effective rehabilitation, socially acceptable. The most serious objection to the operation was the final physiography, a hill and dale formation like cyclopean furrows. In this mining process a shovel removed overburden and placed it on the side as a long furrow before the coal was removed. The next traverse by the shovel again removed the overburden now placed in the hole from which the coal had been removed. Owing to expansion, the returned overburden had a greater volume and a ridge was developed. The final hole filled with water and was stocked with sunnies, bluegills, and, sometimes, bass. So when I arrived in 1949 much of this land was in forest, otherwise rare in the Wabash Valley. Lee gave much land away to the Girl and Boy Scouts, miners' welfare groups, church camps, and other community organizations. He built summer houses for himself and his children's families on lakeside sites.

The project had been a great success. Lee funded research at Purdue and influenced the state of Indiana to pass the first surface mining legislation. After the war, he offered his services to the National Coal Board in Britain for one pound a year.

Thus in my memos to the Coal Board in Scotland I could invoke Hugh B. Lee. What my contribution was I will never know, but the Coal Board instituted a comprehensive policy of land reclamation and was particularly successful with farmland. Many years later a student from the University of Pennsylvania, David N. Skinner, undertook a massive and successful program for coal exploitation underlying farmland in Midlothian, southeast of Edinburgh. In the process agriculture was restored and productivity increased.

When I returned to Scotland there was one modern highway, called the Boulevard. It ran west from Glasgow to Old Kilpatrick, probably fourteen miles. It had the pavement and median strip of a modern highway, but all the intersections were at grade. It had not achieved the grade separation invented for Central Park in New York City by Frederick Law Olmsted and Calvert Vaux in the preceding century.

Traffic volumes were low. However, at a time when the Outer Drive in Chicago was transporting 2,250 cars per lane per hour, 18,000 cars per hour in total, the heaviest traffic in Scotland was Paisley Road West in Glasgow with 800 vehicles per hour. In designing the New Towns, car ownership was assumed to be one car per seventeen families. At that time in the United States, planning practice required one and a half cars per family. There would be changes in Scotland: Could they be introduced to exploit American achievements and avoid their errors?

I well remember a meeting on the subject of traffic and transportation. The dominant figure was Sir Alker Tripp, onetime chief of police for Glasgow. He held that the solution to all traffic problems was the traffic policeman. He pointed out that a crowd of 120,000, watching an international soccer match at Hampden Park, Scotland versus England, could reasonably expect to be home for tea within an hour after the game. No doubt traffic policemen helped, but the success of the system was based on superb public transportation by trains, trams, and buses. Scotland had been colonized by two competing railway lines, the London North Eastern Railway and the London Midland Scottish Railway, which together served every nook and cranny of the metropolitan region. Tramcars served every radial, and Coronation trams traveled at sixty miles per hour on special tracks. Buses served radials and the interstices. There were two competing systems, one public and the other private.

Rapid transit had been effectively destroyed by politicians and the automobile industry in the United States. It seemed imperative that Scotland avoid this error. I wrote a memorandum to this effect to one J.G.S. McPhaill, a senior civil servant. He acted and caused a committee to be formed, chaired by a Glasgow banker, Lord Inglis. I became the staff of one for the Inglis Committee, which in due time produced the Inglis Report.

The next transportation issue involved highway design. The modern highway was an American invention, accomplished by landscape architects, not engineers. The first notable example was the attractive Bronx River Parkway in New York, completed in 1926, for which the purposes were multiple: to achieve the transportation objective of facilitating traffic movement, to provide a gratifying visual experience; and, in this particular project, to rehabilitate the Bronx River and riparian lands. Two brilliant young landscape architects, Michael Rapuano and Gilmore Clarke collaborated with planner Robert Moses in the design and creation of the Westchester County (New York) Parkway System (1922 to 1933), a magnificent exercise in design and engineering. Later the National Park Service designed and built the exemplary Blue Ridge Parkway in Virginia and North Carolina (1931– 1940). Unfortunately, the scale of highway construction after World War II exceeded the capability of the few landscape architects. They were superseded by highway engineers. In the subsequent demonstration of the New Jersey Turnpike, engineers revealed that they lacked the sensitivity, caring, and art to equal the earlier demonstrations, as they do to this day. We are only now implementing Lady Bird Johnson's wildflowers program as a cosmetic redress of some of the engineers' ugliness.

Could Scotland avoid this mistake? It happened that there was a very effective technique, developed by American landscape architects, that facilitated improved designs. Conventional highway engineers, both in the United States and Britain, depended on a centerline profile of the contemplated highway and a number of cross sections. Thus, the engineer could design only at these points but not elsewhere.

The convention of a contour map was well understood, but the invention by an unknown landscape architect was to use contours to depict proposed designs. This concept meant that the plan applied not only to centerlines and sections, but also to the entire area to be planned. Existing contours were shown as dashed lines, proposed contours as solid lines, which permitted calculation of cut, fill, earth moving, and grading. This convention is now universally employed. I exhumed my notes from the courses by Professor Walter Chambers and circulated them. I obtained copies of two seminal books, *A Policy for Design of Rural Highways*, and its urban successor, both by the American Association of State Highway Officials. I also obtained a film on the planning and design of the Garden State Parkway in New Jersey, not entirely exemplary, but novel to Scottish highway engineers.

There was one American concept that I sought to inculcate, that is, "induced capacity," the axiom that any new highway will become saturated. Any new facility induces new and more uses. The application of this principle was invoked during discussions on the proposal to relieve traffic congestion on the road that flanks the western shore of Loch Lomond by improving and building another on the eastern shore. For most of this traffic, the destination is Loch Lomond. Whenever two or more Scotsmen gather for a drink, the urge will arise to sing, "By yon bonny banks and yon bonny braes, Where the sun shines bright on Loch Lomond, Where me and my true love. . . ." Clearly it was the beauty of the loch that should be preserved. I have long held that the natural beauty of Scotland has been well protected by the great conservators of poverty and inaccessibility. But Loch Lomond was only twenty miles from Glasgow. It needed another conservator, indeed a conservative, which Lord Inglis was: "We will not build a highway on the eastern shore, we will introduce modest improvements to the existing highway, conscious that these must not impair the visual experience. We will not induce excessive demand at the expense of Loch Lomond."

Far and away the greatest tragedy in Scotland was housing. Among all the resolutions of the post–World War II Labour government was a massive commitment to public housing. Slums were to be eradicated, and new housing must be provided to enable siphoning from the slums to permit central redevelopment. New towns were major instruments, but every city and town developed plans for housing.

The instinct was noble, as was the sacrifice, which entailed a large expenditure by an impoverished country. The history of housing reform had begun with poor-law tenements during the nineteenth century; it had been inspired by Ebenezer Howard's new towns at Letchworth and Welwyn Garden City and Raymond Unwin's protestation that "there is nothing to be gained by overcrowding." From this, and the Garden City Movement, came a commitment to the magic density of twelve units per acre. Had that been, rather, a commitment to urban, low-rise, multiple family housing, it could have provided many opportunities responsive to places and people. This density had no historical antecedents. Traditional villages were humane at much higher densities, single-family housing at much lower densities.

Unfortunately, the twelve units per acre became dogma and, even worse, a stencil. The geometry of terrace housing, generally four units long, resulted in uniform dimensions: seventy feet face to face, seventy feet back to back, fifteen feet between gables. This geometry offered no opportunities for architecture, and there were no landscape architects; housing plans were thus prepared by draftsmen and junior engineers in municipal departments.

Britain is pocked by these developments, and the analogy is accurate. Everywhere comparison is available between traditional terrace housing and municipal housing estates. For me the most blatant and tragic example was offered by three little fishing villages in Fife: Pittenween, Elie, and Anstruther. In each case there is a harbor and rows of one- and two-story stone houses flanking the street. Houses rise up the slope behind, facing the harbor, generally with a southeast orientation, protected from northwestern winds—an essay of modest common sense, urbane, handsome, humane, tourist attractions. On top of the escarpment rise the public housing projects, all from the same common stencil, looking like broken teeth, forlorn, neither urbane nor handsome, without unity or humanity, unloved, unlovable.

I decided that this matter called for action. My colleagues at the department felt that this approach was so entrenched that it could not be modified. I decided to try. I solicited invitations to give public speeches, first through the Royal Incorporation of Architects for Scotland, later through both Edinburgh and Glasgow colleges for art. The speech began, "The majority of Scottish housing is a travesty of architecture, an embarrassment and shame . . ." It then proceeded to an illustrated indictment in which the virtues of traditional building and foreign examples were compared with the current municipal convention. This attracted attention. A reporter from *The Scotsman*, perhaps the leading newspaper in Scotland, asked permission to publish the speech. This was a sensitive matter. Civil servants may not criticize the government publicly. I would never become a permanent civil servant, however. What could I lose?—my job, and I didn't have another one available. I acted with some prudence. I told the chief architect and planning officer that I would give a speech critical of housing but felt that he would subscribe to its intentions. The speech would be published in *The Scotsman*. He did not demur. The speech was published, and both he and I, separately, were admonished, but a lively debate began. I was asked to write an article, "Open Space and Housing," for the *Architects' Year Book*, the organ of the MARS Group (the British branch of the Congress for International Modern Architecture), and another, "The Site Plan" for the *Architectural Review*.

Perusal of architectural magazines revealed that in other countries a much more successful tradition was emerging in comparable low-cost housing. In the Netherlands, Sweden, Denmark, and Switzerland, multifamily terrace housing had been designed that was more urbane, which conspicuously employed landscape design to contribute to delight and unity. Some part of its success lay in the organization of the site plan, but it was the landscape treatment that constituted the major innovation and success.

The generating idea in these successful plans came from the brilliant mind of an American landscape architect, Henry Wright. It was he, with Clarence Stein, who invented the superblock, first employed in Radburn, New Jersey, and later in Chatham Village in Pittsburgh and Baldwin Hills Village near Los Angeles. This overwhelming idea resolved the conflict of private open space and the automobile. It involved inverting the house plan. Instead of a living room overlooking a little private space and the street, living and dining rooms faced a private garden that subtended common open space. At the back of the house were the entrance, storage, kitchen, stairs, and minor bedrooms. The entrance/backs of houses were served by cul de sacs. The houses thus insulated both people and open space activities from the automobile and from traffic, parking, and services.

The idea had been imported to the Netherlands with, among many other examples, the Frankendaal in Amsterdam by Merkelbach & Elling, for which the landscape architect was Mien Ruys. There were numerous Scandinavian examples and one variation, for steep slopes, the Neubuhl, by Haefli and Moser in Zurich. An illustrated article was developed, circulated to the department, transmitted to the Ministry of Town and Country Planning, and accepted for publication by *Architectural Review*. It was never published.

One problem persisted. No funds were ever allocated for landscape design. I decided to attack this difficulty. The idea was simple. The cost of landscape treatment should be included as a capital cost and amortized over the life of the building. If the idea was appropriate for bricks and mortar, why not for trees, shrubs, lawns, and flowers. But there was the cost to consider. Could it be absorbed?

I obtained plans for a number of exemplary projects, itemized the materials, submitted the plans and quantities to contractors throughout the country, and

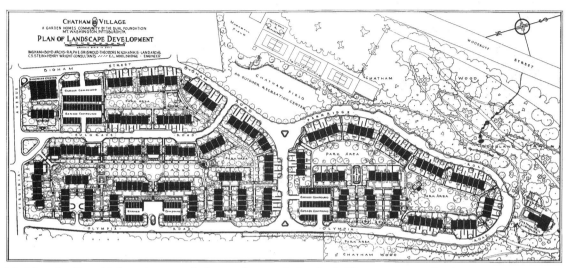

My ideas for Scottish housing were influenced strongly by the brilliant American landscape architect Henry Wright, a 1901 Penn architecture graduate, and the architect-planner Clarence Stein. They had invented the superblock, first employed in Radburn, New Jersey, later on in Chatham Village in Pittsburgh and Baldwin Hills Village near Los Angeles.

Chatham Village was a garden homes community developed by the Buhl Foundation in Pittsburgh. The preliminary planning began in 1930 (plan of landscape development, Ingham and Boyd, architects; Ralph E. Griswold and Theodore M. Kohankie, landscape architects; C.S. Stein and Henry Wright, site planners and consultant architects; and C.L. Wooldridge, engineer).

Pavilion and garden court in the first unit of Chatham Village (circa 1937–1938).

A garden court in the second unit of Chatham Village (May 1937).

obtained their estimates. This was done for a variety of elaborate schemes. The cost, amortized over the thirty-year mortgage period proved to be very modest. The most elaborate plans never exceeded the cost of a packet of cigarettes per family per week. This was a surprise.

The same J.G.S. McPhaill, my friendly senior civil servant, took these calculations to the secretary of state for Scotland and sent a memo to Lord Silkin, minister of town and country planning. Lo and behold, this new rule would apply to all new towns, would be supported with national funding, and would be recommended to all municipal corporations. I wrote an article, "The Cost of Open Space in Housing," which was published in two issues of the *Architects' Journal*.

My several activities, operated through different administrations—hydroelectric power, agriculture, forestry, surface mining, traffic and transportation, and housing—all required contacts with district ministries. So I would follow the progress, or more commonly, lack of progress, of my memoranda by determining their position in the piles of files on the trays of the respective administrators. The daily task was chagrining. Weeks and months would pass without action. It is true that I was impatient. Many years after I left the department, several of these memoranda surfaced and did useful work. But there were no reasons for optimism then.

Planning in Britain

Between 1946 and 1954 British experiments in planning were the cynosure of the world. The New Towns Act of 1946 had created a bevy of new towns around London and a number in Scotland—Stevenage, Harlow, Hemel Hempstead, Crawley, Basildon, Peterlee, East Kilbride, Glenrothes, Cumbernauld, and later, Milton Keynes. In addition, every county, city, and town was required to produce a comprehensive plan, which would be subject to a public hearing and, subsequently, when approved by the minister, would have the force of law. Each plan would be revised every five years.

Paradoxically, the area not subject to planning constituted the greatest success, which was the preservation of agricultural land. This was resolved by a strategic device. Planning fell within the Ministry of Town and Country Planning. The central responsibility was with urban land uses; however, the maps employed to describe these did not include agriculture. Colors were applied to indicate residential, industrial, commercial, and institutional uses, but agricultural land was left white. A prevailing regulation was invoked, which specified that no agricultural land could be transformed into urban land use without permission of the minister. Moreover, local authorities had to demonstrate that no available open land existed within urban zones before such an application could be made. It was also made explicit that the minister would grant exceptions in the cases of new towns, but generally for no other reasons.

Through this device agricultural land was preserved. During periods when the fruits of agriculture oscillated from poverty to wealth, agricultural land was reserved. Now this industry has stabilized within the European Community at a relatively high level of prosperity.

In the United States massive intelligence and much ingenuity have been applied to this problem with a record of total failure. The speculative value of agricultural land for urban uses has been too great a prospect for farmers to relinquish voluntarily, and only a few governmental entities, including Hawaii and Oregon and a handful of environmentally conscious local governments, have shown a willingness to restrict this transformation for the public good. The prodigious urban and suburban growth since the Second World War has largely been at the expense of prime agricultural land.

Whatever problems Britain had or has, this is not one. The boundary between city and countryside has been held. The benefits to society are large: the savings of the social costs of unplanned growth, expensive infrastructure, and high service costs, and retention of an unspoiled countryside. The farmers have not made the great land sale profits of their American counterparts, but they have been permitted to continue farming, and they are assessed and taxed, not on speculative value, but on use value. Furthermore, the constraint on suburban growth has focused development in existing cities. As a result there are no western European equivalents to the South Bronx, North Philadelphia, South Chicago, or much of Washington, D.C.

The new towns probably do constitute a social success. They have provided a large inventory of decent, modest housing in benign environments. The syphon effect did work, and central redevelopment was made possible. New Towns represent a rather low level of architecture, physical planning, and landscape architecture. Redevelopment in the cities shows some greater success. Even Glasgow, one of the meanest of industrial cities, no longer has that infamous slum, the Gorbals, nor any other. Indeed, Glasgow was nominated in 1992 as the European city of culture—quite a transformation from the days of my boyhood.

The price of the new towns has been high. Given the low industrial productivity and the high unemployment rate, it is fair to ask whether it might not have been wiser to invest more in the basic economic capability of the country and spend less for social services, so as not to undermine Britain's capacity to compete in world markets. Low productivity and high social costs are a poor combination. Apparently, Britain has now fallen below Italy in industrial production.

More particular to planning is the creation of a large and stultifying bureaucracy. This was perfectly visible in Scotland forty-five years ago, and perusal of professional literature suggests that it has grown since then. The image is of Gulliver enchained by Lilliputians, initiative constrained by regulation. In contrast, the influence and effectiveness of planning in the United States is more like a cobweb on the frame of a rogue elephant.

British planners do not develop alternative futures; they enforce the law. The following example may be misleading; it may also be illuminating. My brother has a small house in Bearsden, a suburb of Glasgow. It contains three bedrooms, a master bedroom and one each for a son and a daughter. When I visited, the children had to double up. There is an attic which, with two dormer windows, could make two more bedrooms. My brother is an architect and a competent carpenter. He could do the work himself.

The Monkey That Smoked – 1953

In Edinburgh one found many public delights; the Castle, Princes Street Gardens, Crammond, the Salisbury Crags, museums and galleries, but none was more enchanting for children than the zoo. There were not only animals to see, but also camels and elephants to ride. So very often on Sunday mornings Pauline and I would take Alistair to the zoo.

Given that I had tuberculosis, and given my salary I should not have smoked. I had never been required to stop, however, only advised to limit myself to ten cigarettes a day. I suppose then the doctors did not imagine that I would live long enough for this to become a problem. Oh, if only I had been required to stop, and had stopped then. It is my greatest guilt that I continued to smoke until quite recently.

Then, ten cigarettes cost one shilling and ninepence ha'penny. I spent five percent of my salary on these. Each was precious. I numbered and rationed them, one with breakfast coffee, one with midmorning coffee, one after lunch, one for midafternoon coffee, one with sherry before dinner, one after dinner, some for listening to the radio, one reserved for the following morning.

At the zoo the monkeys and gorillas had indoor cages and outdoor enclosures. One Sunday morning I had moved to the back of the outdoor cages for a smoke when I saw a monkey smoking. It was the very picture of guilt. It turned its back to the public view, cupped the cigarette inside its hand, took great sucks with its flattened lips, expelled the smoke, and urgently dispersed the cloud with its paws. Every little boy would recognize the behavior. It saw me smoking, and unmistakably asked for a cigarette. Now each of these was precious; which one was I going to forgo? I passed a cigarette through the chainlink fence. The monkey took it, lit it from the embers of the earlier butt, inhaled with intense enjoyment and threw me a glance of thanks.

I visited him many times. When he was indoors and saw me, he would come outside where I could pass him a cigarette.

"Why don't you?" I asked.

"Planning permission," he replied. "I need permission from Bearsden, Strathclyde Region, and the Department of Health for Scotland. It might even go to the Ministry in London."

"Build the bloody thing, Kenneth. You'll be dead before they discover it."

Teaching

The Royal College of Art in Edinburgh had a distinguished program in architecture. It was run by a quiet but effective man, Ralph Cowan. He approached me early in my stay in Edinburgh and asked whether I would be interested in offering a course in landscape architecture for architects. I was delighted at the prospect. I was offered the splendid honorarium of five guineas, that is, five pounds, five shillings (plus or minus $25.00), not per lecture, but for the course. They would also pay my tram fare.

On the basis of this new largesse I purchased a Stewartry close focus device, which, when attached to my Leica, enabled me to make slides from books and magazines. I reviewed the instruction I had received at Harvard, engaged in extensive reading, and embarked on my first experience of teaching.

It was very rewarding. I had a class of thirty or so; the students were very interested, faithful in attendance, and produced estimable papers. Indeed two of these, James Morris and Robert Russell Steedman, became the first students to enroll at Pennsylvania in my initial class there.

News of the course traveled to Glasgow, whence came a similar invitation with a doubled honorarium and train fare. Now I was amortizing my investment! At Glasgow I came to know Thomas Findlay Lyon, chairman of town planning, a Geddes Scholar and curator of Geddes's papers. Through him I came to learn of Patrick Geddes, whom I found fascinating but difficult to read.

I was at Glasgow for three years. My lectures improved annually, as did my confidence as a teacher. I had never before considered teaching as a serious profession, but, clearly, it had charms.

It was later during this period that I was asked to write a memorandum on the creation of a degree program in landscape architecture to be offered by either the College of Art or Edinburgh University, or by the two jointly. I did this eagerly. There were wonderful resources. The most distinguished British ecologist, Frank Fraser Darling, was at Edinburgh at that time. I discovered that a great biologist, C. E. M. Waddington, whose wife was a colleague of mine, was intensely interested in architecture and landscape architecture. Geology was a powerful department at Edinburgh then; soils were taught at the Agriculture College. There were botanists and horticulturalists galore at the Royal Botanic Gardens, among whom there was strong support for the creation of a department of landscape architecture. Its image was much influenced by the accomplishments of the eighteenth-century practitioners, Kent, Brown, Repton, Price, Payne Knight, Shenstone, and the Scot, John Loudon. A curriculum in a profession with such accomplishments should be introduced.

I submitted the memorandum. Nothing happened. It would be thirty years before it was exhumed.

Life in Edinburgh turned out to be bleak. We lived in a basement apartment with a very fine address, 18-A Abercromby Place, adjacent to East Queen Street Gardens in the "New Town"; that is, the eighteenth-century town as opposed to the medieval one. The apartment was within the Dutch Consulate and was payment for secretarial services provided by my wife.

Six hundred pounds a year could support neither a car nor a telephone, but it did permit a rented radio. Thank God for the Third Program. Rationing constrained expenditures on food. I recall an occasion when Crena de Iongh came visiting, took us out to the George Hotel for a splendid lunch, and spent a sum well over a month of my salary. Our movement was limited to trains and buses and by weather.

Even by Scottish standards Edinburghians are reserved. As a Glaswegian I was considered as foreign as my Dutch wife. Few friendships formed but those that did endured.

One day I was summoned by the chief of the new towns section, an architect named Alex Wylie. East Kilbride and Glenrothes new towns were under way. There was considerable interest in yet another; both the cities of Glasgow and Edinburgh thought that a site near Cumbernauld, between these cities, should be investigated. However, it was likely that this new town would be a satellite of Glasgow and administered by her. Would I undertake the study?

I immediately visited Cumbernauld. It had the virtue of proximity to the major highway connecting Edinburgh and Glasgow. As at East Kilbride several years before, the wind howled, the rain drove horizontally, the whole site was awash. Moreover, the farms were few and scattered. Anthropologists long ago had learned that sparse human settlement bespeaks adverse environments and impoverished resources. I spoke to several farmers whose opinions were united. It was a miserable place, wetter than most, with intractable mud, poor, sour soil, a high water table, few trees, and those wind-pruned.

The Greeks were active colonists and city builders. They had a method for selecting city sites. They found, first, defensible locations; the next criterion was adjacent agricultural land. There, on the prospective sites, they grazed domestic animals, sheep, goats, cattle, and horses, and, after a season, priests selected animals at random, slaughtered them, and examined their cadavers and organs for deformities and anomalies. By this clever device they investigated the availability of nutrients and trace metals and the presence of toxins. Land growing healthy animals would provide healthy food for healthy people. No such sophistication is yet employed in advanced countries.

In Scotland a sieve method exempted prime agricultural land and steep slopes. It was quite elementary. No geology, hydrology, soils, vegetation, wildlife, or archaeology entered into consideration.

Seeing the drenched sheep and cattle and listening to the unhappy farmers was enough to cause me to consider alternatives. Maps, aerial photographs, and, finally, site visits were investigated. Clearly road and rail access to Glasgow was crucial. Next in importance was the availability of water and sewers, and a block of about 20,000 acres was necessary. At Harvard I had been impressed by a book, *American Building*, by James Marston Fitch, which gave great emphasis to the factor of climate in architecture and planning. I had then been instrumental in persuading Harvard University Press to publish *Climate Near the Ground* by Rudolf Geiger, an innovative presentation of the science of microclimatology. I determined to use these perceptions to find an appropriate location.

The ideal site, in classical and Renaissance times, was a southeast-facing slope. That could not be found on the Glasgow-Edinburgh road nor on the south of the Clyde, but north of it were admirable classical sites, south- and southeast-facing, at elevations above fog with beautiful views to the Firth of Clyde and, south, across the Clyde, to the Renfrewshire Hills. On the day I went there, the sun was shining; protected from the wind I lay in heather and exulted in the views. There was Dumbarton Rock, a volcanic cone with a ruined castle atop, ancient capital of Scotland, the gleaming Clyde, and, far out beyond the estuary, the Paps of Jura.

There was one problem: the site was steep. Now this had halted neither Rome, Siena, Frascati, nor San Francisco. This constraint must be transformed into an opportunity; we are not building for popes or cardinals. I recalled a project in Zurich, the Neubuhl by Haefli and Moser, where housing stepped down a steep slope and the flat roof of the lower house became terrace, balcony, and garden of the upper house. This would be the answer. Hanging gardens, stepped housing, each one having the merits of an attached single-family house, each with as much outdoor as indoor space, and the gardens entirely private. If the block was to be composed of four houses in depth, then the occupants at worst would walk down three flights or up one. In a city where the commonest house form was a four-story walk-up tenement, this was not a serious objection. So house plans developed, simple rectangles, L-shapes and T-shapes with different dimensions. They were all modular and could be fitted in various permutations, but all had uninterrupted views to south and east and all had private entrances and gardens. Open space equaled the building area. On the skyline, out of every view but overlooking the

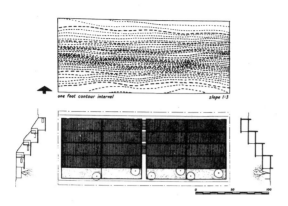

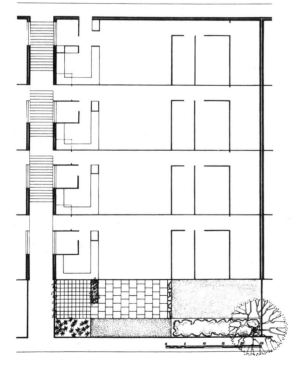

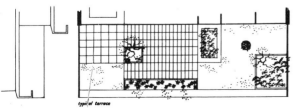

In 1953, fresh from Harvard and the dominance of the Bauhaus I sought to introduce modernist principles to my native land (when I was asked to be involved in the Scottish new town program). I recalled a project in Zurich, where housing stepped down a steep slope and the flat roof of the lower house became terrace, balcony, and garden of the upper house. I designed stepped housing, each with as much outdoor as indoor space, and the gardens entirely private. Simple rectangle, L-shaped, and T-shaped house plans were designed with different dimensions. Here are the rectangle house plans. These houses would be affordable for working class Scots, would have uninterrupted views to the south and the east, and would have private entrances and gardens. I proposed these ideas to the officials responsible for the Scottish new towns but the designs were not used.

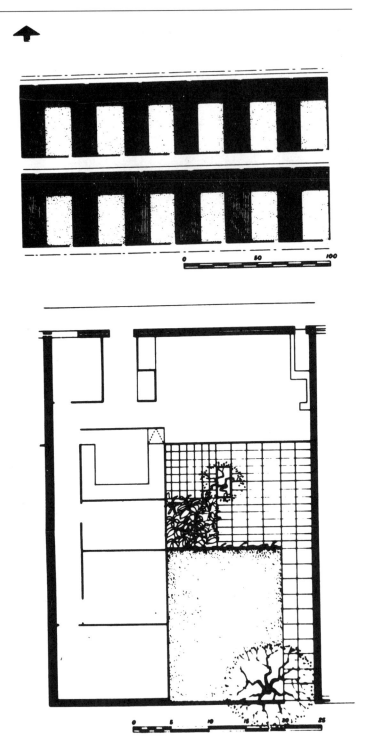

The L-shaped terrace garden house
designs (1953).

The site I selected for the Scottish new town took advantage of the south and southeast orientation of the slope. Single-family homes were stepped up the hillside, with apartment towers at the top.

whole, were towers and slabs for older people, single households, and couples without children. The towers provided views of a landscape of gardens.

Extraordinary economies in construction and costs were achieved by party walls, shared roofs and foundations, and reduced perimeter (the back walls were below grade except for the top structure). The earth-sheltered components ensured energy conservation. I conferred with an architectural colleague, Blanco White (wife of C.E.M. Waddington). She reviewed the plans, and wrote testifying to the economy of construction and the energy saving. The net density that could be achieved was forty dwelling units per acre, much greater than that achieved by the prevailing practice. There would be economies in land cost in addition to building costs.

I submitted the plans to Alex Wylie, chief architect for new towns, who then arranged for me to present the material to the permanent undersecretary, Mr. McGuiness, an Irishman with a Scottish accent. Wylie introduced the idea and gave his endorsement. I was asked to add my remarks. I spoke glowingly of the hanging gardens, the morning-golden windows, the beautiful views, access to workplaces on the Clyde, proximity to Glasgow, the beautiful landscape setting and, above all, of the greater economy of this scheme as compared with conventional building. There was a long silence.

"Well," McGuiness said, "It is certainly revolutionary. There's no doubt about that, and I am impressed by the arguments about its economy, but we can't build this in Scotland. Why, they haven't even built it in England yet."

"Sir," I said. "If the Scots have to wait for the bloody English to build something before we can, this is not the country for me. Good day, sir."

That night I wrote to G. Holmes Perkins.

Dear Dean Perkins,

Do you know of any opportunities which I might pursue in the United States? I find that professional life here is far from gratifying.

Within a week I received a telegram.

Would you be interested in the position of assistant professor at the University of Pennsylvania, teaching city planning, but charged with the responsibility of developing a department of landscape architecture? We can pay $5,000 for a nine-month appointment.

Pauline and I rejoiced. Our son Alistair, now three and a half, in suit, jacket, short trousers, and we, bedecked in our Sunday clothes, had a celebratory lunch at the George Hotel. Alistair behaved splendidly, and the chef brought him a silver tray of petit fours.

But the celebration was premature. Could a person who had tuberculosis be permitted to enter the United States? The rules stated that the condition had to have been stable for one year. Scottish doctors reviewed X-rays and concluded that the evidence supported this contention. The United States doctor in the American Consulate in Edinburgh concurred, but the doctor with the United States Embassy in London did not. Nor did he have to give any reasons. Crena de Iongh decided to intervene on his side of the Atlantic. He enlisted Dean Acheson and his law firm of Covington and Burling to pursue the matter with the Immigration and Naturalization authorities in Washington. This inquiry took a year. Finally, Covington and Burling learned that many favorable applications were being halted by a certain doctor in London, and suspicion arose that the solicitation of bribes might be the explanation. The infamous doctor was fired, and in May of 1954 a letter arrived intimating that I would be granted a visa.

It was almost too late. Perkins had all but concluded that I would be unable to accept the appointment and was negotiating a replacement. But the drama was not concluded. Pauline, as a Dutch citizen, had to apply independently. An X-ray was required, and this revealed a spot on the lung. Was it evidence of disease or an artifact?

It became clear that this matter would not be resolved before I must depart to the United States to assume my position. Should I decline on the assumption that

Pauline would not receive a visa, or should I accept, assuming that she would? This was not an easy decision, but we acted with optimism. (Eventually, I did leave; she and Alistair returned to her home in Amsterdam, and in due time her visa arrived. We were reunited in June of 1955.)

When I advised the Department of Health that I had accepted an appointment at the University of Pennsylvania, I was asked to continue working with the Department until it was necessary to leave for the United States. There was a good deal of relief at my imminent departure. My energy and skill were acknowledged, but my independence and critical faculties were not appreciated. I gave more public speeches and was advertised as professor designate of the University of Pennsylvania. This gave more authority to my remarks and freed the Department from embarrassment at my public criticism of government.

A small ceremony was held before my departure, at which time I was presented with a handsome briefcase. Kind words were said. I decided that this was not the occasion for criticism, thanked my colleagues, wished them well, and left.

Chapter 5

University of Pennsylvania, 1954–1964

The voyage from Southampton to New York was not merely a journey; it was a life decision. I was in the process of changing continents and assuming a new nationality and a new role. Scotland had been my first choice, but tuberculosis had made permanent status impossible in the civil service. Being a civil servant was no guarantee, but my qualified status would forever impede. Moreover, the low level of discourse, the inactivity, and the lack of passion were all infuriating. Yet I had decent qualifications for the role I had abandoned, much more than I brought to my new post. Now I must become a professor of landscape architecture and city planning. I had been a graduate student for four years, but my teaching was limited to lecture courses at Edinburgh and Glasgow. I was ludicrously unprepared to become founder and chairman of a new department. My recollection of the United States was that such improbable things could and did happen, that this was a land of opportunity where energy and initiative were welcomed. I must galvanize every whit of intelligence, every ounce of energy, to justify this generous opportunity.

My thoughts were exciting, but not the journey. The *Nieuw Amsterdam* took ten days to reach Hoboken. There my father-in-law had kindly made a car available, which was waiting on the docks. When we arrived, a dock strike was in progress and there were no porters. In my luggage I had one very large, heavy wooden box, filled with books. I wrestled this aboard the car with much strain and set off. My plan was to reach Wilton, Connecticut, Crena de Iongh's summer house, and, thereafter, the home of friends in North Marshfield, Massachusetts. There was no radio in the car, so I had no forewarning of the storm.

As I drove, it began to rain, soon in torrential sheets accompanied by wild winds, the like of which I had never seen. The windshield wiper was useless; the gale treated the Jeepster like a sailboat and it careened across the lanes of the Merritt Parkway onto the median. Trees fell across the shoulders and inner lanes. This must be a hurricane. I had seen the effects of the 1938 event on the Harvard Forest but had never experienced one. No other explanation could account for this violence. I reached Wilton with some difficulty, but fallen trees made it impossible to drive to the house. I walked there to discover no power and no telephone. I noticed a painful stiffness when I stood erect after driving and great pain when I sat down again. I decided to leave for Massachusetts. The drive involved many detours, power and telephone lines down, fallen trees galore, and flooding. I arrived at my friends' home in North Marshfield and found desolation, the roof demolished, the garage flattened, and gigantic elms strewn like matchsticks.

My poor hosts were in tears. They had spent their adult lives building and planting their place, and that night it was like a battlefield. This was not the time to reveal my ailment. I was in agonizing pain, most notably when I changed position. I could find a balance where pain would diminish, but if I changed positions to either sit or stand it was slow anguish. My condition became evident. "Don't worry," said Jim Craig, "I'll take you to my chiropractor tomorrow."

I slept uneasily; it had been a savage day. I had forgotten about the higher levels of violence in the United States: hurricanes, floods, tornadoes, murders galore, crimes of violence as common as dandruff, and then, of course, Senator Joe McCarthy.

The next day we drove to Copley Square in Boston to see the chiropractor. He was tall, massive, and had a Polish name. The premises consisted of a waiting room filled with documents describing the discrimination and abuse suffered by chiropractors at the hands of orthodox medicine. At long last he led me to the treatment room. He examined me, pulled, twisted, scrutinized the symmetry of my feet, then, without a word, disappeared down a long corridor, only to turn around and charge furiously toward me. He thrust himself into the air. His thumbs hooked under my armpits, then he fell on me. I was dumbfounded. Hurricanes yesterday, mad Poles today. Was this the America I had yearned for?

I looked at him in amazement. He said, "Stand up, stand on the floor." I did; no pain. "You're OK," he said. I was.

I have suffered much from medicine, severed artery, massive surgery, plural effusions, erroneous diagnosis of terminal cancer, and sundry incompetences. This treatment cost five dollars, the best medical bargain I have ever had.

Landscape Architecture at Pennsylvania

In 1954, when I confronted the problem of creating a department of landscape architecture, designing a curriculum, recruiting faculty and a student body, the profession had declined considerably from the eminence that Frederick Law Olmsted had achieved single-handedly in the preceding century.

During his professional life, Olmsted had addressed the problem of the princely patron and designed Biltmore in Ashville, North Carolina, for the Vanderbilts. This project was atypical for Olmsted; much more central were public parks and campus designs. His successors emphasized estates for the new rich of an industrializing America. Conspicuous exceptions were the landscape architects who ran the National Park Service. They, of course, owed much to Olmsted and his sons (Frederick, Jr., and John C., actually a nephew, who was an adopted son). This little service was long dominated by a small band of public service landscape architects, modest, anonymous, yet extremely capable custodians of a large empire, perhaps the best and most constructive civil servants this country has ever had.

I believe that it is accurate to state that no other profession has achieved as rapid a transformation from oblivion to social significance as has landscape architecture. There will be arguments as to the precise event that signaled its emergence, but surely there was a transformation at the end of the seventeenth and onset of the eighteenth century. Doctors evolved slowly over millennia, from shamans to barbers with leeches to present-day physicians. Lawyers had as slow a progression from courtiers engaged in negotiation and adjudication, architects were for long builders and master builders, engineers were first artisans and artificers, but landscape architects seem to have appeared full blown.

The peristyle and atrium gardens of Greece and Rome were architectural adjuncts in which little skill was invested and the great Muslim spaces of Isfahan, the gardens of Alhambra, Generalife, Nishat and Shalimar Bagh were inspired outdoor architectural spaces. In the Christian world medieval cloister gardens, as at San Gall, were developed for culinary and medicinal purposes. The great Renaissance gardens at Frascati, d'Este, Lante, Aldobrandini, and Mondragone were inspired exercises in architecture—terraces, walls, steps, fountains—in which plants were supplementary, although today we agree that it is the garden rather than the villa that excites our admiration. With the work of André Le Nôtre at Vaux le Vicomte and Versailles, the garden is unquestionably the major achievement, the palace a mere focal point in the composition. It could be asserted that Le Nôtre was the first person who could be described as a landscape architect. Whatever reservation could attach to this assertion, that he was merely a green architect addressing the landscape as his subject, no such argument can hold for his English successors who begat the revolution in landscape architecture even as Versailles was being completed. William Kent, Capability Brown, Humphrey Repton, Uvedale Price, Payne Knight, and, not least, William Shenstone were indisputably landscape architects. Such revolutionaries brought a passion to the quest for a unity of people and nature expressed within the English landscape. They seem to have had no identifiable antecedents. They emerged, spontaneously, or so it seems, fully equipped with theory and practice.

So it was in the United States as well, where the first landscape architect, Frederick Law Olmsted, gave the profession its title just over a hundred years ago. He achieved social prominence and distinction early as a writer and experimental farmer, but his first exercise as a landscape architect, Central Park in New York, was an incandescent success. With Olmsted, landscape architecture emerged full blown as a profession in this nation.

In 1950 there were only one or two thousand practitioners worldwide. The dominant figures were École des Beaux Arts designers, products of the American Academy in Rome, engaged in Renaissance revival landscape architecture for the rich. Practitioners also included, as earlier noted, the modest landscape architects in the U.S. National Park Service and, finally, there were the young turks.

These last revolutionaries, almost all rebellious students from Harvard, had a leader, an English-educated Canadian, Christopher Tunnard. He had written articles for the English *Architectural Review* on an emerging modern landscape architecture before the war. These were ultimately assembled as a book entitled *Gardens in the Modern Landscape*. Tunnard joined the faculty at Harvard where he had a significant influence, notably on Lawrence Halprin.

Thomas Church was the first of the reformers. He practiced in California, where he engaged in a modest but thoroughly successful revolution. He observed that the benign climate of San Francisco, Los Angeles, and their surrounds induced an outdoor life-style. He concluded that the areas behind houses should be designed for outdoor living and transformed into places of social intercourse, areas for dining and recreation, with swimming pools assuming a significant role. This inclusion of outdoor living space transformed the internal arrangement of the house. Instead of there being a yard at the rear, this area became the focus, a private space for intense use. Consequently, house plans were inverted—living and dining rooms subtended this new, beautiful, and much-used space. It was a major accomplishment. Moreover, Church worked with small spaces and generally modest buildings and used a novel vocabulary notably free of Beaux Arts conventions. It was eminently adaptable and was widely emulated.

He bred a number of successors, several of whom worked for him. Most notable were Lawrence Halprin, Garrett Eckbo, Bob Royston, and Douglas Bayliss. The eastern wing of this movement included Dan Kiley and James Rose. This group was engaged in the quest for a modern landscape architecture consonant with the revolution of modern architecture.

There was another notable figure, a Brazilian, Roberto Burle Marx. Originally a painter, Marx was induced by Lucia Costa to design the roof garden for the Ministry of Health in Rio, which began his distinguished career as a landscape architect. In 1954 there were two candidates for the honor of the world's greatest landscape architect: Lawrence Halprin and Roberto Burle Marx. Today we must add A. E. Bye and Andropogon.

I consider Lawrence Halprin, Roberto Burle Marx, A. E. Bye, and Andropogon to be the most significant landscape architectural designers of the late twentieth century. Halprin is fascinated by natural processes and used an understanding of ecology as a basis of his work. His approach was more experiential than my ecological science-based method.

Halprin used sketching as a tool to understand landscapes, such as these two drawings for Sea Ranch, 1967. (Courtesy of Lawrence Halprin.)

I have long admired Roberto Burle Marx because he synthesized his pursuit of art with his knowledge of plants. He understood the beauty of native flora, and elevated the use of Brazilian plants to an artform with his designs. The residential garden of Luiz Cezar Fernandes (formerly of Odette Monteiro), Correa, Petropolis, Brazil, designed by Marx in 1949. (Photo copyright Marcel Gautherot; courtesy of Conrad Hamerman.)

Many of my former students practice ecological design and planning. The Philadelphia landscape architects of Andropogon have perhaps taken ecological design the furthest. Andropogon's principals include Carol and Colin Franklin and Leslie and Rolf Sauer. All four once worked for Wallace, McHarg, Roberts and Todd. Carol Franklin and Leslie Sauer have been popular teachers at Penn for many years.

Andropogon designed the master plan for the Crosby Arboretum in Mississippi with Edward Blake, Jr. These drawings illustrate the master plan for Pinecote, the Crosby Arboretum's public interpretive center. *Below left,* a drawing from November 1983, shows the proposed pond and visitor's center. *Below,* from April 1984, shows the proposed pond access road, parking, and interpretive trail loops.

Modeled on a possible past history of the site, the pond simulates the activity of beavers. The existing agricultural ditch was redesigned as a slow, meandering channel ending in a still, dark pool that rises and falls seasonally. Creation of the pond allowed the Crosby Arboretum to display a wide array of Mississippi Coastal Plain plant communities ranging from pond aquatics to wetland fringes. (Plan by Andropogon Associates, Ltd.; drawings by Howard Coale, courtesy of Andropogon Associates.)

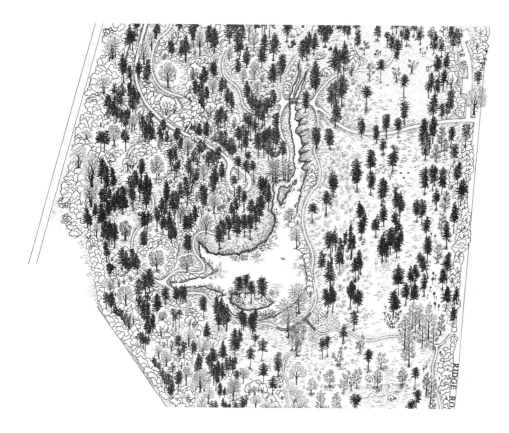

A. E. Bye Designs. *Left,* Ha-ha at Gainesway Farm, Lexington, Kentucky (1975); *right,* Leitzsch Residence, Ridgefield, Connecticut (1958–1960). (Photographs by A. E. Bye.)

Mention should also be made of Stanley White, chairman of landscape architecture at the University of Illinois. He was a brilliant teacher who produced many excellent students, including Hideo Sasaki and Philip Lewis.

There were other practitioners abroad, such as Christopher Tunnard, mentioned earlier, who had designed modern gardens in England for Serge Chermayeff graced with Henry Moore sculptures; G. A. Jellicoe, father figure to British landscape architects, and his protégées, Sylvia Crowe and Brenda Colvin, who broke new ground with rehabilitation of industrial wastelands, coal tips, and quarries, alignment of high-voltage transmission lines, and siting of power stations; and Sir Peter Shepheard, designer of the Festival of Britain and long-time professor of landscape architecture at Pennsylvania. In Italy were Pietro Porcinai and Maria Theresa Parpigliolo; in the Netherlands, Professor J. T. P. Bijhouwer, Nico de Jonge and Mein Ruys; the Dane Hansen; Cabral from Portugal; and the Belgian, Hortha, but numbers were small, even worldwide.

Bigger is not necessarily better, but it is more. Big corporations, institutions, and individuals often carry more weight than their smaller competitors. This was a significant matter for landscape architects. They were overshadowed by the larger profession of architecture, which induced an inferiority complex, much enhanced by the common relationship of architect as client, landscape architect as consultant or subcontractor.

Based on historical experience, there was an inversion of value. The single figure of André Le Nôtre dominated the late French Renaissance; Kent, Brown, and Repton had transformed an entire country in the eighteenth century. Olmsted made a greater beneficent contribution to the nineteenth-century American environment than all of the architects in the United States, and the national parks were an unparalleled gift—the selection, planning, and design of the most powerful and beautiful landscapes in the nation.

These facts were generally unknown to architects or, if known, the implication was not acknowledged. Architects assumed unquestioned primacy; landscape architects were allotted a supporting role.

The task then was a large one, to found and develop a department of landscape architecture in a major university. Yet perhaps I was alone in considering it important. The university commitment was modest, a three-year appointment to an assistant professorship with a starting salary of $5,000 for nine months. Such appointments are notorious. The rule is, up or out. I had three years.

The first problem was the low esteem of the profession, vis à vis architecture, in the academic community and in society at large. This status may have been unjust. The accomplishments of landscape architecture, performed by only a few practitioners, deserved more recognition, but the fact of the matter was that they were either unknown or lightly regarded.

This modest reputation held true in universities. With the notable exceptions of Harvard and the University of California at Berkeley, landscape architecture was usually an undergraduate curriculum in land grant colleges. Moreover, these departments were often within schools of horticulture or agriculture, and waifs in these.

Such departments did not attract the brightest students. In the postwar years recruitment selected persons whose families engaged in the nursery business, landscape contracting, agriculture, and forestry. From such candidates there did emerge distinguished professionals, but these were exceptions. The bulk of candidates performed benignly but modestly. Yet, this may well be the time to observe that landscape architecture may be exceptional in that its least competent practitioners are unlikely to cause human suffering or inflict social losses. Medicine, engineering, law, and architecture can make no such claims. The cost of liability insurance for medicine is sufficient testimony; failed dams and bridges provide evidence of engineering incompetence. How many lawyers are in jail? How many more should be? And, of course, some of our most conspicuous architects have had their buildings razed as social hazards. There should be more.

Failure in landscape architecture projects may mean disappointment, dead trees, shrubs, and plants, or perhaps an unfortunate design on a landslide area or floodplain, but on the whole, failures will not be life-threatening.

The first objectives of the department were clear: to recruit brighter, more ambitious students than were entering the profession elsewhere, to examine crucial social problems that were not being addressed by society or resolved by practitioners; to attract the most distinguished landscape architects and designers as visiting professors, and, finally, to obtain support for the venture within the university and the community.

There was one very large decision to make. Should the proposed program be undergraduate, graduate, or both? Harvard's was the sole exclusively graduate program. The undergraduate curriculum was the norm. As a result, Harvard had staffed the faculties of most schools and had a "farm" system. Its alumni sent the best B.L.A.s (Bachelor of Landscape Architecture) to Harvard for graduate study. It would be unwise to compete for these recruits. More than a decade would pass before Penn graduates supplanted Harvard as the major source of teachers. While fees at Pennsylvania were similar to Harvard, they were multiples of those charged by public universities. A new undergraduate program would be at a competitive disadvantage against North Carolina State, Penn State, Georgia, Iowa State, Illinois and, not least, Berkeley. These schools were large and they were cheap.

The next decision proved to be most effective—to select and actively recruit architects as the core of the student body. If the selection process was successful, we could achieve several objectives simultaneously. Experienced graduates of architecture would be dominant in a school with a large number of undergraduate architects. They would clearly be superior to them; there would be no inferiority complexes. This choice could also select students with qualifications superior to the Harvard admissions criteria. Finally, by selecting excellent architects, candidates would enter as skilled designers. Teaching design is by far the most difficult task in all curricula. The challenge would be to transform skilled architects into landscape architects.

During the following year the idea was given great support by Lewis Mumford, a visiting professor at Pennsylvania. He led faculty discussions on the subject of education, including professional education. He examined the undergraduate architectural curricula at Penn and elsewhere and categorized them as "rag bags." He recommended abandoning undergraduate professional education, admitting B.A. and B.S. candidates with a general education, the appropriate intelligence, motivation, graphic skills, and visual imagination. His recommendation for a graduate professional program was accepted and realized. So the program would be graduate, initially selecting architects as its principal recruits.

The Graduate School of Fine Arts

In my life I have experienced much good fortune. Discovering landscape architecture was one instance; certainly, being admitted to Harvard lacking the necessary credentials was another. Being invited to join the faculty of the School of Fine Arts at Pennsylvania was yet another. Here again my credentials were modest. As I was a foreigner, I was cheap. American salaries looked prodigious from the vantage of Scotland, and that was my major asset. Beyond this I had demonstrated commitment and energy, but I had no experience as a practicing professional landscape architect. My Scottish experience had been in planning, my landscape

Although I was active in practice during the late 1950s and early 1960s, my main focus was building the Department of Landscape Architecture and Regional Planning at the University of Pennsylvania. Dean G. Holmes Perkins had gathered many of the young talents in the world to teach architecture, landscape architecture, and planning at Penn. This photograph is from a Penn city planning jury, circa 1956. *From left to right,* the seated jury includes: Louis I. Kahn, Bob Mitchell (who was chair of city planning at Penn), Preston Andrade, and me. William L. C. Wheaton, who was later dean at the University of California-Berkeley, is standing and pointing to the student's drawing. (Photograph by Joseph Nettis.)

architectural engagements had been in policy. However, competition was not strong. Of the students of landscape architecture at Harvard during my stay there were few who achieved national distinction; Hideo Sasaki, Bob Zion, and Bob Breen are conspicuous.

Perkins left Harvard to become dean at Penn in 1952, at the time when Walter Gropius was asked to retire. This had caused a furor. The rules held that persons of international distinction could be retained on a year-by-year basis. Gropius's reputation certainly met that criterion, so the faculty and student body were dumbfounded when President Conant requested his resignation. Of course, I have now reached this situation myself. At seventy I became emeritus; my contract with the university ended.

At Harvard there were massive sympathetic resignations accompanying the Gropius departure, and Perkins took advantage of the situation to persuade brilliant faculty, young and old, to join him at Pennsylvania. Harold Stassen, then president at Penn, gave him carte blanche.

So William L. C. Wheaton, Martin Meyerson, Blanche Lemco, and Robert Geddes arrived from Harvard, plus Paul Rudolf as an annual visitor. Sasia Nowicki and George Qualls were drawn from North Carolina State, Rimaldo Giurgola from Rome, Robert Le Ricolais from Paris. These comprised the second wave of modern architecture, transferring primacy from Harvard to Penn. So too in planning, Robert Mitchell, first executive director of the Philadelphia Planning Commission, became chairman. Wheaton directed research, and Martin Meyerson, Charles Abrams, Chet Rapkin, Herbert Gans, William Rafsky, Jack Dyckman, Erwin Gutkind, Britton Harris, Howard Lapin, with Mumford as visiting professor, constituted a planning faculty without peer in the United States.

Perkins's plan was simple and direct: year one, expunge the École des Beaux Arts tradition and introduce a new program in modern architecture; year two, introduce city planning; year three, establish a curriculum in landscape architecture. His hierarchy of importance followed this order—architecture dominant, planning next, and landscape last. He had further plans, first, to divest the program in music to the college. Art historians were offended by being servants to architecture; he gave them a department. After some years of trial, he abandoned the teaching of interior design.

There is no doubt that the School of Fine Arts at Pennsylvania was the creation of G. Holmes Perkins. He had a clear vision, and he worked to achieve it with total dedication and considerable success. Among all of the testimonies that he deserves, none is greater than acknowledgment of his capacity to discern distinction, often in young persons but among older ones too, those who had not been accorded appropriate opportunity or recognition. Among the former are Geddes, Meyerson, Dyckman, Gans,

In 1958, Dean Holmes Perkins of the University of Pennsylvania organized a conference on urban design criticism. Held in Rye, New York, the conference involved several Graduate School of Fine Arts faculty and other prominent planners and designers. *From left to right,* participants include: Lewis Mumford, me, J. B. Jackson, David A. Crane, Louis I. Kahn, G. Holmes Perkins, Arthur Holden, unidentified member of Dean Perkins's staff, Catherine Bauer Wurster, Leslie Cheek, Jr., Mary Barnes, Jane Jacobs, Kevin Lynch, Nanine Clay, and I. M. Pei. (From *Architecture,* January 1959; courtesy of the Architectural Archives of the University of Pennsylvania. Photograph by Grady Clay.)

Nowicki, Qualls, and, later, Robert Venturi, David Crane, and David Wallace. Lou Kahn is the most conspicuous among the lightly regarded who were found and elevated, but Erwin Gutkind, Bob Mitchell, Robert Le Ricolais, August Commandant, Charles Abrams, and Chet Rapkin all achieved high distinction with Perkins.

Very early after my arrival Perkins introduced me to John M. Fogg, botanist, plant geographer, and director of the Morris Arboretum. He in turn impressed me into the campus landscape committee. He was a splendid scientist and teacher, an enthusiast. Knowing of my charge to create a department of landscape architecture and of the need for scholarships, he effected an introduction to Mrs. Laura Barnes. This lady was the spouse of Alfred Barnes, who had made a fortune with Argyrol, a disinfectant used in World War I, and amassed a world famous collection of Impressionist paintings. His collection was displayed in small rooms in his home, badly hung, poorly lit, and sometimes three high on the walls. Mrs. Barnes actively disliked the paintings. She recoiled from acres of Renoir and Rubens flesh. Her passion was trees. She had created an excellent private arboretum at her home on Latches Lane in Merion, and gave instruction in horticulture and landscape architecture to gentleladies and suburban matrons. In this she was supported by Jack Fogg and a local landscape architect, Joe Langran.

I was invited to tea. Mrs. Barnes, Jack Fogg, and I sat at a table in the garden. We were served cucumber and watercress sandwiches. My mission was explained. I expanded on the topic, the necessity of recruiting superior candidates, the high cost of tuition, the availability of financial support in other departments and schools. As we finished the tea she said, "Young man, I will provide support for eight students to the value of free tuition and a stipend of $500." That was $1,000—magnificent then, but trivial today, with tuition not $500 but $20,000, living expenses not $500 but in excess of $5,000.

However, it was this generous gift that made possible the search for the superior candidates who held degrees in architecture. An advertisement was written and published in every architectural magazine in the world, offering free tuition and a stipend to accepted candidates. The response was marvelous from Britain, Norway, Australia, Turkey, India, Sweden, the Netherlands, and elsewhere, but not a single American applied. Some part of the explanation lay with the London *Architectural Review*, which regularly published articles by Nicholas Pevsner on historical landscape architecture, H. F. Clarke who wrote of the nineteenth- and twentieth-century experience, and Christopher Tunnard who aspired to a modern landscape architecture. The American architectural press had no counterparts then, nor has it since. The candidates, it transpired, were familiar with eighteenth-century English accomplishment, but uncertain about contemporary practice. Nonetheless, they believed that the knowledge of landscape was an essential skill for the practice of architecture, still a revolutionary conception. Architects have never been instructed in environmental sciences and are not yet now.

The selected candidates all had superb records, all had professional experience. Such candidates would achieve esteem in the school, the university, and, ultimately, in society. Out of the eight, two are now deans, one a chairman, another a distinguished practitioner who is a member of my school's Board of Overseers, and the remaining quartet have achieved splendid reputations.

They set the tone for the department and for subsequent recruits, who maintained these high standards. The second class produced a dean, two chairmen, two professors, and four practitioners of distinction. Today, almost forty years later, the department has graduated more than 1,000 students, who include 11 deans, 31 chairmen and directors, and at least 140 professors teaching in institutions throughout the entire world. They have created a dozen or so new programs worldwide and include a significant number of partners, associates, and practitioners in distinguished offices, private and public.

I arrived at Pennsylvania in the summer of 1954. I was an assistant professor of city planning, charged with the role of introducing a curriculum in landscape architecture. I rented an apartment in Chestnut Hill, The Cherokee, designed by Oscar Stonarov. My apartment held only a borrowed bed. I needed little more, as my wife and son were still in Amsterdam. I had no office, no secretary; there were no students, no budget. The first year was devoted exclusively to designing a curriculum, raising scholarship funds, recruiting a student body, and creating a new department. All of which was done, on the whole, successfully. Certainly the accession of a brilliant student group of distinguished architects was revolutionary in landscape architectural education.

The objective of the first five years was the assimilation of the best practice, historical and contemporary. This was much affected by a grant which I obtained from Chadbourne Gilpatrick of the Rockefeller Foundation in the second year. The purpose was to create an illustrated bibliography of professional work. This grant also provided funds to support authors in contributing to a literature on the subject, among them Gordon Cullen and Ian Nairn from the *Architectural Review* in London and the Dutch architect, Aldo van Eyck. The importation of distinguished practitioners also characterized this period—Phillip Johnson, Garrett Eckbo, Bob Royston, Douglas Bayliss, Gordon Cullen, Ian Nairn, Aldo van Eyck, and Karl Linn. This too was novel and effective. No other school had so resolutely employed distinguished professionals as continuous visiting critics.

The choice of problems was also crucial. Great efforts were made to find and pursue current and conspicuous social problems. The plan for Seagram Plaza in New York was topical, the location of a new type of national park at Cape Hatteras was challenging, the development of the projected Penn Center Plaza in Philadelphia was an important local issue, and redemption of the Schuylkill adjacent to downtown Philadelphia and recovery of an island in Manayunk were both popular issues. Not least was the investigation and proposal for the new National Independence Historic Park in Philadelphia, for which Lewis Mumford was a critic.

During these five years there were, at any time, only two simultaneous design studios, yet it is fair to say that the vast majority of studios had significant effects on the real projects and received a considerable amount of public attention and approbation.

There were many essential chores: the creation of a library, subscriptions to magazines worldwide, the initiation of a slide collection using the 35-mm color slide innovation. This was accomplished economically by providing film to students who, during their peregrinations in their native lands, selected the images of conspicuous buildings, plazas, and gardens. So was a slide collection created.

Sir Peter Shepheard

The most distinguished teacher of landscape architecture was Sir Peter Shepheard. He taught at Penn from 1959 to 1995 and spent eight years as dean of the school, from 1971 to 1979. He was knighted by Queen Elizabeth, elected president of the Royal Institute of British Architects, was president of the Institute of Landscape Architects, and was a member of the Royal Fine Arts Commission.

He has an impressive number of realized projects, including the landscape for the Festival of Britain, Lancaster University, numerous projects for the London Zoo, Landsbury Housing, the De Witt Wallace Museum in Williamsburg, consulting for the Morris Arboretum, Longwood Gardens, and, not least, the Blanche Levy Park, the heart of the Penn campus.

Perhaps Peter Shepheard's greatest distinction is his immoderate modesty, an attribute seldom found among architects. While architects generally show their work at the drop of a hat, Peter can be induced to show his work only upon direct request. He is a lifelong photographer, and his slide collection displays his perception and his erudition. He has arranged his slides into a series of lectures on a number of subjects—trees, walls, steps, paving, hedges, fountains, light and shade. Each illustration is exemplary and reveals his preferences. He eschews bombast and virtuosity; he selects modesty, simplicity, appropriate materials and form. If ever there was a book waiting to be published, it is the series of illustrated lectures developed by Peter and presented over the past twenty-odd years.

Another example of his exemplary teaching involves his phenomenal ability in drawing and painting. He is an artist of some note and has illustrated books on birds and plants. Indeed, when the British Council received a request for a show of British drawings to be exhibited in Russia, they asked Peter to design a show based on his drawings.

Not only can he draw like an angel, but he has a prodigious visual memory. That is, he can sit on a stool, surrounded by a class, and draw bird, fish, tree, shrub, insect with dumfounding detail and accuracy from memory. He can do the same with famous buildings, gardens, and spaces.

He uses this phenomenal ability in a totally unique process of teaching. The students begin their exercise with a map and program statement, and Peter gives desk criticisms to them. He asks each student about the concept for the scheme. He scrutinizes the plans, sections, and perspectives that have been done, then he unrolls some tracing paper and proceeds to construct a plan and perspective from the student's work. "Is this what you have in mind?" he asks. "Why, no sir." The student then begins to modify the illustrations. So it continues; the plan and the dimensional representations proceed in unison with criticism by Sir Peter.

This method is seldom employed. It requires a degree of drawing skill that is very rare, too rare to become a conventional tool. Yet three-dimensional design requires such skill. Without it, the designer depends too much on plans and section, which cannot explain experience in space and time adequately.

In the case of Sir Peter Shepheard, there are no surprises. The perspectives he draws of projects are identical to their realization. This is a great skill, to which he has devoted his life.

He has yet another accomplishment. He is always a constructive juror. At most architectural juries the faculty frequently show their brilliance at the expense of the students. Yet however unhappy a student's project is, I have yet to hear a single destructive criticism from Shepheard. If there is any merit to be found, he will find it. Teaching involves strengthening the confidence of the students, which Sir Peter does to a remarkable degree.

At the conclusion of the first five years, there were clear accomplishments. The department had been created, and although its permanent faculty were few and modest, the visiting professors were all of national distinction, the student projects were being published and affecting events, and their accomplishments contributed to a rising reputation. But numbers and funds were small, and I experienced a growing apprehension. Some part of this may have evolved from lectures by three ecologists whom I invited to speak, Robert McArthur of biogeography fame, who later came to Penn, and Paul Sears and Edward Deevey, both then at Yale. But I believe the larger hesitancy derived from the collaborative studio undertaken in 1959. This cast doubt on the adequacy of the principles, data, and perceptions employed in the orthodoxy of the three professions, architecture, landscape architecture, and planning.

The West Philadelphia study, which I undertook at Penn with graduate students in architecture, landscape architecture, and planning, induced much thoughtful review. This study was conducted and supervised by many of the leading lights in the professions. Steen Eiler Rasmussen, the elderly distinguished Danish architect-planner, was in charge, David Crane was the innovative urban designer; and Robert Geddes was the bright star of architecture. In addition, the students were interpreting insights from collateral courses given by W.L.C. Wheaton, Martin Meyerson, Herb Gans, Jack Dyckman, Chet Rapkin, Charlie Abrams, and others.

It was clear that I was in the presence of the intellectual leadership of architecture and planning in the United States. Yet it was just as clear that there were serious deficiencies. The first was the absence of any concern with the environment. (Perhaps attention to solar orientation was the single exception.) Consider the environment now: earthquakes in Los Angeles and San Francisco, hurricane damage from Hugo and Agnes to Andrew, the devastating floods in the Mississippi basin, forest fires, land and mudslides, and general perturbation in climate. The total disregard for the environment was then a serious omission.

Karl Linn

Karl Linn might well be the most stimulating and original of all the teachers of landscape architecture during the history of the Penn landscape architecture program. Born of German Jewish stock, his parents ran an experimental nursery. They migrated to Israel before the war where Karl obtained a degree in agronomy from the Technion. He joined a kibbutz, then left it to join the British merchant marine. When war ended he went to Basel, Switzerland, to study psychology. Back in Israel he made an arrangement with a woman who sought to emigrate to the United States. At that time agricultural laborers were welcome, so Karl married the lady and took her to the United States, where they were divorced. Karl obtained employment with the New York City Parks Department as a gardener and, in addition, began to design handsome gardens for rich residents of Long Island. It was at this time that I learned of his accomplishments and invited him to come to Pennsylvania and teach landscape architecture.

His originality was manifested immediately. He gave a short, one-week sketch problem and required students to design their preferred environments. Almost every student had credentials in architecture, so their utopias were to contain both a built and a natural component. The class was polyglot, including, among others, a Welshman, William Roberts; a north country Englishman and Rosicrucian, Denis Wilkinson; a Swedish count, Carl Frederick Wachtmeister; an Irishman, Phillip Shipman; and a South African, John Ross from Witwatersrand.

Linn forbade his students to identify their drawings. The burden of the exercise was to demonstrate to the students that each of them had a personal utopia, that most of these had ethnic identities. He would identify the authors from the unnamed drawings: a beech forest with a carpet of bluebells—English or Welsh— by Bill Roberts; a boreal forest by Count Frederick Wachtmeister; bald hills with rivers—Ireland, of course—the work of Phillip Shipman. So he proceeded, infallibly. In truth, within each student was a utopian vision which he or she would seek to realize. This was a source of problems, said Linn. You should seek to realize your client's utopia, not your own.

Moreover, he stated, each person has a characteristic psychological state. It is important to recognize this, because your purpose is not to fulfill your psychological preferences but those of your clients. However, you should learn of your own psychological states. To demonstrate this point he reorganized the presentation, explaining that the class included a full range of psychological states, from extreme introversion to extroversion. Wilkinson had created a cave; hides hung on the walls and carpeted the floor. There was a large fire, and through an aperture would be seen the forest. "A Womb with a View," said Linn—a peak of introversion. Locations graded from deep in the forest, its edge and clearings to open landscapes, culminating in a modern home cantilevered over the Pacific—the acme of extroversion.

This presentation impressed the class and me.

The next demonstration of his psychological view was Linn's assertion that there was an inherent dignity in building and improving the environments in which people lived. He believed that improvement to the status of the black poor in North Philadelphia could be achieved by restoration of buildings and the creation of humane environments.

Toward this end he conceived of the Peace Corps and transmitted the idea to Bobby Kennedy, who gave it to President Kennedy. He also originated the Domestic Peace Corps, which was not accepted.

Vest pocket parks are another of Linn's contributions.

There was a time when the entire faculties and student bodies of landscape architecture, architecture, and city planning at Pennsylvania were continuously engaged in creating vest pocket parks in North Philadelphia. Unfortunately, the ills of society were beyond the remedies that Linn could dispose—discrimination, poverty, unemployment, police brutality, not to mention hopelessness. These were not soluble with cobbles, marble steps, shrubs, and trees. Indeed the spaces so arduously and skillfully created ultimately became battlegrounds for competing gangs.

The epitaph for the enterprise was not Linn's failure but rather the lack of appropriate energies and devices to solve this intractable problem, which went unheeded by all levels of government and private agencies.

Linn's own history also shrank. He has a messianic character. His aims were valid and challenging. He could mobilize his helpers into prodigies of effort. Inevitably, when projects became either too demanding or unsuccessful, the participants withdrew, which induced Linn to stronger exhortation, sometimes with criticism and aspersion, and passion withered. A great pity. Here was a wonderfully passionate and skillful man whose only failure was his inability to recognize that the task required greater skills and more resources than he could apply. Nonetheless, he was a powerful teacher and practitioner. He made his mark on the education of landscape architects, at Pennsylvania and at many other institutions.

Yet just as serious was the total absence of any effort to elicit the responses of inhabitants to the existing environment or to their needs and desires, preferences or aversions. The process operated as if the architects and planners knew best what society required or, even worse, regardless of what the inhabitants wanted, they would receive the current dogma of architecture and planning in the forms invented by Le Corbusier, Mies van der Rohe, Walter Gropius, and Ludwig Hilberseimer.

This realization led to a questioning and rejection of much of my education. This was an important and disturbing matter. However, I resolved to act to improve the situation. My responses took several avenues and consumed the next five years.

It would probably be an error to array the problems hierarchically as if I had firm conceptions of the areas to be pursued and of their relative significance. This was not so. I surely had a firm view of the deficiencies, but I was entering unfamiliar new fields—and so many of them. Thus I advanced where I could rather than where it might be most advantageous.

Certainly the most powerful act I initiated was to offer a new course in the fall of 1959 entitled "Man and Environment." I originated the conception and was the impresario. Most of the lectures were given by guest speakers; I introduced and concluded each segment. All other lectures were provided by visiting professors. The subjects were the scientific conceptions of matter, life, and man; the views of God, man, and nature in the major philosophies and religions, and, last, an examination of the interaction of man and nature, mainly ecological. This became the forum for my continued education for a quarter of a century. It, in turn, begat the television series for CBS entitled *The House We Live In* and provided much of the

Genesis Revisited

When I first studied Genesis at sixteen, the crucial terms were, as I remember them, "God made man in his own image, made he him; God gave man dominion over all life; God enjoined man to multiply and subdue the earth." There was no ambiguity here. Yet, hesitant to believe that this was the Christian message, I deferred to my minister, the Reverend John M. Graham. He offered no alternative. It was much later that I discovered the terms "anthropomorphic" and "anthropocentric." In 1962, when I reopened the subject in my course, "Man and Environment," and invited theologians from all faiths, it was my hope that one of these scholars would find an alternative view in scripture. They all failed. Now convinced that the burden of the Creation story was formally accepted in both Judaism and Christianity, that no alternative had been proposed, I began to lecture on the fact that Genesis had no correspondence to reality, no survival value; that, indeed, it might be the greatest injunction for suicide, genocide, and biocide. It was the injunction for cataclysm, not interdependence.

I lectured widely on this subject from 1962, the origins of man and environment.

I spoke at the Cathedral of Saints Peter and Paul in Philadelphia, Bryn Mawr College, the National Council of Churches in Saint Louis, an ecumenical conference at Riverside, in New York City, and elsewhere. A lecture entitled "Man and Environment" was given to the American Society of Orthopsychiatrists in 1961 in Los Angeles. It was subsequently published as a chapter in *The Urban Condition*, edited by Leonard Duhl, in 1962.

In 1967 Lynn Whyte, Jr., the famous historian, wrote a very important paper, published in *Science*, entitled "The Religious Origins of the Ecological Crisis." This was an authoritative review of the issue, written by a reputable historian. In contrast, I could claim no authority, only quote the opinions of the various theologians whom I had invited to address the subject, although some, such as Tillich, Weigel, Heschel, and Watts, were very distinguished indeed.

So I can claim to have introduced the subject of the implications of the Creation story in Genesis four or five years before Whyte. There is no doubt, however, that he buttressed the argument and gave it authority. It still awaits formal repudiation, but at last this matter is being discussed.

scientific basis for *Design with Nature*, written in 1967, which in turn propagated the movie *Multiply and Subdue the Earth*.

The religious inquiry initiated in "Man and Environment" and represented by dominant theologians in *The House We Live In* included Margaret Mead, Abraham Heschel, Gustave Weigel, Paul Tillich, Swami Nikhilananda, and Alan Watts. My involvement in religious attitudes to environment generated a lively response. First came an invitation from the Cathedral of Saints Peter and Paul in Philadelphia, next, from Bryn Mawr College, and, later, from the National Council of Churches, Riverside Theological Seminary, and many others.

In 1961 I was invited to join the Committee on Environmental Variables and Public Health of the National Institutes of Mental Health (NIMH). This brought me into the company of a distinguished group, involved in environmental health, mainly of social scientists. This activity produced the book entitled *The Urban Condition*, edited by Leonard Duhl, in which my chapter was entitled "Man and Environment." This involvement encouraged me to introduce another new course, entitled "Ecology of the City," in an attempt to focus ecologists, ethologists, and epidemiologists on the problems and remedies of the urban plight. "Man and Environment" was immensely successful, growing to 250 students. "Ecology of the City" never achieved great success. It was clear that scientists were not attracted to the city. I pursued this subject, but it was not until 1973 that it blossomed into the NIMH grant, "Experiment in Anthropology." We still await the creation of a national focus on this intractable and growing problem.

Certainly the most powerful, and possibly the most influential inquiry was into ecology. Early in my first five years at Penn, I invited ecologists to address the students. In 1959 I negotiated a contract with the Urban Renewal Administration, predecessor of the U. S. Department of Housing and Urban Development (HUD), to undertake a research study entitled "Metropolitan Open Space from Natural Processes." This investigation relied on a rudimentary knowledge of geology, physiography, hydrology, soils, vegetation, and land use. Nonetheless, it was a precursory exercise in ecological planning. Next followed a project using ecology as the basis for landscape architecture, advanced by Lewis Clarke, and in the following year, I introduced this new conception in the study and plan for Harvey Cedars on the New Jersey shore, the culmination of my first decade at Penn. At last a body of principles had been discovered, a foundation was available. On this we could build. Here was a conception and method that could produce useful work. Happily, David Wallace, my classmate in planning at Harvard, had been a member of the review of the Harvey Cedars project. He was impressed. In Baltimore he had directed the Greater Baltimore Committee and conceived of the Charles Center Redevelopment. Many of his colleagues on the Greater Baltimore Committee lived in the bucolic Green Spring and Worthington Valleys. They were appalled at the prospective destruction of their beautiful land by the completion of the Jones Falls Expressway, which would bring downtown Baltimore to within twenty minutes travel. They sought advice from Wallace. His skills were as a brown-fingered planner; in manipulating money, legislation, power, and urban planning, he felt insufficient. Needing some green-fingered skills, he asked me to join him. Thus began Wallace-McHarg Associates and their first job, "Plan for the Valleys." So now, not only was there direction for teaching and research, but the basis for a new professional career.

Metropolitan Open Space 1957–1959

The inquiry into metropolitan open space had its origins in the West Philadelphia study. This research revealed that the current dogma of modern architecture and contemporary practice in city planning and landscape architecture were not only dogmatic and inadequate but also myopic. It did not require any special skill to see that the overwhelming problem consisted of uncontrolled metropolitan growth, which, in scale and destructive ability, far exceeded the urban problems being pursued. I had published an article in the *Annals* deploring the despoliation of nature, entitled "The Place of Nature in the City of Man." It advocated simply that natural phenomena and processes that perform valuable functions for man, without his aid, be recognized and perpetuated within the metropolitan fabric. In addition, it observed that much metropolitan land was often unsuitable for development and that, if those rules were observed, a continuous and productive system of open space would permeate the metropolis and provide its skeletal form.

This proposal came to the attention of William McLaughlin of the Urban Renewal Administration. He requested a proposal for an investigative research project, "Metropolitan Open Space from Natural Process," which would, in addition, examine the implications of such policy for the housing market, transportation, land use law, and urban form. The proposal was submitted and subsequently approved, and I directed the metropolitan open space study from 1957 to 1959. I believe that it was a landmark for funded research by a landscape architect in the late 1950s.

The program was quite simple. We would identify rivers, streams, lakes, ponds, and their flood plains, wetlands, aquifers and aquifer recharge areas, steep slopes, forests, woodlands, and prime agricultural lands. We would recommend that these be either prohibited to development or constrained to meet certain specifications

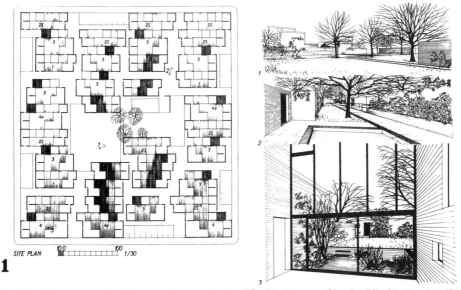

THE COURT HOUSE CONCEPT

My work of the late 1950s and early 1960s can be characterized as mostly traditional landscape architecture. However, I was experimenting with new ideas for urban housing design, ecological garden design, and campus planning. The Court House Concept was a project I pursued for the residential development of a city block using court houses, with special consideration of private and public open spaces. (1959, Ian L. McHarg, landscape architect; drawn by Anthony J. Walmsley.)

as an exercise of the police powers that provide governments the authority to regulate land use to protect the public health, safety, and welfare.

With two landscape architects, Donald Phimister and Frank Shaw, all of the parameters for the Philadelphia metropolitan region were mapped and subsequently overlaid. The resulting pattern was examined by housing market analyst William Grigsby. His conclusion was that such a policy would canalize but not constrain growth. Anthony Tomazinis examined the effects on transportation. He too concluded that the open space system would affect but not provide serious limitation to transportation facilities. William Roberts examined alternative suggestions, notably William Findlay's wedges-and-corridors theory. He concluded in favor of the natural process approach. He also investigated nodal settlement patterns within the proposed open space system. Ann Louise Strong, environmental lawyer, considered the legislative requirements, the municipal ordinances, that must be followed in order to realize the proposal. Finally, Nohad Toulon digitized the nat-

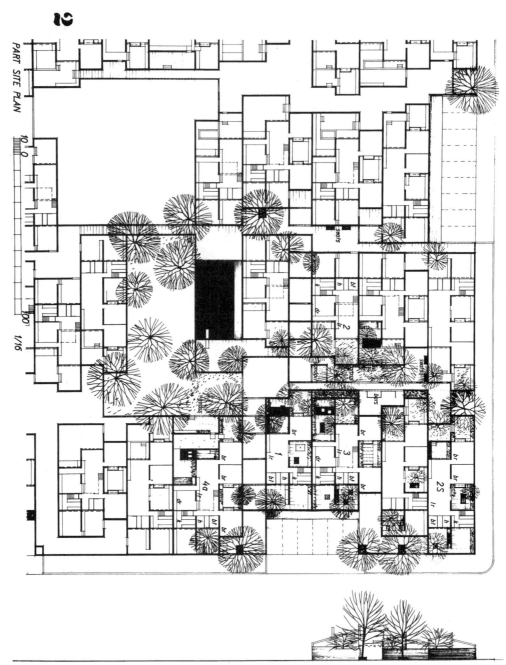

STREET ELEVATION

Concept for urban houses with courtyards, plan of one quadrant. (1959, Ian L. McHarg, landscape architect; drawn by Anthony J. Walmsley.)

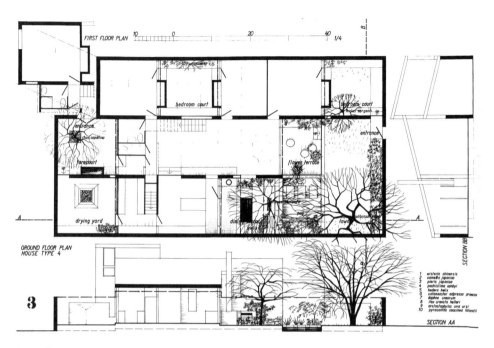

Court house concept, typical house and garden plan. (1959, Ian L. McHarg, landscape architect; drawn by Anthony J. Walmsley.)

ural resources data with punch cards and computed areas for each parameter and their combinations. His calculations were employed by Bill Grigsby and Anthony Tomazinis. This was the origin of what would become computerized ecological planning: Geographic Information Systems, or GIS.

The project was finished in a year, but a decade elapsed before it was published. At that time, while its message remained valid, the growth in environmental sciences, particularly ecology, was remarkable, and their implications for planning had been significantly recognized. "Metropolitan Open Space for Natural Process" had been superseded before it was published.

However, in the late 1950s, the study was a move toward an ecological view. It did employ natural science; it did address regional problems. It was an important precursor.

Southwark

There is often a chasm between an ideal and the institution designed to realize it. Such was the case with the conception of managing the environment. Certainly the

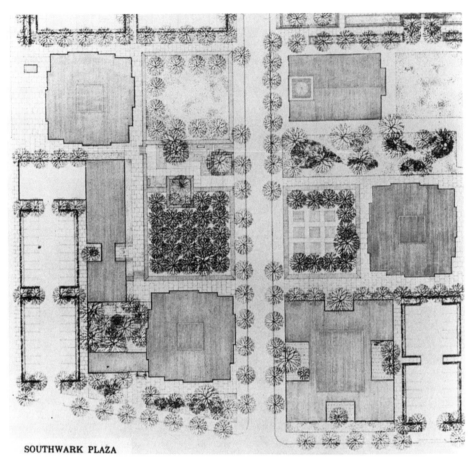

SOUTHWARK PLAZA

My concepts for urban housing were used in the Southwark Public Housing Project in Society Hill, Philadelphia, Pennsylvania, with the architects Oscar Stonarov and Frank Haws. (1959, drawn by Ian L. McHarg, landscape architect; from University of Pennsylvania, Graduate School of Fine Arts Exhibition and catalogue, 1960; courtesy of the Architectural Archives of the University of Pennsylvania.)

idea that the environment should be monitored and regulated to protect human health and well being was a laudable intention. This conception was introduced at a conference in Airlie House, Virginia, led by Russell Train and attended by the most distinguished environmental scientists of the nation. From it emerged the National Environmental Policy Act and the Environmental Protection Agency (EPA), laudable and successful. But the creation of the new institution encountered some serious obstacles. It so happens that any new governmental institution must first incorporate existing agencies and superfluous candidates from other units of government. Here is a device whereby the failures, misfits, time servers, and rejects can be disencumbered and relocated. Unfortunately, this inventory filled the majority of the new positions—not a propitious beginning. So when I first walked into the EPA offices I was distressed, but not surprised, by the level of science and planning knowledge I encountered. Had my colleagues and I had the opportunity to examine the institution that would emerge from our decision, we might have been somewhat hesitant. However, with the notable exceptions of Ann Gorsuch-Burford, the EPA has performed adequately. It has often been reluctant to enforce the law, and it does so without much inspiration or enthusiasm. However, the advent of William Reilly and the heightened sensitivity to the environment did offer promise.

Other institutions have been even less successful. Perhaps the most conspicuous example is public housing. This is an arena with a lineage of reformers originating in nineteenth-century England with poor-law housing. It received an enormous stimulus from two young women in the immediate postwar period, Catherine Bauer, professor of planning at Harvard, and Dorothy Montgomery, a Philadelphian. They effectively wrote the Housing Act of 1949, which produced the Public Housing Agency and a plethora of related projects. No one can deny the passion, energy, and intelligence of these young women, but it was compassion that best explained their accomplishments. Their goad was the persistence of slums during the period of housing emancipation for the middle and working classes achieved by the FHA, VA, and uniform payment mortgages. Good housing, they believed, should extend down the economic ladder.

This cause was also espoused by modern architecture. Catherine Bauer married William Wurster, architect, dean at MIT, later dean of the College of Environmental Design at Berkeley, and leader in the Bay Region tradition of humane domestic architecture. Dorothy Montgomery married Robert Montgomery of Montgomery and Bishop, a Philadelphia firm also identified with humane housing.

However, humane interest came into conflict with the current architectural ideology. Modern architecture had a dogmatic attachment to high-rise building: Gropius in the Seimenstadt, Le Corbusier with La Ville Radieuse, the Voisin Plan, later Unité d' Habitation, Mies van der Rohe, with the Lakeshore Apartments. The dogma had a landscape component, that high-rise buildings liberated land for human use. The prototype was of towers and slabs in a vast expanse of empty lawn. Brasilia is of, course, the largest realized expression of this idea.

There was another idea which was current but never achieved widespread acceptance. As noted earlier, Henry Wright, landscape architect, and Clarence Stein, architect, developed the concept of the superblock, a plan whereby low-rise housing was served by culs-de-sac to which houses turned their backs, facing, first, private gardens and, beyond, common open space. It was, and remains, an inspired idea. The first realization at Radburn, New Jersey, was prosaic architecture and landscape architecture. The planning concept deserved approbation, the architecture and landscape architecture did not. For this reason the idea did not become popular. It was the image of tower, slabs, lawn, and the slogans of Le Corbusier, "Le pacte est signé avec la Nature," "Espace, verdure, soleil," that won the commitment of young architects everywhere in the world.

The reality of public housing clients was very far from this dream of slabs and towers in a green plain. The occupants, predominantly black and poor, had a unique social structure: families consisting of one or more women, not necessarily related, large numbers of children, and transient adult males. Was this architectural archetype appropriate for such households? Peter, now Sir Peter, Shepheard, the architect of Landsbury Housing for the Festival of Britain, was one of few modern architects in Britain who opposed high-rise housing for low-income families. He objected to the famous Pimlico project by Powell and Moya, and those by Derek Ladsun and others. He demonstrated that he could equal the density of high rises with low- and medium-rise housing and create humane environments sustaining to family life. His empirical rule was that the height of housing should be controlled by the position of a mother, leaning out of a window, able to communicate to her child on the ground. Oh, that such a rule had been employed.

Of course, the error has now been discovered, Pruitt Igoe in Saint Louis, the proud product of a famous architect, Yamasaki, has been demolished. Yet, it was one of the purest expressions of the dogma.

I encountered a paradoxical problem when in 1959 I was invited to be landscape architect with Oscar Stonarov for a public housing project named Southwark. The history of this project is illuminating. A national competition involving architects and developers was initiated for Society Hill, Philadelphia by the Philadelphia City Planning Commission.

Oscar Stonarov's submission won. However, as a result of negotiations with the developer, the award was withdrawn and the second prizewinner, I. M. Pei, architect, and William Zeckendorf were selected.

Oscar Stonarov was a presence. Imprinted by Frank Lloyd Wright, he wore the flat-brimmed Wright hat and a string tie. He was quite bald and given to violent expostulations and gestures. Characteristically, he would arrange a meeting to review a project, arrive very late, and immediately deface drawings and destroy models while shouting wild criticisms. His aide, Frank Haws, was quiet, soft-spoken, deliberate, careful, and industrious. It was he who did all the work. How he survived the temperamental behavior of Stonarov we will never know.

Yet Stonarov had done good things. He was an early advocate of planning for Philadelphia with Robert Mitchell and Edmund Bacon. He had done admirable conversions of Baltimore row housing and alleys. He was a staunch supporter of public housing. Violent in life, Stonarov died violently in a plane crash with Walter Reuther in 1970.

Stonarov had invested a large sum in the competition. He adroitly took the rejected plans to the Philadelphia Housing Authority and persuaded its members that these could be employed for their Southwark Public Housing Project, not far from Society Hill and of similar size. The question of whether housing types for upper- middle-class occupants were appropriate for welfare households apparently never arose. My task was to fit the buildings on the site—three towers, a number of two- and three-story terrace houses, and a community center. Denied the right to question the appropriateness of the high-rise apartments, I directed my passion

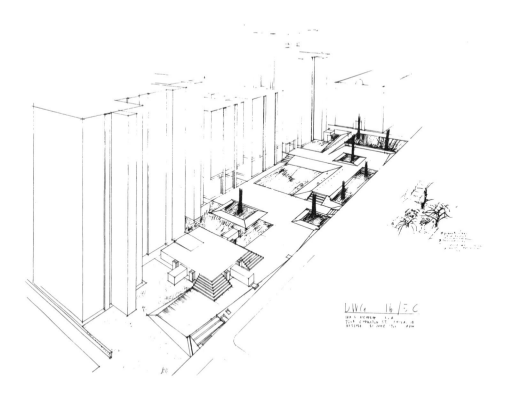

Drawing of entrance development of the University of Pennsylvania Medical Research and Botany (Richards) Building. (1960, Louis I. Kahn, architect; Ian L. McHarg, land-scape architect; drawn by Anthony J. Walmsley.)

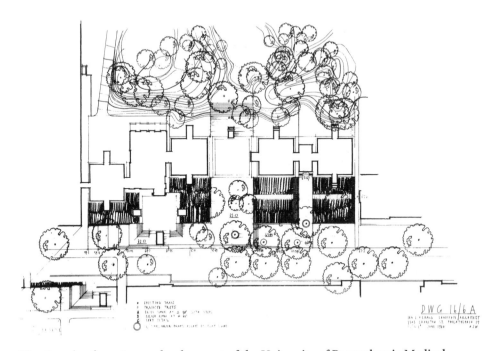

Planting plan for entrance development of the University of Pennsylvania Medical Research and Botany (Richards) Building. (1960, Louis I. Kahn, architect; Ian L. McHarg, landscape architect; drawn by Anthony J. Walmsley.)

to provide gardens for the low-rise occupants and as rich an environment for the project as I could create.

The scheme was a calamity. It did not select a responsible and appreciative population. Murder, rape, molestation, and other crimes of violence, drugs, graffiti, and vandalism were commonplace, so much so that the towers were condemned and evacuated. Now tens of millions are scheduled to be spent on rehabilitating these buildings. Meanwhile, the Society Hill Towers built by Pei at less cost have vastly appreciated in value and need no expensive repairs. The town houses, which originally sold for $45,000, now sell for $300,000.

Catherine Bauer climbed Mt. Tamalpais and was found dead there; Dorothy Montgomery has gone too. Their image of humane housing for poor people remains unrealized. Their splendid efforts were thwarted by an architectural dogma and deeply insensitive institutions.

There was always another option, strangely not then considered. As suburbs expanded, there grew a legacy of abandoned inner city housing. Property values fell, rental properties became surplus, an increasing housing stock reverted to city ownership following tax delinquency proceedings. Surely, this was the appropriate vehicle for public housing. Yet, at that time, when FHA and VA mortgages were abundant for new housing, mortgages were not available for conversion or restoration. Public housing did not exploit this opportunity.

Given two choices— one, to select and congregate the socially disadvantaged, and the other, to diffuse these households into existing neighborhoods where the original population could provide both example and constraint— surely the latter showed more promise. This idea is now, belatedly, accepted, at a time when negligible sums have been appropriated for public housing.

If there are reservations about EPA, there are none about HUD. This is an institution that has been totally emasculated. It serves no useful purpose whatsoever. The dreams of model cities and new towns no longer have a place in government. Indeed, the subject of the state and future of cities is being ignored.

Ecology Emerges

In the summer of 1955 I obtained my first commission, the design of the plaza and fountain for the Pennsylvania State Office Building in Philadelphia. For this project I created a private office with never more than two employees, students or recent graduates, and this continued modestly until joining David Wallace, creating Wallace-McHarg in 1962. Those who worked for me were uniformly excellent and their subsequent careers fulfilled their early promise: Jim Morris and Robert Steedman, partners in Edinburgh, perhaps the most distinguished office in Scotland. David N. Skinner, later dean at Edinburgh; Michael Hough, first chairman at Toronto; Michael Langlay-Smith, partner in the largest office in Europe; William Roberts, partner of Wallace Roberts and Todd in Philadelphia; Frank Shaw, distinguished landscape architect in England and occasional teacher at Penn; Donald Phimister, practicing in Philadelphia, and Anthony J. Walmsley, teacher at Penn, and notable practitioner in New York.

I suppose that during my first decade I was obtaining the cream of commissions in landscape architecture in Philadelphia, but that is a small boast. Yet in spite of their modest numbers and size, they exhibited purpose and direction. In scale, they ranged from a large garden, the Greenfield Estate, to a small urban space at Penn; Woodland Avenue, an urban park system in Southwest Washington, D.C.; a suburban shopping center, Cheltenham; the Southwark public housing project with Oscar Stonarov; a plan for the twenty-mile Philadelphia waterfront on the Delaware River; and the open space study for the Philadelphia metropolitan region.

It would appear that the Metropolitan Open Space study had the largest effect, certainly on me, as a precursory ecological enterprise. It laid the foundation for the Plan for the Valleys, the Potomac and Delaware River Basin studies. The Plan for the Philadelphia Waterfront had no effect on Philadelphia, but ideas generated then were to emerge and be applied to Baltimore Inner Harbor, the Lower Manhattan Plan, and the Toronto Waterfront. The Delaware study was an early assertion that the largest latent resources in many cities lay in derelict and abandoned waterfronts. The Cheltenham Shopping Center study also had no effect; it was not realized as designed. Yet its conception was valid. Conventional plans were doughnuts, a sea of asphalt parking surrounding shops inside a mall containing benches, fountains, and planted panels. The Cheltenham project asserted that the maximum contrast with the pervasive aridity of parking lots could be achieved with a rich natural landscape replication— forests, streams, waterfalls, luxuriant vegetation, shrubs, flowers, and water in movement. This was the first shopping center for the developers. It was a large gamble, and they sought convention. Northland and Southland in Detroit by Victor Gruen were their idols. Yet here was another incipient ecological instinct, abstraction and replication of native ecology. Southwark had no such generating idea. There the purpose was to induce a green verdant environment into urban housing. With a working- or middle-class population it could have been successful. A public housing population was inappropriate, and it failed, more, I should add, because of housing than landscape. Southwest Parks in Washington consisted of central arcaded spaces with pergolas containing lakes and several islands. The scheme derived its form from attempts at climate control, through the use of arcades and shade, water and evaporative cooling, vegetation in view but not accessible for deleterious use or vandalism. Here, too, was a move toward ecology. Of all these projects the Greenfield Estate was the most original. It was concurrent with the Metropolitan Open Space study and employed the same principles, but at a project scale—nature is the gardener's best designer, true for garden or metropolis.

The Greenfield property consisted of a large site, part of the hill in Chestnut Hill, extending to Fairmount Park and the Wissahickon Creek. The original house had been remodeled; children's rooms were furnished by George Nakashima. Edward Stone had built a pool and pool house. The new Mrs. Albert Greenfield wanted a garden. I proposed to extend the Wissahickon woodlands up the slope to the top of the hill and to recover and reconstruct a watercourse that would proceed in waterfalls, rills, and pools to the creek below. The geology was Wissahickon schist, but not exposed. My colleague, A. J. Walmsley, found a rock face destined to be covered by condominiums nearby, recorded each rock, and planned reconstruction of this formation in the garden. The vegetation was entirely native. Adjacent woodlands provided the vocabulary: beech, hemlock, oak, hickory, ash, halesia, cucumber magnolia, dogwoods, spice bush, wild azaleas, and ferns galore. At that time plants for landscape projects were selected from nursery catalogues, a wide range of exotica, seldom linked to each other by any environmental association. Dominant native plants were rarely available. My instruction in plants had been all but absent at Harvard. Experience was limited to the Arnold Arboretum, a facility where long-separated and distant members from various ecosystems were assembled into unfamiliar taxonomic association. It favored exotic materials at once inappropriate and unavailable. Generally, landscape plans reflected this bias, employing the same vocabulary. *Acer palmatum atropurpureum,* tormented willow, and European lindens appeared and reappeared, irrespective of place. However, this plan was quite novel; it utilized only native vegetation. Mrs. Greenfield was ecstatic. She wished the garden to be built,

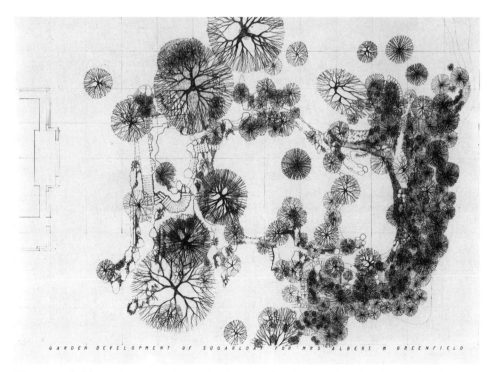

GARDEN DEVELOPMENT OF SUGARLOAF FOR MRS ALBERT M GREENFIELD

The Greenfield Garden. The schematic planting plan for a rock and water garden for Mrs. Albert M. Greenfield in Philadelphia. Although the garden was not built, it was in planning it that I was able to explore the application of knowledge about regional ecology to design. (1959–1960, Ian L. McHarg, landscape architect, with Anthony J. Walmsley.)

The Greenfield Garden. Sketches illustrating (1) the lake at the foot of the garden from the "look-out," (2) stepping stones and waterfall below the "Birch Pool," and (3) the "landing stage" and "headland" with stepping stones in the foreground. (1959–1960, Ian L. McHarg, landscape architect, with Anthony J. Walmsley.)

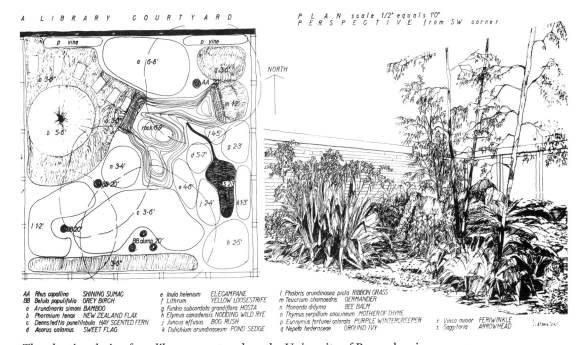

AA Rhus copallina   SHINING SUMAC
BB Betula populifolia   GREY BIRCH
a Arundinaria simoni   BAMBOO
b Phormium tenax   NEW ZEALAND FLAX
c Dennstedtia punetilobula HAY SCENTED FERN
d Acorus calamus   SWEET FLAG

e Inula helenium   ELECAMPANE
f Lithrum   YELLOW LOOSESTRIFE
g Funkia subcordata grandiflora HOSTA
h Elymus canadensis NODDING WILD RYE
j Juncus effusus   BOG RUSH
k Dulichium arundinaceum POND SEDGE

l Phalaris arundinacea picta RIBBON GRASS
m Teucrium chamaedris   GERMANDER
n Monarda didyma   BEE BALM
o Thymus serpillum coccineum MOTHER OF THYME
p Euonymus fortunei colorata PURPLE WINTERCREEPER
q Nepeta hederacea   GROUND IVY

r Vinca minor   PERIWINKLE
s Saggitaria   ARROWHEAD

The planting design for a library courtyard on the University of Pennsylvania campus.
Throughout my career at the university, I did some work on the Penn campus. In contrast to the Greenfield Garden, plant selection for this design was decidedly ecologically
incorrect. At the time, I was more concerned with the arrangement of plants in space
and their display value than the use of appropriate native species. (1959, Ian L. McHarg,
landscape architect, with Anthony J. Walmsley.)

but not her husband, Albert Greenfield, king of Philadelphia real estate operators,
who said, "Go to Paris, buy some clothes instead."

There was then a sympathy for the ecological view in these exercises of the fifties.
This sentiment was innocent of scientific ecology, but there was a strong instinct and
a presumption in favor of the natural— a fertile field awaiting elaboration.

Man and Environment

In 1946 to 1950 when I was a student, the agents of charge were initiated which
would engender the suburban explosion, but the effects were barely visible then.
On my return to the United States in 1954, the transformation was conspicuous.
The ingenious invention of equal mortgage payments, FHA and VA mortgages,

Eisenhower's interstate highway program, and prosperity had transformed millions of acres of farmland into tract housing and strip development. Ranches, split levels, gas stations, diners, sagging wires, and billboards—great swathes of farmland were transformed into low-grade urban tissue. Sadly, each annular ring of new development was encysted by successive rings, and nature, so dearly sought, was successfully expunged. This process could never succeed. It was only the newest, the richest, and most distant suburbanites who would temporarily savor the edge of pastoral nature.

Earlier development had been subject to controlling influences. The necessity of living within walking distance of work and church or synagogue applied in the nineteenth century; suburban railroads later produced nodes of development around stations; electric streetcars with greater acceleration and shorter intervals between stops produced all but continuous urbanization, but only along radial highways. However, it was the automobile that made the interstices accessible and extended the effective distance, vastly amplified by new highways. There was an explosion of growth.

The remedies of architecture, city planning, and traditional landscape architecture might on occasion produce islands where development was sensitive to nature, where buildings were organized to provide humane and handsome spaces, but these would be rare exceptions. Indeed the prevailing dogma in architecture gave no reason to believe that such an approach was likely. However, the bulk of development was performed by builders without any contribution by either architects or landscape architects, so the remedy did not lie in the design profession. Nor was the trend effectively constrained by municipal planning ordinances.

Robert Potter and Ruby Buick, students at Penn some decades later, made a movie that demonstrated urban growth in a most dramatic way. Beginning with maps of the primeval landscape occupied by the Leni Lenape Indians, they simply plotted urban development and filmed it at a constant speed. Seventeenth-, eighteenth- and nineteenth-century growth proceeded slowly but inexorably leading to the explosion after World War II. The symbolism was simple: nature was white, urbanization, black. The original nucleated villages were swallowed by the expanding city, whose tentacles and growth extended with terrifying speed and scale. And they continue to this day.

Clearly, if there was to be a remedy there must be a profound change in social values, notably, attitudes to nature and conceptions of what constitutes a humane environment. The subject of inquiry had to be vastly enlarged. My response to this challenge was to design a new course, required for landscape architects but open to architects, city planners, and urban designers. It was entitled "Man and

Environment." This was first offered in 1959 at a time when there were no persons identified as environmentalists and certainly no environmental lobby, when the Sierra Club was intent on preserving the American wilderness, notably in the West. The Audubon Society was preoccupied with birds. The Conservation Foundation was alone in the concern for world population, world agriculture, the threat of another dust bowl, the problems of environmental destruction, all presented in the *Plundered Planet* by Fairfield Osborne. So the decision to offer a course devoted to the attitudes of society to God, man, and nature was, at best, ambitious; at worst, or perhaps more accurately, presumptuous. Yet it was a success from the start, became a *succès de scandale* and taught, perhaps, to three or four thousand students. It persisted for more than two decades.

The role of professor has one significant privilege, the opportunity to design courses. Clearly, these must contribute to the curriculum, they must respond to student needs and interests, but it is often possible to satisfy these aims while addressing the major purpose, the continued education of the instructor.

In my case, it was apparent that my education at Harvard, while necessary, was insufficient. The skills I had acquired were notably deficient; in particular, there was a complete vacuum in environmental science. But there was an even larger omission, the absence of any serious investigation into the attitudes of people to the environment. Environmental destruction, already extensive, was accelerating. The agrarian values of pioneers and founding fathers had fueled deforestation of a continent, extinction of the passenger pigeon, decimation of buffalo, and more. The values of the current materialist, technological society contained even fewer safeguards. Here was a fit inquiry for a quarter of a century.

"Man and Environment" permitted me to invite the most distinguished speakers in the environmental movement for the illumination of students and the development of my own knowledge. It also became a dominant subject of inquiry in the school, attracting architects, planners, landscape architects, urban designers, and many undergraduates. There were three lectures per week, thirty-six in total, of which I gave six, as well as an introduction and conclusion and a summary and review of each of the four segments. The first segment considered was the scientific view of the evolution of matter, life, plants, animals, and man. The second topic was the views of God, man, and nature in animism and pantheism, Judaism, Catholicism, Protestantism, Islam, Tao, Shinto, and Zen. In the third segment the physiological and psychological relationships of man and nature were presented. The final subject was the ecological view, later organized as atmosphere, lithosphere, hydrosphere, and biosphere, plant, animal, and systems ecology.

The time I spend with students is most valuable and challenging to me. The only occasion I wore the kilt was when I was best man at the 1957 wedding of James Morris, a Scottish student in my first class at Penn. I am dancing with Jean Roberts, wife of William Roberts, my former student and partner.

When the course was first given in 1959 to a class of twenty-five students, faculty were drawn from Penn and the surrounding region. It grew tenfold and ultimately attracted the most dominant spokesmen on these topics from the entire country.

As mentioned earlier, in 1959 the environment was not a topic, there was no lobby, there were no persons identified as environmentalists. There were conservationists, although very few; ecologists were fewer still. Those precious few who would give intellectual leadership to the environmental movement were intent on learning of the operation of natural systems. Tending to exclude man as a source of destruction and pollution, they felt forced to narrow their inquiry and so excluded important areas—meteorology, geology, hydrology, and soils—and focused on plants and animal interactions.

"Man and Environment" placed ecology at its center, but broadened the area of inquiry into a larger biophysical environment, and, not least, included human attitudes toward the environment.

The course evolved continuously. One important device was to inform each speaker of the topics that preceded and followed. Transcripts of previous addresses were circulated. Addresses became more integrated. The subject of environment emerged in both science and public consciousness; more and better environmental science was developed. And there were dramatic discoveries—sea floor spreading, continental drift, all subsumed later in plate tectonics, plus systems ecology, ethnology, and ecological ethnography. I well remember inviting Harry Hess from Princeton to address this new geological hypothesis on plate tectonics. My colleagues in geology at Penn were aghast. "Next you will be inviting Velikovsky!" Why didn't I? He has been vindicated, at least, in part.

The speakers included a core who came year after year and others who spoke occasionally but, in sum, those who participated are a Who's Who of theology and science. Harlow Shapley, John Wheeler, Tulio Regge, Steven Weinberg, and Gaylord Harnwell, then president at Pennsylvania, spoke to the evolution of matter, a story more miraculous than scripture ever imagined. The evolution of life began with Penn's provost, David Goddard, followed by incandescent addresses by George Wald, and Theodosius Dobzhansky, René Dubos, Harold Blum, and Phillip George spoke on occasion. Carleton Coon was then at Penn and annually addressed the evolution of man. Margaret Mead, Irving Halowell, Loren Eiseley, Ray Birdwhistel, Yehudi Cohen, and others spoke to the attitudes of "primitive" people to the environment. Year after year, Barrows Dunham addressed polytheism in Greece and Rome, an address enriched in every presentation. Mordecai Kaplan, Abraham Heschel, and Jack Cohen were among the spokesmen for Judaism, Gustave Weigel and a Catholic layman biologist, Vincent De Their, spoke for Catholicism. Paul Tillich presented the Protestant view. Islam was presented mainly by Arthur Upham Pope, with occasional presentations by Hosein Nasr and Ettinghausen. Shinto and Zen were most frequently addressed by Alan Watts, Albert Stunkard (a psychiatrist at Penn, recommended by Susuki), and Wing T'sit Chan. Morse Peckham treated medieval Christianity and the Enlightenment, Robert Spiller, Emerson and Thoreau. The subject of physiological relationships between man and environment were presented throughout the history of the course by Francis Woidich, frequently supplemented by John Calhoun and Jack Christian. The psychological relationship was brilliantly revealed by Erich Fromm, but, generally, speakers for this subject were hard to find. The last block of lectures presented the ecological view and, in fact, provided an appropriate climax. Here, at last, was a coherent body of evidence and theory on the relationship of organisms and environment. The speakers constituted the leadership of this science: Paul Sears, Pierre Danserau, Edward Deevey, Frank Fraser Darling, Paul Shepherd, Stanley Cain, Robert McArthur, René Dubos, Tom and Eugene Odum, Paul Ehrlich, and others. The final lecture was given by poets. In the early years Kenneth Rexroth was the

Howard Nemerov

Some speakers impress you with their confident delivery, clear command of the subject, and reasoned development of the salient points. Not Howard Nemerov.

His delivery was tentative, self-deprecating, hesitant. His hands shook, and the audience immediately sought to express their sympathy and engagement with reassuring expressions. But this approach was finely calculated. His speeches, which gave the impression of being extemporaneous, were, in fact, brilliantly choreographed. Hesitations, long pauses, asides, were all precisely written into his lecture notes. The effect was sensational and so was his subject.

Why should a poet conclude a lecture series dominated by theologians and scientists? Poets knew little of those matters, but if there was any reason, it must repose in metaphor. A metaphor is only a little story in which something known is used to describe some other, unknown or less known. Metaphors are the core of poetry.

"My own perception of the power of metaphor was crystallized by an interesting experience. Sitting at a table, looking out the window, I saw an unfamiliar bird. It was sparrow-like but pale red. Was it a purple finch? I consulted Peterson; the drawing and the bird did not agree. Then I saw the asterisk. It said, 'A purple finch looks like a sparrow dipped in raspberry juice'. Conclusive."

Can you imagine dipping a sparrow in raspberry juice? Someone did, to great effect. Metaphors are powerful, but dangerous. If their power derives from comparison between the known and unknown, then the accuracy of the known is crucial. Yet language contains errors. The names of the known often veil its attributes. Daphne is a flower; Daphne is a Greek goddess. What attribute of Daphne describes the little shrub, what of the plant describes the goddess? Errors are common: brutes are not brutal and savages are not necessarily savage. What of ignorance of God, spirit, soul, truth?

Yet we have no choice. Language could be made more exact, but that would be a long task. In the meantime we must continue to use metaphor, which Nemerov did in his own poems: the sun and the planets, a revolving disc, like a gramophone record, spinning and singing its celestial song. Does it, like the record, stop? And when?

speaker, but on the greatest number of occasions it was Howard Nemerov, who gave a brilliant lecture entitled "Metaphor."

The emphasis of the course changed over the years. Ethology was introduced by Robert Ardrey, George Skaller, and Peter Marler. Epidemiology became an important area of inquiry and was addressed by J. Ralph Audy, Alexander Leighton, Leo Srole, John Cassell, Leonard Duhl, and Jack Geiger. A new conception of economics compatible with ecology emerged, with Kenneth Boulding as originator and including Herman Daly, James Weaver, and Hazel Henderson. World populations and resources also emerged as a significant inquiry, addressed by Paul Ehrlich and Georg Borgstrom.

As time went by, the years, the theologians became embarrassed, and, one by one, declined invitations to address the class. The reason was clear: the students held strong conservationist views, in many cases at a level that could be described as religious, yet the theologians could find no supporting evidence in scripture and were conscious of this inadequacy. In contract, the scientific expositions amplified the understanding of the miraculous in nature. No scriptural description of the supernatural could remotely compare to the scientific view. The initial hope to find support from the formal religions was generally abandoned. Science, notably ecology, seemed reasonable as an attitude to the world and, simultaneously, numinous. The spirituality of matter, life, and biosphere was not incompatible with the ecological view; indeed, it seemed a logical extension.

The students' selection of topics for their papers was illuminating. People with strong religious identities and faith sought confirmation within their own religions. Among Christians, Catholics were best able to find representatives whose views conformed to their own conservation ethics. St. Francis, Duns Scotus, Johannes Erigena, Gerard Manley Hopkins, and Theilhard de Chardin were frequently selected. Protestants had few choices: Wordsworth, Emerson, Thoreau, and Schweitzer, only the last being assertively Christian. For Jews, the problem was enormous. Aaron David Gordon, Russian founder of Zionism, had been presented by the Reconstructionist rabbi, Jack Cohen. His assertion that Jews must return to the land to find God attracted many students. Other Jewish students examined the Nabbateans, the Essenes, and the kibbutz.

Islam is the most nature-oriented monotheism. The Paradise Garden plays a profound role, and the preservation of natural areas by religious injunction provides an important distinction from both Judaism and Christianity. Among monotheists the Islamic students had, perhaps, the easiest task in reconciling their traditional religion with this new ecological view.

Tao, Shinto, and Zen were widely selected by religionists, atheists, and agnostics alike as religious views entirely in consonance with ecology and conservation. Animism, animitism, and pantheism were pursued, in myriad expressions among American Indians (notably Pueblo), Bedouin, Taureg, and Dogon cultures, people of Polynesia and Micronesia, Eskimos, Lapps, and other peoples.

Many students selected global problems, population, world agriculture, soil erosion, natural calamities, radiation, and pollution. By far the largest number of topics selected were ecologist-conservationists ranging from George Perkins Marsh to Paul Sears, Fairfield Osborne, Aldo Leopold, Rachel Carson, Marston Bates, Paul Ehrlich, Garrett Hardin, Frank Fraser Darling, Edward Deevey, and G. Evelyn Hutchinson.

With no teaching assistants, my Christmas vacations involved a prodigy of gifts: insights into a multitude of subjects, revealed in some two hundred papers. I can, to this day, often identify ex-students from the papers they submitted to "Man and Environment."

The House We Live In

In 1959, "Man and Environment" was an ambitious venture. I suppose it was possible because it was initiated by a small professional school. No important department such as biology or geology could ever have offered such an extensive course with impunity. Landscape architecture, however, did not engender jealousy. An unthreatening stature and treatment with benign neglect have been vital factors in the development of the department, and in my own.

Today, the subject of the environment fills television news and cocktail conversation. It was not so then. I believe that the thousands of students who took "Man and Environment" made a modest contribution.

The first offering of "Man and Environment" was an exciting success. I was in the process of planning a repeat when I received a call from George Dessart of CBS Philadelphia. He had learned of the course: Could it be presented as a television series, perhaps twelve episodes? I would be empowered to pay first-class travel and living

During 1960–1961, I was the host of *The House We Live In* television series on CBS. I interviewed many of the world's leading thinkers about human-environment relationships, focusing largely on religious, ethical, and philosophical issues. Astronomist Harlow Shapley and I are pictured here on the set of *The House We Live In,* October 1960. It was Shapley who discovered that the sun and the earth are located in the Milky Way.

expenses and the appropriate honorarium to invited speakers. I agreed eagerly. Here was an opportunity to invite world figures to discuss the environment and a powerful medium to disseminate their ideas. The series was called *The House We Live In.*

The biggest obstacle was not simply my lack of connection with these international figures, but their improbable connection with my field. I well recall a phone conversation with Sir Julian Huxley, then in Nairobi.

"Hello, Sir Julian, my name is Ian McHarg." (Silence.) "I am a professor of landscape architecture at the University of Pennsylvania." (Silence.) "I have been authorized to produce a television series on man's relationship to the environment for CBS in Philadelphia." (Silence.) "I would like you to give the final address on evolutionary humanism."

"Why, that is interesting."

"Paul Tillich, Erich Fromm, Harlow Shapley, and Margaret Mead have all accepted the invitation."

"Very interesting. Do tell me what dates you have in mind."

It was a great success. At two o'clock each Sunday afternoon a very large audience became immersed in this deep and comprehensive inquiry into our planet and our relationship with it, that is, the house we live in. This was the first network presentation on the environment.

The format was simple and powerful. The series considered the evolution of matter, life, and man. It reviewed the attitudes of "primitive" man to God, man,

Psychologist Erich Fromm
and I on the set of
The House We Live In,
October 1960.

and nature, the attitudes of Judaism, Catholicism, Protestantism, and the Hindu and Buddhist views. Man's psychological and physiological needs were discussed. A conclusion was drawn from the preceeding presentations.

We invited the most distinguished spokesman for each of the subjects. Harlow Shapley, Harvard astronomer, who located the planet Earth eccentric within the Milky Way, discussed the Big Bang theory, the evolution of matter—hydrogen, helium, lithium, beryllium, and boron, continuing up the periodic table—a breathtaking creative act. David Goddard, biologist and provost at Pennsylvania, introduced life and death, the improbable process by which a modest group of chemicals became animated, reproduced themselves, and developed an instrument for imperfect replication by which mutation and evolution would proceed.

The physical evolution of man was presented by Carleton Coon, perhaps the world's primary physical anthropologist: tree shrew, tarsier, lemur, autralopithecus, man; the sparse record of skulls and bones comprising the fossil record; brain, eye, opposing finger and thumb, tools, generalist, omnivore, inheritor of the earth.

Adaptations by our ancestors and so-called primitive man were the subject of Margaret Mead's presentation. While she conceded the harmony of pantheist peoples with the environment, she warned that modern technology would replace traditional views without remorse. The major religions were examined for their attitudes to God and nature. The spokesmen were famous, venerable, gentle, and mostly unhelpful. Abraham Heschel, Gustave Weigel, and Paul Tillich presented the anthropocentric, anthropomorphic view in Judaism and Christianity with neither conviction nor persuasion. But it was important that the subject be presented and reviewed. The answers did not lie there.

Fromm and Selye did better with the psychological and physical needs of people for nature. Julian Huxley integrated the whole with his plea for evolutionary humanism, a response to the way the world works, integrated into a benign view of man in nature. Incremental and constant, the evidence accumulated. The picture was coherent, comprehensible, and persuasive.

A thirteenth program was presented consisting of salient points from the series. A second series was then created including Loren Eiseley, Lewis Mumford, Arnold Toynbee, Theodosius Dobzhansky, Frank Fraser Darling, Jack Christian, John Calhoun, A. M. M. Payne, Leonard Duhl, W. L. C. Wheaton, Luna Leopold, and Kenneth Rexroth. The series was widely shown by CBS affiliates and subsequently given to PBS, where it persisted for a decade. A careful viewer would have observed that while the distinguished spokesmen approached the subject of man and environment from different vantages, there was an enormous area of agreement. Western man was arrogant, destructive, careless, oblivious to the miraculous system he inhabited. He indeed acted as if he believed that he was the apex of the cosmic pyramid, the planet his to plunder. One could say man made God in his image and justified his license to do what he wished. Shapley, Goddard, Coon, Weigel, Eiseley, Tillich, Fromm, Mead, Huxley, Dobzhansky, and Darling have gone, and now Mumford. They have gone; their perceptions remain. The tapes were to have been destroyed, but were not. They are in the possession of the Library of Congress.

Each encounter in taping the series was miraculous for me. The great men and women exceeded their reputations for wisdom and, considering the eminence of their status and my modest rank, they were extraordinarily kind to me.

I would meet them at the airport, take them to hotels, have lunch and dinner, at which I would identify all of the speakers and the topics and discuss the specific subject for each speaker. I read extensively in preparation and received an education from these wonderful encounters.

Each had a story. Huxley looked like a small gnome. He alternated between high seriousness and high humor. He had a storehouse of funny, often ribald, stories of the great and famous. The one that made him laugh hardest involved Clement Atlee. The prime minister and his wife were in India, meeting Nehru. As the leaders converged, one of Nehru's aides attached himself to Mrs. Atlee. "How often do you have elections?" she asked. He looked very embarrassed. Again, she asked, "How often do you have elections?" "Madame," he said, believing he heard "erections," "that is rather an indelicate question, but as you ask repeatedly, I must answer. Evely morning."

Margaret Mead presented a new problem. No male guests had ever requested or received makeup. When Margaret Mead arrived on the set, the director was ready to film. "Where is the makeup?" she asked. The cosmetician arrived. Now, as her matrimonial history testifies, Margaret Mead had a serious romantic past, but, in her seventies, I had not considered her as a romantic figure, simply a formidable scientist. Yet, as the cosmetics were applied—powder, blush, eyelid pencil, eye shadow—wrinkles faded, eyes became larger, color was heightened. She shed years and was suddenly a younger, vital woman. I moved forward in my chair.

It was Gustave Weigel who produced the greatest drama. He was then represented as the leading liberal Catholic theologian, director of the Woodstock Seminary. We discussed the subject: the Catholic view of creation and attitudes toward God, man, and, most central, to this discussion, Nature.

In our conversation, Gerard Manley Hopkins, Duns Scotus, Johannes Erigena, St. Francis, and Albert Schweitzer were invoked for a new and appropriate Christian relationship to nature. But, in the television presentation, Weigel abandoned these and insisted on a totally literal interpretation of the Creation story in the first chapter of Genesis: to paraphrase, "God made man in his own image—gave him dominion over all living things—and ordered him to multiply and subdue the earth."

The format was standard. I would introduce the great man or woman and topic; thereafter the speaker would continue for twenty-five minutes. I would then offer a prearranged question; the great man or woman would answer. Then I offered thanks, the music swelled, and we went off.

Weigel pursued his archaic course; I ground my teeth. He finished. I did not offer the prearranged question but, a novel one: "Dr. Weigel, the faithful look to you for guidance, yet there are massive contradictions. Would you recommend the literality of Genesis or a quite different view, the life and example of St. Francis?"

"If I had known I had to deal with an irascible Gael, I would not have accepted this invitation."

"But you did accept. What is your answer?"

"I would recommend St. Francis."

"Thank God, and thank you, Father Weigel."

Ecology for Landscape Architecture 1961

Given the dominance of architecture in the Penn Graduate School of Fine Arts, the strong Department of City Planning, and the preponderance of architects studying in landscape architecture, it was appropriate that landscape architecture should first focus on urban problems. Seagram Plaza, with Phillip Johnson, and Independence Historic Park, with Lewis Mumford, were followed by Ian Nairn and Gordon Cullen whose essays on townscape in the *Architectural Review* had drawn wide attention and admiration. In addition, the Dutch architect, Aldo van Eyck, who had transformed abandoned urban space into playgrounds in Amsterdam, joined this search for a more humane city and the contribution of landscape architecture to this quest.

In 1959 there was a schoolwide collaborative project involving faculty and students of architecture, landscape architecture, and city planning under the direction of Steen Eiler Rasmussen. This exercise proved conclusively that the engagement of the three professions was essential to solve urban problems. In fact, in each of the solutions the landscape conception was the essential ingredient. The first objective

---

FACULTY

Ian L. McHarg, B.L.A., M.L.A., M.C.P.,
*Associate Professor of Landscape
Architecture,* Chairman.

John M. Fogg, Jr., Ph.D., Sc.D.,
*Professor of Botany, Director of the
Morris Arboretum.*

George B. Tatum, M.F.A., Ph.D.,
Associate Professor of the History of Art.

Karl Linn, M.A., Dip.Agri., Dip.Psy.,
*Assistant Professor of
Landscape Architecture.*

George E. Patton, B.S. in L.A.,
Lecturer on Landscape Architecture.

Research Staff

Gordon Cullen,
Dip.Arch.

Ian Nairn, B.S.

Aldo van Eyck,
Dip.Arch.

Ian L. McHarg, B.L.A., M.L.A., M.C.P.

B. Michael Brown, Dip.Arch., M.L.A.

Denise Scott Brown, Dip.Arch., M.C.P.

Visiting Critics, 1957-61

Gordon Cullen

Dan Kiley

Philip Johnson

Garrett Eckbo

Peter Shepheard

Robert Royston

Lewis Clarke

Robert Mackintosh

Lawrence Enersen

Douglas Baylis

By 1960, I had coalesced a quite diverse faculty, listed here in a Graduate School of Fine Arts Exhibition Catalogue on the occasion of the American Institute of Architects' 1960 convention in Philadelphia. (Courtesy of the Architectural Archives of the University of Pennsylvania.)

had been achieved. Landscape architecture had achieved esteem in the school and within the university.

However, it required no great perception to note that the greatest emerging problems were metropolitan and rural rather than urban. FHA and VA mortgages had unleashed massive development in communities, without planning. An unprecedented and prodigal decentralization was in process. Solutions required a more extensive understanding of the environment and skills greater than those disposed by urban design.

While ecologists were invited to speak to students, Paul Sears and Robert McArthur in 1959 and Ed Deevey in 1961, I had not then observed the relevance of this emerging science for landscape architecture.

In 1961 I hired a bright English landscape architect, Lewis Clarke, to teach a six-week program at Penn. He had obtained a diploma in architecture from the University of Newcastle, where he had studied landscape architecture under Brian Hackett. If anyone deserves recognition for having introduced ecology as the underlying science for landscape architecture, Brian Hackett is the primary candi-

Influenced largely by Lewis Mumford, I had also developed a rather pessimistic
view of trends in American settlement by the early 1960s. This view of New York
City from a cemetery in Queens is an illustration for the Penn Department of
Landscape Architecture, from a detail of a poster from the exhibition and catalogue
for the 1960 American Institute of Architects Conference in Philadelphia. (Courtesy
of the Architectural Archives of the University of Pennsylvania.)

date. Clarke had two obsessions. The first was hydroponics, which he assured us would solve the world's food problems. The second was ecology. This he proposed to employ in undertaking a plan for the real project under way to build Levittown in nearby Bucks County. His class included a small but distinguished group: Michael Hough, later chairman at the University of Toronto; Phillip Langley, dean of the University of Senegal; Timothy Cochrane, a deaf person who devoted his life to designing for disabled children in London; Michael Langlay-Smith, partner in the largest firm of landscape architects in England; Frank Burgraff, navigator on a SAC bomber, later chairman at Arkansas; Lois Sherr, with a successful practice in New York, a major contributor to Expo and Habitat; and A. J. Walmsley, professor at Penn with a large and successful practice also in New York. Their project was intellectually triumphant, but neither Mr. Levitt nor anyone else paid any attention to it—their loss. However, I was powerfully persuaded.

It was noteworthy to observe that while there was no thought given to ecology in the design of Levittown, a budget of $17.00 per house for landscaping produced the most dominant and humane component of the environment.

I decided to test this new direction and chose a site at the New Jersey shore, Harvey Cedars. It was only one of many communities suffering a massive postwar assault of second homes. The class for this project too was small but brilliant: Michael Laurie, later chairman at Berkeley; Peter Ker Walker, partner with Dan Kiley; Roger Clemence, dean of graduate programs at Minnesota; Geoffrey Collins, partner with Derek Lovejoy; Ayre Dvir, professor at the Technion in Israel; and William Oliphant, a very successful practitioner in Tennessee.

An ecologist, William Martin, was hired, and his contribution was enormous. He introduced us to physical oceanography, marine biology, meteorology, geomorphology, hydrology, soils, vegetation, and land use. Not least, he showed us that sand dunes are ephemeral. Successive photos revealed that, during the era of air photography at least, most of Harvey Cedars had been under water, a link between bay and ocean, but there were islands with thickets and woodlands that had survived for many decades. This ecological study revealed where building could safely occur and where it could not. In fact, with the exception of a hotel, all houses had been located in areas of extreme hazard, which, simultaneously, had accomplished the maximum environmental damage. Why should it be otherwise? The lure of the sea proved irresistible, notwithstanding the clear evidence that no New Jersey shore community retained either a First or Second Street—they had long ago succumbed to hurricanes and storms. At a meeting in Harvey Cedars, the class presented their findings to the community on where to build, where not to build, how to build, and how to manage beach, dune, trough, backdune, and bay. The very next visitor following our departure was Hurricane Agnes. As I wrote of the event at the time, "A violent storm lashed the entire northeast coast from Georgia to Long Island. For three days sixty-mile-an-hour winds whipped the high spring tides across a thousand miles of ocean. Forty-foot waves pounded the shore, breached the dunes, and filled the bay, which spilled across the islands back to the ocean. When the storm subsided, the extent of the disaster was clear. Three days of storm had produced eighty million dollars worth of damage, twenty-four hundred houses destroyed or damaged beyond repair, eighty-three hundred houses partially damaged, several people killed, and many injured in New Jersey alone. Fires subsequently added to this destruction; roads were destroyed, as were utilities."

There were, of course, other significant losses, not least the expectation of income from tourism, the major economic base of the New Jersey shore. In addition, this resort, a recreational resource for the region, looked like a battlefield. For the majority of people the damages were compounded because little was recoverable from insurance. Many people made mortgage payments on houses that had been bulldozed into the bay. Yet all of this disaster was caused by people through sins of commission and omission. Immediately after the disaster, giant bulldozers pushed the wrecked houses into the bay or burned them in great funeral pyres, sand dunes were reformed, streets exhumed from under the overburden of sand, and, slowly, houses reappeared to fill the selfsame sites of those that had been swept away. The commonest problem was the exposure of foundations; those houses that had sat high on the dune, commanding a view of the sea, found the sand swept from under them, and there they stood, floors fifteen feet above the sand, grotesquely leaning, supported on their exposed telegraph-pole foundations. But not all of them. In a remarkable example of wisdom and virtue rewarded, in those rare cases where the dune was stable and unbreached, clothed in grasses, the houses endured, suffering only broken windows and lost shingles. Some learning did result from this event, and a more careful attitude to shore development emerged, which was later incorporated in the federal Coastal Zone Management Act of 1972. One group, however, learned very much indeed. It may well have been a major turning point in landscape architectural education and practice. The students in that class resolved, along with me, then and there, that ecology would provide the fundamental basis for the practice of landscape architecture and regional planning thereafter.

The experiment was conclusive. We had transcended superficial diagnosis and prescription; here we had achieved an understanding of natural processes and the implication of these for human use. The search for a discipline had been successful.

An Ojibway View

In the summer of 1962, my family and I went off on a summer vacation to Lake Temagami in northern Ontario. The trip was an adventure. We drove in a Volkswagen camper, which had a table and two bench seats where the boys, Alistair and Malcolm, read and played cards during the day. At night the space could be made into beds, in which they slept. The VW was underpowered. It was a fine downhill car but decidedly slow on uphill sections of the road. We had to drive all night to reach Temagami by morning. We even cooked and ate a three-course dinner on the move. At Temagami we parked the truck, took the motor launch, the Gray Owl run by an Ojibway, first to the Hudson Bay Post at Bear Island and thence to Treasure Island, where we had reserved a cabin, Dove Cottage.

We set out on a three day-trip to the north arm of the lake, across the portage to Lady Evelyn Lake, across another portage to Diamond Lake, and then back on to Lake Temagami and on to Treasure Island. We decided to go in one canoe. Pauline took the bow, I took stern, the boys, five and twelve, amidship on wooden wannigans, red-painted boxes that contained our provisions. It was a calm day. I had never seen the lake like glass before; not a ripple was to be seen. We set off, paddles in unison, across lovely, clear, clean water, the bottom visible and magnified. After an hour or two we espied a furrow far ahead in the water. What could it be? Was it possibly a large lake trout on the surface, a pike, a muskelunge? Improbable. We decided to investigate, turned the bow and paddled toward the furrow. Something was swimming. From where to where? There was a headland behind and a little island ahead. The furrow

aimed at the island. As we came nearer, we saw that it was an animal swimming—a chipmunk. We pulled alongside. I offered the paddle to the chipmunk. It accepted, climbed on the paddle, walked up the handle, climbed from my hand to my knee, shook itself, climbed to the floor of the canoe, jumped on the wannigan, walked on Malcolm, crossed to Alistair, climbed forward to Pauline, back to Alistair, to Malcolm, and then to my knee, where it deposited a small pebble of excrement. We began paddling to its destination, and as we came to the island, we saw a campsite and an old man fishing.

"Ahoy," I called. "Will you take a chipmunk ashore?"

"Yes," he said. "A bear just swam away from here this morning. I'd be glad to have the company."

So I offered the paddle to the chipmunk, and down the shaft it climbed, into the water. Paddle, paddle, left and right, a little furrow behind it, the chipmunk swam to the shore. Once more it shook itself, looked at us, turned, and walked away.

Many years later I was having lunch with Irving Hallowell, the great anthropologist at Pennsylvania. I knew that he had done his initial field work with the Ojibway. I told him the chipmunk story. He said, "If you told that story to a Ojibway, he would have said that is most unusual behavior for a chipmunk. So much so that it was not a chipmunk. He would have concluded that it was the reincarnation of someone very close and precious, someone who wanted to see you and your family. And the pebble on your knee was a gift, an appreciation." Could it have been my mother, who never saw her daughter-in-law or her grandchildren?

In 1960 it would have been difficult to find an ecologist who would join an applied department. However, a resource economist would be palatable, certainly to the powerful planners. So, their aid was enlisted and I was authorized to institute a search. In 1962 I appointed Nicholas Muhlenberg. He had a bachelor's degree in forestry from Michigan, a master's in conservation from that university under the tutelage of Stanley Cain and Marston Bates, both distinguished ecologists, and a Ph.D. in resource economics from Yale. In addition, he had been a research scientist for FAO in Geneva and in New Zealand had undertaken research for Resources for the Future.

Muhlenberg was the first faculty member in the Penn Graduate School of Fine Arts who was informed in ecology and familiar with the literature and many of the scientists. His advent was thrilling for students and faculty alike. He introduced us to E. Lucy Braun, *The Forests of Eastern United States* within days of his arrival; Cain, Dansereau, Sears, Deevey, and Hutchinson were quickly added. We were engaged in a quest. Suddenly we all knew that we had found our future. Nick gave direction to our tentative exploration. Here was a body of knowledge that must be incorporated into the curriculum. Here at last was the theoretical basis for the practice of landscape architecture.

Moreover, the class to which Muhlenberg introduced this new science was brilliant, passionate, and immediately enthralled. Their intellectual leader was Narendra Juneja, an Indian architect from Delhi who later became a professor at Penn, an associate at Wallace, McHarg, Roberts and Todd, my right arm, dear friend. Carol Levy, now Carol Franklin, a Smith graduate, was the passionate leader and is now a prominent practitioner with Andropogon and crucial member of the Penn faculty. David Streatfield, English architect, chair at the University of Washington today; William Wilson, president of Synterra; Howard Grist, Welsh architect, and Glen G. Caldaro completed this marvelous class.

Never did students so warmly welcome a new professor as this class did Nicholas Muhlenberg. My response was every bit as enthusiastic. He would be our intellectual leader, and he looked like Adonis. As he introduced titles and their authors, I would compile names and ascertain addresses and invite these ecologists to speak at Pennsylvania. For thirty years, three speakers a week converged on Pennsylvania and contributed their wisdom. We were interested not only in their ideas, but also in the applicability of their perceptions to planning and design. We were avid for perceptions and principles that could guide decisions on land use. We sought problems that were amenable to solution—where and where not to build, how much to build—and we sought data and principles to assist us in this endeavor.

We all subscribed to ecology as the unifying discipline, and knew that studies of the environment of necessity had to be inter- and multidisciplinary. We recognized that the university gave access to science and that actual projects provided the occasion to apply science to planning problems. Here was a wonderful reciprocity: information came from the department and was applied in the studio. Where successful, the process was incorporated in revised teaching. This arrangement guaranteed that the method would continue to improve—more and better data, improved intelligence, and higher skill all guaranteed a lively educational experience. Each year a contingent of bright young people, incorporating the environmental sciences, planning, and landscape architecture, came to Philadelphia determined to assimilate this ecological planning method and determined to improve it, which they did, year after year.

Chapter 6

Design with Nature, 1964–1970

The completion of a decade at Pennsylvania in 1964 was a milestone: the department had forty-five students, still a tiny permanent faculty, and a procession of distinguished visiting professors. "Man and Environment" was perhaps the most exciting course in the school, if not the university. The department had proclaimed ecology as its fundamental discipline. I was engaged with David Wallace in establishing a private office, and the first project, Plan for the Valleys, had been acclaimed. The plan for the Inner Harbor of Baltimore was to receive more widespread public attention.

The next five years proved to be critical. In 1964 the Ford Foundation proposal was written, which, when funded, made it possible to recruit a faculty of natural scientists within the Department of Landscape Architecture. In 1965 I participated in the Potomac Task Force, beginning the department's commitment to studies of the Delaware River basin. In 1966–1967 I took a sabbatical to write *Design with Nature*, published in 1969. Following the Ford grant in 1965 a new curriculum in regional planning was introduced, with natural scientists selected as students. Certainly, the publication of *Design with Nature* was a fitting climax of my life to date. The book raised me from obscurity and gave prominence to my person and my views.

Wallace-McHarg Associates— Plan for the Valleys

David Wallace was enrolled in the Ph.D. program in planning at Harvard during my period there. He had bachelor's and master's degrees in architecture from

Pennsylvania, and had served with the Army Corps of Engineers. His dissertation on race and housing was remarkably prophetic.

He became executive director of the Philadelphia Redevelopment Authority and created the first project generated by the new redevelopment regulation. He then went to Baltimore as executive director of the Greater Baltimore Committee, where he conceived Charles Center, the first dramatic example of central city redevelopment.

Many of the leading citizens in Baltimore lived in the Green Springs, Worthington, and Western Run Valleys, north of Baltimore, the bucolic landscape captured in the film *National Velvet.* At this time the Maryland State Highway Department had designed the Jones Falls Expressway, a radial running due north to the Beltway. This would bring the pastoral paradise to within twenty minutes' driving time of downtown Baltimore. The rural residents, aghast at the prospect, asked Wallace for help. He concluded that this required skills additional to those he possessed. At about that time he had accepted the position of professor of city planning at Pennsylvania, where we renewed our friendship. He participated as a juror on the Harvey Cedars project and was, as he reported, powerfully persuaded by the ecological planning method developed for that problem. Would it be efficacious for the Valleys? Would I join him in partnership? Our first commission would be a plan for the Valleys.

At that time, I rented a three-story Victorian house. It had three rooms on the third floor and this became our office. Before we found better facilities, or, rather, until we could afford them, fourteen people worked in these rooms. It was there that the Plan for the Valleys was completed, as well as the Plan for Baltimore's Inner Harbor, with which, indeed, our partnership, Wallace-McHarg Associates, was created in 1962. Wallace is older and much more distinguished than I when I joined him. It was then a constant source of annoyance and indignity that many clients believed that there was a single figure, Wallace McHarg.

If Harvey Cedars was the first university project to apply ecology to planning, the Plan for the Valleys was the first professional application in which I employed ecology. The ecology used was quite elementary, but it proved to be adequate; the plan was a success. Lewis Mumford wrote a flattering introduction to the report, which did much to expand acceptance of the method.

The Green Spring, Worthington, and Western Run valleys lie in the Crystalline Piedmont just north of the Beltway in Baltimore. The seventy square miles constitute a particularly beautiful bucolic landscape. Its genius lies in the broad valleys in pasture, framed by forested slopes defining the plateaus. Here is the locus of the Maryland Cup, Milady's Manor, and the Maryland Hunt. Expensive horses and cattle graze in the pastures defined by white rail fences, handsome stone

houses sit barely visible among the trees, rural roads fold over the gently undulating landscape.

Suddenly the Jones Falls Expressway was focused like a rifle at the Valleys. It was
as if the Homestead Act were proclaimed anew and every developer in the region
stood poised, awaiting the blast, ready to urbanize, expunging beautiful farmland and
centuries of decent husbandry. This was, indeed, the fate of the entire surround, as
can be seen today, but not of the Valleys, which more than thirty years later still retain
their pastoral beauty.

In 1962, however, the inhabitants of the Valleys lived in terror; their legacy was
under threat. What would be done? A group of residents met to confront the test and
devise a response. They first sought David A. Wallace, executive director of the
Greater Baltimore Committee, inspired planner, source of the Charles Center redevelopment concept, my fellow student and friend. He asked me to join him in devis-
ing what came to be known as the Plan for the Valleys. The client group constituted
themselves into the Green Spring and Worthington Valley Planning Council. We had
barely begun when we confronted a crisis. The completion of the Jones Falls Expressway, linked to the Beltway, provided an inevitable location for a regional shopping
center. Baltimore's leading developer, James Rouse, immediately perceived this opportunity. He approached the landowner with an offer to purchase. The consequences
could be grave. If the transaction were to be consummated, a sewer would certainly
be built to service the facility and this would stimulate urbanization of the Green
Spring Valley. Fortunately, the owner was coerced into retaining the land, thus thwarting the regional center. No sewer was ever built, and time was bought to undertake
the planning study.

Although there were four valleys, there was effectively only one ecological problem. A cross-section transect through ridges and valleys revealed the same condition.
The ridges and side slopes were uniformly Wissahickon schist, the valley was limestone, Cockesville marble. Vegetation and land use conformed to these factors. The
rich limestone-derived soils were in pasture, grazed by horses and cattle. The slopes
were too steep to lumber and remained in forest, and the generally flat plateaus were
being farmed—cropland, hedgerows, and woodlots—inhabited by bona fide farmers.

The problem was an inspired opportunity for a neophyte ecological planner,
and the solution was plain. The Valleys were valleys because they were limestone, the
ridges were ridges because they were Wissahickon schist. The limestone was an
aquifer, and the schist had much less water, contained only in fractures and fissures.
Moreover, the limestone aquifer, Cockeysville marble, was unconfined. It was continuous with Lake Roland, Baltimore's water supply. Normal development would
have selected the valleys, then septic tanks would have polluted groundwater, Lake

Roland, and the water for Baltimore. Sewers in a valley are only a more technolog-ically advanced method for polluting groundwater. So the solution was simple: Prohibit septic tanks and sewers in the valleys. The plateaus were eminently suited for development; there were no serious problems of groundwater contamination, no flood plains, no steep slopes, fewer problems of erosion and sedimentation, and little forest. There were also wonderful views, good foundation conditions, and soils suitable for septic tanks. Between the ridges and the valleys were forested slopes, whose steepness had inhibited logging. These areas could support low-density development.

The study was much more comprehensive than this summary suggests. Market analysis, growth allocation, computation of alternative plans for unplanned and planned growth—all of this was brilliantly examined and resolved by David Wallace. Today, more than thirty years later, the Valleys remain green, gratifying residents and consultants alike.

There was one proposal that was not implemented. Would that it had been. It must have been inadequate in some way, because it was not accepted. The idea was my own. I believe it is fair to say that public planning, notably zoning, has pro-tected very little; it is, at best, a delaying procedure. The Plan for the Valleys was a private plan, but its success depended on public action, as in the prohibition of septic tanks and sewers in the valleys. This action did provide benefit to the preser-vationists, but what of the poor bona fide farmers on the plateau? They would welcome development, notably, community services, and they were not averse to selling land at a profit.

There were three social groups, each occupying a physiographic province. The very rich, with horse farms and Black Angus, occupied the valley floors; the upper middle class lived on the forested slopes, deriving benefit from the beautiful valleys manicured by the very rich. On the plateau, poor farmers worked modest farms.

Growth would certainly occur. The plan advised that growth be limited to hamlets and villages on the plateau. Now, if the landowner of the selected site received a windfall, should his neighbors be denied any benefits? To avoid this feast-or-famine situation, it was proposed that real estate syndicates be established from ridge line to ridge line, across each valley. Each group of people within these boundaries for the Green Spring, Worthington, and Western Run valleys would comprise a syndicate. They would capitalize the value of the aggregate of land and buildings. Each member would have stock equivalent to his or her property value and concede development rights to the syndicate. Areas deemed appropriate for development would be identified. The syndicate could either sell land, subject to a plan by a developer, or act as developer itself. Whatever stratagem was employed, the profits from development would be distributed proportionately to all stockholders.

I thought this a very persuasive idea, but it lacked an essential ingredient. Each valley with its ridges was a physiographic unit; each contained three distinct social groups—very rich, upper middle class, and working class—but it was not a community, not a social unit. The relationship of the farmers to the rich was to provide grooms, house servants, and farm laborers. The rich had no contact with the middle-class professionals, and little with farm families. Nor did the lawyers and stockbrokers have much contact with the farmers.

Had the people within each unit constituted a community, it might have worked. But it was not to be. They were geographical neighbors only, in space, not a society. Yet today, without the syndicates, the green valleys persist, anomalies in a surrounding sea of suburban tissue.

Now, more than thirty years after my exposure to Baltimore County and the Valleys, I find myself ensconced in precisely the same environment. Chester Valley in Chester County, Pennsylvania, is identical to the Green Spring and Worthington valleys, with the same Precambrian geology, the same Wissahickon schist ridges, the same broad valleys of Cockeysville marble, the same northeast–southwest trend.

In contrast, however, no threat comparable to the Jones Falls Expressway developed to menace West Marlboro Township. It is more distant from Philadelphia than are the Valleys from Baltimore, and it benefits from another very effective planning device, the efforts of the hunting fraternity. It is strange that this group never surfaced as an important agent in Baltimore County. In Pennsylvania it was the members of the hunt who were the principal actors in a dramatic land-use conflict and resolution. I am a gratified benefactor of the solution.

In the 1920s the agricultural fraternity in Chester County was in crisis; farmers were close to bankruptcy. Into this circumstance came one Plunkett Stewart, his pockets bulging with large-denomination bank notes. He proceeded to buy whole farms for cash and amassed five thousand acres. His plan was to sell intact farms to landowners who would agree to support a hunt and arrange their properties to satisfy this need. His plan was accomplished, and many of the new landowners, refugees from Chestnut Hill, retained the bona fide farmers as tenants. Horses became dominant in the new agriculture, and dairy herds were replaced by beef cattle, Black Angus and Herefords. A new land use, mushroom farming, emerged, mostly concentrated in Kennett Square. Among those induced to buy property was one Mr. Clayborne, owner of the King Ranch in Texas. A devoted huntsman, he organized the Pennsylvania King Ranch to pasture his Getrudis cattle en route to market. And he could ride with the Cheshire Hunt.

During the 1980s, it was decided to sell the King Ranch. The news caused terror in the community. Would this rural enclave be developed? Growth was expanding, from both Philadelphia and Wilmington. The threat was real. This is where my wife Carol, our son Ian William and I entered the scene, looking for a site to build.

Frolic Weymouth, character, portraitist, driver of carriages, determined to avert disaster. He created a consortium, which bought the King Ranch. Its members resolved to sell the property in intact farms. First, Weymouth created the Brandywine Conservancy. Would-be buyers were required to transfer the development value of their properties to the Conservancy. Through this device the land would remain undeveloped in perpetuity. Most properties were two hundred and more acres, but there were two of 35 acres each. One was contiguous with a 600-acre forest preserve, the Laurels. This property was selected by my clever wife. We bought it and on it we built our home. Carol found an Amish barn builder, Rueben Reihl, and worked with him to select an appropriate barn, which was dismantled and then reassembled to become our home. Carol was architect and general contractor.

The real estate syndicate proposed for the Valleys in 1962 did not work, although the environment has been miraculously preserved. The Brandywine Conservancy, however, did work in the late 1980s. Now 15,000 acres have been eased and the process proceeds. Of course, unlike the Valleys, this area has not had to deal with a proposal to accommodate growth in areas deemed to be propitious. In 1962 the idea of creating a village, such as advanced in the Plan for the Valleys, was not evocative. Andres Duany and Elizabeth Plater-Zyberk have now brought this alternative into widespread and serious consideration.

The Inner Harbor, Baltimore

The second project by Wallace-McHarg Associates was the Inner Harbor. It has become a resounding success, but I should establish immediately that my contribution was modest; the conception was developed by David Wallace and later augmented by Tom Todd and William Roberts.

When one Sunday morning in 1962 I visited the site, I surveyed an array of derelict piers and buildings, abandoned railroad tracks, raw sewage in the Jones Fall, and floating excrement in the foul Inner Harbor. But the water reflecting the sky, and Federal Hill, across the water, was a small redemption. Here indeed was a

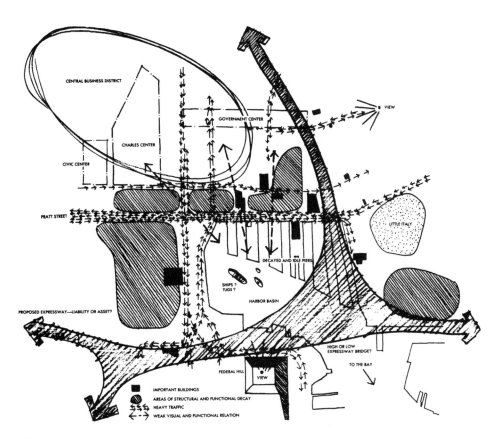

Diagram of problems and opportunities for the 1964 Inner Harbor Plan conducted
for Baltimore by Wallace-McHarg Associates, under the direction of David Wallace.
(drawing by Thomas Todd; courtesy of Wallace Roberts and Todd.)

Wallace-McHarg Associates began work with the Baltimore Inner Harbor in 1964.
The succeeding iterations of the firm (Wallace, McHarg, Roberts and Todd; Wallace
Roberts and Todd) continued to work on various plans and designs for the Baltimore
Inner Harbor through the 1970s and 1980s. David Wallace was the intellectual and creative leader of the Inner Harbor work. I helped to stop an expressway originally planned
for the same place that the Inner Harbor now occupies. Widely regarded as one of the
finest examples of late twentieth-century American urban design, Inner Harbor is a significant result of three decades of leadership by David Wallace and a testimony to the
quality of work of the firm that began as Wallace-McHarg Associates and now exists as
Wallace Roberts and Todd. In addition, Inner Harbor is an important example of how
environmental activism can result in a better place for people to live. My energy and
access to power helped to prevent a mistake. My partner helped to transform the place
into a vibrant downtown.

A view of Baltimore Inner Harbor in 1976 from south shore promenade (Photograph by Wallace, McHarg, Roberts and Todd; courtesy of Wallace Roberts and Todd.)

powerful latent resource. Water quality could be transformed from repugnance to charm. It was a site gravid with opportunity, and I so affirmed and gave my opinion in favor of redemption. This was my largest contribution.

My other contribution was to obtain the aid of Lady Bird Johnson in rejecting a Department of Transportation proposal that would thwart the plan to restore and develop the facility. Persuasion is a useful planning tool, but retribution can be even better.

When the original plans and model for the Inner Harbor of Baltimore were well-nigh completed, a bombshell struck. The State Highway Department announced plans to build an interstate that would bridge the throat of the Inner Harbor. It would cross the water with a series of little columns. Head room was limited to motorboats, there would be no *Constellation,* no frigates, no visiting ships. The dream for a revitalized Inner Harbor was threatened with total destruction.

The mayor, members of the council and the planning commission, the two United States senators from Maryland, and other dignitaries assembled to review our plan. It was agreed that the mayor would present the Wallace-McHarg plan as the city plan and oppose the highway and bridge. In the interim a bridge designer,

Lev Zetlin, was hired and with Wallace-McHarg redesigned the highway and the bridge to permit access and serve the Inner Harbor's future.

A meeting was convened to discuss the matter. Governor, mayor, senators, and prominent businessmen, with Wallace and McHarg, on one side, faced the federal representative, one Mr. Fink, the state highway commissioner, and the engineering consultants. First the mayor presented the plan, and the rest of the group affirmed their support. Then up spoke Fink. "Indeed, there is merit in your plan, but if you want our money, you will take our highway and plan."

I decided to take the matter to Sharon Francis, assistant to Lady Bird Johnson. Here the Bureau of Public Roads was flouting governor, mayor, senators, and the city of Baltimore, planning to destroy the latent possibility of regeneration of the Inner Harbor at great public expense. Surely a regional director could not overrule the wishes of governor and mayor, state and city? Would Mrs. Johnson intervene? Indeed, she would and did. During the following week the news emerged. Fink had been fired. The highway department's plan was abandoned.

Lady Bird, I-95, and the Bureau of Public Roads

In 1966 I received an invitation to give an address at the Institute for Advanced Studies at Princeton. The invitation came from Romer McPhee, one-time legal counsel to President Eisenhower and brother of the yet-to-be-celebrated author John McPhee. I must wear a dinner jacket and black tie. There was no mention of an honorarium. But as the Institute evoked Einstein, this was an awesome invitation. I accepted.

My address postulated two states within which all systems, from cell to biosphere, oscillated. The first was called syntropic-fitness-health and the second entopic-misfit-morbidity/death. This conception was based on Darwin's assertion that the surviving organism was fit for the environment, and the elaboration of this axiom by Lawrence J. Henderson, that, as the world consisted of an infinitude both of organisms and environments, there was a necessity for every system to find the fittest available environment, including both matter and organisms, to adapt it and adapt itself. The definition of a fit environment was one in which the greatest number of needs of a user were provided by the environment as found, in which the least work of adaptation was required. The audience appeared surprised, but they seemed not to have detected any heresies; at least, no comments were made.

However, it was made immediately clear from the first question that the interests of the audience lay not in cosmic formulations but in very parochial problems:

"Mr. McHarg, are you aware that the state highway department of New Jersey proposes to extend I-95 across the Delaware at Scudders Fall Bridge and thence to the Raritan, traversing the heart of Princeton? Is there an ecological solution to this problem, and, moreover, can you discover an ecologically sensitive route in six weeks?"

"Yes, indeed," I answered. "While I have never undertaken a route selection problem, I am confident that it is possible to array the region, its environmental and social factors, evaluate them, and select a route that incurs the least costs and provides the maximum benefits, or to conclude that costs exceed benefits and no highway should be constructed."

The next day Romer McPhee called. "Proceed; we require the solution before the public hearing six weeks hence."

At that time I had two brilliant young colleagues, both initially architects, both graduates of landscape architecture at Pennsylvania: an Indian, Narendra Juneja, and an Australian, Lindsay Robertson, both of whom, sad to say, died young. We devised the method together.

The area of the study was 600 square miles, from the Delaware to the Raritan, bounded by Sourland Mountain and Route 1, defined by the origin and destination of the Interstate-95 link. First, we undertook an inventory of climate, geology, hydrology, soils, vegetation, and wildlife. This was mapped. Next, we interpreted the data in each of these realms with an emphasis on the implications for an interstate highway. Fog, snow, ice, and inversions were clearly important in the consideration of climate, so we located areas of cold air drainage, frost and fog pockets, and areas of snowdrift. The presence of such factors would mean a cost, their absence a benefit. Similarly, bedrock types and surficial geology were evaluated for foundation conditions and for cost of excavation. Diabase and argillite would require blasting and would be very costly; sand and gravel would be cheap. Moreover, sand and gravel would provide a benefit, as these materials could be employed in highway construction. Physiography was similarly evaluated. Any slope in excess of three percent was a cost; the greater the slope, the greater the cost in cut and fill. Hydrology focused on the costs of stream and river crossings. First-order streams have no tributaries, second-order streams have first-order tributaries, and so on. Low-order streams can be crossed by culverts, high-order streams require bridges, and bridge costs escalate with stream orders. Moreover, highways pose problems for water quality: road salt, effluent from combustion, heavy metals, and more. Can we avoid the social costs of degrading water quality? Soils were similarly appraised: depth to seasonal high-water table, depth to bedrock, shrink-swell, shear strength, susceptibility to erosion. Vegetation was arrayed in a gradient of values using age, condition, species types, and number. Wildlife habitats were similarly arrayed. Historical buildings, places, and spaces and scenic quality were evaluated, as were land value, residential quality, and agricultural and recreational areas.

This was an original approach. Conventional highway engineering at that time addressed a narrower problem, concentrating on slope categories, property ownership, land value, and highway design. Environmental factors and environmental impacts were not then considered. The inclusion of meteorology, geology, physiography, hydrology, soils, plant and animal ecology, and limnology was revolutionary. Even more foreign, however, was the conception that the values of the impacted population should be factors in determining what constituted a cost or benefit. At that time alignments were presented at public hearings, perhaps with alternates, but the public had no role in establishing values. Community members were not asked what they might be prepared to sacrifice, what they would fight to the death to preserve. The alignments represented the values of highway engineers, oblivious and unresponsive to environment or people.

In the 600-square-mile area there were many distinct constituencies with quite definite value systems: Hopewell, Pennington, Princeton, Millstone, and Manville, among others. It became important to recognize these factors, and a simple and ingenious method was developed to resolve the problem. The intention was to seek the alignment having the least social cost. Therefore, all of the factors that had been interpreted were arrayed in degrees of potential cost on a gray scale; the greater the cost, the darker the tone. Each map was presented on transparent mylar with transparent tones. These would be superimposed, the second on the first, the third on the first and second combined, until all ten maps were superimposed. The lightest area would be the alignment of least social costs. However, we had found that there were different attitudes as to what constituted a cost, and indeed, as to the ranking of factors. So we devised a method. Thirty-five-millimeter slides were made for each factor map. Members of each township group, in Pennington, Hopewell, or elsewhere, could include the factors they wanted and exclude those they did not. Moreover, if it were necessary to give additional weight to a certain factor, many negative factors would increase blackness, their absence, the presence of white, propitious areas. A group preoccupied with historic preservation, or another concerned with agricultural preservation, could include several illustrative slides, effectively weighting the selected factors. The procedure included making a black-and-white print from the selected slides that revealed the least social cost alignment for a particular group. Meetings were held between the various groups. God must favor ecological planners for, in all the value sets, the same white trumpet shape, running from the Delaware along the base of Sourland Mountain, revealed an alignment least costly in terms of both the natural environment and the social values of the discrete constituencies. Moreover, it even cost less than the alignment designed by the state highway department—for its officials, the final blow. Their alignment transected everything near and dear, would violate not only the town of Princeton but college and university as well, and would cost more than the ecological alternative.

The public hearing convened to a standing-room audience. The highway engineers revealed the proposed alignment. This upper-class audience reacted like irate football fans—shouting, jeering, shaking fists, howling threats and imprecations. Romer McPhee stood up to say that the community categorically rejected the alignment. They had discovered an ecologically sensitive route and would submit this formally to the state highway department.

This was all very well, but what would be the effect? State highway departments were rich, powerful, and arrogant. Highway contracts and contractors were built into the political process. They could not easily be dissuaded or stopped.

I decided to call Lady Bird Johnson. She was a fan of mine, taking notes during my speeches, assuring me that she would persuade the president to a more ecological viewpoint. I spoke to her assistant, Sharon Francis: "We can win a battle for the environment on the playing fields of Princeton, we can beat the Bureau of Public Roads, the state highway department and the highway lobby." Sharon assured me that Mrs. Johnson would act, and she did.

At that time the highway fund was engorged with money. There was an effective alliance between the Bureau of Public Roads, the American Association of State Highway Officials, the state legislatures, and the highway construction industry. President Johnson determined that he and Congress should control this collusion and for this reason, among others, caused the creation of the U.S. Department of Transportation. The I-95 study emerged during discussions on the creation of the Department of Transportation. Then two significant events occurred. Rex Whitton, administrator of the Bureau of Public Roads, resigned, and Alan Boyd was nominated first secretary of the new Department of Transportation.

I had phoned Sharon Francis on a Thursday. On Friday morning I received a telephone call from Rex Whitton. I had been nominated as a candidate for his position as head of the Bureau of Public Roads. Would I be available for an interview? Clearly, I had been nominated by Mrs. Johnson, a very effective method for establishing my credentials. Hardly had I put down the phone when it rang again. Alan Boyd, secretary of transportation wanted to know whether I could present the ecological route selection method to him, his staff, the senators and congressmen of New Jersey, and Mrs. Johnson. I told him that I had arranged to have my suit dry-cleaned and have a haircut, that I had made an appointment on Monday with Rex Whitton and could amortize my investment by making the presentation thereafter. It was arranged.

Narendra, Lindsay, and I set off for Washington with our mylar map show-and-tell. First, I had a meeting with Rex Whitton. He was attended by his two assistants, Bridwell and Shotwell. He told me the salary, not impressive; the duties, very impressive; and asked if I was interested. The purpose of this meeting, clearly, was merely to establish my credentials. This had been accomplished. I had been nominated as a candidate for administrator of the Bureau of Public Roads. I could use the meeting constructively. I was not interested in the position, but I did think I could improve this shining hour by advising the administrator and his assistants on how the BPR could avoid causing great damage to the American environment and its cities. I recommended that they hire physical and biological scientists to interpret environments and compute the environmental and social costs of all contemplated projects. This was the genesis of environmental impact assessments, and the Interstate-95 study was probably its earliest exercise. It was not a gratifying encounter for Mr. Whitton, but it so happened that his next two experiences, in rapid succession, were to be much worse.

The next event was the presentation to Alan Boyd, his staff, senators and congressmen from New Jersey, Mrs. Johnson, Sharon Francis, and Rex Whitton.

The procedure was simple. A base map was mounted on a large light table. The method was explained. Map 1, with geological constraints, was superimposed with physiography; then hydrology, soils, vegetation, and land use followed, layer upon layer, the dark tones revealing costs and constraints, the white areas revealing opportunity. When it was finished, the least-social-cost route was visible to everyone, a white arc as clear as a bone in an x-ray. It incurred few environmental costs, it conformed to community values, and it cost less than the official proposal.

Alan Boyd spoke. "A most succinct and lucid presentation. I concur completely."

The political contingent assented.

Boyd turned to Whitton. "Rex, how much do you spend annually on research?"

"Hundreds of millions."

"Mr. McHarg, how much did your study cost?"

"Six thousand dollars."

"Mr. Whitton, aren't you embarrassed that such an effective method can be developed at such a modest cost when your bloated expenditures have produced nothing comparable? I would suggest that you ask Professor McHarg if he would address your staff and explain his method to them because, assuredly, it will be employed hereafter."

The President's Chair 1966

In 1966, when Lyndon Johnson convened the White House Task Force on Conservation and Natural Beauty, Laurance Rockefeller organized a meeting, at which I was one of the speakers. The conclusion would require Rockefeller to present the decisions of the task force to the president. The event was scheduled for the White House lawn. The dignitaries assembled—led to their seats by very senior army and naval officers, heavy with gold braid—the speakers, the cabinet, the Supreme Court, and selected guests. Hardly had everyone been seated when it began to rain. Mrs. Johnson told the audience that the event perforce must move indoors to the East Room. Secret Service men led the procession. I was in good shape, among the first to enter. I proceeded to the front row of seats, when Mrs. Johnson spoke to me. "Professor McHarg, I hope Lyndon will listen to your proposals; they will help to keep America beautiful." I listened respectfully. While we were engaged in conversation, the room filled. Stewart Udall and Orville Freeman were pushing for seats, television crews were dragging in cameras and cables. It was clear that not all members of the audience could be seated. The aisles were crowded. Suddenly the room became quiet, and the audience, at least all who could, sat down. I sat beside Mrs. Johnson, uneasily. Two Secret Service men preceded the president. The first approached me and said, "Sir, that is the president's seat." I rose straight up into the air, hovered for a millisecond looking for a place to land, and found it, a piano stool. So there I sat, tremulous in embarrassment, with no escape possible. Laurance Rockefeller presented the conclusion of the task force, speaking to the president and the audience. The president, however, made his replies to neither the audience nor Rockefeller, but to me. I sat there, trying to shrink into invisibility, as the president, looking at me over his bifocals, assured me of his splendid intention to keep America beautiful.

I agreed. I would be at South Main at 2:00 P.M. to present the method to his staff. I went off to lunch at the Cosmos Club with Romer McPhee, and we toasted Mrs. Johnson and our success with dry martinis.

That afternoon, I stood at the entrance to the auditorium with Rex Whitton. Truculent engineers converged on the doors, their anger evident. I was pushed—was it intentional? The auditorium filled. Rex Whitton spoke. "I have experienced a great humiliation this day. An entirely new method, described as an ecological route selection method, was displayed to the secretary, his staff, the political leadership of New Jersey, and Mrs. Johnson. It shows our current method to be wholly inadequate. We are required by the secretary to learn this new method. Ten thousand copies of the study will be circulated to all DOT, BPR, and state highway departments. I now ask Professor McHarg to describe the method."

Recall the fury of the upper middle class at the Princeton public hearing, and you have some idea of the anger that highway engineers engendered in conservationists. They were brutal, destructive, stupid, and, above all, arrogant. I was not in a forgiving mood.

"I welcome the opportunity to describe the ecological planning method for highway route selection," I began, "but, first, I have to reveal my loathing of you and your kind. If you all had a fatal paroxysm, I would find it difficult to mobilize a single tear. You have been engaged in an onslaught against the American environment, you have dismembered, dissected and destroyed significant areas of American cities. Your depredations must end. There is no reason that the American public should pay so dearly to have their environments attacked by such insensitive bullies. You must learn about the environment, both natural and social. You must ask nature whether you may build, where and how, but you also must ascertain from those who will be impacted, what are their perceptions, values, needs, and desires. Only then will you be able to design highways fitting to the land, fit for people. And so now I will show you how." And I did.

Scenic Highways 1967

A proposal was made to create a system of scenic highways in the United States. President Johnson turned to Laurance Rockefeller to convene hearings on this matter and advise him. Rockefeller invited three speakers to give testimony: Holly Whyte, author, journalist, and authority on open space; Philip Lewis, a distinguished landscape architect from the University of Wisconsin who had studied corridors extensively; and me. There was a dinner in Chevy Chase the evening before to rehearse testimony and decide who would address which topics. Laurance Rockefeller gave me rather specific advice. "Mr. McHarg," he said, "you have a reputation for being plainspoken, even hyperbolic. I would not advise you to change your character during your testimony." So advised, I appeared the following day shaven, dry-cleaned, polished, and belligerent. While denied the opportunity to give testimony, the highway lobby was there in full force, the Bureau of Public Roads, the American Association of State Highway Officials, the Portland Cement Institute, the Asphalt Institute, Caterpillar Tractor, and others.

I was introduced. Laurance Rockefeller spoke: "Mr. McHarg, you have had extensive experience in highway planning. The president would welcome your advice as to the wisdom of constructing a system of scenic highways."

"Mr. Rockefeller, do you happen to know where all the scenic areas of the United States are?"

"Why, yes, Mr. McHarg, I think that I could have those identified."

"If you do, sir, please, for God's sake, make sure such information does not fall into the hands of the Bureau of Public Roads, for surely they would destroy them all."

"Come now, Mr. McHarg, isn't that rather extreme?"

"Indeed not, sir, you are so insulated by wealth and power that you do not know how ultimately depraved these highway engineers are."

"Oh, really, Mr. McHarg" (how well he turned the screw).

"Sir, there is a profound psychic flaw in highway engineers. What psychic trauma explains their behavior I do not know, but it would appear that they have a deep insecurity as to their masculinity which can only be appeased by mutilating mute nature."

"Surely, Mr. McHarg, that is too extreme."

"No sir, my experience has been both extensive and intensive, so much so that I have coined a definition of highway engineers, which, if not entirely accurate, does reveal the loathing of environmentalists like myself for the breed of highway engineers."

"You have a definition?"

"A highway engineer can be defined as a person who, if struck a blow with a four-pound hammer on one ear could not transmit a reverberation through to the other ear audible with a stethoscope."

"Mr. McHarg, what would you do without hammer and stethoscope?"

"Why, sir, I supposed I would be satisfied with medical evidence of brain damage."

"Thank you very much, Mr. McHarg."

No scenic highways were ever built.

Ford Foundation

By the mid-1960s, ecology was slowly touching the public consciousness. One consequence was that in 1964 Gordon Harrison of the Ford Foundation was entrusted with the responsibility of investigating the field and determining whether it was worthy of foundation support. To that end he invited a number of persons, prominent in ecology and resources, to a four-day conference in New York. These included Paul Sears, René Dubos, Edward Deevey, E. Max Nicholson, Frank Fraser Darling, and others, including me. The conference addressed general problems of the environment but focused on the contribution ecology could make. Each evening an exquisite dinner was arranged in a fashionable restaurant. I doubt whether all of the invited guests had ever been together in a single room before, and these meetings and dinners were incandescent. This was an unprecedented focus on the environment.

While I contributed my wholehearted endorsement of ecology, for whatever it was worth, my own supplication was directed toward its application. I was firmly committed to ecology as the scientific foundation for landscape architecture, but I also submitted that it could perform invaluable services if employed in environmental and regional planning. I recommended that persons with initial degrees in the various environmental sciences be recruited into programs of regional planning and their discrete sciences, either physical or biological, be expanded and augmented and, most important, focused on contemporary problems. Such a program would require a multidisciplinary and interdisciplinary faculty.

Two years elapsed, during which Harrison secured approval from the Ford Foundation to embark on a grant program to support ecology and its application. I received a letter inviting me to make a proposal.

The first proposal made in 1966 was a modest one, simply the description of a method of recruiting the necessary faculty members. This consisted of identification of the leading figures in the constituent fields of environmental science. Each would be requested to nominate a candidate, and the group would collectively review documentation, interview candidates, and recommend prospective faculty. The interviewers included William Reifsnyder, meteorologist; John Hack, geologist; M. Gordon Wolman, hydrologist; Whittaker and Bormann, plant ecologists; Edward Deevey and Lamont Cole, animal ecologists; Ruth Patrick, limnologist; and Waldo Tobler and David Simonette, representing the field of computation and remotely sensed imagery. The procedure took three days. The proposal was funded, the conference convened, all invitees attended, and the selection was made.

The chosen faculty included William Lowry, biometeorologist; Robert Giegengack, geologist; Thomas Dunne, hydrologist, Ronald Hanawalt, soils scientist; Arthur Sullivan and Estella Leopold, ecologists; and E. Bruce MacDougall, computer science and remotely sensed imagery. Given this faculty, the next tasks were to describe the courses and curricula in ecologically based regional planning and to work with the faculty to identify their teaching and research roles. It took almost a year to review the application, and it was not until 1967 that the grant was made. The request had been for $1 million; the grant was for half that sum.

Yet this was a landmark event. For the first time a Department of Landscape Architecture could recruit a faculty of distinguished natural scientists sharing the

ecological view and determined to integrate their perceptions into a holistic discipline applied to the solution of contemporary problems. In addition, the grant
supported the creation of a curriculum in regional planning that consequently
recruited candidates from the natural sciences.

The accomplishment was large; it was also adventurous. Had Biology sought to
hire three physical scientists, there would have been deep opposition from Geology.
The reverse would have been as true. I sought a meeting with my president, Gaylord
Harnwell. Ford would fund the creation of a natural science faculty in landscape
architecture. Could it be approved? He was a large, tweedy, pipe-smoking Philadelphia Quaker. He put his arm around my shoulder. "Ian," he said, "there are only
two things that matter. Your plans must bring glory to the university and should not
cost us money. If you can raise the funds, proceed. You have my blessing."

The accomplishment was significant and unusual. An applied professional
program had been selected rather than a department of science. What an unlikely
program to create the first interdisciplinary and multidisciplinary faculty focused
on environmental problems. Indeed, the magazine *Science* described this program
as unique in the country, perhaps in the world.

The grant transformed education in environmental problems. The step was
widely imitated, notably in landscape architecture and engineering, and there were
spawned innumerable programs in environmental science, man and environment
and more. All expanded the uniform-discipline approach and incorporated several
distinct natural sciences. Yet no program exceeded that at Pennsylvania in the
range of disciplines represented.

I can find no words but praise for Gordon Harrison and the Ford Foundation,
but I do have regrets. Halving the grant request meant that the contemplated
faculty could not be entirely recruited. The reduction also removed support for
interdisciplinary unfunded research, and this was a tragic loss. So meteorology,
hydrology, and animal ecology were not permanently incorporated, and these
constituted serious omissions. Research granting agencies were at that time resis-
tant to supporting interdisciplinary studies and are not widely supportive even
today. In the 1960s, it was necessary to relieve faculty of teaching to fund such
interdisciplinary work. The fund grant was inadequate. Faculty were required to
pursue research grants within their independent disciplines, unable to exploit
the larger perceptions represented by their collective wisdom. There was little
research employing the combined range of perceptions, with one exception, the
Medford Study, undertaken in 1971.

I believe that it is correct to state that this integrated faculty accomplished a
revolution in education, notably in landscape architecture and regional planning,

Andy Warhol's Visit to Penn

There was an occasion in 1965 when the Institute for Contemporary Art of the University of Pennsylvania arranged an exhibit of the work of Andy Warhol. It would be held in the Furness Library of the School of Fine Arts. Many of the exhibits were thought to be too valuable to be shown, so there was quite a lot of empty wall space. Nonetheless, the reception preceding the opening was a mob scene, a rock band pulsed, and, suddenly, Andy Warhol appeared at the top of a spiral staircase. He surveyed the admiring throng and, with a regal gesture, threw his sunglasses to them.

A dinner followed the reception arranged by Mrs. Gates Lloyd, a prominent Philadelphian and patron of the ICA, Institute of Contemporary Art. This was held in a downtown apartment. I arrived; here again was a mob. I viewed the scene and found few familiar faces, when I was joined by a man slightly older than I. "I am Gates Lloyd. You look like the only person here I can talk to, have a drink with. Let's find a seat." I learned something of Gates Lloyd, but he did not reveal that he was with the Central Intelligence Agency. Had I known, we could have had a very interesting conversation, although not necessarily gratifying to him.

There was an announcement. "Dinner will be served, please be seated." We found our cards. I found myself facing Andy's companion, a very thin young woman with bare breasts. Her development was modest, no greater than my own. Suddenly, there was an ado outside. In marched waiters from Bookbinder's restaurant, bearing lobsters and bibs. Around each neck a bib was tied, and suddenly our topless beauty was rendered decorous.

Mrs. Lloyd had solved the problem brilliantly: no confrontation; lobsters bring bibs— bring lobsters, fast!

but also affecting city planning, engineering, environmental science, and more. Had it been possible to facilitate the faculty in research, I believe that the benefits would have been even more dramatic. The dilemma persists with us to this day.

I am frequently introduced as the father of ecological planning. Fatherhood requires insemination, but for me the Ford grant application was the seed, the grant the fetus, and ecological planning the child.

The Potomac 1965–1967

Secretary Stewart Udall invited the American Institute of Architects to nominate members for a Task Force on the Potomac. The nominees were mainly architects; Arthur Gould Odell, then AIA president, Edmund Bacon; R. Max Brooks; Donn Emmons; and Francis Lethbridge. The urban planner Frederick Gutheim, the geographer Edward Ackerman, hydrologist M. Gordon Wolman, engineer Thornedike Saville, and Grady Clay, editor of *Landscape Architecture*, were, with me, the nonarchitectural constituency. Both Gutheim and Ed Bacon had illustrious careers as urban planners.

President Lyndon Johnson recommended that "a sweeping model plan be made of the Potomac, to be exemplary to the nation."

The composition of the task force, with a preponderance of architects and city planners, ensured that a major effort would be invested in urban and metropolitan problems and opportunities. The Palisades above Key Bridge, Georgetown, and Foggybottom; Rock Creek, the Monumental Core, Anacostia, and Harbor, all received detailed examinations and proposals.

The regional viewpoint was represented by Ackerman, Wolman, Saville, and me. However, we confronted a serious problem. While the architects could appraise urban design problems by site visits, review of plans, and proposals, the data necessary for a regional investigation were much more extensive. A staff was necessary. The Department of the Interior would not provide the staff; even worse, Interior was ignorant of ecological planning.

I conferred with faculty and students. Were they interested in undertaking a year-long ecological planning study of the Potomac River basin, effectively acting as staff to the task force? The response was unanimous. The rewards were that student work might influence national policy and the product would be published as it was.

This was a great challenge. Earlier studies for TVA and the Columbia River had omitted ecological data, and we knew of no prior studies that sought to employ such data as a basis. We had to invent a method. Of course, this revealed my ignorance of the extraordinary accomplishments of Charles Eliot. My earlier experience in 1959 with the research on metropolitan open space had employed modest tenets of geology, physiography, surficial hydrology, and vegetation. Now, six years later, from innumerable lectures in "Man and Environment" and "Ecology of the City," it became clear that the data set must be much more encompassing: meteorology, geology, geomorphology, groundwater and surficial hydrology, soils, vegetation, wildlife, limnology, and, where appropriate, physical oceanography and marine biology.

The study plan was developed. We would first review the entire Potomac basin, next we would examine each of the physiographic regions in greater detail—the Allegheny Plateau, the Ridge and Valley Province, the Great Valley, the Blue Ridge, the Piedmont, and the Coastal Plain. We would proceed by selecting typical sites within each region for more detailed study; among them would be the Washington metropolitan region.

The class, eleven in number, was superb. I recall them by associating each with the regions they studied: Richard Westmacott and Joachim Tourbier, English and German (peas in a pod), the Allegheny Plateau; Griet Terpstra from Drenthe in the Netherlands and Sarah Manwell from Connecticut, the Ridge and Valley Province; Louise Kao from Taiwan, the Blue Ridge; John Seddon from St. Louis, the Great Valley. A quartet studied the Piedmont and the Washington metropolis: Derek Bradford and John Chitty, English architects, James Sinatra and Chuck Meyers, both American. The Coastal Plain was addressed by Gary Felgemaker from Illinois.

The quality of student classes waxes and wanes. There seems to be no explanation, no prediction possible. Transcripts, portfolios, and letters seem incapable of predicting a class that will fuse into a marvelously effective, complementary, and productive association. Yet such was this class. Its members launched themselves into this adventure with unqualified enthusiasm.

Today Bradford has been dean and chairman at Rhode Island School of Design and is now a professor; Sinatra is chair in Melbourne; Westmacott and Tourbier are professors at Georgia and Dresden, respectively. Terpstra teaches and practices in England; Manwell, who is now Mrs. Bradford, teaches and practices at Rhode Island School of Design in Providence; and Chitty, Seddon, Felgemaker are all distinguished practitioners, Chitty in London, Seddon in Singapore and Felgemaker in Los Angeles.

The decision for landscape architects to undertake a river basin study was revolutionary. Until that time the experience of the profession in the United States was generally limited to the project scale—gardens, parks, and urban open space. I had made a great leap in studying a metropolitan region, although unknown to me then, my distinguished predecessor, Charles Eliot, had done so half a century earlier. The Potomac constituted an enormous enlargement of scale, unprecedented in the history of landscape architecture. Indeed, we were embarking on an exercise in regional planning, an expansion of professional responsibility. But large-scale conceptions were not foreign; the landscape architects of the eighteenth-century English landscape tradition had cumulatively accomplished transformation of a country, Olmsted had conceived of a system of national parks, and Benton MacKaye had proposed a massive open space system encompassing the eastern United States.

We embarked on the exercise with passion. Here was an appropriate opportunity, we could enlarge our skills. If successful, we could contribute to national policy, we could create a new discipline for the profession.

Our first task was organizing the profusion of data that were being collected. Each discipline had its journals and products. How could this superabundance be organized? Even better, could it be investigated in a causal way wherein each step contributed incremental understanding of succeeding layers? In this predicament, I concluded that chronology might be the most effective unifying device. Let us reconstruct the past to explain the present. Let us begin with the oldest evidence and proceed. Moreover, we wished to record change: All that is now has been, and is in the process of becoming. The first decision was to embrace chronology. This produced confirmatory evidence. We found that the earliest events, mainly of geological history, had pervasive and influential effects, not only on physiography, soils, and vegetation, but also on the availability of resources. The next decision was the "layer cake" representation, in which the region being studied was treated as though it consisted of multiple layers. These were, of course, the discrete disciplines of the environment. The world is a whole, divided only by science and language, but these are obdurate divisions, each discipline limited to a single layer. Yet it was the whole that concerned us. So we constructed layer cake models. The oldest geologic evidence, five hundred million years of age, was represented in Precambrian Wissahickon schist; next lay surficial geology, the glacial events of the Pleistocene age, a million to ten thousand years ago. These could be reinterpreted in the next layer, which was groundwater hydrology. The expressed surface of bedrock geology and the veneer of glacial materials produced the next layer of physiography, causally related to the foregoing layers. Precipitation, gravity, and physiography resulted in surficial hydrology; soils followed; then the structure of plants, responsive to physiography, soils, slope, and aspect; and, finally, wildlife, largely related to habitat and the structure of vegetation associations. Climatic factors were pervasive but, in the layer cake model, they formed a crown—microclimate, mesoclimate, and macroclimate. Estuaries included limnology, oceans required physical oceanography and marine biology.

If such layers are represented in transparent materials, causality becomes evident. Bedrock geology will be reflected in physiography. Mountains, hills, valleys, escarpments, and faults will then be seen in resultant elevations, slopes, aspects, and characteristic features. The geology will reveal and explain presence, absence, abundance, and quality of groundwater. Given knowledge of geology and climate, the presence or absence of lakes and the abundance of streams become comprehensible. Soils derive from parent material, glaciation, aeolian and fluvial processes, physical characteristics reflect position on a section, high to low. Plants synthesize all of the foregoing, and species and ecosystems are responses to environmental variables, notably, the relative abundance of water, as well as elevation, slope, and aspect. Wildlife relates directly to the vegetational structure. Layer after layer contributes meaning. No layer is comprehensible without access to that underlying. This concept is an enormously useful invention, with which I am very pleased and which I have retained unchanged. It is at once an invaluable organizing principle, an unequaled learning device, and a most revelatory instrument for understanding the environment, diagnosing, and prescribing.

The study was a landmark; it developed the ecological planning method. Selection of physiographic regions as the major structural elements was proven to be the appropriate strategy. Chronology and the layer cake method were confirmed, as was the litany of descriptors—meteorology, bedrock and surficial geology, groundwater hydrology, physiography, surficial hydrology, soils, vegetation, wildlife, and land use. The method was shown to be effective at the scale of river basin, of physiographic region, and of metropolitan area.

Major suitabilities were revealed. The Allegheny Province, mountainous, forested, and with lakes and high-quality water, revealed predominately recreational opportunity. The Ridge and Valley Province, with parallel ridges, steep slopes, and narrow flood-prone valleys, was dominated by coal mining and its attendant problems—environmental degradation, stream acidification, and flood vulnerability, not to mention poverty. This area was clearly distinguishable from the neighboring Great Valley, with its extensive agriculture, rich soils, and broad streams, neutralized from passage through limestone. The Blue Ridge, with the oldest rocks, densely forested, represented another scenic and recreational opportunity. The Crystalline Piedmont contrasted with the flat limestone, with its undulating physiography, dissected by the Potomac, at whose tidal limit sat Washington. Last, the flat coastal plain and the estuary, with its distinct geological history, marine-deposited sands and gravels, abundant groundwater, characteristic forests, and, above all, its fishing and other water-related recreational opportunities.

The study revealed structure and meaning in the landscape and offered the ability to understand, to ascertain attributes, to evaluate these, and to determine areas of intrinsic suitability for all prospective land uses.

But it was not to be. Although Secretary Udall was pleased with the plan and sought to institute a federal-state compact for the Potomac, he was opposed by the two senators from West Virginia, who rejected federal intervention and were successful in thwarting the idea.

Curriculum

The curriculum in landscape architecture at Penn followed an evolutionary process. It began with the recognition of the extraordinary accomplishments of the eighteenth-century English landscape tradition, the transformation of an entire countryside, and its development in the nineteenth-century United States with the powerful contributions of Olmsted and Eliot. A further step saw ecology embraced as the scientific and philosophical basis for the profession. This involved no repudiation of the historic examples; the eighteenth century had employed a rudimentary but effective ecology. The next great leap was the "experiment in anthropology," funded by the National Institutes of Mental Health, which led to the expansion of ecology to include people, human ecology. This too was simply an augmentation. The employment of ecology and human ecology was applied to planning, where it was obviously efficacious. The last, and continuing, curricular quest is to develop ecological design. Parallel to these advances has been the effort to develop computerized ecological planning and, ultimately, design.

It was concluded very early that introduction to the ecological method should be the foundation of the curriculum and should be presented to students upon entry. An ambitious exercise in group teaching was devised, engaging the entire scientific faculty. Instruction would be offered in meteorology, geology, hydrology, soils science, and plant and wildlife ecology. A special calendar was devised to permit offering a dozen or so modules, short courses in each of the environmental sciences, an irreducible minimum but presented at a consonant level with emphasis on integration. Simultaneous with formal instruction, students would be allocated to sites within regions where they could employ their knowledge of each of the environmental sciences to learn how the places came to be, how they worked as interacting biophysical systems, and to investigate the implications of this knowledge for human use and planning. Each site was the subject of a number of field trips.

Given the novelty of the method, and its value in the learning process for the faculty, it was appropriate that the first exercises address river basins. Here striking variations could easily be discerned, even by neophytes. In the initial exercises the physiographic regions provided examples wherein uniform natural histories had produced characteristic geology, hydrology, soils, vegetation, wildlife, and other resources. First in the Potomac, later in the Delaware, the same Allegheny Plateau, Ridge and Valley Province, Blue Ridge/Reading Prong, Great Valley, Crystalline Piedmont (including the Triassic Basin), and Coastal Plain provided the contrasting environments. Because of the oil embargo in the early 1970s, far-flung sites were later abandoned in favor of metropolitan ones. Yet here it was possible to find examples from the Inner and Outer Coastal Plains, the Triassic Basin, the Limestone Valley, and the Crystalline Piedmont. After a decade, the method had been formalized, the faculty had achieved a considerable degree of understanding of all the contributing disciplines, and discrimination was finer, so the contraction of scale was possible and appropriate. The method was now capable of handling large-scale, largely rural regions but was just as efficacious when applied to metropolitan regions and sites.

Design with Nature 1966–1967

In the spring of 1966 I received a conference call from Russell Train, then president of the Conservation Foundation, and his chief scientist, the noted ecologist Raymond Dasman. After some pleasantries, Train said, "Ian, Ray and I have decided that the time has come for a book on ecology and planning." I agreed.

Martin Luther King, Jr.—Iowa 1968

Some events have dates engraved on them. Such was my speech in Ames, Iowa. The itinerary was a complicated one, which involved flying to Salt Lake City by way of Chicago, from Salt Lake City to Iowa, also by way of Chicago, thence to Minneapolis and home. The weather intervened; a massive snowstorm covered the East and Midwest. We took off without incident, but traffic was stacked in Chicago. When the plane arrived, my connection had departed. The next flight might just get me into Salt Lake City to give an after-dinner speech. It did not. The speech was rescheduled for the following morning, which delayed my departure. We left Salt Lake City in sunshine but quickly rediscovered yesterday's snowstorm and found conditions unchanged in Chicago. The plane arrived very, very late but it did land. However, the airport closed down, and my flight to Ames, Iowa, was cancelled. I walked to Butler Aviation and inquired whether there was a charter. Indeed, it had been used until this very day by Eugene McCarthy, the presidential candidate—twin engine, pilot, and copilot. Could they guarantee my arrival by 7:00 P.M. at Ames? They

could. We set off, back into the buffeting storm and headwinds. I was sitting at a table in the cabin, drinking a martini, smoking, when the pilot joined me. "Mind if I have a drink?" he asked. The plane was careening like a leaf in a strong wind. "I do indeed mind, not on your bloody life." He was actively displeased and showed it. He returned to the cockpit but soon reappeared. "We are not going to make it on time, but someone called Margharita Tarr will give a one-hour lecture on Machu Picchu until your arrival."

We pitched and tossed to Ames and finally landed in a snowstorm produced by the plane's propellers. The copilot opened the door. I descended, followed by the pilot. We stood together at the foot of the steps, and a group came toward us, among them my host, Jim Sinatra. But it was not he who came forward first. Someone rushed to the pilot and said, "You are chartered for Atlanta, go back to Chicago right away, Martin Luther King has been assassinated." "That'll teach the black bastard," the pilot said. I swung and hit him square on the mouth.

"We think that you are the man to write it."

"No way, I am totally incapable of writing about ecology. I am not an ecologist."

"Ian, we think you can do it, and we have a proposal. If you request and receive a sabbatical next year, we will pay you $20,000."

Twenty thousand dollars was then, as now, a serious sum. This was an unexpected but challenging prospect.

"Come and discuss it."

I did, and I was persuaded. My request for a sabbatical was granted, and at the end of classes I began to write. First I wrote a synopsis for consideration by members of the Conservation Foundation. With their approval, I submitted it for publication in *Landscape Architecture* under the title "Design with Nature: An Ecological Basis for Landscape Architecture."

I Quit When the War Ended—1969

It was in 1969 when the Army Corps of Engineers decided that they had to respond to public resentment for their insensitivity to the environment. The Corps' history of large-scale hydropower projects, was widely criticized as "Big Dam Foolishness," and could not continue, so General Wheeler, then chief engineer, convened a closed conference in New York for all of the district engineers in the country to discuss how best the Corps could improve its environmental record. I was one of three persons invited to address them. George Harzog, head of the National Parks Service, began. He was, as were they, a southern old boy. Harzog chided them and cajoled them; for the most part he got along with the Corps, but there were points of friction—the Florida Barge Canal and the Everglades, for example. Next to speak was Ruth Patrick, the most distinguished limnologist in the country. Soft-spoken and erudite, she drew upon countless studies of the rivers of America that she had undertaken. Implicit in her remarks was the observation

that the Corps knew little of rivers as physical processes and nothing of them as biological systems. Her wisdom, science, and language were far over the heads of the audience.

Now there was only one more chance. Clearly, it was time for the two-by-four approach—a blow to the testicles to get the mule's attention. I began: "How fortunate that this meeting is not open to the press. I can therefore reveal my antienvironmental past. I was once an army engineer. In the British Army, to be sure, but from 1939 to 1946 I was an Army Engineer. In this capacity I certainly modified the environment, notably with high explosives. I blew up bridges, ports, harbors, railroads, trains, buildings galore. I blew up lots of things which I was ordered to destroy. I also blew up things for which there was no great necessity. I enjoyed big bangs. I came to enjoy changing the environment explosively. But, gentlemen, the difference between you and me is that I quit when the war ended."

The period 1966–1967 was a propitious time to write *Design with Nature,* for a number of seminal ideas were surfacing simultaneously. The book offered the opportunity to assemble, integrate and present these as a new way of looking at the earth. Vladimir Vernadsky had advanced the conception of the biosphere, Teilhard de Chardin had invented the term *noosphere* for the skin of consciousness enveloping the planet. Geologists were beginning to describe the lithosphere, hydrologists the hydrosphere. The general term *atmosphere* was being redefined as the envelope of gases encircling the earth. The theory for this integrated view had its basis in *The Fitness of the Environment,* written at the turn of the century by Lawrence J. Henderson. George Wald wrote a new introduction to a reissue, with topical comments. G. Evelyn Hutchinson had promoted a lecture, "Geochemical Cycles"; Paul Sears, Raymond Fosberg, and, most important, Harold Blum had addressed energetics, entropy, and the particular role of life that Buckminster Fuller described as *syntropy.* Tom and Eugene Odum had introduced systems ecology.

Of course, the greatest insight of our lives came in 1969, when we first saw the earth from the moon. Lewis Thomas spoke for us all. His response was, "The earth is alive, it is alive."

I immediately sent a request to NASA asking permission to include the famous first photograph of the earth, which was used as the back page of the dust cover of *Design with Nature.* I believe this was its first employment in a book.

These and other ideas were converging; the sum of ideas from the "Man and Environment" course formed the basis for the manuscript. Two chapters presented the theory and were central to the burden of the work: "The Cast in the Capsule," a description of the major actors and processes comprising the earth, and "The World Is a Capsule," an application of the processes in capsule experiments to simplify and dramatize the salient earth processes. These preceded the Biosphere II experiments by more than two decades. Indeed, the book included a provocative discussion of a space station, based on an abstracted farm, a subject only recently under serious investigation by NASA.

In many ways, this was one of the most gratifying years of my life. I worked at home. I established a discipline of 2,500 raw words each day and reserved an hour or two each morning for correction and expansion of the previous day's text. Sometimes I completed my task by noon, but often I worked into the wee hours.

I sent the outline and drafts to Dasman. He was pleased, but I was growing more and more frightened. The book was becoming presumptuous, as the evidence I was compiling was impelling me to make greater and greater denunciations and claims. I had begun writing to landscape architects and planners, but the evidence was pushing me to address larger problems and wider audiences. After all,

I had a modest reputation, but here I was questioning prevailing values, methods, and processes, not only at the regional and national levels, but on a global scale.

I needed help. The wisest man I have ever known was Lewis Mumford. I decided to present my predicament to him. The book was getting out of hand, leading me into areas where I had no authority. I was uncertain that I could finish it, and I needed support and advice.

His response was wonderful. "Indeed, Dear Ian, in a good and proper world you would not be asked to write this book, but the world is vastly imperfect and you may be the one person who will write it. It should be written, you can write. I enclose my comments for your consideration, but my best advice is that you solicit invitations from Harvard, Yale, Berkeley, and elsewhere, present your ideas and be guided by the response." Which I did. The response was warmly gratifying. I settled down and completed the book. It was finished at the appointed date. Then I submitted it to the Conservation Foundation, where it languished for almost a year.

One officer at the Foundation was with the Natural History Press, and it was assumed that this press would publish the book. But with his departure from the Conservation Foundation, the connection was broken. The Foundation did not transmit the manuscript. It was then advised by Ray Dasman that I should assume the initiative to have the book published myself. I had received many offers: Curley Bowen of MIT Press, Praeger, Houghton Mifflin, Thames & Hudson, and, later, Jake Page of Natural History Press, all showed interest.

In every case the offer was to print 15,000 copies and give me ten percent royalties. I had one problem that no one could answer. The book depended on graphics. All of the case studies required maps, many of which would be incomprehensible without color. Could I write into the contract the numbers of graphics—four-color, three-color, and two-color? No one could or would allow this. The editors and publishers may have known spelling, colons, and semicolons, but they knew little about printing or color.

An art printer friend of mine, Gene Feldman, printed catalogues for museums. He also taught printmaking at Penn. I conferred with him. Could he specify a book that would retail at $12.00, print for $5.00, with a run of 5,000; identify signatures of four, three, and two colors and halftones, specify paper weight, binding, and dust cover? Indeed he could. He introduced me to the mysteries of signatures, forms, color separations, folding, and cutting. Together we produced a dummy.

No full color was possible; only one signature of three colors could be afforded. For this schema the manuscript had to be rewritten to correspond to the location of the graphics. We chose an eleven-by-eleven-inch format and divided each page in nine squares. We selected a typeface that provided 110 words per segment, 330 per column, 1,000 per page.

Given my inability to write specifications into a contract, I decided to publish the book myself. My expectations were that the sale of 5,000 copies (my most ambitious expectation) would pay all costs. (In fact, more than 350,000 have been sold and the book was reprinted in 1992 with a new preface.) I designed stationary so that typing corresponded to the dummy text. I then hired employees at my firm, Wallace, McHarg, Roberts and Todd (which had evolved from Wallace-McHarg Associates in 1969), to make maps, plans, diagrams, and color separations and to undertake the pasteup of the dummy. I paid my partners cost and overhead for these services, but no profit. As many of the projects illustrated in the book had been performed by this partnership, I trust and hope that the resulting publicity made ample repayment for their relinquishing profit.

It took one year to produce a photo correct dummy with all illustrations, separations, and captions, ready for publication. I decided to try direct-mail sale and produced a brochure, which was sent to all members of the American Institute of Architects, American Society of Landscape Architects, American Institute of Planners, the Conservation Foundation, Audubon Society, and Sierra Club.

This worked very well; checks flowed into my home. My wife and sons packed books into cartons and took them to the post office. Two or three thousand orders had been filled when I received a call from Natural History Press and its parent, Doubleday, saying they would like to distribute *Design with Nature*. If I delivered books to their warehouses in Virginia at a cost of $5.60 each, they would buy 5,000 copies.

This would end the peonage of my wife and sons, but instead of making $7.00 a book, I would make $.60 plus $1.20 in royalties. Yet surely Doubleday could do a better job of distribution than I. At least I thought so then. But this meant I would have to sell four times as many books just to pay the costs of my printer and the office. The book was selling like hotcakes, but neither my family nor I wished to become booksellers, so I assented.

The Doubleday staff had little confidence in the book. They ordered printings of 5,000. The first printing was sold out before it arrived in their warehouse, as was the second and the third. They had none for Christmas. I suggested that they print a run of 20,000, which would have reduced the printing cost to $1.50. No, they continued to reject these large economies and profits, and continually ordered 5,000-book printings. I offered to pay for any unsold copies. In vain. So it goes.

But go it did, so much so that the new president of the Conservation Foundation, Sydney Howe, strapped for funds, wrote me a letter stating that, as the

Multiply and Subdue the Earth

I was vacationing with my family on Barney's Joy Farm, Padenarum, Massachusetts, with a VW camper and a tent on the promontory overlooking Naragansett Bay, when our campsite was invaded by a visitor, Austin Hoyt, a director for WGBH of Boston. He had received a substantial grant from the Ford Foundation to do a television show on the environment and had been referred to me. I had just completed the manuscript for *Design with Nature*, and I gave him a copy.

When next I heard from Hoyt, his grant had been confirmed and he had concluded that I should play a significant role in his film. He would draw from *Design with Nature* for the conservationist/ecological tone and present three of my projects—Plan for the Valleys in Baltimore County, Maryland; the ecological study for Minneapolis-St. Paul, Minnesota; and Sea Storm and Survival, Harvey Cedars on the New Jersey shore.

The other contributor to the program was Alfie Heller, prominent California conservationist, publisher of *Cry California*. He discussed the Hawaii Land Use Law and the threats to Lake Tahoe. We filmed in Maryland, on the New Jersey shore, in the Muir Woods near San Francisco, in the Sawtooth Mountains of Colorado, in Taos, New Mexico, and Hawaii.

I carried cameras and batteries, reflectors and manuscripts. The crew consisted of Austin Hoyt, the photographer Peter Hoving, and Peggy Zappel.

In January 1969 the program was aired, first to the northeast from Boston, next from Denver to the midwest, and finally from San Francisco. It received rave reviews and was made into a film. Five hundred copies were

printed, which were so popular that a six-month waiting period resulted. The Audiovisual Center of the University of Indiana in Bloomington, Indiana, distributed the copies. For years, every meeting of conservationists began with this movie.

This project held several magic moments. I made a statement to Austin, saying that the continent was empty. He asked me how to show this. I said, "I will find a site, either in Colorado or New Mexico. Let us plan it when the aspens are in their full glory." I first tried Taos, but the foliage was not at the right stage. Then I inquired about Grand Junction. Yes, the aspens would be at their peak on the weekend. We went to Denver and thence to Grand Junction. We hired a charter with a landscape architect for a pilot and proceeded up the face of the Grand Mesa, bathed in luminous gold, succeeding to the plateau with its turquoise lakes and Englemann spruce. It remains an epic experience to this day, colored by the golden, lustrous, quaking aspen leaves. How poignant that these delicate trees were lumbered to make bomb crates for Viet Nam.

We went on to Taos, where the shaman awaited. He would present the Indian view. A graduate of the University of Chicago, head of Indian Affairs with an office in that city, he had returned to his home in Taos. He would discuss the Pueblo view of the environment. He spoke very, very slowly. His silences were cut, but the spliced tape revealed erratic head movement, so his speech was deleted and he was made into an audience for me. He accepted this role. His reward was that the TV publicity on the sacred lake, then in Forest Service hands, caused it to be returned to the Taos Pueblo.

In Muir Woods I had to declaim against the Creation story in the first chapter of Genesis. My craggy face was to be photographed against the bark of a giant redwood, illuminated by a shaft of sunlight. My message was on a card taped under the camera lens. As I looked, I could see my own face, which undid me. We kept trying again and again, looking for illuminated trunks, trying for one good take.

> God made man in his own image,
> made he him; man was given
> dominion over every walking,
> flying, swimming creature; man
> was enjoined to multiply and
> subdue the earth.

The movie is now on videotape. I showed it to graduate students at Harvard during the spring of 1994. There I was, with a full head of brown hair, a bushy moustache, energetic, given to hyperbole and colorful language. Although almost thirty years old it remains remarkably topical. It seems that we have learned little.

Foundation had funded the writing of the book, it was entitled to the income, and, as I had clearly made money from the venture, he wanted the $20,000 back and the royalties. I kept the royalties, but returned the $20,000.

I suppose the only time I ever received an iota of attention from Doubleday was when I was nominated as a finalist for the National Book Award in Science. However, this matter caused me a good deal of embarrassment. Two authors whom I adulated, Loren Eiseley and René Dubos, had been on the short list but had succumbed. Alvin Tofler's *Future Shock, Design with Nature,* and *Science in the British Colonies* were the finalists. I was so embarrassed that I avoided meeting Eiseley, who was colleague and friend. I had also discontinued asking René Dubos to speak to my students for the same reason. Generous both, they congratulated me without rancor and we were reconciled.

I do not know the deliberation of the jury, but the secondhand report I received was that the "people" people supported Tofler, the "nature" people supported *Design with Nature,* but neither could obtain a majority. In the end, *Science in the British Colonies* (a posthumous work) was selected.

Design with Nature sells well to this day and has been described as the most widely used text for architects and landscape architects. I have observed no effects on the former.

The best encomium I have ever received for *Design with Nature* involved the daughter of a friend, Julius Fabos of the University of Massachusetts, who was in Melbourne as a visiting professor. His daughter attended school there. One day she returned for lunch. "Daddy, I was studying geography today and we were talking about one of your friends, Ian McHarg. We were studying *Design with Nature.*"

The book was very well reviewed; indeed, there were several hundred reviews, with only one bad criticism. I was accused of prostituting science. As a nonscientist I had thought that I had been meticulous in my treatment of scientists and their data. The ecological planning method that was developed was seized immediately and is practiced throughout the world. The theory I labored so hard to develop received too little mention, yet I still hope that it will receive attention. I believe that the underlying theory holds the promise for a vastly enlarged and improved planning method.

The book has been published in hardback and paperback, printed and reprinted, translated into French, Italian, and Japanese and printed in these languages, and translated into German and Spanish but not yet published. To my astonishment, while it is now more than a quarter of a century old, the work has not yet been superseded.

When the book was first written, there was no enabling legislation that required ecological understanding and planning. The book contributed to the efflorescence of environmental legislation, so that the method is probably more applicable now than when first written. Moreover, it has increasing relevance for countries only now confronting the crisis of the environment and the need for ecological planning.

My bibliography has grown to cover more than twenty pages. This is evidence of a productive writing career. Yet there is one entry that overwhelms all others— "Ian McHarg, *Design with Nature.*"

That book includes a relatively short experience in the United States, from 1954 to 1968, whereas my subsequent experience has been much longer, over twenty-five years. In this subsequent period have occurred many of my proudest accomplishments: Woodlands New Town, Pardisan, A Comprehensive Plan for Environmental Quality, and the Medford study, yet *Design with Nature* remains my single most powerful identification.

Chapter 7

The Environmental Decade

Some events are exhumed and can be reexamined. Searching for the World Cup Final in July 1994 in Tempe, Arizona, I switched channels, only to stop at a most familiar sight. Celebrating the moon walk along with Howard K. Smith, Bill Moyers, and Marshall McLuhan, there I was with a brown Van Dyck beard and a full head of hair, assuring the audience that the greatest benefit of the moon mission was to see that lonely orb, the earth, and accept the charge to cherish it.

By the 1970s I had become something of a public figure. Participation in the *Today* and *Tonight* shows, with Mike Douglas, and Dave Garroway, plus the impact

After the publication of *Design with Nature*, I became a frequent guest on television talk shows. With Mike Douglas on the set of *The Mike Douglas Show* (1969).

of my movie *Multiply and Subdue the Earth* on PBS had introduced me to a wide audience. My television series *The House We Live In* had twenty-four episodes and was distributed to all CBS affiliates before going to PBS. I was profiled in *Life, Time, The Wall Street Journal,* and *Smithsonian* and was included in an article in the *The New Yorker* by Anthony Bailey. Moreover, *Design with Nature* had been selected as a finalist for the National Book Award and was selling well.

I continued to give speeches around the country to large and enthusiastic audiences. The largest, of 30,000 people, was in Fairmount Park in Philadelphia on the original Earth Day, with George Wald, Senator Edmund Muskie, and Alan Ginsberg.

April, 1970: Earth Day

What an exciting time that was, the great and unexpected efflorescence in environmental sensibility. Of course, there had been precursors, many of them— George Perkins Marsh, John Muir, Frederick Law Olmsted, Charles Eliot, Gifford Pinchot, Fairfield Osborne, Benton MacKaye, Paul Sears—but it was not until a small lady with pale blue eyes in the Department of the Interior wrote *Silent Spring* as a series of articles in *The New Yorker* that the movement mobilized. After the publication of Rachel Carson's powerful work, suddenly interest in the topic of the environment was universal, but the number of speakers available was quite small. For decades the demand had been minuscule, and it had taken a considerable obsession to maintain enthusiasm through such a period of indifference. Paul Ehrlich, Barry Commoner, René Dubos, Ralph Nader, and I were the frontline troops and we crisscrossed the country giving lectures to enormous and excited audiences. Standing ovations were commonplace, the audience confirming their commitment to the cause with cheers and applause.

For me, the culmination of the movement was Earth Week, and within it, Earth Day. Philadelphia had by far the largest and most successful program. On the very day that Gaylord Nelson intimated his plan for Earth Day, the faculty and students of our department sent a telegram committing ourselves to participation. A committee was formed, headed by a young hydrologist and regional planner from Vanderbilt, Austan Librach. Soon an executive director was hired, a lawyer and city planner, Ed Furia. The king of Philadelphia hippies, Ira Einhorn, joined the group and played a major role. My task was to identify the speakers and invite them to participate. Ralph Nader, Senator Ed Muskie, George Wald, Frank Herbert of *Dune* fame, Paul Ehrlich, René Dubos, and Alan Ginsberg were all invited and accepted.

One of the largest original Earth Day, actually then Earth Week, celebrations was held
in Philadelphia. This was a counterculture event organized by hippies and students.
Neither hippie nor student, I was nevertheless quite involved.

   Left to right: Thatcher Longstreth, Earth Week Committee; Director Austan S. Librach,
Earth Week Committee; Executive Director Ed Furia; and I, announcing the first
Earth Day at the University of Pennsylvania Graduate School of Fine Arts Auditorium
(1970, photograph courtesy of Austan S. Librach).

All of the regional institutions participated. Penn, Temple, and Drexel; Villanova,
LaSalle, and St. Joseph's; Haverford, Bryn Mawr, and Swarthmore. A calendar of
events for the week was scheduled. On the day before Earth Day, a celebration was
organized in front of Independence Hall, where I read the Declaration of Interdependence, followed by an address by Ralph Nader.

   On the following day—clear sky, sunlit, warm but not oppressive—30,000
people converged on the Belmont Plateau in Fairmount Park. Men and women,
old and young, children and dogs arrayed themselves on the hillside facing a large
scaffolding stage with a gangplank to the lonely lectern and its bevy of micro-

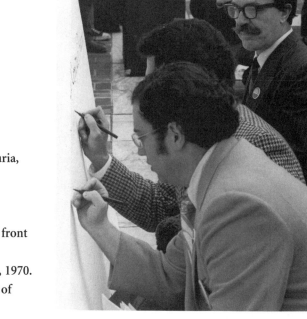

Austan Librach, Ed Furia,
and I, signing the
Declaration of
Interdependence at
Independence Mall in front
of the Liberty Bell,
Philadelphia, April 21, 1970.
(Photograph courtesy of
Austan S. Librach.)

phones. A band, Redbone, played. Television cameras were mounted, microphones
and speaker system were tested, and Wald, Muskie, Herbert, Ginsberg, and I assembled in a tent. The excitement was palpable. I began to address the crowd:

> Why must I be the person who brings the bad news?
> My propositions are simple.
> You have no assurance of a future.
> The views of man and nature which permeate the entire western culture are the reason.
> Our view of man and nature does not correspond to reality, has no survival value, indeed
>   it is the best guarantee of the extinction of man.
> Man is an epidemic, multiplying at a super-exponential rate destroying the environment
>   upon which he depends and threatening his own extinction.
> He treats the world as a storehouse existing for his delectation, he plunders, rapes, poisons
>   and kills this living system, the biosphere, in ignorance of its workings and its funda-
>   mental value.
> The survival of the human race is contingent upon categorical rejection of this cultural
>   inferiority complex that is the western view and its replacement with the ecological
>   view—man in nature. This reveals the ways of the working world and shows our igno-
>   rant interventions as self mutilation, leading to suicide, genocide, biocide.

Earth Day, Fairmount Park, Philadelphia, thirty thousand people, April 22, 1970. (Photograph courtesy of Austan S. Librach.)

I used the term "man" then. Today, I might use human instead. Even so, western *man* has been, and remains, the biggest culprit. *He* retains the most power to inflict damage to the environment. It is the whole human race who suffers.

At dusk, the first Earth Day was over. Those who had attended filled plastic bags with the debris of the day. They left no litter. The great exodus formed two chains, one on each side of the Schuylkill River. Columns of people carrying candles and singing made their way downstream to the Philadelphia Museum of Art and then diffused into the city.

Of course, there was a product from this great public manifestation. It took the form of federal legislation. There was no doubt that the greatest enemies to the American environment were government agencies. Among the first that should have been constrained was the Atomic Energy Commission, which, touting energy too cheap to meter, had elaborate plans for peppering the country with reactors, irradiating the population and the environment, ringing the Pacific and Atlantic coasts, the Gulf, the Great Lakes and the major river systems. Operation

Ploughshare was a plan to use atomic bombs for "peaceful" purposes: to dig new Panama Canals, blast huge new ports in Alaska, and to compress and release natural gas. The U. S. Army Corps of Engineers, architects of big dam foolishness and the destruction of environments, were advocates of the Florida Barge Canal, Tom Bigbee, and the draining of the Everglades, and were the grantors of permission to drain and fill wetlands. The Bureau of Reclamation was as culpable in the West, and there were other enemies, as well: a Forest Service fond of board feet but reluctant to practice multiple uses, a Bureau of Public Roads engaged in remorseless destruction of city neighborhoods and rural environments, the Department of Agriculture, shamelessly colluding with cattle and forest interests in the impoverishment of rangelands, through the mining of topsoil, and poisoning by fertilizer and pesticide. The National Environmental Policy Act addressed such public agencies. They were required to undertake environmental impact analyses and show the anticipated consequences of their proposals. The environmental impact analysis was my invention, and it alone caused many misbegotten projects to be aborted. This may have been the finest product of the act. EPA was created, as was the Council for Environmental Quality, the Clean Air Act, the Clean Water Act, the Surface Mining Control and Reclamation Act, the Coastal Zone Management Act, and more followed. These were the positive products of this passionate endeavor. We could say as Churchill did of the RAF pilots in the Battle of Britain. "Never . . . was so much owed by so many to so few." But who won the battle? Why, the flower children—dirty, unkempt, on drugs, promiscuous, unlikely moralists. And where were the dominant churches and synagogues, Christians and Jews—somewhere else?

An Evolving Faculty, An Evolving Practice

Bill Roberts and Tom Todd joined David Wallace and me and WMRT became the acronym for the firm that grew from Wallace-McHarg Associates. Its reputation had risen. It was perhaps the dominant office performing city planning, urban design, and landscape architecture during the 1970s. Earlier projects had come to fruition, Plan for the Valleys had been widely acclaimed, Baltimore's Inner Harbor had been substantially completed and was praised, the Plan for Lower Manhattan would breed Battery Park City, and the new town of Woodlands would become the first example of ecological planning for development. The plan for Pardisan would involve creating a new institution, incorporating not only botanical and zoological gardens, aquarium, and planetarium but also a Museum of Natural History and Academy of Natural Science. Through the university, the Medford study would be conducted—an ecological planning study to prepare appropriate ordinances. This model would be used later by WMRT in the Lake Austin and Sanibel studies.

The Penn Department of Landscape Architecture and Regional Planning was described in *Science* as having "national, perhaps international primacy." It was identified as perhaps the best example of inter- and multidisciplinary education in the United States. There was a surfeit of applications to the department. Many candidates had Ph.D.s, and even more had master's degrees before admission. We regulated the numbers: sixty landscape architects, sixty regional planners. We selected the student body to include all of the environmental sciences, physical, biological, and soils. We solicited architects, landscape architects, and, increasingly, persons with skill in computation. Standards were very high, as was enthusiasm.

We had accomplished the incorporation of physical and biological science into the instruction of design and planning. By the mid 1970s the social sciences of ethnography and anthropology were increasingly being integrated into human ecological planning, as in the Hazelton and Kennett Square studies, and this development held great promise for better informed prescriptions.

Of course, this explosion of environmental concerns reflected society at large. That most unlikely environmentalist, Richard Nixon, had given us the National Environmental Policy Act, the Environmental Protection Agency (EPA), and the Clean Air and Clean Water Acts. These were followed by legislation on coastal zone management, surface mining, and more.

Perhaps now is the time to discuss my colleagues in this effort. Ideas were developed at the university, wherein was the repository of knowledge in the sciences, and their application was accomplished by WMRT. Data generated by the office were more accurate, methods more precise. Hypotheses were tested and if successful, were immediately incorporated into teaching. Through this method, research and development continued. Every project, either in the department or at the office, was seen as a research investigation.

At WMRT, David Wallace, the founder, was the dominant and most distinguished of the partners. He had asked me to join him to supplement his own powerful skills. Older than me by two years, he held bachelor's and master's degrees in architecture from Penn, a doctorate from Harvard, was the first director of the Redevelopment Authority in Philadelphia, and later became executive director of the Greater Baltimore Committee. By the 1970s, Wallace was, indisputably, the dominant city planner in the United States. The success rate of his planning projects was legendary. However, he never received the praise he deserved, perhaps

The Lower Manhattan Plan

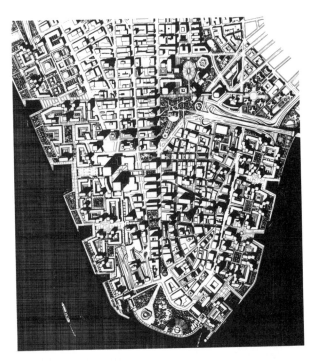

In 1966, Wallace, McHarg, Roberts and Todd completed the Lower Manhattan Plan for the City of New York. David Wallace was the partner-in-charge with Bill Roberts, Tom Todd, and me participating as consulting partners. The plan led to the creation of 110 more acres in lower Manhattan. The Hudson River portion of the plan was later realized in the Battery Park City redevelopment, but the East River portion was not. (Photograph from Wallace, McHarg, Roberts and Todd, 1966, "The Lower Manhattan Plan.")

Conceptual drawing of Lower Manhattan Plan by Tom Todd. (Photograph from Wallace, McHarg, Roberts and Todd, 1966, "The Lower Manhattan Plan.")

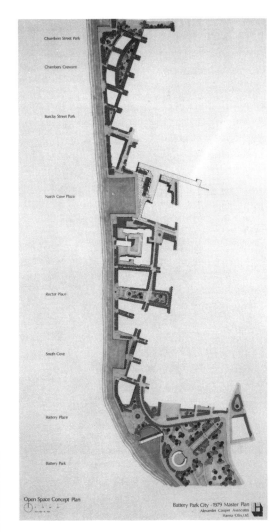

Chambers Street Park

Chambers Crescent

Barclay Street Park

North Cove Plaza

Rector Place

South Cove

Battery Place

Battery Park

Open Space Concept Plan

Battery Park City · 1979 Master Plan
Alexander Cooper Associates
Hanna/Olin, Ltd.

The Lower Manhattan Plan had a great influence on subsequent planning and design undertakings, such as the redevelopment of Battery Park City, designed by Cooper Eckstut Associates (formerly Alexander Cooper Associates), Hanna-Olin, Ltd., and other firms. (1979 Master Plan for Battery Park City; courtesy of Hanna-Olin, Ltd.)

In the early days of Wallace-McHarg, we were invited to prepare a plan for Lower Manhattan. The City Planning Commission was the formal client; the actual client and donor was David Rockefeller and the Lower Manhattan Businessmen's Association. They were appalled. The piers at the waterfront were derelict, warehouses had been abandoned, and light industry had fled along with the Fulton Fish Market. There appeared to be two surviving institutions: Pace University and the New York Stock Exchange. This was not a fit setting for the world's financial center. Either it would be improved or they would leave.

New York wrote the conditions of the contract, and they were severe. We must establish an office in New York; travel, living costs, and telephone calls between Philadelphia and New York were disallowed. We must submit work in increments; following approval we would be paid.

Wallace and I were then professors. We had little capital. The necessity of establishing a New York office posed considerable risk. Our ability to pay salaries was conditional upon the city's prompt payment for services. We did indeed perform promptly and well, and the work was highly regarded by the Planning Commission and David Rockefeller, but no payment appeared. Calls to the comptroller elicited sympathy but were not productive. Yes, we had completed the work; yes, we were entitled to payments; but the bureaucracy in New York was slow and cumbersome. We must wait. We were in peril, several months had elapsed without payment. One morning Wallace received a call from the comptroller. He was very sorry about the inconvenience caused by delays in payment, but there was a remedy. He would mail to us a list of New York lawyers who were familiar with the system. Any one of them could *fix it*. They would probably cost about thirty thousand dollars. *Fix* did not register. Wallace noted that the city had written the contract, we had performed as required, and the city was obliged to make payment. Why was a lawyer required? We lost a lot of money.

My contribution to the plan has been realized, but not quite as intended. I concluded that a strategy that introduced massive amenity to the Hudson waterfront and made it accessible

might induce landward improvements. I therefore proposed that the city fill from bulkhead (the land) to the pier-head line (the limit of development in the water). The city would charge to permit disposition of demolition and other materials, create a park with a marina, and sell a portion of the land for development. And so it did, with such little control that foundation conditions varied from marble to grapefruit rinds, and too greedily, for the park shrank to an esplanade. However, Battery Park City emerged, and the Hudson waterfront was made accessible.

Battery Park City Esplanade, looking north. (Photograph by Felice Frankel, courtesy of Hanna-Olin, Ltd.)

General Wheeler U.S.E.

On one occasion in 1969, the president of the University of Pennsylvania received a letter from the chief of the Army Engineers, General Wheeler, insisting that I make a public apology for remarks made, deemed excessively critical to the Corps. These remarks, published in a Philadelphia newspaper, were, I thought, rather mild. I had merely suggested that two groups in the Corps were working at cross purposes and would do well to talk to each other. One group, responsible for channel widening, deepening and dredging of the Delaware River, was disposing dredged material into marshes and wetlands, destroying flood storage, diminishing the river's width, and thereby thwarting the objectives of that other contingent of the Corps responsible for flood control.

The request was transmitted to me, without comment, by President Meyerson on a most propitious day. I was able to reply.

Dear General Wheeler,
How nice to hear from you again.
I understand that you insist that I make a public apology for some recent remarks. I fear, sir, that your request for an apology has been addressed to the wrong person. I observed in the newspaper today that Russell Train, administrator of the Environment Protection Agency, stated that the Army Corps of Engineers has not yet, to date, prosecuted a single person under the provisions of the Refusal Disposal Act of 1899. This leads Mr. Train, the American people, and me to conclude that the pollution to the oceans bordering this nation, the Great Lakes, and all navigable rivers and harbors is entirely due to the negligence of the Corps. I believe this to be a shameful indictment. Could you possibly disagree? What is the remedy? Well, in another military society the remedy is hara-kiri, ceremonial disembowelment. In our society we cannot insist on this, but you and your colleagues might give it serious consideration.

in part because of the declining reputation of city planning. A more likely reason was the escalating concern with the environment and my reputation for ecological planning. This recognition elevated me, and I began to receive the bulk of public attention and approbation. This was very unkind to Wallace who was full-time partner, while I was a full-time teacher and part-time partner. My person and projects were receiving the bulk of public attention and applause.

Much of the work identified with David Wallace, the Inner Harbor and Lower Manhattan, was done in partnership with Thomas Todd, a skilled architect and urban designer. William H. Roberts, a Penn graduate and chairman for the department during my 1968 sabbatical, performed a complementary role to mine. As noted, I spent only one day a week in the office during the academic year and worked there full-time during holidays. My method of ecological planning devolved responsibility to participants by subject, thus Robert Giegengack studied geology, Arthur Johnson soils, Jim Thorne ecology, Dan Rose ethnography, and other scientists addressed their own subjects.

Through this method I designed the study, developed the budget, and identified the personnel. My remaining tasks were to review the data and interpretations, participate in the planning process, and present the study to the client. As I did little, save contribute to the final report, my role was not very time-consuming. I could direct several projects simultaneously, employing only one day per week. Of course, this could not have worked without the day-to-day supervision that William Roberts provided. He became a very skilled and effective ecological planner. In particular, he was effectively the leader for the Sanibel project. The method was drawn from the Medford study, but Victor Yannacone and Arthur Palmer, who provided the legal expertise for Medford, were replaced by attorneys Fred Bosselman and Charles Siemon.

The Amelia Island study employed the ecologist Jack McCormick, who identified and selected the team of natural scientists and a brilliant group it was. The method used was my ecological planning method, but the application was accomplished by William Roberts. My limited role included the first reconnaissance and the final presentation. As for the study of Wye Island in the Chesapeake, I made no contribution whatsoever; it redounds entirely to William Robert's credit.

In addition to the contributions of the partners, were those of a marvelous procession of employees. Without exception Penn graduates, landscape architects and regional planners, they contributed to the evolution of the natural sciences and their interpretation. These people are identified here without hierarchy. Their positions in the listing are random, with one exception. Narendra Juneja, from the Delhi School of Architecture, revealed his brilliance as a student in a brilliant class, became one of the first and best employees of Wallace-McHarg Associates, a graduate, an associate professor, my good right hand. We developed a deep affection and marvelously complementary roles. Narendra knew what I could do, what I could not, and what he could do or cause to be done. It was a most gratifying relationship, which terminated when he died in 1981, never to be replaced.

Michael G. Clarke and Jonathan Sutton performed roles as job captains for many projects. Michael had a bachelor's in forestry from Michigan, a master's in conservation (really ecology), and had served with the Army Corps of Engineers. He was in charge of a wide array of projects, conspicuously the 208 planning study for Colorado, the Skippack Watershed, Lake Austin, and Dover and Wilmington, Vermont. Jonathan was a Penn architect. His major contributions were with me on the Woodlands project and with William Roberts on Amelia Island and Sanibel.

The Federal Territory and its National and Regional Context

The National Context

Location of the new federal territory of Nigeria and its national and regional context. (International Planning Associates, 1978, "A New Federal Capital for Nigeria, Report No. 2, Site Evaluation and Site Selection.")

The 1978 plan for Abuja illustrates the interdisciplinary nature of Wallace, McHarg, Roberts and Todd during the 1970s, showing how an extensive, careful site analysis can contribute to thoughtful design. Wallace, McHarg, Roberts and Todd were part of an international consortium of firms that planned and designed the new capital of Nigeria, Abuja. Thomas Todd was the partner-in-charge, and I coordinated the ecological analysis for the site selection and planning.

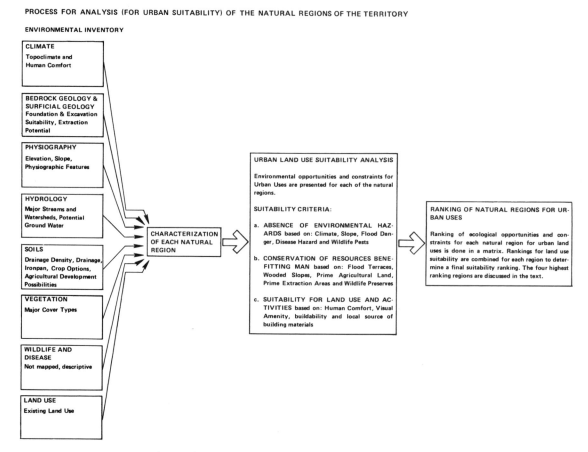

Process for analysis for urban suitability of the natural regions of the new federal territory of Nigeria. (International Planning Associates, 1978, "A New Federal Capital for
Nigeria, Report No. 2, Site Evaluation and Site Selection.")

Carol Franklin and Leslie Sauer brought their gifts of perception and passion to a wide variety of projects. In the Woodlands project it was they who analyzed soils, depth to fragipan, and demonstrated the basis for vegetational distribution. They also contributed to the development of the coverage and clearance ratios.

E. Bruce MacDougall and Lew Hopkins developed the computerized route
selection study for the Wilmington Outer Beltway. This was a successful demonstration of the proposition that any planning solution is determined by the value

system of the problem solvers. Three senior highway engineers of the Delaware Department of Transportation demonstrated three distinct alignments, thereby reflecting individual and explicit values attributed to the many descriptors of the environment.

Richard Nalbandian held a master's in geology from MIT. He was resident geologist-hydrologist for many projects. In particular, it was he who calculated the natural water budget for the Woodlands project and participated in the design for the new town urban hydrology, which worked with incandescent success.

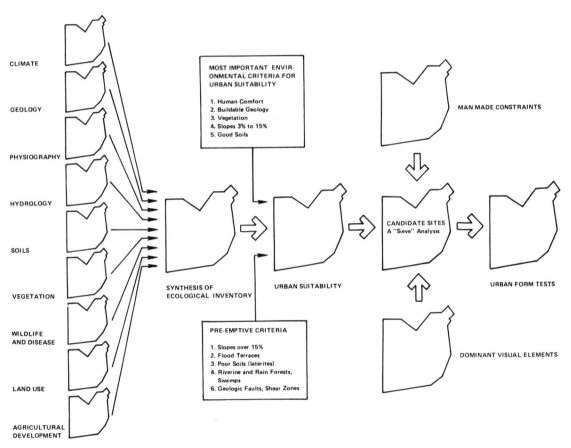

Diagram of the process of site selection for the new federal territory of Nigeria. (International Planning Associates, 1978, "A New Federal Capital for Nigeria, Report No. 2, Site Evaluation and Site Selection.")

Site of the proposed parliament buildings in Abuja. Wallace, McHarg, Roberts and Todd were part of an international consortium responsible for Abuja. (International Planning Associates, 1978, "The Master Plan of Abuja, The New Federal Capital of Nigeria.")

View of the proposed parliament buildings from the central area of Abuja, drawn by Thomas Todd in 1978. Wallace, McHarg, Roberts and Todd were part of an international consortium responsible for Abuja. (International Planning Associates, 1978, "The Master Plan of Abuja, The New Federal Capital of Nigeria.")

Rhavindra Bhan, an Indian architect from Delhi, was right hand to Narendra Juneja, and this team assumed total responsibility for graphics, symbols, colors, and reproductions.

WMRT was a prolific publisher; there were dozens of studies published in addition to annual promotional reports. The agent who designed dummies and undertook graphic selection and reproduction was Jane Laughlin.

This catalogue of participants would be profoundly inaccurate if it failed to include Lenore Sagan, long-time administrative assistant to the Department of Landscape Architecture and Regional Planning at Pennsylvania and surrogate mother to the student body. She learned the names of students and spouses, found them living accommodations, jobs, and employment after graduation. Thereafter she monitored their children, promotions, careers, and changes of address. The number she shepherded is large, well over a thousand students. No other person has had such a deep emotional involvement with past graduates and knowledge of current students.

The period from 1969 to 1974 was another tempestuous quinquennium. The department, released from strictures as to size, increased to 120 graduate students—half landscape architects, half regional planners. The faculty included twenty-four persons spanning physical, biological, and social science, architecture, landscape architecture, city and regional planning. An equivalent of fourteen faculty members were budgeted to the department. Earlier plans had come to fruition. Here, at last, was the requisite range of environmental scientists.

The notion of an instant faculty, however, had not been realized. Members joined the ranks as individuals. Nick Muhlenberg, a resource economist, was an established faculty member in 1963. Jack McCormack, ecologist and part-time faculty member, came in 1964. Robert Giegengack, originally appointed to geology, was shared beginning in 1966, and in the same year Archie Reid became the first full-time plant ecologist in the department. The hydrologist nominee accepted the position, but a Fulbright grant required him to leave the country. So we lost Thomas Dunne, now a world famous hydrologist. In 1968 the soils scientist, Ronald Hananalt, arrived, and two years later systems ecologist Arthur Sullivan and E. Bruce MacDougall, geographer and computer scientist, assumed their roles. In that year, William Lowry, biometeorologist, came as a visiting professor with a view to assuming a permanent position, but personal problems intervened and he departed.

With these accessions, the natural science faculty was in place. Yet almost immediately there ensued the experiment in anthropology whereby the National Institutes of Mental Health made a grant of a half million dollars to expand ecology into human ecology and to institute a curriculum in health planning. This initiated another intense faculty search for an ethologist, ethnographer, cultural anthropologist, and epidemiologist. Under the leadership of Yehudi Cohen of Rutgers, a succession of anthropologists proceeded to investigate and develop human ecological planning. David and Vera Mae Frederickson, in the spring of 1972; Cohen, in the fall of that year; and in 1973, Martin Silverman of Princeton,

Loren Eiseley:
When God Became Natural

The anthropologists and archaeologists at Penn were an unusually gifted group. Loren Eiseley, Irving Hallowell, Anthony Wallace, Young, Dyson, and Carleton Coon—I came to know them all, but I found a particular delight in Loren Eiseley. He was quiet, large, round, serious and thoughtful, an insomniac. He had revealed enormous perception and poetry in his *The Immense Journey*. He had also revealed an astonishing childhood. His father, a failed farmer in rural Nebraska, was an itinerant Shakespearean actor. He had begotten a son by a first marriage and had later remarried. His second wife, Loren's mother, was deaf. She made barbarous and incomprehensible noises. As his father was regularly absent, Eiseley grew up lacking conversation with people and, thus, talking to birds and insects. This family was so remote and so idiosyncratic that not even the minister visited them. He was rescued by the teacher at his one-room school, who perceived an unusually gifted boy, directed him to a

good school and thence to the University of Chicago.

In 1962 he gave the Dewey Lecture, which was subsequently published with the title *Mind as Nature*. I lunched with him at least once or twice each year. One of these meetings followed the publication of *Mind as Nature*. I was moved by the book, not least by the dedication to the schoolteacher who had recognized and nurtured him. She was alive, well, and present at the Dewey Lecture.

We talked about his book, the thesis of mind as natural, and I exclaimed, "Loren, surely you see the inevitable title of the sequel." "What is that?" "Why, 'When God Became Natural.' "

The Quakers say, "There is that of God in every man." Better to say, There is that of God in everything. Natural is billionsfold greater than conventional ideas of the supernatural. God is natural. No one could have written it better than Eiseley.

Final landscape architecture jury at the University of Pennsylvania, May, 1976. *From the left:* Laurie Olin, Colin Franklin, me, Rolf Sauer.

Jury at the University of Pennsylvania, 1979. *From the front:* me, Bob Hanna, Nick Muhlenberg.

With a student at Penn jury in 1979.

At my office in the Department of Landscape Architecture and Regional Planning, University of Pennsylvania, circa 1979.

(Photograph at upper left courtesy of Deborah W. Dalton; others by Becky Young.)

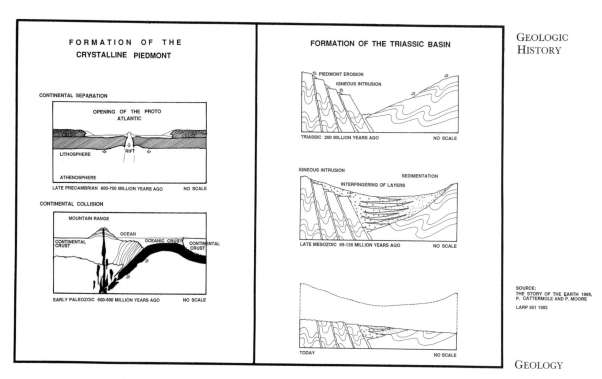

SOURCE:
THE STORY OF THE EARTH 1985,
P. CATTERMOLE AND P. MOORE
LARP 501 1992

GEOLOGY

Geologic History, from the fall 1993 LARP 501 studio. (1993, Kim Douglas, Ken Keltai, Lisa Miles, Jeanne Thompson, and Rob Staudt, Department of Landscape Architecture and Regional Planning, University of Pennsylvania.) In the 1960s, I initiated an ecological inventory and analysis course for landscape architecture and regional planning, called LARP 501. The interdisciplinary studio was offered each fall at Penn. During the 1970s, Jon Berger took responsibility for coordinating the course with a team of scientists and designers. Art Johnson, Nick Muhlenberg, Ruth Patrick, and Robert Giegengack, among others, contributed to the scientific content of the studio. Dan Rose, an ethnographer, and Setha Low, an anthropologist, significantly strengthened the human ecology component, and Jorge Sanchez-Flores, then John Radke, and later, Dana Tomlin added geographic information systems to the course. After Jon Berger left Penn, Frederick Steiner coordinated LARP 501 for a year; then I assumed leadership again.

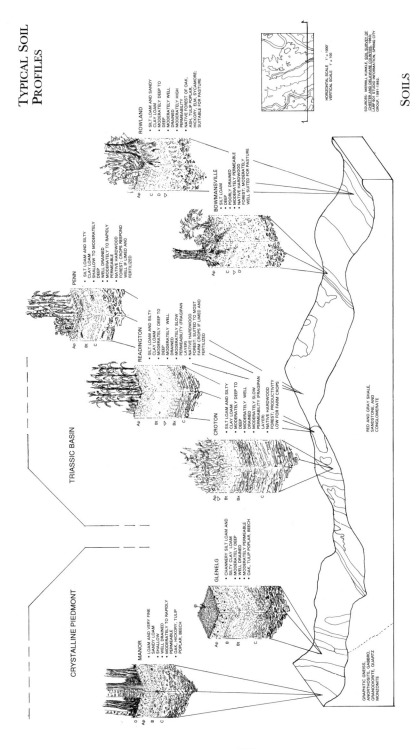

TYPICAL SOIL
PROFILES

SOILS

HORIZONTAL SCALE 1" = 1000'
VERTICAL SCALE 1" = 100'

SOURCES: MERRIL KUNKLE, SOIL SURVEY OF CHESTER AND DELAWARE COUNTIES, 1963; LARP 501 STUDIO INFORMATION, SPRING CITY GROUP, 1991-1992.

Typical Soil Profiles, from the fall 1993 LARP 501 studio. (1993, Kim Douglas, Ken Keltai, Lisa Miles, Jeanne Thompson, and Rob Staudt, Department of Landscape Architecture and Regional Planning, University of Pennsylvania.)

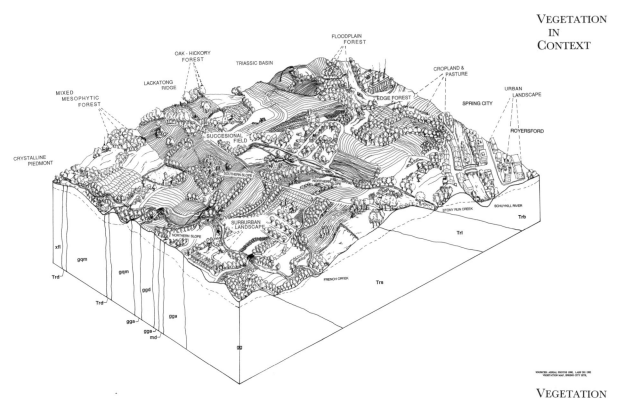

VEGETATION

Vegetation in Context, from the fall 1993 LARP 501 studio. (1993, Kim Douglas, Ken Keltai, Lisa Miles, Jeanne Thompson, and Rob Staudt, Department of Landscape Architecture and Regional Planning, University of Pennsylvania.)

focused on application to landscape architecture and Jay Ruby addressed regional planning. Anthropologist Frank Vivelo followed, succeeded in 1974 by the permanent faculty member, the ethnographer Dan Rose. One year later, Setha Low, medical anthropologist, completed the quest.

Within a decade the department had been transformed to include a wide range of natural scientists and a compatible group of social scientists, united with landscape architects and regional planners to create a theory of human ecology and employ it to enhance human health and well-being.

Design had always been seen as central to the curriculum in landscape archi-

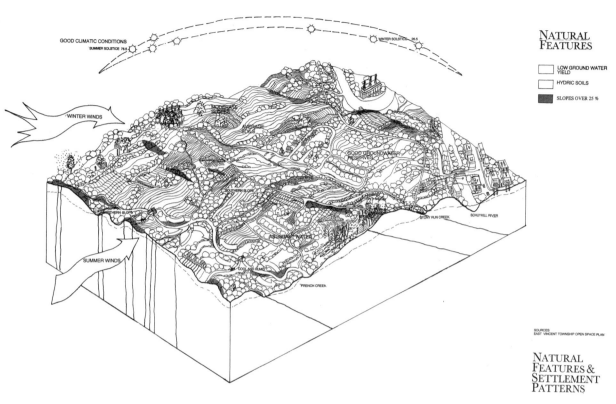

NATURAL
FEATURES

LOW GROUND WATER
YIELD

HYDRIC SOILS

SLOPES OVER 25 %

SOURCES
EAST VINCENT TOWNSHIP OPEN SPACE PLAN

NATURAL
FEATURES &
SETTLEMENT
PATTERNS

Natural Features and Settlement Patterns, from the fall 1993 LARP 501 studio. (1993, Kim Douglas, Ken Keltai, Lisa Miles, Jeanne Thompson, and Rob Staudt, Department of Landscape Architecture and Regional Planning, University of Pennsylvania.)

tecture. Indeed, over the years the instructors constituted leadership in the design profession. In the 1970s and 1980s, Sir Peter Shepheard, Robert Hanna, Laurie Olin, Carol Franklin, Jon Coe, A. J. Walmsley, A. E. Bye (an annual visitor), and I constituted a design faculty beyond compare. Penn had not only a unique group of physical, biological and social scientists, but an exceptional design team as well. The personnel were at hand to accomplish the revolution in human ecological planning. Ecological design achieved less success, although what success did occur was the product of Carol Franklin and Leslie Sauer of Andropogon, and Jon Coe of Coe, Lee, Robinson, Roesch.

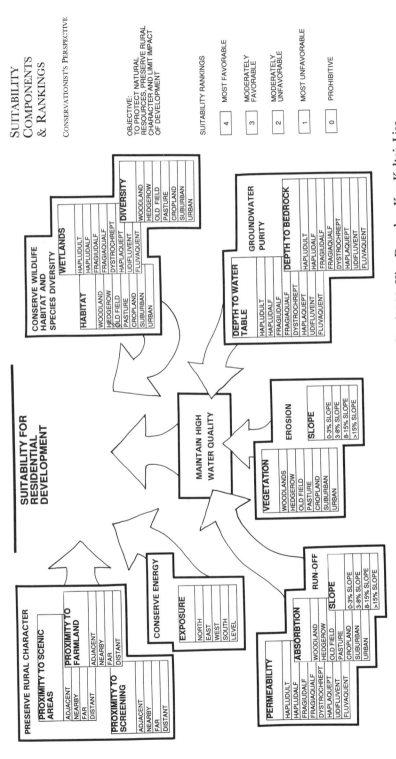

Suitability Components and Rankings, from the fall 1993 LARP 501 studio. (1993, Kim Douglas, Ken Keltai, Lisa Miles, Jeanne Thompson, and Rob Staudt, Department of Landscape Architecture and Regional Planning, University of Pennsylvania.)

Women in Landscape Architecture at Penn

During my reign as chairman of landscape architecture and regional planning, the proportion of women increased in both the student body and the faculty. Ruth Patrick, the queen of American limnology, was an adjunct professor for decades. Her courses on physical limnology and aquatic biology and a summer field course were taken by the brightest students. She was a powerful role model for young women. Carol Franklin and Leslie Sauer, principals of Andropogon, taught the "Plants and Design" course for decades. It became the central instruction in ecological design. They were powerful lecturers, articulate, intelligent, persuasive. If only they could have been cloned. Setha Low, medical anthropologist, taught courses in behavior, planning, and design and participated in studio projects with Laurie Olin, Bob Hanna, and Jon Coe. She led the introduction of methods from anthropology into landscape architecture. Her summer field work in Costa Rica informed her students of variable attitudes, expectations, and uses of space by different cultures. Anne Spirn, a Penn graduate who taught at Harvard and wrote the wonderful *The Granite Garden,* assumed the Penn chair in 1985. She in turn hired Katherine Gleason, a Cornell landscape architect and Ph.D. in archaeology from Oxford. For many years Sally Anderson, a Ph.D. in geology from Pennsylvania, gave a superb module in geology for entering students; she also contributed to the summer course in field ecology.

So with Ruth Patrick, Carol Franklin, Leslie Sauer, Setha Low, and Sally Anderson, the faculty had reached gender parity in all but studio design. There were, unfortunately, no female equivalents in the design studios at Penn to Peter Shepheard, Bob Hanna, Laurie Olin, A. E. Bye, or Jon Coe. However, the process is under way. Elsewhere, Penn alumna and graduates of other schools—Linda Jewell, Cora Olgay, Sue Weiler, Beth Meyer, and Justina Boughton—offer this promise.

Over twenty years, the female landscape architecture faculty at Penn rose from zero to near parity, and the same process could be seen in the student body. In 1954, my first year at Penn, there were two female students, Joan Taylor and Ty Learn. For the past two decades the students have been more or less equal in gender. I can recall when the change occurred.

During the first decade, the number of young women was limited to one or two per class. It was a "man's work" world, according to the bias of the time. Most Ivy League schools other than Penn enrolled only men, and most architectural schools had a quota for women architects. Penn's architecture program, however, was totally exclusionary. Indeed, the mother of a provost of Penn, Thomas Ehrlich, fulfilled the requirements for an architectural degree but was awarded a degree in fine arts instead. It was not until the 1980s that she was awarded the degree in architecture that she had long ago earned and deserved.

The tactic of soliciting architects into our Master of Landscape Architecture (M.L.A.) program proved very successful. These students quickly acquired a reputation for skillful design. But, with the introduction of science, notably ecology, it became clear that an architectural student body was inappropriate for a curriculum based in the environmental sciences. So a new three-year M.L.A. program was introduced for persons lacking a first professional degree. These B.A. and B.S. candidates were highly intelligent, lacked any antipathy to science, and brought new insights to bear. The three-year program attracted a wider audience, and, I realized immediately, it contained a significant proportion of young women. I came to appreciate that here was a pool of high intelligence and passion, which could make a serious contribution to the profession. I therefore changed my tactics and began to give serious attention to women as a major source of recruits among the B.A. and B.S. candidates.

I well remember the event in 1960 that changed recruitment at Pennsylvania and, indeed, had a profound and beneficial effect upon the profession and its education.

The occasion was the faculty meeting to consider applications, approve admissions, and award scholarships. For the latter, applications were arrayed in rank according to transcripts, letters, and portfolios. The documents available did not permit selection based on either race or gender. I alone knew these factors. I participated in the selection—number one, two, three, four, five. I was astonished; I could restrain

myself no longer. "Gentlemen," I said, "when are we going to select the first male?"

This was the threshold. The proportion of young women rose from being scant and uneven to the situation today, maintained now for several decades, wherein half of the students are female.

Not only has equality of the sexes in the profession resulted, but the same equality has come to be reflected in education and leadership. Debbie Dalton was dean at North Carolina State, and now is dean at the University of Oklahoma (in fact, she is the first female dean in the university's history); Angela di Parodi was dean at Maracaibo, Venezuela; Anne Spirn, Linda Jewell, Lois Brink, and Monica Kuo are or have been department chairs; Carol Franklin, Leslie Sauer, Jestina Boughton, Anu Mathur, Lyda Caldas di Borrero, Barbara Morehouse, and at least twenty other Penn alumna are all professors. Neither the profession nor professional education is any longer an exclusively male domain. Clearly, Pennsylvania has made a major contribution to this important development.

B. Y. Morrison Award 1971

In 1971 I received a notification from the United States Department of Agriculture that I had been awarded the B. Y. Morrison Medal. I had never heard of it, but I was very much impressed by the previous recipients, who included René Dubos. The presentation would take place in Portland, Oregon. I was asked to give an address that would subsequently be published. The audience would be the annual meeting of a wildlife and range management group. I accepted. However, the selected date caused a serious problem. I had to fit this in with a meeting in Harrisburg with the governor, a trip to New York for meetings with UN, Ford Foundation, and FAO officials, and a conference on the urban environment in Buffalo. So my itinerary would have to include traveling to Oregon from Philadelphia and returning the same day. It was possible. It involved a flight from Philadelphia to Chicago, change of planes in Chicago for the flight to Portland, where a helicopter would await to fly me to the roof of the hotel, the site of the speech. It looked perfectly feasible, however, an unexpected factor caused complications. An unseasonable storm blanketed the United States with torrential rains and high winds. We set off from Philadelphia, whereupon the pilot announced that strong headwinds would delay our arrival in Chicago. Sure enough, our plane and others arrived late and departures were thus delayed. Yet it still seemed possible to reach Portland, give my speech, and return. But the headwinds persisted, and the projected time of arrival extended threateningly. The cluster of Mount Hood and its companions is not reassuring during a descent through thick fog, buffeted by high winds, but we landed in a drenched Portland. My hosts loaded me aboard a waiting helicopter, which rose aloft immediately. I looked around and quickly discerned the towers of the city. They were receding. I shouted over the engine noise, "Aren't we going downtown?" "Yes." "But we are not." "This machine has a forward speed of 100 knots and we have a 120-knot wind." We were going backward. Then we began to tack, seeking shelter from the wind at low altitudes, and made progress. We landed on the roof, descended in the elevator, and entered the auditorium with an audience of perhaps two thousand waiting. My watch disclosed that I had forty minutes before I must leave. My speech had been prepared and rehearsed. It ran for an hour. The walk to the auditorium, introduction, and adjusting the lavolier microphone took ten minutes. I now had thirty minutes to give a speech. My prepared speech focused on the interest of the audience. It was quiet and, for me, thoughtful, unlike the polemic that was my contribution to the environmental movement at that time. I could not possibly edit that speech to thirty minutes, I had to retreat to familiar themes. And so I did. It is a matter of record that I used ten thousand words in thirty minutes. Almost all of it was an excoriation of the Department of Defense, of this and other countries, General Overkill, Dr. Strangelove, the putrescences engaged in chemical and biological warfare, captains of industry who poisoned our environment, and so on.

The speech was well received, and I made my way out of the auditorium during a standing ovation—but not to the roof. The helicopter pilot had decided that if he took the 'copter up it might be difficult to bring it down before we were over the Rockies. So we drove to the airport where a twin-engine charter awaited. We flew to a rendezvous in Seattle with a United flight from Honolulu. Would they hold the United flight? They would, but only for so long. Yet, long enough; the plane landed on a taxi strip and drove right under the wing of the big jet. An attendant met me with a striped umbrella, and I climbed aboard. So I was able to travel to New York, go to the Ford Foundation, where I learned that an award of $500,000 had been given to my department, fulfilled my schedule, and returned home.

U. S. Steel

In 1970 I received a very angry letter from the president of United States Steel, taking exception to some remarks made about the carelessness of American industry to the environment. The letter asserted that U.S. Steel was central to the American economy and was indeed sensitive to the environment. Moreover, the writer proposed to send a vice-president with films that would convince me of the error of my allegations. I replied:

Dear Sir,

Thank you for your kind offer, but it is unnecessary. I have a very effective personal monitoring system for the environmental effects of our most conspicuous steelmakers. When I fly north from Philadelphia, I peer through my window and observe a plume of rust-red smoke and a rust-red river, I know I am above Trenton and Fairless Steel. When I fly west from Philadelphia and note a rust-red plume in the air and telltale ruddy water, I can identify Pittsburgh Steel. When I fly south from Philadelphia and there again are these rust red trademarks, I know I am above Sparrows Point, Baltimore. So, sir, keep your vice-president and movies at home. When I can no longer infallibly identify my location from your industrial excrement, I will so inform you. Sincerely.

Some months later I began to receive a large number of requests for copies of my speech. Among them, one letter had an enclosure, a notice the Government Printing Office would not distribute copies of "Man, Planetary Disease" by Ian McHarg. I asked my administrative assistant, Lenore Sagan, if she had seen copies of the speech. Yes, indeed; she produced a package of reprints. I examined one. It had very pretty drawings of wildflowers in the margins, and there was the speech, more or less as given. I learned later that Senator Proxmire had quoted from the paper and asked rhetorically why the government should publish such an excoriation of itself. Why, indeed? It was censored. Ms. Sagan concluded that copies were collectors' items. She sold them for a fair price and paid for office coffee for years from the proceeds.

But that was not the end of it. In the spring, censored or not, I received a consignment of hybrid azalea plants. It transpired that B. Y. Morrison had been a noted horticulturalist, and the plants had come from the U. S. Department of Agriculture, sponsor of the award.

Children and Youth, 1971

Also in 1971, President Nixon convened a White House Conference on Children and Youth. To my astonishment, I received an invitation to participate. This was surprising. I had never been able to say a kind word about Nixon and had frequently made public remarks that were very uncomplimentary. And, of course, he had censored my publication, "Man, Planetary Disease."

However, I accepted. My serious reservations about the president were exceeded only by self-doubt. What contribution could I possibly make to the problems of children and youth? My experiences with young people were personal, limited, and not professional. The most obvious concerns clearly were drugs and alcohol, homicide and unemployment, but, to my surprise, the quality of the environment young people would inherit was deemed to be an important issue.

The first meeting was held at the Irvine Ranch in Southern California. Helicopters flew participants from John Wayne Airport to Irvine, where, without cars, we were effectively prisoners. Security was strict and it was extremely difficult to leave. But this was not too painful, as there were many fascinating and lively participants.

The committee to which I was allocated was concerned with the environment. The chairman was Russell Train, head of the Council of Environment Quality, later to succeed Ruckelshaus as administrator of the EPA. The members were admirable, thoughtful, and constructive. However, each committee had a government "observer." Ours was the porcine and baleful John Ehrlichman, who growled and objected when any adverse comments were made about either government or industry. I had previously made a comment, published in *Life* and *Time*, that American industry should be toilet trained. Thus, my observations were generally rejected by Ehrlichman, but not only mine, so after some hours Train told him sternly, "Shut up, you are an observer, not a participant."

On the final day of the conference there was a plenary session, at which each chairman was to report the results of the committee's deliberation. It was announced that the president would attend. Sure enough, as we delegates milled about outside the auditorium, a large helicopter appeared above us. At the same time, converging on the ball field where the helicopter would land was a ragged procession bearing placards for black power, Indian power, and human power, peace signs, and various obscene comments about, and instructions to, our president.

The helicopter vacillated above. Many of the delegates joined the column of demonstrators. There was a quick decision, the hovering observers concluded that this would not be a friendly reception. The helicopter, bearing the president, left.

This event affected the choice of the site for the second session. It would be held at a YMCA camp in Estes Park, Colorado, an isolated area with only one entry. It could be easily guarded. There would be no demonstrations at Estes Park.

Still, there was a visitation. Delegates converged from American Samoa, Hawaii, Puerto Rico, the U. S. Virgin Islands, Alaska, and throughout the United States.

Only the Alaskans were properly equipped, for—in full summer—there was a massive snowstorm. It was so severe that delegates could not walk from their huts to the meeting rooms. Soon there were air supply planes overhead; food, drink, parkas, and military cold weather clothing fell from the sky. You took your life in your hands being outdoors, but muumuu-clad Hawaiians, along with the rest of us, donned army overcoats and all were warmly clad.

As the event began, we learned that the environment committee had been augmented by Rogers Morton, secretary of the interior. Ehrlichman had gone; now Morton, the administrative spokesman, was a participant. Housed in a small cabin, we began the day with enough firewood, coffee, and cigarettes. Morton now filled the role of Ehrlichman, rejecting any criticisms of industry or government. The rest of the committee found itself constrained by his negative comments: he was a very large man and he was secretary of the interior.

The day wore on, it was very cold. The firewood ran out, then the coffee. Irritation began to show. Later still, the last cigarettes were gone. There was a sense that the meeting should conclude. I addressed Rogers Morton. "Mr. Secretary," I said, "You can be of great help to me. I have spent my mature life finding and selecting brilliant students from all over the world and designing years of instruction in order to make them competent landscape architects and regional planners. But, look at you, one moment innocent of the environment, bagman for the Republican party, and now, here you are, the custodian of the national environment, the country's leading environmentalist. If only I would transform my students into environmentalists as easily and quickly as you did." He towered over me, a full head taller; he had a mind to grab me, thought better of it, turned on his heel, and left.

Confrontation: Addressing the Fortune 500

One day in 1972 I received a telephone call from an editor of *Fortune* magazine. He informed me that a forthcoming issue would be devoted to the environment. Now in 1972 this was an important innovation. Up to that point, the environment had been resolutely avoided by *Fortune* historically. I congratulated the editor and American industry on their belated discovery. He continued: *Fortune* planned an address on the environment, to be given to representatives of the Fortune 500, to coincide with its issue concerning the environment. Would I address this meeting?

It would follow dinner at the Four Seasons Restaurant in New York City, and he mentioned an impressive honorarium. I accepted. As a Presbyterian I was aware that the guilty need to be censured and offered salvation. I was delighted at the prospect of censuring these dominant figures in American industry and welcomed the opportunity to prescribe the ecological view as a passport to salvation.

I had given the lecture many times. It had been published as the B. Y. Morrison Award lecture by the U.S. Department of Agriculture as "Man, Planetary Disease." However, I never had such an appropriate audience as was provided by *Fortune*. All of the giants were represented and, of course, those corporations that operated nuclear establishments were prominent. Du Pont ran the Savanna River Plant, Westinghouse was in charge of Hanford. Monsanto, Rockwell, and Martin Marietta, not to mention the University of California at Berkeley, which ran Los Alamos and Livermore, were also represented.

The speech began by invoking an image conceived by Loren Eiseley long before man had penetrated space. He imagined a first lonely astronaut, viewing the earth from space, a tiny orb about the size of a dime, sunwashed, alone in an infinite black surround silently rotating, blue-green with verdure and maritime algae, accompanied by a halo of atmosphere—a green, celestial fruit; the earth, our home. As the astronaut returns, he discerns lesions on the earth's life body—wounds, suppuration, welts, necrotic tissue. He perceives that these are the works of man and asks, "Is man but a planetary disease?" Indeed, he thinks, this may be too kind. There is an epidemic afoot, multiplying at superexponential speed, destroying the environment upon which he, with all life, depends.

I recalled my horror at first hearing this story. I looked about me at friends, faculty, students; were they pathogens, agents of disease, epidemics? Surely not, but there were institutions and men whose fulfillment threatened the survival of humans and all life. None were more dangerous than the nuclear warriors, General Overkill and his kin, irrespective of race, color, or creed, who sought continuously to rob national treasuries to expand that obscene lethal capability. Enabled to kill every man, woman, and child many times over, they were not content. They must amass ever greater arsenals. General Overkill and his scientific minions, the Dr. Strangeloves, were indisputable evidence of man, planetary disease; man, epidemic.

I recommended that these nuclear warriors should be considered subhuman, pathogens, ambulant pus. Their children should not kiss them, their wives should not admit them to bed, their ministers, priests, and rabbis should not administer final rites. Upon their death there should be no sorrow, merely dignified exaltation.

Of course, there were many other excoriatables, evidence of planetary disease, but, these, pillaging the world's resources, inducing the massive pollution of rivers, oceans, and atmosphere, imperiling the survival of an infinity of creatures, were not comparable to the nuclear warriors. They were not pus but, rather, people covered in scabs—in a word, scabrous. Among these were the captains of industry who comprised the audience. "Gentlemen," I began (there were no ladies),

> Gentlemen, I have observed you at the reception and during dinner. I have seen you handle hors d'oeuvre, drinks, knives, forks, spoons, napkins, even finger bowls. I feel certain that before coming to this event most had a shower, changed clothes, dabbed the underarms with a deodorant, applied a touch of cologne. In sum, your personal hygiene meets impeccable standards. May I make a bargain with you on behalf of the American people and the American environment? I believe that they would permit a reasonable reduction in your personal hygiene, say, forswear the second shirt, underpants, and handkerchief. I believe that you might be permitted to burp in public, even fart, without causing any serious damage to the environment. However, as compensation for the relaxation of your impeccable standards of personal hygiene, we might ask that in exchange you make a massive improvement in your standards of corporate hygiene. You must cease and desist from voiding millions, perhaps billions, of tons and gallons of excrement into the environment. Gentlemen, you are incontinent. There are two explanations: the first is senescence, the second infantilism. If you are senescent we can only await your demise impatiently. If you are infantile, can we assist you to dispose of your corporate wastes in ways less destructive to the environment?
>
> Gentlemen, the time has come for American industry to be toilet trained.

There was a long silence.

I imagine that it was at this point that the editor concluded that my address would not be published. Nor was it. The words were too strong. American industry expected approbation; it had no taste for criticism.

Yet, this was the appropriate audience for my sermon. While there are megadevils, there are also more widespread agents culpable for the destruction of the environment. Among the scabrous is an identifiable component—the automobile, facilitated by the internal combustion engine and the petroleum industry. This was the overwhelming source of pollutants and the cause of the prodigal exhaustion of nonrenewable resources. The audience included representatives from Detroit and the major oil companies. I continued:

> Gentlemen, I would like to make a bargain with you on behalf of the American public and the American environment.

Members of the audience stiffened. After all, the first bargain had not been warmly received.

> What America needs from you is modest, nonpolluting locomotion. However, you provide locomotion that is distinguished by the massive pollution it provides for very limited transportation. Indeed, your only success is the amount of pollution

produced for any unit of transportation. The explanation for this may be found in
your advertisements. In every case, a lightly clad nymph will induce us to buy new
cars with the implication that one such nymph will grab you from behind the wheel,
throw you under the nearest bush, and ravish you to an ecstasy beyond understanding. Your failure in providing adequate transportation and reducing pollution is
explained by your assumption that you are selling, not cars and locomotion, but
aphrodisiacs.

   If this claim were true, the price would not be too high, but in the absence of
any effective demonstration as producers of aphrodisiacs, why don't you address the
problems of providing nonpolluting and economical transportation? Better, please
address the objective of diminishing the threats to the environment produced by
transportation and industry.

Now this was a group distinguished by arrogance, incompetence, and stupidity. You think my accusation is extreme, but consider. During my stay at Harvard I
studied economics from such luminaries as Schumpeter, John Black, John Kenneth
Galbraith, and Seymour Harris. We considered the elegant confluence of factors—
coal, iron, limestone, water, labor force, transportation costs and market, which
explained the dominance of Detroit. Had I then asserted to any of the economists
that the Japanese would purchase American scrap, transport it to Japan, make
superior and cheaper automobiles, then transport these to the United States and
undercut American cars, I would have been called an idiot. Yet this is what happened. The largest and most successful automobile manufacturers in the world
allowed Japan to undersell them, to produce cheaper, better cars with better mileage
and less pollution.

   The oil and chemical industries did not fare much better. The disasters at
Bhopal, Times Beach, Love Canal, and the *Exxon Valdez* added to the explosion in
carbon dioxide, sulfur dioxide, and nitrous oxide contamination, plus the prolifer-
ation of herbicides, fungicides, pesticides, organophosphates, chlorine bond, and
more. Had the nuclear cataclysm occurred, and nuclear winter ensued, there is no
doubt that this would have been the greatest calamity in human history. God be
praised, it has not happened. However, the environmental consequences of the
petroleum, automobile, and oil industries have contributed to world warming,
increased climatic violence, desiccation, inundation, pollution, toxins, and ozone
attenuation. Planetary diseases, indeed. So, I continued:

Perhaps the most widespread evil is the Western view of man and nature. Among us,
it is widely believed that man is apart from nature, superior to it; indeed, evolution
is a process to create man and seat him on the apex of the cosmic pinnacle. He views
the earth as a treasury that he can plunder at will. And, indeed, the behavior of
Western people, notably since the advent of the Industrial Revolution, gives incon-
trovertible evidence to support this assertion.

Surprisingly, at least to me, was the discovery as a young man that the most succinct expression of this view reposes in the Creation story from Genesis.

"God made man in his own image, made he him. God gave man dominion over all life, over every walking, swimming, flying thing hath man dominion. God said, 'Multiply and Subdue the Earth.'"

This Judaic text was absorbed virtually unchanged into Christianity. The major differences were the Christian introduction of otherworldliness, absent in Judaism. Life on earth was thought to be a probation for the life hereafter, which diminishes the import of human actions on earth. The other Christian contributions were chastity and monasticism, which operated similarly. Life on earth was only the stage for a moral play. Success led to paradise. The earth was without enduring significance.

It was clear that the Judaic-Christian theme elevated people to a shared divinity. Nature was seen as the enemy of Jehovah—pagan, carnal, savage, an inducement to sin. The golden calf symbolized the declaration of war between Jehovah and nature: "Ye shall make no graven images." These were nature gods. There is one God, and that God is Jehovah. Banish pagan nature forever.

The objective was the subjugation of nature. The caprices of nature, bringing flood, drought, pestilence, disease, and death were deemed to be unendurable, their effects were to be terminated. Let us bring nature to her knees, let us terminate these calamitous events. Indeed, let us subdue nature, bring her to heel.

It required technology to achieve this end. Lewis Mumford insisted that the aim of the Western quest for technology was to rule nature. Of course, the organ that distinguished humans from things and other creatures was that huge, convoluted cerebellum, the human brain. It was this above all that justified man's insistence upon supremacy. It was brains that would lead man to bring nature to submission. No more earthquakes, volcanos, tsunamis, hurricanes, epidemics. Would disease and death be banished too? It is an unbearable conceit that people would believe that these great planetary processes are initiated to harm them, to give pain. Surely it is better to understand these natural processes, and act accordingly.

I have invented a parable to illustrate the paradox of brain. Let us assume that the brain has totally failed. The great nuclear power antagonists are engaged in a squabble. One of the warriors determines to resolve the matter conclusively. A white-coated, lily-livered warrior, deep in some bunker, presses buttons. Silos open and myriads of rockets, myriads of missiles, arch through space. Immediately, the recipient responds. The world trembles from the gigantic explosions. Mushroom clouds cover the sky, all is smoke and dust, gradually settling. In this postatomic calm it transpires that all life has been extinguished, except that within a deep leaden slit, long inured to high-level radiation, persist a small colony of algae. These single-celled, photosynthesizing creatures, almost as old as life, perceive that all creatures save themselves have been eliminated. The world is a graveyard. They are the single hope for the recovery of life. It may take all of three billion years of incorporation, mutation, and natural selection to recover yesterday.

When this awful prospect is finally understood, the algae come to a spontaneous, unanimous conclusion, "Next time, no brains."

Should there have been such a postmortem, some questions could have been asked. Is the human brain the apex of biological evolution? Or, in contrast, is it akin to a spinal tumor? Had the event occurred, there is no doubt about the conclusion. How much better is the evidence for the tumour hypothesis. It has not happened. Nonetheless, we must recognize that people are on trial, the human brain is on trial.

Certain insects have examined this subject before. There are antecedents to the cockroach and the social insects—bees, wasps, ants, and termites. The behavior of the social insects is genetically determined. There is no free will among termites. Cockroaches do exhibit independent behavior. Which way should we go? A frontal lobotomy would bring man into the genetic behavior category of the social insects. Is there another way? Can brain and man show how to live in and of nature, not as a parasite or a pathogen, but as a creature fulfilling a symbiotic role, akin to an enzyme?

Let us hope and pray that this is so.

So now I had delivered the indictment. Man, the planetary disease, global epidemic. Western views toward humankind and nature are a great illusion, a cosmic inferiority complex. The heart of the heresy derives from our most holy scripture. And finally, brain, the proudest emblem of human evolution, may be akin to a tumour.

This was the pattern of the Presbyterian sermons of my youth. Sin, guilt, punishment, hell, and damnation. But finally, there is forgiveness. There is absolution if you repent.

Wherein lies salvation?

At this point, I lit a cigarette. There was a gasp. Consider what damage I was inflicting on my lungs. How delicate for those people who shared with Edward Teller the confident assertions made to President Reagan. "Mr. President, the United States can survive a nuclear war with Russia. Less than half of the American population will be killed." He did not mention that the survivors might well envy the victims.

I observed that their solicitude for my lungs was very touching, but I would prefer their solicitude for the earth and the human species.

But now was the time to open the door to salvation.

I told the Martin Marietta story. In the early 1960s the great Philadelphia architect Louis I. Kahn and I were commissioned by Martin Marietta in Baltimore. Our role was to find an appropriate location for RIAS, their research arm, and to design this facility. Lou and I met at the Baltimore and Ohio station in Philadelphia and entrained for Baltimore. The dining car attendants welcomed us aboard, served coffee immediately, and then a leisurely breakfast. Soon thereafter Lou became stimulated by the coffee and began a two-hour, charismatic lecture.

We were met by the Martin Marietta realtors who engaged us in the search for sites. Our preference was for a peninsula overlooking Chesapeake Bay. During this search I came to meet an employee of the company whose research objective was to design a system to support an astronaut to and from the moon. He was one of that crew of German rocket scientists who had been offered positions with NASA to lead America to salvation in space.

This man had made a plywood simulation of a rocket, on the top of which was the capsule designed to support the astronaut. At that time it was believed that the journey might be quite long and would require a recirculating system. It was this which he had designed.

The capsule could accommodate one astronaut. In the lid was an electric light, simulating the sun. As electricity is only fossilized sunlight, this idea was not too remote. A helical aquarium lined the walls of the capsule, containing algae (he who laughs last) and decomposers. The system worked as follows. The sunlight falls upon the algae, which use carbon dioxide, water, air, and light to fix carbon, and then expel oxygen. The astronaut breathes air, consumes oxygen and exhales carbon dioxide, which the algae absorb. Thus there is a closed cycle of oxygen and carbon dioxide. The astronaut drinks, then pees into the aquarium; water condenses on the outside and is collected by the astronaut—a closed cycle of water. The astronaut hungers, he collects some algae and eats. In due time he defecates into the medium wherein live the decomposers that reduce the wastes into nutrients employed by the algae, which grow, and which the astronaut eats. Here is a closed cycle of food. There is one input—light; one export—heat. Oxygen, carbon dioxide, water, food, wastes, and nutrients go round and round.

I looked at this experiment in awe. This was a simple caricature, but all of the essential actors were here. This is the way the world works, as I told the Fortune 500 audience.

Of course, the experiment failed. It was too simple to survive. The lesson in nature is redundancy. Should one species fail, be assured that another will fill the role. But the capsule experiment failed to simulate the richness and the redundancy of natural systems. In nature the species comprising ecosystems have survived all of the exigencies their ancestors have encountered. They contain all of the adaptive strategies to deal with all circumstances previously experienced. There is a lesson to be learned here. We live with a myriad of cotenants of this phenomenal earth who have come to learn how to regulate physical and biological processes in ways that are beneficial to life. It should be chastening to learn that the earth was aflower before the advent of man. The biota today are participants in self-regulating processes which seem to be benign. Nature is a remarkable system; it has no explicit laws, no police, no prisons, no hierarchy nor authority, yet there is interdependence, cooperation, symbiosis, perhaps even altruism. It is unbelievable that man cannot find a cooperative role, but to do so we must learn how the world works, diminish the damage of man's intervention, learn self-regulation, seek to become an enzyme in the biosphere, and help to maintain evolving ecosystems. This was the period of the two-by-four approach, recommended for the training of mules: a blow to the testicles gets their attention. This I quite clearly did. I did not make friends, but I did influence people.

Some days after the Fortune 500 event I began to receive outraged letters.

Resolution: The Ecological Model

The purpose of the lecture to the Fortune 500 was to strike terror in the hearts of our villains of the environment. For too long they had been profoundly oblivious of the subject, having derogated it to an externality. The hubris of industry and economics relegated all of philosophy, natural science, religion and, not least, the environment itself, to an irrelevance. However, by the 1970s, times were changing. There had emerged a substantial and vociferous environmental lobby, mostly young and thoroughly irreverent. Our corporate and governmental leadership, having long ignored this constituency, was to receive a massive shock. My role was to contribute to this reluctant transformation, and I did, with relish. The comment, "The time has come for American industry to be toilet trained" received much attention and approbation.

However, the excoriation was only the introduction to my sermon. I myself needed to find the path of salvation. I had earlier concluded that in ecology lay the answer, but I needed a stronger theoretical formulation. When it was developed, it was clearly unsuitable for audiences like the Fortune 500. It required university audiences, preferably with knowledge of biology and interested in the environment. It was to these audiences that I addressed the conclusions of the "Man, Planetary Disease" lecture, entitled "An Ecological Model."

Entropy is the center of the second law of thermodynamics. In short, it states that all energy is destined for disorder. Whatever its original state, it will ultimately be zero degrees Kelvin, random in a random cosmos. There is also a contrary theory. The English physicist Stephen Hawking speculates that "perhaps deep in black holes, energy is constantly renewed." We need not take sides on this issue, although it would be more symmetrical if matter behaved as does life.

It is certainly true that all energy is destined for entropy. In every energetic transaction there is an increase in entropy. However, this is not the only consequence. While entropy will increase in all transactions, in some of these, matter and energy will increase the level of order. A favorite example of physicists is the conditions of the early cosmos which, it is thought, was composed of only hydrogen and helium. A galactic event, it is hypothesized, involved an explosion wherein matter was raised in order so that at the end of the event, while there was a massive increase in entropy, all of the elements, in addition to hydrogen and helium, were present: lithium, beryllium, boron, carbon, nitrogen, and oxygen to complete the periodic table. So there could be two products of energetic transactions; one was certainly an increase in entropy, and the other was characterized by the creation of new elements. Once described as neg-entropy, this condition has a better title, invented by Buckminster Fuller: syntropy. Thus the evolution of matter is a syntropic act, creative.

If we consider the evolution of life, it is immediately clear that life employs energy. Life is a process, but living is also machinelike. In the processes of living and evolution, energy is employed; entropy results, but that is not the only consequence. Organisms adapt, and we see the procession of algae, fungi, lichens, liverworts, mosses, club mosses, ferns, gymnosperms, and angiosperms. In this evolutionary process the creatures incorporated sunlight with carbon dioxide and water into their beings. Most energy left as heat, but the residuum was the increasing amount of information embodied in the genetic accomplishment of plant evolution. Thus the evolution of plants was also a creative process. Clearly this is as true for animals. So evolution contributed to entropy, but the energy employed was transformed into the genetic characteristics and roles of plants and animals. These represent the syntropic product of the evolution of matter and life. In sum, evolution has been and is a creative process.

We think of creativity as being an attribute of poets, painters, and playwrights, but it appears to be an attribute of matter and life, certainly of evolution. The next step in this model formulation was to discover a criterion with which to measure the degree wherein processes, physical and biological, are either syntropic or entropic.

The criterion was first advanced by Charles Darwin and later by Lawrence J. Henderson. Darwin laid the foundations with his assertion, "The surviving organism is fit for the environment." This statement has avoided contradiction for more than a century. Furthermore, it was augmented. At the turn of the century, Henderson published *The Fitness of the Environment*, in which he states, among many other important things, that while Darwin is correct, his statement is insufficient. Given the infinitude of environments and organisms and the necessity of accommodation to both, Henderson recommended that there is a necessity for all organisms to find the fittest available environment, and adapt it and the self to accomplish a better fitting. A fit environment was described as one which, as is, provides the largest needs of any system or organism. Thus, successful adaptation requires the least work by an organism in comparison with any and all competitors.

Such fitting is a least-work, maximum success solution. In any environment, therefore, there will be one organism whose needs are best supplied by that environment and where the necessary work of adaptation will be less than for any competitor.

Presumably, this quest for fitness applies to cells, tissues, organs, organisms, ecosystems and, of course, all types of human institutions. It appears that this criterion of fitness includes a thermodynamic challenge. If success is a least-work solution, then successful fitting is creative. We can now discern the presence or absence of syntropic fitting, and its antithesis, entropic misfit. This, then, is the measure of survival and successful evolution.

Is there a further criterion by which we can appraise whether cells, organisms, and institutions either have or have not accomplished syntropic fitting? Some part of the answer lies on Darwin's assertion. Survival is the first criterion; extinction measures failure. Can we use this criterion but vary it to accommodate different time scales?

If we apply the question to algae, the time scale would be two or more billion years. Yes, algae are successful. The question applied to fish and reptiles would require a shorter time scale, and yield the same answer. In every epoch some species disappeared, but life continued unabated. Birds, amphibia, and mammals are successes of shorter periods. Simians are comparatively young; australopithecus and humans are only a million or so years old. These newcomers are recent successes. As we move the time scale to include the living, the criterion should change. The question, are you healthy? remains the same, only the time scale has changed. So perhaps we can employ this concept of health and disease as the criterion for syntropic-fitness-health, or its antithesis, entropic misfit, disease and death.

There are three definitions of health. The first, routinely employed by doctors, is the absence of disease. This gives no attribute to the presence of health, only to its absence represented by disease. G. Scott Williamson, the great English biologist and creator of the Peckham Health Center in London in the forties, insisted that health was a positive state, not merely the absence of disease. His health center facilities were free to families who would submit to examinations. These persuaded Williamson that certain individuals and families seemed inordinately healthy, and more immune to disease than their neighbors. He found these states to be localized not only in individuals, but in families and groups. He defined this concept of health as the ability to seek and solve problems. It was subsequently augmented, I believe, by J. Ralph Audy of the World Health Organization, who suggested that health was revealed by the ability to recover from insult or assault.

These are complementary depictions, and very compatible with syntropic-fitness-health. Is health, then, successful adaptation as measured by syntropic fitness? Is it evidenced by the ability of organisms to find the fittest available environment, adapt it, and adapt themselves to accomplish a syntropic fitness? I suggest that it is. We can then review systems at the levels of cells, tissues, organs, organisms, and species and conclude whether they are healthy or not. This syntropic criterion would assure us of their creative process with health and the prospect of survival and success.

Now it is clear that adaptation is the subject, that fitting is the crucial activity, and that successful fitting requires selection of the most propitious available environment and subsequent modification, both of the environment and the self. This activity, when accomplished satisfactorily, is creative, and its reward is the presence of health.

The human equivalent to adaptation is ecological planning. That is, the environment is disassembled in response to its fragmentation by science. Each of the constituent factors in each layer can be interpreted as either propitious, neutral, or detrimental for a specific use or user. The locations where all or most of the propitious factors exist, and where none or few detrimental ones are present, is deemed to be the most fit environments. That is, the location containing most of the desirable factors, and none of those to be avoided, constitutes the selected region. It requires less work of adaptation than any other available.

But there is more to adaptation than selecting the most advantageous location or ecosystem. It will be necessary to adapt that environment to make it more fitting, if for no other reason than that it will change, as will the user.

Certainly, adaptation of the organism to better fit the environment is basic. Improved movement, running, swimming, flight, burrowing, jumping, all provide examples that continue today. I once saw a kingbird diving into a small pond to catch minnows. She seldom caught any; she was thoroughly inexpert as compared with a kingfisher. I saw her teach her brood to fish. This was an important adaptation. Presumably, kingbirds have alternate food sources. Next comes adapting the environment, which ranges from building nests, burrows, and beaver dams, to improving soil tilth, aeration, and water-holding air passages, culminating in the most accomplished adaptation of the environment, represented by coral reefs. The Great Barrier Reef is perhaps the largest, a geographical phenomenon, made by these minute plant/animals transforming sterile environments into the richest and most beautiful known on earth. Theirs is an exemplary case of successful adaptation, a challenge to humankind.

For people, the kind of mutation and natural selection occurring in nature at large continues. One of the most dramatic examples is the physiology of Japanese women. Japan's historical ideal of feminine beauty has long been visible in Japanese artworks and theater. However, the women in the audience with whom I shared a theater performance in Tokyo in 1993 looked totally different from the characters on stage. These women resembled European and American women much more than traditional Japanese.

However, we reserve selective breeding for sweet peas, corn, cattle, horses, and pigs. The selection and creation of hybrids plays an important role in agronomy. Recombinant DNA promises to augment this role in fundamental ways, as it is faster than hybridizing and breeding. Few young people seeking spouses investigate the genetic properties of spouses-to-be. The only group devoted to such scrutiny were members of royal families, who were not successful in breeding for beauty, handsomeness, courage, or intelligence. Hemophilia seems to be the most conspicuous accomplishment of selective royal breeding in Europe.

So the conscious manipulation of physiological mutation and the editing of natural selection has not been widely employed in modern society. Some selection is accomplished by youths sharing environments, important public schools and colleges, neighborhoods, clubs, and affiliations, but this is different from the royal selection patterns. And these more random selections can encourage diversity, especially if groups are not excluded because of race. Diversity is afterall a positive attribute of any healthy ecosystem.

Behavioral adaptation is the next available mechanism. Here innate behavior is considered, a major element often controlling breeding and occupation of territory. Subject to trial and error, selected by natural editing, innate behavior is a crucial mode of adaptation. Undoubtedly, much human behavior is involuntary—heart rate, inhaling and exhaling, hunger and thirst (and the responses, eating and drinking), the sex urge, the need for relief and defecation, and more. Of course, many of these processes are affected by medicines, but I do not think that conscious manipulation of innate behavior is considered to be an appropriate instrument for improved adaptation.

The final instrument is cultural adaptation, including voluntary modification of behavior. This method is the most plastic of all; it can change rapidly and, indeed, has changed, through the communications media alone. Conversation, letters, telegraph, telephone, radio, television, satellites, and computers are all dramatic examples of human adaptation and profound ability to change. Cultural evolution includes language, religion, philosophy, science, literature, art, incorporating the knowledge and value systems of societies. It is this instrument that gives humankind the greatest power to shape the environment, not only for ourselves but for all creatures and systems.

The works of humankind have traditionally not been respectful to the environment; indeed, Western man has been an archdestroyer. Can we use the conception of syntropic fitness, revealed in health, as a model, the search and accomplishment of fitting and fitness as an objective, the promise of health as a measure of success?

If so, can we return to Darwin and Henderson and recapitulate the challenge? Find the fittest available environment, adapt it and the self to make it more fitting? What human activity most closely corresponds to this admonition? Surely, planning and design—the search for fit environments. Planning and design seek to better adapt environments, challenge us to discover new institutions, and provide the human prostheses for successful adaptation.

Sanctification: The Conversion of General Overkill

In speeches, I have for years excoriated General Overkill and Dr. Strangelove as the embodiments of the anthropocentrism I so deeply loathed. The assumption that humankind is the apex of the cosmos and the pinnacle of evolution, and the belief that the earth is a structure that people are licensed to plunder, were among the heretical views that made Western man the greatest threat to life and people of all historical time.

So it seemed that these anthropocentric ideas should be abandoned and a more fitting view replace them. Of course, the ecological view promised the salvation I sought. But could General Overkill and his minion, Strangelove, be converted to the ecological view? If these two extreme figures could be converted, it would be reasonable to expect that lesser demons would be convertible too.

So I imagined a method of conversion. I entitled it "The Greatest Fireworks Show on Earth." It would be held approximately on the Fourth of July at Cape Canaveral. We would assemble all of the archdestroyers, the General and his cronies, those who insisted on robbing national treasuries to increase their obscene lethal capability—the greatest threat to life and humankind. Then we would bring in Strangelove and his colleagues, all the lesser Philistines, captains of industry responsible for Times Beach, Love Canal, Bhopal, and the Exxon oil spill, to join the group, as well as the operators of nuclear plants at Hanford, Savannah River, Brookhaven, Rocky Flats, and other such installations.

When these emblems of man, planetary disease, have been assembled, the first order of business is to weigh each one. For they are going off into space, each in a capsule on a Saturn rocket. The capsule will be fueled by sunlight and will contain a biomass of algae and bacteria equivalent to each astronaut. So weighed, each, with his allocation of algae and microorganisms, is installed. To the sound of military bands playing the national anthem, the president announces, "Let us celebrate our independence and interdependence." He then presses a button, and the rocket blasts off, the capsules diverging into space.

After the deafening roar of the rocket engine subsides, a careful listen may detect an audible sigh of relief. For all of the earth's animals, plants, and microorganisms are responding to the departure of man, planetary epidemic.They are safe from depredation, the enemy is far in space, disarmed, effectively emasculated.

In my fantasy, my interest in the scenario was to convert these archdestroyers, but my attention was mainly directed to General Overkill. I could hear him talk to his companions.

"Algae, microorganisms, you know that I am divine; you are not. It says so in the Bible: God made man in his own image, made he him." The algae turned its chloroplasts to the sun, the decomposers addressed the detritus. They were mute. The General had lots of time. He therefore addressed this matter of the selective allocation of divinity. Now, he was enclosed in a recirculating system. All of the elements moved from member to member. Time passed, and at some point there was a good chance that all the matter that had made up the General at the onset of the voyage was now algae and bacteria. Conversely, all that had been algae and bacteria was now recognizably General Overkill. The General considered this matter. It would appear that if divinity applied to only one member, this distinction would hold true for only an instant of time. Thereafter the distinction between people, algae, and bacteria would change. Could divinity be determined only by a clock and calendar? The General concluded, "Now hear this: Aboard this spacecraft, divinity is pervasive. If there is divinity, all are divine."

I nodded. The General spoke again, he was considering the license contained in Genesis. Having disposed of the insistence of divinity as exclusively human, he was prepared to address dominion. Dominion, clearly, is the exercise of power by one who possesses it over a subject who does not. Dominion is the sergeant major's approach—"Do it or I will punch your teeth down your throat." The General considered this assertion. It was not useful in the capsule. Any dominion, any mutilation of the creatures on which he depended would have a consequence for him. Now, generals cannot shrink nor are generals necessarily masochistic. So General Overkill announced his conclusion: "Aboard this spacecraft, there will be no dominion. We are totally mutually interdependent, and our relationship must reflect this realization. The algae and bacteria are closer to me than mother or wife. An appropriate relationship is as symbiotic cotenants of the earth."

Once more I nodded. The General addressed the last pillar of the Genesis story: "Ye shall multiply and subdue the earth."

Multiply, of course, is appropriate; it is central to biology. Yet there should be some control of numbers. Elsewhere I have written that numbers should be limited to those who can be cherished. But *subdue*, implying subjugation, is another story. It means putting every man, woman, and child to the sword, burning homes and villages, and enslaving captives. If dominion is a punch in the mouth, subjugation is a knife between the ribs, aimed at the heart and turned. Subjugation is the insect under the heel, scrunched. Subjugation is nonnegotiable—terminal.

It did not take long to consider the consequences of subjugation in the capsule. Death to algae or bacteria would be death to the General. He had no wish for death. If life he sought, there could be no subjugation.

"Now hear this," came the announcement. "Aboard this spacecraft there will be no subjugation."

It does not take much wit to see that if this parable was understood by the General, it should be understood by his archdestroyer colleagues as well, silently experiencing conversion in lonely space. If true for them, surely it is as true for the rest of us. Aboard spaceship *Earth*, if there is divinity, it is pervasive. The biophenomenal world is probably the nearest manifestation of God that we are likely to experience. Here, there should be no dominion; there should absolutely be no subjugation. That is appropriate only for suicide, genocide, biocide, Armageddon.

There was a long silence; then I spoke to the General. "After your lengthy deliberation, have you come to a new understanding of the world?"

The General paused, then replied, praying:

> Sun, shine that we may live.
> Earth, our home.
> Oceans, ancient home.
> Matter, of this is the cosmos, sun, earth, life, and man made.
> Atmosphere, protect and sustain us.
> Clouds, oceans, rain, rivers, and streams, replenish us,
> erstwhile sea creatures.
> Plants, live, breathe, and grow that we may
> live, breathe, and eat.
> Animals, kin and ancestors,
> Decomposers, reconstitute the wastes of life
> and the dead that we may endure.
>
> Amen.

"General, we are going to bring you home," I said. "You have displayed an understanding of the way the world works. You have learned reverence. There is reason to believe that you will be deferential, perhaps reverential to nature henceforth. Come back to earth. You are free to exercise your creative will to maintain the biosphere, its creatures, the health and welfare of humankind, to participate with us in the dream for fulfillment.

Welcome, home, General."

Would that we could achieve such a conversion globally.

Edinburgh—A Proposal Exhumed 1970

In 1970 I was invited to give the annual discourse to the Royal Institute of British Architects (RIBA) in London on May 12. This placed me in the highly elevated company of Louis Kahn, Le Courbusier, and Frank Lloyd Wright. I accepted. Hardly had the invitation settled when I received a letter from the vice-chancellor of Edinburgh University. "Dear Professor McHarg, I note that you will give the RIBA Discourse in London. Could you be persuaded to come to Edinburgh and give a talk here, where once you taught? We can pay your train fare and offer you a modest honorarium."

"Where once you taught," indeed. I was an assistant planning officer (temporary) in the Department of Health for Scotland from 1950–1954. "Temporary" was the stigma of having had tuberculosis. Such people could not become permanent civil servants.

During my first year I had been asked to give twelve lectures on landscape architecture to architectural students at Edinburgh. For this I would receive my tram fare and five guineas (maybe fifteen dollars), not for a lecture, but for the series. I gave twelve lectures for three years at Edinburgh and for two years in Glasgow. The effort netted me thirty-five pounds, say $185, and a number of marvelous graduate students.

The RIBA Discourse was the reason for my trip to Britain. It went well enough, but it was not the main event. When I contemplated my audience in Edinburgh, I confronted an enormous throng, and my whole life lay before me. My brother, sisters, school friends, soldiers I had fought with, fellow officers, patients who had suffered with me in the Southfield Colony for Consumptives, students I had trained at Pennsylvania were all present. I sensed their question, "Why did you leave us, what do you have to say for yourself?"

I well remember why I had left. I had received an ultimatum. My wife, Pauline had suffered the poverty of an annual salary of six hundred pounds and a basement apartment, but it was the weather that had finally overwhelmed her. She said one morning, "Ian, I have something to say to you. It will be very painful; think before you reply. Scotland is uninhabitable and I cannot live here any longer." I thought, yes, the woman has reason, and I have reason, too, the unwillingness of the Department of Health to undertake imaginative planning. I sat down immediately and wrote a letter to G. Holmes Perkins, my chairman at Harvard, then dean at the University of Pennsylvania. In short, I asked, did he know of any opportunities in the United States? He replied all but instantly, "Come to Pennsylvania, teach planning and set up a department of landscape architecture. We can offer you $5,000 for a nine-month appointment." That explained the departure. But how could I be exonerated? While a lecturer, I was asked to prepare a memorandum on the subject of establishing a department of landscape architecture in Edinburgh. I had undertaken a modest survey. There were bountiful resources, including Frank Fraser Darling, one of the greatest ecologists in the world; a great biologist with a strong interest in the environment, C. E. M. Waddington; the geographer Arthur Geddes, son of Sir Patrick, the founder of modern planning; and a renowned Department of Geology with many botanists at the Royal Botanic Garden and soil scientists at the Agricultural College. The resources were abundant, interest was keen, and it required only resolve and the acquisition of a landscape architect to launch the venture. But it was not to be. The memorandum died, or so it had seemed.

My exoneration was simple. Not having been afforded the opportunity to train landscape architects in Scotland, I had been so enabled at Pennsylvania, where I had trained the majority of landscape architects, not only in Scotland, but in England, Wales, and Ireland as well. This comment took only a minute of the speech but relaxed the audience. Deserter I might be, but not without some redemption. The speech went well. The Scots are not usually demonstrative, but I received an ovation. It was doubly welcome. Then came the vote of thanks from the dean of architecture, "I would like to invite Professor McHarg to lunch with deans and myself at the Staff Club tomorrow."

The lunch was splendid—cock-a-leekie soup, smoked trout with horseradish, a very good white wine, coffee and cheese. As we sipped coffee, the vice-chancellor arose and tapped on his glass with a silver coin. The deans and professors quieted.

The plan of 1953 had been exhumed. Now after the passage of well over 20 years, the belated invitation would be offered. The vice-chancellor spoke. "Gentlemen, there is only one reason for this occasion, only one question to ask Professor McHarg. Sir, could you be induced to return to Scotland to fulfill your plan of 1953?"

"Sir, I fear that the trauma inflicted on me by my last sojourn in Scotland was so severe—a Siberian winter, poverty, and a monumental resistance to change—that the only condition under which I could return to Scotland would be as an American tourist, willing and eager to provide such assistance as I can, gratuitously. But send me students, I will be delighted to train them."

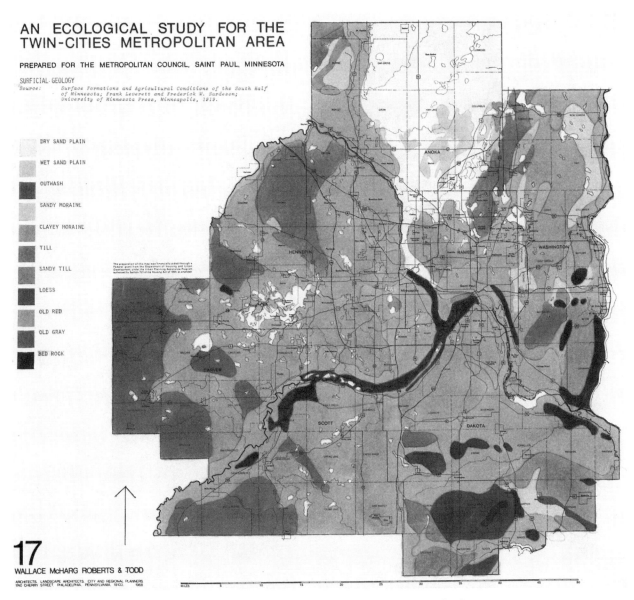

AN ECOLOGICAL STUDY FOR THE
TWIN-CITIES METROPOLITAN AREA

PREPARED FOR THE METROPOLITAN COUNCIL, SAINT PAUL, MINNESOTA

SURFICIAL·GEOLOGY
Source: Surface Formations and Agricultural Conditions of the South Half
          of Minnesota; Frank Leverett and Frederick W. Sardeson;
          University of Minnesota Press, Minneapolis, 1919.

DRY SAND PLAIN
WET SAND PLAIN
OUTWASH
SANDY MORAINE
CLAYEY MORAINE
TILL
SANDY TILL
LOESS
OLD RED
OLD GRAY
BED ROCK

17
WALLACE McHARG ROBERTS & TODD
ARCHITECTS, LANDSCAPE ARCHITECTS, CITY AND REGIONAL PLANNERS
1740 CHERRY STREET, PHILADELPHIA, PENNSYLVANIA, 19103   1968

The ecological study for the Twin Cities Metropolitan Region of Minnesota is the first
comprehensive regional assessment of its kind. The study was undertaken in 1968–1969
for the Metropolitan Council of the Twin Cities Area by Wallace, McHarg, Roberts
and Todd, under my direction.

Surficial geology of the Twin Cities Area at the scale of 1:250,000. (1969, Wallace,
McHarg, Roberts and Todd; map courtesy of the Metropolitan Council of the
Twin Cities.)

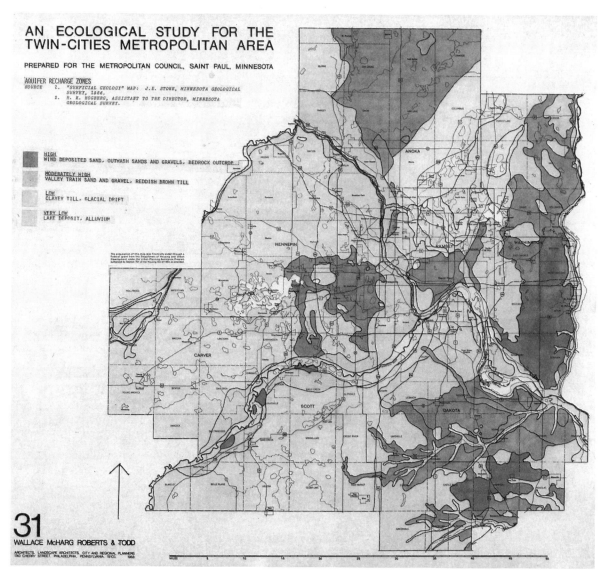

Aquifer recharge zones of the Twin Cities Area at the scale of 1:125,000.
(1969, Wallace, McHarg, Roberts and Todd; map courtesy of the Metropolitan
Council of the Twin Cities.)

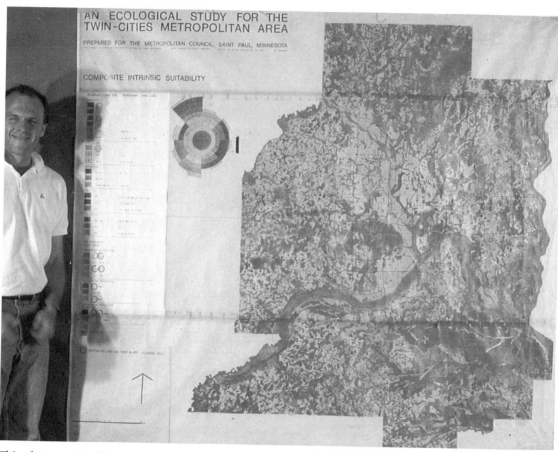

This photograph of the composite intrinsic suitability map of the Twin Cities Area was taken at the Design Center for American Urban Landscape. This suitability analysis was the first of its kind for a metropolitan region. Design Center staff member Tom Hammerberg is standing beside the six-by-six-foot map with a scale of 1:62,500. The map contained 27 colors. The scale and the use of color were unique for their time. (1969, Wallace, McHarg, Roberts and Todd; photograph courtesy of the Design Center for American Urban Landscape, University of Minnesota.)

George Mitchell—The Woodlands

On October 13, 1970, I received a telephone call from a Mr. George Mitchell of Houston, Texas. He had acquired more than 200,000 acres of forest land surrounding Houston and proposed to build a new city. On the advice of my former student and his director of planning, Robert Hartsfield, Mitchell had selected me to plan it. Now, at that time, there were many efforts to build new towns. Reston, the first, had succumbed to bankruptcy and had been acquired by an oil company. Columbia, in Maryland, was beset with problems of cash. Soul City, Flower Mound, and others were in various states of disrepair. I suggested to Mitchell that the most critical factor was cash. After all, building a new town required massive investments for years before any return would be forthcoming. In short, we should discuss his financial resources.

Now, as it transpired, this was singular impertinence. George Mitchell was an oil and gas multimillionaire, indeed, a billionaire, while I was then a professor as I am today. However, he came to Philadelphia, sat by my fire, had a drink, and reassured me as to his financial resources. They were formidable. He told me more, about his father who was born in Greece and had come to the United States where he laid rail in Louisiana. The gang foreman could not pronounce his name and renamed him Mitchell. He in time married a Greek lady, begat two sons who graduated from Texas A & M. George's degree was in petroleum geology. After service in the Pacific, George took his savings to Houston, invested prudently in oil and gas ventures, and prospered. Meanwhile, he also bought forest land in and around Houston, requiring it only to pay taxes by logging selected lumber, and appreciate in value.

This was a time of new environmental sensibility. The environmental factor had not been important in the earlier new towns of Reston and Columbia, but it was now. Moreover, there was a large carrot. The Urban Growth and New Community Development Act of 1970 had a Title VII, which provided $50 million of loan guarantees for developers of new towns. This grant procedure gave great import to environmental factors, and may very well have been the reason for my firm's being selected. The study had to be exemplary, and it was. This was a beautiful site, a splendid oak-pine forest contrasting with the short grass prairie of Houston. A surveyor confirmed the appellation of a stream, Panther Creek. He met a panther there. But this site was distant from Houston; could it support development, in terms of both market and ecology? We would investigate.

I began an ecological study, and it soon became apparent that surficial hydrology, soils, and vegetation constituted a closely linked system and were crucial to the study. As we proceeded, William Gladstone embarked on market analysis, first the metropolitan region, next the northern sector, and last the catchment adjacent to the site. Persons moving to employment in Houston were identified and questioned as to housing preferences, acceptable travel time, environmental requirements, and more.

On investigation, the problem presented unusual difficulties. Conventional development had been sporadic in the oak-pine forest and almost universally unsuccessful. The reason was simple. In this flat land a fragipan, an impenetrable layer, lay on or close to the surface, so that drainage was impeded, there was little or no percolation, and it was so flat, and drainage so immature, that after intense storms, water lay on the ground until it evaporated. The local saying was that the only way you could predict where it would flow was by knowing the direction of the wind. In this situation the conventional engineering response was to lower the water table. To do this, drainage ditches were dug; these were very ugly, very expensive, but quite efficacious. The water table dropped—and the trees died. As it was the forest that constituted the attraction of this region, the solution was inadequate. Another stratagem must be invented.

There was another problem as well. Houston is beleaguered by floods. Although annual rainfall is only thirteen inches, the annual hurricane visitation produces intense precipitation with single events often equal to the average annual precipitation, and this causes widespread flooding. The land owned by George Mitchell lay upstream on a tributary of the San Jacinto system, which regularly flooded Houston. As urbanization always increases runoff and flooding, conventional development would have exacerbated Houston's plight. So George was admonished: build your new town, but you may not increase the discharge from Panther Creek into the San Jacinto. This required an entirely novel approach, but that was not all. The marine sediments that underlie Houston and the new town site consisted of continuous layers, all water bearing. Should George withdraw water from this aquifer, the tall buildings in Houston would sink—no small embarrassment to George, who occupied the penthouse of One Shell Plaza. So any water withdrawn from the aquifer must be recharged.

To the best of my knowledge each of these was a novel problem for planning. It was downright unfair to have to confront them all on a single site.

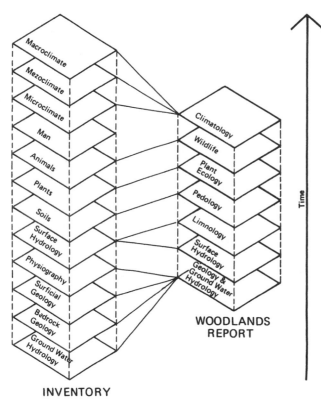

Layer Cake Representation of Phenomena

A landscape combines natural and cultural processes that can be represented by the "layer cake" model. This prototype model was used in the 1971–1974 ecological planning of the Woodlands New Community in Texas. I was responsible for the ecological inventory, with Narendra Juneja, Richard Nalbandian, Dennis McGlade, Doris Zorensky Cheng, and Jonathan Sutton playing important roles. I worked on the layer cake concept for the Woodlands, represented in this drawing, with Narendra Juneja. The new community planning was conducted for George Mitchell of the Woodlands Development Corporation in Houston. (Wallace, McHarg, Roberts and Todd, 1974, "Woodlands New Community: An Ecological Inventory.")

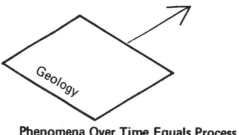

Phenomena Over Time Equals Process

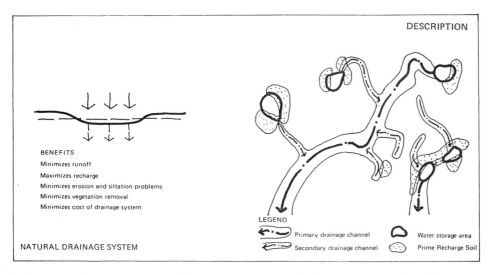

BENEFITS

Minimizes runoff

Maximizes recharge

Minimizes erosion and siltation problems

Minimizes vegetation removal

Minimizes cost of drainage system

NATURAL DRAINAGE SYSTEM

DESCRIPTION

LEGEND

← ··· → Primary drainage channel   ⌂ Water storage area

⟵ ··· Secondary drainage channel   ⊙ Prime Recharge Soil

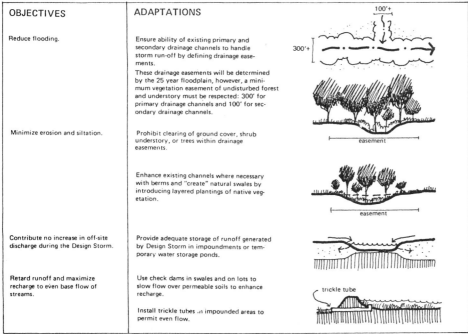

OBJECTIVES	ADAPTATIONS
Reduce flooding.	Ensure ability of existing primary and secondary drainage channels to handle storm run-off by defining drainage easements. These drainage easements will be determined by the 25 year floodplain, however, a minimum vegetation easement of undisturbed forest and understory must be respected: 300' for primary drainage channels and 100' for secondary drainage channels.
Minimize erosion and siltation.	Prohibit clearing of ground cover, shrub understory, or trees within drainage easements.
	Enhance existing channels where necessary with berms and "create" natural swales by introducing layered plantings of native vegetation.
Contribute no increase in off-site discharge during the Design Storm.	Provide adequate storage of runoff generated by Design Storm in impoundments or temporary water storage ponds.
Retard runoff and maximize recharge to even base flow of streams.	Use check dams in swales and on lots to slow flow over permeable soils to enhance recharge. Install trickle tubes in impounded areas to permit even flow.

A summary of the analysis of hydrology used during 1971–1974 in the ecological site planning of the Woodlands New Community in Texas. I was in charge of the site planning, with Richard Nalbandian, Colin and Carol Franklin, Leslie and Rolf Sauer, and Jonathan Sutton playing important roles. (Wallace, McHarg, Roberts and Todd, 1973, "Woodlands New Community: Guidelines for Site Planning"; drawn by Colin Franklin.)

In summary, we had to discover a method of development that would not increase runoff and would not lower the water table and, finally, we must accomplish artificial recharge of all water used so as to eliminate subsidence.

But God smiles on ecological planners.

The first problem involved computing the natural water budget—precipitation, percolation, storage, runoff, evaporation, and transpiration. Next we had to devise stratagems whereby the water budget for the new town would parallel natural conditions. This required that all water courses, sinks, swales, and flood plains would remain undeveloped in perpetuity. All new construction—roads, golf courses, house sites—must be designed at densities that did not exceed the natural recharge of soils and employ their water storage capability, and, most important, the rare Boy and Splendora soils, which had no fragipan and were, to all intents and purposes, sumps, should be the foci for all surface drainage systems. Finally, detention and retention ponds were necessary and the cross section of swales should be designed to accommodate extreme events. As indeed they did. [On two successive years, after portions of the new town were built, there were events of thirteen inches' precipitation in twenty-four hours. The pools were brimful, as were the streams and swales, but twenty-four hours later only the sediment on leaves showed the extent of inundation. There was no flooding in Woodlands during those occasions when Houston was closed down by floods.]

The geohydrologic-soils analysis led to determining that proportion of the land wherein urbanization could occur while maintaining the natural levels of percolation and runoff. Where the fragipan lay on or near the surface, the addition of asphalt, concrete, and housing would have no appreciable effect. In the areas of highly permeable Boy and Splendora soils, which were sinks, no development could occur, and so a gradient from 0 to 100 percent coverage was developed with corresponding soil categories—an approach quite original and thoroughly efficacious.

This is a profoundly simple concept, to determine densities and land use from the geohydrological properties of the soils. I do not know of another such example, then or since. And from the perspective of twenty years later, it has worked very well indeed.

The next subject was the development of a clearing ratio. Obviously building a new town would require felling trees. Which ones and why these? The forest association provided a gradient directly related to fragipan and water table. The highest, finest willow and water oaks and the densest stands of yaupon lay on the Boy and Splendora soils, grading from a domination of deciduous species into monocultures of pines as the fragipan surfaced. When exposed, there were no woody plants, only Waller ponds and wet meadows.

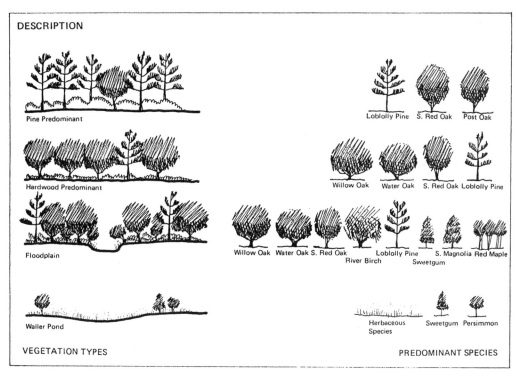

DESCRIPTION

Pine Predominant

Hardwood Predominant

Floodplain

Waller Pond

VEGETATION TYPES

Loblolly Pine   S. Red Oak   Post Oak

Willow Oak   Water Oak   S. Red Oak   Loblolly Pine

Willow Oak   Water Oak   S. Red Oak   Loblolly Pine   S. Magnolia   Red Maple
                                      River Birch   Sweetgum

Herbaceous   Sweetgum   Persimmon
Species

PREDOMINANT SPECIES

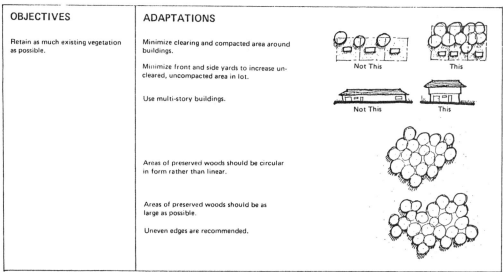

OBJECTIVES

Retain as much existing vegetation as possible.

ADAPTATIONS

Minimize clearing and compacted area around buildings.

Minimize front and side yards to increase un-cleared, uncompacted area in lot.

Use multi-story buildings.

Not This   This

Not This   This

Areas of preserved woods should be circular in form rather than linear.

Areas of preserved woods should be as large as possible.

Uneven edges are recommended.

Some general guidelines for the site planning of the Woodlands New Community, Texas. (Wallace, McHarg, Roberts and Todd, 1973, "Woodlands New Community: Guidelines for Site Planning"; drawn by Colin Franklin.)

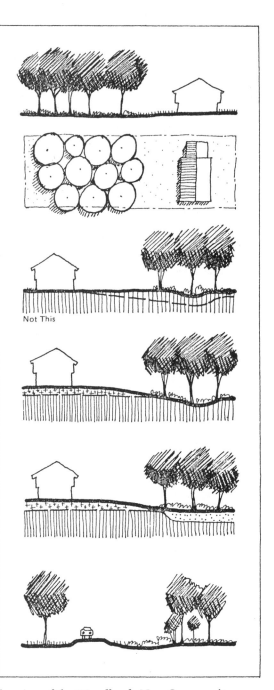

Uncleared woods need not be exempted from salable real estate. Buildings may be located on the periphery of these stands and lot lines may be extended into them.

Cutting to achieve drainage is only acceptable when it does not necessitate cutting below grade at existing drainage channels or recharge soils.

Fill cleared areas to achieve drainage and direct runoff to recharge soils. Trees cannot be retained if existing grade is changed.

Roads may be used to direct or impound runoff.

Swales may be sited along roads to minimize disturbance.

Some general guidelines for the site planning of the Woodlands New Community, Texas. (Wallace, McHarg, Roberts and Todd, 1973, "Woodlands New Community: Guidelines for Site Planning"; drawn by Colin Franklin.)

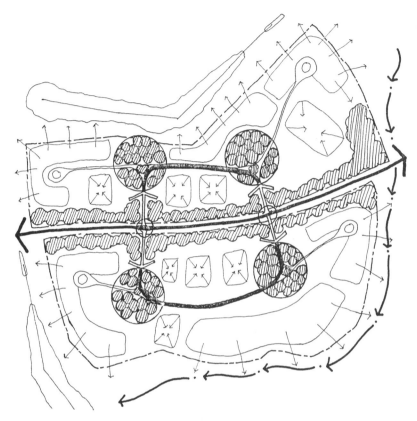

Design concept for a neighborhood in the Woodlands New Community, Texas. (Wallace, McHarg, Roberts and Todd, 1973, "Woodlands New Community: Guidelines for Site Planning"; designed by Colin Franklin and Jonathan Sutton.)

The Woodlands in 1994. (Photograph by Lisa Carol Hardaway and Paul Hester.)

The popular evaluation corresponded to the scientific one. The greatest species number and richness of wildlife habitat and beauty reposed in the vegetation on the Boy-Splendora soils; this was the expression of wealth in Houston, epitomized by the River Oaks Development. Uniform pines were common, held to be of little value and equated with poverty. So clearance conformed to coverage, with the exception of the Waller pond and wet meadow extremes, where no clearance was permitted. Elsewhere 100 percent clearance of pine with fragipan near the surface and zero clearance on the water-willow oak climax was planned.

Specific numbers were allocated to both clearance and coverage for all soil, physiographic, and vegetation conditions. The proportions and locations of clearance and coverage determined placements for housing, roads, golf courses, community facilities, and more.

When the water budget was completed, the formula for allocating densities based on runoff, coverage, and clearance calculated, and retention and detention basins swales specified, the solution was presented to George Mitchell and his staff. They were skeptical. What did landscape architects and ecological planners know of hydrology? How could they succeed where engineers had failed? George asked his engineering consultants, Espey Associates, to run our solution through their computer and advise him of their results. Another meeting was convened, and Espey reported, albeit with some embarrassment, that the system worked.

George looked at me and said, "All right, natural drainage works, but what does it mean to me?"

"First, George, it means you'll get $50 million from HUD and, second, it will save you even more money. For instance, you won't have to build a storm drainage system. This will save you $14 million for the first phase alone."

George looked to the Espey people for confirmation. They nodded. He looked at me, and it was clear that I had made a convert. Here was a new and powerful advocate for ecology and ecological planning, as he has indeed become.

The Woodlands now has a population of 30,000 with 10,000 jobs. The forest is intact, the hydrologic system is in balance. The architecture is the conventional California-developer type, but the population is very gratified, as is the developer. Woodlands continues to attract an ever-increasing proportion of the Houston housing market. Best of all is the demonstration that it is not only possible, but profitable, to design with nature. Nothing beats the combination of righteousness and profit.

Golf Balls and Alligators

Wallace, McHarg, Roberts and Todd received an invitation to undertake an ecological planning study for Amelia Island, Florida, just off Jacksonville, in 1971. Bill Roberts directed the master plan development. Jack McCormick, the ecologist, was an incredible man, an enthusiast who had expanded into ecological planning. He was responsible for the scientific team for ecological inventory of Amelia Island. He was uniquely well prepared for this role. Jack's research had concentrated on the ecology of the coastal plain, mainly in New Jersey. He was familiar with the coastal plain region as a generic system with characteristic problems and opportunities.

Jack selected the entire scientific staff for the Wallace, McHarg, Roberts and Todd team: a physical oceanographer, a marine biologist, a geologist, and a hydrologist, but he reserved ecology for himself. Among the scientists he hired was the leading authority for the painted bunting, whose homeland was Amelia Island. It was already clear that this was a most intolerant environment, indeed, the only area where development could occur was on Holocene dunes.

Bill Roberts, along with Jonathan Sutton and other landscape architects, developed the plans with meticulous attention to the ecological consequences. The sound, marshes, forests, and habitats would persist without detriment. However, there were difficulties,

among which was the necessity for at least one golf course. The client group to whom the project was addressed included retired golf-playing generals and admirals, Southerners all. Roberts and Sutton concluded that the golf course would best be located in the trough, between the major dunes. This was a region dominated by large live oaks and an understory of palmetto. It was a constraining site. For the proposal to work, fairways needed to be narrow, greens small, and alignment selected so as to protect the majestic live oaks. When this was done, Pete Dye was hired to realize the plan, which he did admirably.

However, in the middle of the site was a small community, American Beach, with a few hundred persons, mostly black children. They entertained visitors by luring alligators into view by lobbing them marshmallows. Who will ever know what was the more effective lure, marshmallows or little children? In due time, the golf course was complete. A competition was organized. Celebrated golfers and residents teed off. Little white marshmallows attracted alligators. So you can image the scene of golfers and alligators converging. You will agree that golf balls are no substitution for marshmallows. So it was a convergence of angry alligators and trepidatious golfers. Course rules were developed; all alligators over fifteen feet were relocated, presumably to ecological sites without golf balls.

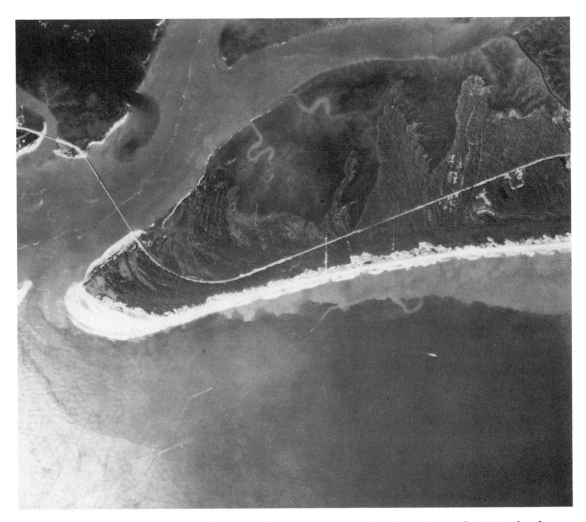

Aerial photograph of Amelia Island, Florida, before development. The pioneering early 1970s plan for Amelia Island was directed by William Roberts of Wallace, McHarg, Roberts and Todd.

Roberts was responsible for the plan and design for this new community, with Jonathan Sutton and others making contributions. Jack McCormick selected the team of extraordinary natural scientists who conducted elements of the ecological inventory. Wallace, McHarg, Roberts and Todd prepared the plan for Charles Fraser, who developed the Sea Pines Company of Hilton Head, South Carolina. I regard the Amelia Island plan as Bill Roberts' masterpiece. Bill was my student and partner. He was also acting chairman at Penn while I was on sabbatical leave, writing *Design with Nature*. Bill's work with Amelia Island is a wonderful example of designing with nature. (Wallace, McHarg, Roberts and Todd, 1971, "Amelia Island, Florida: A Report on the Master Planning Process for a New Recreational Community"; photograph courtesy of Wallace Roberts and Todd).

Master plan for the new recreational community in Amelia Island, Florida. (Courtesy of Wallace Roberts and Todd.)

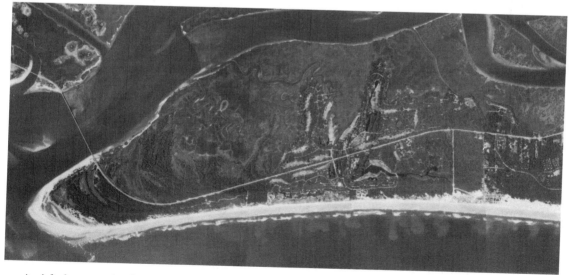

Aerial photograph of Amelia Island Plantation in 1983, illustrating how the development followed the Wallace, McHarg, Roberts and Todd master plan. (Photograph courtesy of Amelia Island Plantation.)

Amelia Island in 1994.
(Photograph courtesy of
Amelia Island Plantation.)

Planning for Human Health

Not everyone makes an immediate connection between the National Institutes
of Mental Health (NIMH) and landscape architecture or regional planning. If it
is true that tranquility, introspection, and well-being are some of nature's gifts,
perhaps the link is not remote. But such was not the reason for a telephone call I
received in June of 1973 from Dick Wakefield of NIMH. He had a proposition.
Ecological planning had developed very well and was efficacious, he said, but it
concentrated on physical and biological science. Could it not be extended to include
social science and people? Moreover, could it not focus on planning for human
health and well-being? This seemed reasonable, but difficult. I had experienced
several years of graduate social science at Harvard and concluded that most of it
was oblivious to the environment, could not perform useful work and that much
of it, notably economics, was antithetical to the ecological view. Wakefield persisted: surely there were compatible views within the social sciences that could

transform ecology into human ecology and enrich planning. He suggested a lot of money, a million dollars, and my interest was galvanized. Would I write a proposal? Indeed I would, and fast.

The proposal operated in a step function. My colleagues and I had concluded that geomorphology synthesized physical processes and that ecology synthesized both physical and biological processes. How could we extend this model to include people? We determined to use adaptation as the unifying theme. The plant and animal ecologists, limnologists, and marine biologists all subscribed to physiological adaptation through mutation and natural selection. The zoologists also included behavior as an adaptive strategy for animals and humans. As behavior was central to humans, our first step should be the acquisition of an ethologist, a specialist in animal behavior. Ethology was a small though lively science that had produced novel insights from intensive observation, new theories, and disproportionate numbers of Nobel laureates. Clearly, human behavior must have its origin in animal ancestry, thus particular relevance might accord with the primates. Given some understanding of underlying animal behavior, could we expand it to people? Yes, ethnography did this exactly. The literature of ecology was familiar to ethologists, and their literature was shared by ethnographers. What insights could they provide of human behavior drawn mostly from simple societies? Such societies are those where people and environment are likely to be in good shape, wherein there is not likely to be any threat to the rest of us. The problems are with developed societies whose environments are bad, getting worse, and are imperiled, as are we all. This is the realm of cultural anthropology, notably of those who have abandoned the idyllic lure of Polynesia and Micronesia and address contemporary American problems. Yet the string of disciplines has become too extended; is there someone who can make a circle and join social science back to climate, geology, water, soil, plants, and animals? Of course, such a person is either an epidemiologist or a medical anthropologist. He or she cares about climate and health, geopathology and background radiation, soil nutrients and pathogens, water, plants, and animals as food and drink, pharmaceuticals and disease vectors, but the primary concern is with humans and their health.

So the proposal was written, but the grant was made for a half million dollars, not one million, and, with the erroneous assumption that we could acquire the ethologist from departmental funds, we proceeded. The objective was to create a curriculum in human ecological planning directed to human health and well-being.

The enterprise was led by Yehudi Cohen, author of *Man in Adaptation*. He recruited a succession of brilliant anthropologists, ethnographers, and medical anthropologists: David and Vera Mae Frederickson, Martin Silverman, Jay Ruby, Frank Vivelo, and, ultimately the permanent faculty consisting of Dan Rose, ethnographer, and Setha Low, medical anthropologist.

Hardly had the work began when I was summoned to Washington. NIMH was seriously interested in my venture, but the Institutes had bigger plans. They would like to induce a distinguished university with a powerful medical school to turn its attention to the subject of planning for human health and well-being. Untold sums of money would be available, not only from NIMH but from the Johnson Foundation and others. Would I try to interest the Medical School of the University of Pennsylvania in this prospect?

I had, at that time, a grant from the Ford Foundation of a half million dollars that was fully discretionary. Its general purpose was to fund recruitment of natural science faculty and initiate a graduate program in ecological planning for persons with qualifications in physical and biological science. I conferred with Gordon Harrison of Ford, who approved this courtship of medicine. The plan was to rent the Sinkler estate in Chestnut Hill, a transported Elizabethan house, provide a splendid, expensive catered lunch twice a month, and invite the leadership of the university to listen to addresses by luminaries in the field of health, epidemiology, and health policy.

J. Ralph Audy, John Cassell, Alexander Leighton, Leonard Duhl, Hinkle, Sarjent, Petrakis and John Greiger were invited. Also invited were President Martin Meyerson; the vice-president for Medical Affairs, Robert Dripps; Provost Stellar, Albert Gelhorn, dean of Medicine; his two vice-deans; the chairman of Medicine, Bud Relman; the chairman of Psychiatry, Albert Stunkard; Sociology's Renée Fox; from Community Medicine, Robert Leopold; and the director of the Leonard Davis Institute for Health Policy.

The Sinkler house was charming, with splendid rooms and furniture, fires burning, good food and drink. The speakers were excellent. Discussion was stimulating, and there was an immediate interest in the idea. Each speaker reinforced the central recommendation that medicine could not await the delivery of the patient to the hospital, it must intervene in these processes in society that so persistently produced the sick, the maimed, and the dead. Moreover, medical education must include knowledge and concern for those conditions that affect human health and well-being. This enlarged concern required medicine to join others engaged in the conduct of human affairs who were equally interested in human health and well- being. The group could include engineers, architects, planners, landscape architects, lawyers, sociologists, and political scientists, not to mention meteorologists, geologists, seismologists, hydrologists, soil scientists, plant and animal ecologists, and toxicologists.

Indeed, the addresses and comments of the participants gradually focused on the idea that the university should raise a flag and identify those persons involved in its scientific or professional schools who were involved with human health and wished actively to ameliorate it.

Given this emergency consensus, John Geiger was asked to assume the responsibility for developing a new medical curriculum based on this innovation. Geiger had recently accepted the Nobel prize on behalf of Physicians for Social Responsibility, was currently at City University of New York Medical School, previously head of community medicine at SUNY, and earlier at Tufts. A man of great wisdom, energy, moral power, and funny to boot, he deserves eternal bliss for his astonishing solutions to starvation in Bolivar County, Mississippi. Here he first wrote prescriptions for food—eggs, bread, butter, meat—and then created agricultural cooperatives, wholly black owned, producing soul food. He built privies and dug wells, constructed model homes for $3,000, set up transportation systems, and initiated adult education, all in the name of health, and all with brilliant success.

Geiger worked with a will; he interviewed all the dominant members of the university and medical hierarchies, produced drafts and revisions. Then came the fateful meeting at Penn to resolve the proposal—when the free lunches would be transformed into university policy. There had been an unexpectedly large measure of agreement. Bud Relman, chairman of Medicine, had invested his heart and hopes in the laboratory; he was neutral, but he would not be an adversary. The director of the Leonard Davis Institute, who was the only strong adversary, was dying. The rest approved.

During the week of the meeting, convened by President Meyerson, the whole construction fell apart. Robert Dripps, vice-president for Medical Affairs, died of a heart attack while playing tennis; Albert Gelhorn resigned, as did his two vice-deans, Bud Relman moved to the *New England Journal of Medicine,* and Albert Stunkard went to Stanford.

Thus we had an acting vice president and an acting dean of Medicine, who could not act. The rest had gone, leaving a president and a provost without even a quorum, let alone a consensus. There was no vote, no action.

Yet it could have been otherwise. There had been consent; there was certainly little dissent. Here was an opportunity to do just what was needed. But, no, irresolution ensued, the whole construct fell to the floor, shattered, never to be reconstructed, at least not by me.

Progressive Architecture Jury

Progressive Architecture (P. A.) holds an annual competition and makes awards for architecture and planning. In the fall of 1971, I was juror for planning and urban design. My fellow jurors were a distinguished crew. Rimaldo Giurgola, Eliot Noyes, M. Paul Friedberg, John Johansen, I. M. Pei, John Andrews, and David Crane, among others. I was close to Giurgola. He and I had joined Penn together in 1954; I had helped him find an apartment near my own. We were colleagues, neighbors, and friends.

The first problem the jurors confronted was to distinguish architecture from planning. A room was filled with submissions—which was which? "Easy," I said. "Everything that appeals to the brain is planning. Every submission based on images and appealing to the eyes alone is architecture." So advised, janitors separated the submissions. The planning jury reviewed their smaller task and found nothing worthy of commendation. There would be no planning awards for 1971. But the architects were beleaguered, confronted by a huge pile of boards in the middle of a room. Giurgola, on learning that we had finished, asked if we would help his group. "I am not an architect, Aldo." "Never mind, you have been on many architectural juries. You can do it." So I picked up a pile of boards and made my selections— worthy of consideration, unworthy. Each juror moved around the piles, similarly discriminating. Ultimately, the selected submissions were hung, the jurors checked them in concert and awarded prizes. When we withdrew for drinks and dinner, Aldo said, "What did you think of the jury?" "I thought it was terrible." "Why?" he asked. "No one looked at the back of the

boards to read the programs, the clients' preferences, or any other information." "How would you do it?"

"Aldo, I have been thinking about that very subject, and I have a proposal to make. First, the submission of nominees should be made by gratified clients, each with at least five years experience of the building nominated. Nominees should be elicited through nationwide advertising. The criteria for selection should be based on the enhancement to life accomplished by the building. The jury should select candidates from these nominations and solicit submissions. I will give an example of an award-winning submission. A client writes:

Gentlemen, I wish to submit Mr. John Doe for a P. A. Award in Residential Architecture. I have a wife and two children, eighteen and fifteen. Seven years ago, we lived in a three-bedroom apartment. My mother-in-law died, and my wife received a small inheritance. I qualified for a V A loan. We resolved to build a house. We learned of a young architect from a friend, interviewed and hired him. Our first problem was finding a site. It transpired that this young man had studied environmental science. He knew about climate, rocks, soils, vegetation, wildlife, and, with information on land values, we examined several prospective sites. We found one we loved and bought it. We set up tents and spent our weekends there considering views, slopes, location for the house, terraces, and room views. During this time, the architect came to know us as a family, learned of our needs, preferences and aversions, and offered us a number of alternative arrangements. The plans developed; we participated in their evolution and were enthralled by the design process. Finally, five years ago, the house was built and we moved in.

Now we can report. The house has transformed our lives; first the children. In the apartment, they had been underfoot. There was no escape. They were not attractive. We had to spoil them for the sake of peace. Now they have a little wing and share a playroom. The architect introduced them to a microscope, a herbarium and aquarium. They have their own music, mercifully distant, their own access. They have been transformed, no longer spoiled, they are charming and delightful young people, and bright.

Next food. In the apartment it was television dinners. The kitchen offered no opportunity for inspired cooking. Now the kitchen is the heart of the house, skylights and hanging baskets, herbs on the kitchen windows, a mini-greenhouse, copper pots and pans, arrays of herbs, cherry counters. The kitchen is a joy of splendid food and smells.

Music was impossible in the apartment. Children's noise and music, acoustics, competition with TV, all made it impossible. No longer, the children's separation solved TV and rock. We now have music in living, dining and bedroom. It is an important part of our lives. Finally sex. In an apartment with thin walls there are constraints. Sex was seldom and humdrum. No longer. The master bedroom is a lovely space, wonderful views, skylights for the night sky, stars and moon, a fireplace, candlelight and music.

"Give that man a prize," I say, "that's what architecture is all about." It won't happen. Architecture is about style not life.

Medford

At registration there was always a procession of students awaiting counsel. On one such occasion, I noticed the new face of a much older man. In due time he sat down and said he wished to apply for admission to landscape architecture. His name was Arthur Palmer. "May I ask how old you are?" "I am sixty-two, are there any age limitations?" "None." "What must I do to apply?" "Complete the application, submit transcripts, three letters of recommendation, and a portfolio." "You will have them in a few days." And I did.

High intelligence is commonplace among our applicants, and we considered only A and high-B candidates; letters are valuable too, but only if you know the reputation of the authors. However, because graphic skill is the rarest commodity, it was the portfolio that I customarily examined first. Palmer's was bulky, containing

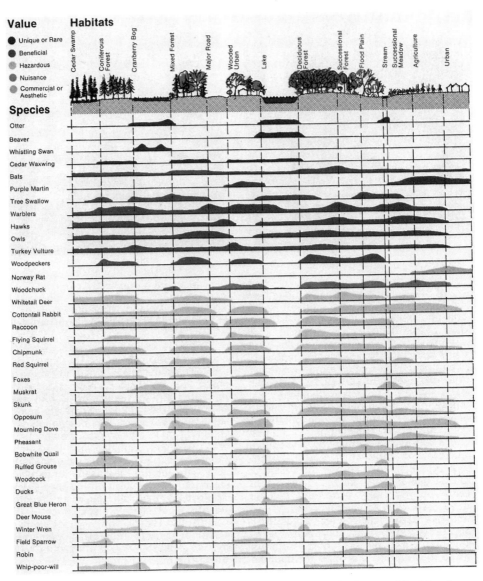

Occurrence and abundance of selected wildlife species in Medford Township, New Jersey. (Narendra Juneja, 1974, "Medford: Performance Requirements for the Maintenance of Social Values Represented by the Natural Environment of Medford, N.J.")

For many years Narendra Juneja was my closest professional associate, both at the University of Pennsylvania and at Wallace, McHarg, Roberts and Todd. I was the principal investigator of the development of innovative ecological-based performance standards for Medford Township, New Jersey. The study was conducted through the University of Pennsylvania Center for Ecological Research and Design, and Narendra was the author of the 1974 report.

pencil drawings, watercolors, and a sequence of photographs, mainly gardens—pools, steps, walls, flower borders, minor buildings. It became clear that there were two sites, one in fashionable Long Island, the other in Bar Harbor, Maine. These, it emerged, were Palmer's residences, where he had applied his energies. He was both client and landscape architect, and quite skilled. Next were his transcripts, all from Yale for an A. B. and a J. D. Last came his letters, the first, "To whom it may concern," was from Franklin Delano Roosevelt. It said simply, "My appointment of Arthur Palmer as undersecretary of War. . . ." The next letter was from Henry Stinson, secretary of War: "The American people will never know their indebtedness to Arthur Palmer." The last letter was from the then-president of Yale, Griswold. He wrote, "The most exciting professor of law during my studies was Arthur Palmer."

Arthur Palmer was admitted. He became the key to the development of ecological planning studies in designing environmental law.

The great gift of ecological planning was our ability to learn how natural systems had evolved and how they operated, but the most immediate benefit was the discernment that permitted evaluation of regions or sites as tolerant or intolerant for specific land uses. This discrimination provided two perceptions; the first was the degree of fitness for any prospective land use in the environments as found and, linked with predictability, the cost, benefits, and consequences of any contemplated action in the region under study.

It was this perception that motivated Harvey Cedars, Plan for the Valleys, and the Potomac and Delaware River Basin studies. However, when it became clear that certain environments were profoundly intolerant and comprised hazards to life and health or high social costs, the question emerged, could there be regulation responsive to these situations? Active faults, landslide areas, flood plains, subsidence, hurricane zones, and fire-prone forests were obvious examples. Yet it was not enough to identify these environments. Could regulations be introduced to constrain or limit development?

This issue became clear in the early 1960s. There was then no field of environmental law, but there was one lawyer intensely interested in the subject—Victor Yannacone. Yannacone and his father had a legal practice devoted to insurance claims in Islip, New York. This was his livelihood but not his passion, which was reserved for the environment. Yannacone, George Woodwell, Ann Strong and others had created the Environmental Defense Fund in 1967 and courageously embarked on several crusades: the prohibition of the use of DDT to kill Colorado beetles on Long Island and averting the use of an atom bomb to compress natural gas in Rulison, Colorado. I invited Yannacone annually to speak on the subject of envi-

RUNOFF MANAGEMENT

No alteration permitted of the amount of surface runoff presently occurring, both under normal precipitation as well as under intense storm conditions, as identified in Runoff Management Chart. Excess runoff to be recharged locally into the ground through the use of recharge ponds or injection wells.

RUNOFF MANAGEMENT CHART

EXISTING CONDITION — Excess Runoff in inches produced during the most intense hour of 10 year recurrent 24 hour rainfall by a prospective land use; and the percentage of site area required for withholding it, to allow its infilteration locally within three hours

COVER TYPE	SOIL GROUP	PLAYFIELD ETC. RUNOFF	INFILTERATION CLASS I	II	III	IV	2 ACRE RESIDENTIAL RUNOFF	INFILTERATION CLASS I	II	III	IV	1 ACRE RESIDENTIAL RUNOFF	INFILTERATION CLASS I	II	III	IV	½ ACRE RESIDENTIAL RUNOFF	INFILTERATION CLASS I	II	III	IV	¼ ACRE RESIDENTIAL RUNOFF	INFILTERATION CLASS I	II	III	IV	CROPLAND RUNOFF	INFILTERATION CLASS I	II	III	IV	INTENSIVE URBAN RUNOFF	INFILTERATION CLASS I	II	III	IV
1 thru 4 All Forests and Upland Successional Meadow	A	0	0	0			0	0	0			0	0	0			0·02	0	0			0·12	1	2			0·20	1	3			2·00	10	33		
	B	0·02	0	0	1		0·12	1	2	6		0·16	1	3	8		0·20	1	3	10		0·40	2	7	21		0·44	2	7	23		1·90	10	32	100	
	C	0·04		1	2	7	0·16		3	8	27	0·24		4	13	40	0·28		5	15	47	0·43		7	23	72	0·43		7	23	72	1·58		26	83	263
	D	0·04			2		0·09			5		0·24			13		0·29			15		0·47			25		0·64			107		1·44			76	
5 Lawns, Parks etc.	A						0	0	0			0	0	0			0·02	0	0			0·12	0	2			0·20	1	3			2·00	10	33		
	B						0·10	1	2	5		0·14	1	2	7		0·18	1	3	9		0·38	2	6	20		0·42	2	7	22		1·89	10	31	100	
	C						0·12		2	6	20	0·20		3	10	33	0·24		4	13	40	0·39		6	21	65	0·39		6	21	65	1·54		26	81	257
	D						0·05			3		0·20			10		0·25			13		0·43			23		0·60			100		1·40			74	
6 2 Acre Residential	A											0	0	0			0·02	0	8			0·12	1	2			0·20	1	3			2·00	10	33		
	B											0·04	0	1	2		0·16	1	3	8		0·28	1	5	15		0·32	2	5	17		1·78	9	30	94	
	C											0·08		1	4	13	0·12		2	6	20	0·27		5	14	45	0·27		5	14	45	1·42		24	75	237
	D											0·15			8		0·20			10		0·38			63		0·55			92		1·35			71	
7 Pasture	A											0	0	0			0·02	0	0			0·12	1	2			0·20	1	3			2·00	10	33		
	B											0·08	0	1	4		0·12	1	2	6		0·26	2	4	12		0·26	2	4	14		1·72	9	29	86	
	C											0		0	0	0	0·04		1	2	7	0·19		3	10	32	0·19		3	10	32	1·34		23	71	223
	D											0			0		0·05			3		0·23			12		0·40			21		1·20			63	
8 1 Acre Residential	A																0·02	0	0			0·12	0	2			0·20	1	3			2·00	10	33		
	B																0·04	0	1	2		0·24	1	4	13		0·28	2	5	15		1·74	9	29	92	
	C																0·04		1	2	7	0·19		3	10	32	0·19		3	10	32	1·34		22	71	223
	D																0·05			3		0·23			12		0·40			21		1·20			63	
9 ½ Acre Residential	A																					0·10	1	2			0·18	1	3			1·98	10	33		
	B																					0·20	1	3	11		0·24	1	4	13		1·70	9	28	90	
	C																					0·15		3	8	25	0·15		3	8	25	1·30		22	69	217
	D																					0·28			15		0·35			58		1·13			60	
10 Farmstead	A																					0·03	0	1			0·11	1	2			1·91	10	32		
	B																					0·04	0	1	2		0·08	0	1	4		1·54	8	26	81	
	C																					0·05		1	3	8	0·05		1	3	8	1·20		20	63	200
	D																					0·09			5		0·26			14		1·06			56	
11 ¼ Acre Residential	A																										0·08	0	1			1·88	10	31		
	B																										0·04	0	1	2		1·50	8	25	79	
	C																										0		0	0	0	1·15		19	61	192
	D																										0·19			10		0·97			51	
12 Cropland	A																															1·80	10	30		
	B																															1·46	8	24	77	
	C																															1·15		19	61	192
	D																															0·80			42	

Light shading indicates absence of any soils with such Hydrologic Soil Group/Infilteration Class combination.
Dark shading indicates no increase in runoff by alteration of existing condition by prospective land use.

Runoff management chart for Medford Township, New Jersey, invented by Narendra Juneja.

(Narendra Juneja, 1974, "Medford.")

ronmental law. He was certain that English common law, the U. S. Constitution, and municipal police power gave total support to regulating the environment in order to protect health and welfare and those resources highly valued by communities. I was convinced; I spoke on the subject on every possible occasion and awaited the chance to apply the concept.

So it was with enormous enthusiasm that I responded to the first opportunity. I received a call from Ephram Tomlinson, the mayor of Medford, New Jersey, in 1971. He would like to visit me. When he arrived, accompanied by two young lawyers from the community, Messrs. Haughey and Harp, I listened to their story. Medford is a small town in the New Jersey Pinelands, with a charming village at its center and a population of 10,000—many blue collar workers, many young professionals, and some farmers. My visitors were frightened of the future, wondering whether their bucolic environment could survive. The evidence said no. Medford was charming and green, but each trip to Philadelphia revealed heightened suburbanization, reaching its zenith in Cherry Hill and then evolving to the urban pathology of Camden. Would this wave engulf them? What could they do?

I had no reservations in my reply: Undertake a meticulous ecological inventory, identify the quality of the environment now—its climate, geology, water, soils, vegetation, wildlife, its historical buildings, its high scenic quality as a public good—analyze the tolerance and intolerance of environments, determine performance specifications, and write ordinances based on the police power reposing in the municipality. When these are passed, undertake to prepare a plan based on the new powers.

Tomlinson took the idea to the town. He recommended a levy per family to pay for the study. It was approved, and we were authorized to proceed. The entire scientific faculty of the department participated: Robert Giegengack, geology; Seymour Subitsky, hydrology; Ron Hanawalt, soils; Michael Levin, plant ecology; Robert Snyder, animal ecology; and Ruth Patrick, limnology. The project director was Narendra Juneja, and his deputy, W. Robinson Fisher, and some twenty graduate students participated, among them an anthropologist, Jane Fajans, who was responsible for the ethnographic history. Yannacone and Palmer were responsible for environmental law.

Enthusiasm for the study was intense, and it was easy to recruit public support, notably from high school students. Temperature, humidity, precipitation, and wind speed and direction were measured; water samples were taken from lakes, streams, and wells; soil pits were dug, vegetation and wildlife inventories undertaken,

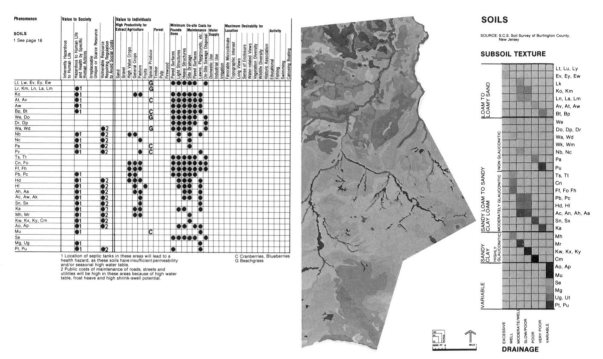

Soils analysis for Medford Township, New Jersey. (Narendra Juneja, 1974, "Medford.")

historical buildings identified and recorded. For a year Medford was thick with faculty and students undertaking inventories.

A sequence of presentations was organized, each dealing initially with a single topic. Giegengack began the series to an overflow audience at the high school, and they were immediately enthralled. Plate tectonics was novel then, the idea that Africa and Europe once pressed on the American coast was revelatory, the emerging Atlantic, orogeny to the west, towering mountains, a sequence of seas in the Triassic, all were engrossing. Next came the Pleistocene, ice sheets, New Jersey now above sea level, tundra and taiga, the front of the glacier a hundred miles away. The audience envisioned mammoths and mastodons, saber-toothed tigers, giant sloths, then the regression of the ice sheet ten thousand years ago, the migrating warmer climes, the emerging forest types proceeding to today. There it was, the land perfectly comprehensible, formed largely under the sea, of quartzite sand, flat, acid, poor in nutrients, a gigantic reservoir of groundwater. The series had had a fascinating beginning.

After the presentation on geology, Subitsky gave a talk on water, and his message was as dramatic: Water is key to New Jersey and Medford. He told of the porous soils, thousands of feet deep at the shore, permeated with water, contained by deep bedrock and by the heavier sea water, an incalculable resource but vulnerable where the aquifer surfaced.

Physiography followed. Certainly, it was no surprise to the audience that Medford was flat, that there were no rocks save where people had brought them. There were, however, anomalies; high ridges with gravel revealed ancient watercourses. That which had been low now provided elevations. And, of course, surface water was in reality only exposed groundwater.

Soils were presented by Ron Hanawalt. They were mostly marine derived, but there was a significant distinction based on the proportion of clay. This threshold revealed a line: more clay, better prospects for agriculture, and more water retention. There were peats and mucks and the alluvium of flood plains; soils and water were highly acid.

Levin introduced vegetation, and here too was drama. The threshold between the deciduous forest and the pines was distinct, showing a powerful contrast. A number of factors were involved: nutrients, poor soils, high porosity, drought as a consequence and, mediated by the evidence of clay, as a response to fire. As Jonathan Berger (with John Sinton) would later write in *Water, Earth, Fire,* these were the three dominants in the New Jersey coastal plain. There was also important introduced vegetation, commercial cranberries and blueberries.

Robert Snyder, pathologist of the Philadelphia Zoo, presented wildlife, responsive to both deciduous and oak-pine forest: abundant deer and small mammals, endangered snakes and frogs, and timber rattlesnakes, whose location he would not divulge lest they be extirpated.

The last element of the inventory was the region's ethnographic history, the Lenni-Lenape Indians, water transportation, small clearings, active burning, the advent of the Europeans in Medford (mainly English Quakers), hunting, lumbering, agriculture; then water power, bog iron foundries, charcoal, glass making, saw and grist mills (denuding the landscape of trees), extensive agriculture (which thereafter declined), forest regeneration, the emergence of Medford Lakes and summer homes, and then suburbanization, still at its early stage when the study began. I presented a summation with maps, sections, and illustrations, revealing the evolutionary processes that had culminated in contemporary Medford, their dynamics, and the implication for land uses.

The presentations were well attended and extensively published in the local newspapers, and the political process produced a powerful conservationist constituency.

Meanwhile Yannacone and Palmer had interviewed each of the natural scientists to review their data and establish the implications. What hazards to life and health were involved? What regulations were appropriate to protect society? Conscious of the takings issue, the allegation that to regulate land use required compensation, both gentlemen investigated performance specifications. This did not involve specific prohibition but the necessity of meeting standards—discharge not more than x feet per second, recharge not less than y inches per year, no more sediment than z tons per acre, nitrates limited to a maximum of 45 forty-five parts per million, and more.

Ordinances can guard against hazards to life and health and protect cherished attributes, but they cannot induce positively good development, they can only avoid error. To compensate for this deficiency, it was decided to undertake suitability analyses and determine which areas were most suitable for all prospective land uses. Studies were made for housing of very low, low, intermediate, and high density; commercial and industrial land uses; recreation, agriculture, and forestry. Then the community was enabled, not only to regulate damaging and costly development, but to induce appropriate development into propitious areas.

Do Americans have the inalienable right to drown, burn, mutilate, and bury their children, friends, and neighbors? Do municipalities have such rights? Surely not; the Constitution requires that government ensure the health and welfare of all citizens. So municipalities should forbid or constrain development on flood plains, in active seismic areas, in locations susceptible to landslides, mud slides, subsidence, in areas of fire-prone forests, hurricanes, tornados, and tsunamis. Should there not be regulation to protect the maintenance of community resources—ground and surface water, mineral resources, prime agricultural land, aged forest stands, habitats of valuable, rare, and endangered species, historical buildings and places? Note that these areas are seldom subjects of planning control. It was not until the Plan for the Valleys in 1962 that constraint of development in flood plains and on aquifer recharge was advocated.

However, it became clear that ecological planning studies for river basins and metropolitan regions that identified hazards to life and health or the presence of community values did not constitute a remedy. Clearly, there had to be an examination of the police powers that could be invoked to constrain development. We

SUITABILITY CRITERIA: RECREATION AND URBANIZATION

Development Type	Paved Surfaces (Foundations)	Light Structures	Heavy Structures	Site Drainage	Paved Surfaces (Maintenance)	Lawns, Playgrounds, etc.	On-Site Sewage Disposal	Domestic Use	Industrial Use	Irrigational Use	Favorable Microclimate	Topographic Interest	Long Views	Sense of Enclosure	Water-related Views	Vegetation Diversity	Wildlife Diversity	Historic Association	Educational	Fishing	Swimming	Canoeing	Boating
URBANIZATION																							
Rural Urban		■					■	○			■	■	■	■	■	■	●	●					
Suburban	○	■		■		■	●	○			○	○	○	○	○	●	●	●					
Clustered Suburban	■	■		■	■	○		○			○	●	●	●	●	○	○	●					
Urban	■		■	○	○				○				●		●			●					
RECREATION																							
Intensive				■	○	■					○												
General				○		○					●	■	■	■	■	■	●	●	●				
Natural											■	■	■	■	■	■	■	■					
Cultural and Historic																		■	■				
Water-Related																				○	○	○	○

■ Critical   ■ Preferred/Compatible
● Optional   ● Preferred/Partially Compatible
○ Desirable   ○ Desirable

Suitability criteria for recreation and urbanization in Medford Township, New Jersey. (Narendra Juneja, 1974, "Medford.")

concluded that emphasizing the potential effects of development on health and welfare was the most plausible course. The threat to regulation, was, of course, the "takings issue." That is, should a unit of government forbid or constrain development, it must recompense the landowner for his loss of value. Such payment would have made our strategy hopelessly costly.

Victor Yannacone, my long-time adviser, held that it was not a loss of right to prohibit murder and crimes of violence; why, he asked, was this different from avoiding death by drowning, earthquake, hurricane, and other such phenomena? So we decided to interpret natural processes to determine their intrinsic hazards to life or health, and then to consider the possible effects of social policy. For instance, social policy may result in poisoning groundwater or in raising the water level, thus increasing the threat of flooding.

Yannacone and Palmer wrote many ordinances, but only one was submitted to the electorate. It was approved. This was the Medford subdivision ordinance. It stated that any developer must analyze the ecological study and undertake an environmental impact analysis. The immediate result of its passage was that all of the bad developers fled Medford. Medford provided a difficult environment, with the water table on or near the surface throughout and extensive wetlands and flood plains. The requirement to be responsive to these factors and, where necessary, to employ mitigating devices such as detention and retention ponds, enhanced recharge, and limits to coverage and clearance, all proved too difficult, and they moved to less regulated environments. For those developers who remained, there was a task of education, an introduction to ecologically sensitive planning and design. An office was established at the university to help developers assimilate the ecological inventory and respond. Narendra Juneja directed this activity, and Carol Reifsnyder was the single full-time employee, frequently assisted by many graduate students. The effort was an unqualified success. Despoliation of neighboring communities proceeded apace and provided an immediate contrast. There was one consequence of the study that was not anticipated. The guarantee of the quality of the environment proved to have a high market value. This was a unique and invaluable assurance. As a result, the prices of homes escalated. Fortunately, the historical tradition of Medford had bequeathed a considerable legacy of low- to moderate-income housing, and so it was able to withstand the state standards for "fair share" housing, whereby standards were set for the availability of low-cost housing.

The first ecologist in Penn's landscape architecture department was Jack McCormick, a brilliant and irascible fellow. He was passionately committed to the New Jersey Pinelands and to the wetlands. If ever a plaque is cast for the founder of the New Jersey Pinelands Reserve, it should be for Jack McCormick. He died of a heart attack in a paroxysm while attacking some minion of the U. S. Fish and Wildlife Service. He was also instrumental in saving Tinicum Marsh and creating the Fish and Wildlife Service's first environmental center. He left us two significant legacies: Tinicum Marsh and the Pinelands National Reserve, his finest work, astonishing accomplishments.

As the border of the Pinelands transected Medford, the larger, southern part became a public reserve. The enabling legislation emulated the Medford study, but as its criteria were developed exclusively to preserve ecosystems, and particularly water quality, the Pinelands' permitted residential densities were much more stringent; one unit per thirty-nine acres in the preserve, one unit per ten acres in agricultural zones. In addition, there were performance specifications. Development could not adversely affect water quality or quantity, vegetation, or wildlife habitat. The preferred residential environment, adjacent to lakes in the oak-pine forest, was effectively prohibited to development. Route 70 marks the boundary, not only of the park but also of the threshold between nutrient-poor soils in oak-pine forest and the richer clay soils to the north in agriculture. Development was perforce channeled into farmland. As most of the township was constrained for development, the entire market was pressed into the non-preserved, agricultural land, and at higher densities. The township responded by providing public sewers and water. Not coincidentally, many of the key contributors to the Pinelands comprehensive management plan were Penn ecological planning and landscape architecture alumni, notably Cecily Kihn, Ricki McKenzie, John Rogers, Robert Pierson, Jon Berger, and the firm Andropogon.

There was a political revolution following the study. Initially, the government was innocent of environmental values. The ecological study changed that, and many of the conspicuous environmentalists successfully ran for office. There followed a period of intense conservationist policies and actions. The advent of the Pinelands Preserve effected a dramatic reduction in available developable areas at a time when the housing market and housing prices were escalating. Then the prevailing mood changed to echo Ronald Reagan, and the conservationists' primacy was eroded. Pro-development forces assumed ascendancy, where they remain today. The burden of their purpose is to attract and concentrate commercial development along the major highway, Route 70, and to assume that this will support adjacent multifamily housing.

Later, in 1989, I was invited to review the planning process, re-examine the township plan, and explore the utility of computers for the development review process. I studied the history and concluded favorably, the village of Medford had recovered and was much improved. Development, since the study, had been remarkably sensitive to the environment, and although conservationism had relinquished power to the development forces, environmental factors were still operating effectively. This is an excellent demonstration that it is possible for people to understand their environment and regulate its use to protect health and welfare, to maintain cherished places, buildings, and environmental quality. Moreover, in Medford's case, the effort involved no economic costs. Indeed, there were and are substantial economic benefits in addition to protection of the environment.

Of course, I deeply regretted that my involvement with Medford was limited to the one-year ecological study. I had hoped that with the acceptance of the study and the passage of the ecological ordinances, I would be retained to prepare a plan

Giants in Chains

In 1973, during the oil embargo, I received a telephone call from a deputy attorney general in Washington, asking whether he could come to Philadelphia to discuss a matter with me. Indeed. So, some days later we lunched at La Terrasse, a favorite watering hole for Penn faculty and students. The government was being sued under the provisions of the Surface Mining Act, he told me, and then asked whether I would be a witness for the government. I was familiar with the Act. Its intentions were thoroughly admirable. It sought to ensure that the process of open-cast mining was so organized as to mitigate environmental degradation. However, the writers of the Act, undoubtedly lawyers, were clearly unfamiliar with mining, geology, and physiography, for they had written that "land should be returned to the original contour." The intention was clear: cut down the forest, strip the overburden, stockpile it, remove the coal, replace the overburden, and plant it to forest. On flat land this could work like a charm. However, much of the coal in the East is found in the Ridge and Valley Province, parallel ridges where coal and poverty live, called Appalachia. Coal seams frequently surface on the steep slopes. When coal is stripped from such slopes, nothing short of concrete can return the overburden to the original contour of the native rock. A much better condition would have required companies to regrade the mining operation to satisfy local needs, provide new social values. All of the villages and towns in this region are, of necessity, located within narrow valleys in flood plains, threatened not only with the hazards of a coal economy and poverty, but with floods as well. The creation of flood-free, generally flat land would be more valuable than a reconstituted slope. However, the Act was adamant: return the land to its original contour. It was clear that I could have been of some use in helping to write the Act, but I would not be a useful witness for the government, indeed an adversary.

This impasse disturbed me. How could we derive benefit from the occasion? Here I was, in the company of a deputy attorney general. I was unable to provide remedy for the case at hand. Could I offer remedy for any other problems?

There was one current issue in which remedy seemed necessary. During the oil embargo the presidents of all of the leading oil companies declined to sell oil to the U.S. Department of Defense. "My friend," I said to the deputy attorney general, "we can justify your trip from Washington. I propose the following scenario. The president organizes a dinner to which the presidents of all of the oil companies are invited. The president plans to make an important announcement, and so the affair will be televised. The television announcer identifies each of the corporate giants as they assume their seats, wreathed in smiles. The president rises: 'Ladies and gentlemen, I think it important that we begin this occasion with the Pledge of Allegiance.' The assembly rises; each person places his right hand over his heart and says, 'I pledge allegiance . . .' at which point a bevy of federal marshalls enters the room, and handcuffs and leg-chains each corporate president. The president speaks: 'Having refused to sell oil to the Department of Defense of the United States, you are charged with treason. Take them away.' "

The deputy attorney general looked at me, his face drained, his eyes large. He breathed deeply, indeed, he gulped. "God," he said, "You can't do that." "We should," I said.

and, certainly, hoped that I would participate in the planning process thereafter. It was not to be. I had but one chance, and it was remarkably effective. I now feel confident that this method can provide a similar service for any town and, now, with an enlarged capability.

Computation

In the early 1970s, spatial computation was in its infancy. Digitizing was undertaken with cells that introduced a basic error. Cells could only record the presence of a single property, so that the dominant property of a given location would be recorded, and all other properties would be omitted. Moreover, nature is not rectilinear, but the cells were; lines became sawteeth. Even more difficult, the majority determination often failed to represent continuous features—rivers could appear, disappear, reappear as might beach ridges, highways, powerlines, and other features. The graphic output was as abject: typewriter keys were overlaid to provide texture in a caricature of gray scales; typewriter ribbons were the only source of color. So at the time of the Medford study, it was not appropriate to employ computers. Much has changed in the interim, and an exciting prospect is now visible. One of the biggest problems with ecological planning is the expense. The only people who choose to meet the cost are those who are rich and those who are beleaguered and must undertake a study whether or not they can afford it. The computer offers the promise of being able to undertake such studies much more accurately, with more data, more interpretation, more complex analysis, faster, better, and possibly cheaper than by conventional manual methods.

Today it is possible to digitize in polygons, to produce plots of geology, hydrology and soils, vegetation, wildlife, land use, to produce automatically plots of slope, aspect, and insolation categories, to make a three-dimensional digital terrain model and view it from any height or direction. It is possible to make block diagrams with sections, and it is also possible to drape rivers, soils, vegetation, wildlife habitats, and land use on the three-dimensional model. Most important of all, it is possible to initiate "queries," to ask questions of the system. The object can be as simple as identifying single attributes or as complicated as establishing the concurrence of many attributes to show correlations between several factors. The technology facilitates the search for pattern and meaning.

It is possible to review any proposed subdivision and undertake an impact assessment, largely automatically. In the 1989 re-examination, Medford was interested, so my colleagues, Jonathan Berger and John Radke and I developed a demonstration. The proposal recommended that the entire ecological inventory be digitized. The repository for data would be in the university minicomputer lab and the town was to purchase a microcomputer and a plotter. The township could then undertake computerized planning functions. Any procedures beyond the capability of the township's PCs would be undertaken by minicomputers in the lab. Although the town authorized a demonstration and budgeted money, it never requested a presentation, and there the investigation died.

Many of my colleagues, including Peter Shepheard, Laurie Olin, Bob Hanna, Carol Franklin, and Leslie Sauer, collaborated in a major renovation of the Penn campus landscape in the early 1980s. This 1980 drawing is of the then-proposed Blanche Levy Park by Peter Shepheard. (Drawing courtesy of Sir Peter Shepheard, from the collection of the Architectural Archives of the University of Pennsylvania.)

However, this is the face of the future; it will come to be. The original, handsome report was published in 1974, entitled "Medford." Authored by Narendra with contributions by many Penn students and faculty, it became the bible for the township and remains so to this day. It effected the creation of the Pinelands Preserve, was a model for the 1990 New Jersey State Plan, and was employed as the basis for many other studies, including Lake Austin, Texas, and Sanibel, Florida. In the latter project, not only was an ecological study accomplished, but new ordinances were passed and employed in the creation of the comprehensive plan. All of these have been unqualified successes.

Japan 1973

In 1972, Premier Kakuei Tanaka of Japan wrote a book entitled *Building a New Japan*. Its central thesis was that many of the ills experienced by the population came as a result of excessive concentration. His recommendation was that the population, industry, and commerce should be distributed throughout the entire archipelago. Tanaka proposed to subsidize any industry that chose to participate. He would fund the construction of new facilities and purchase the abandoned plants.

Someone in his entourage revealed a concern with the environment. This subject was delegated to the premier's colleague, Governor Hirata. In turn, he requested me to come to Japan to review the project. He made a most generous offer. I declined, as my wife was very ill in the hospital. Two further offers were made, each with an increased honorarium. My friend, and doctor to my wife, Larry Meltzer advised me that I could go to Japan but only for a short visit, which I did.

On the first day I met all of the members of the cabinet. Each described his own role in realizing Tanaka's plan. After each presentation I asked quietly, "What facts of the environment have you included in your deliberations?" There were no answers, only smiles. The second day was given to more detailed presentations by members of the cabinet: reports on transportation—airports, trains, docks, harbors, and highways—new towns, and even industrial facilities. I repeated my request, "What environmental data did you employ in your land use decisions? After all, Japan is a very violent country; volcanoes, earthquakes, tsunamis, floods, and subsidence are all common. Surely these factors should be employed in your analysis and planning." There were no replies, only smiles.

The next day there was a presentation, which I had organized, not only to the cabinet, but to leaders in both government and industry. Perhaps one thousand persons occupied the hall where the reigning scientists of all the environmental disciplines spoke, describing their knowledge of the environment of Japan: meteorologists, geologists, hydrologists, pedologists, plant and animal ecologists, marine biologists, limnologists, and physical oceanographers. The sum of their knowledge was impressive, yet not one of these scientists had been engaged by the government in the proposal to "rebuild Japan."

I observed this profound deficiency. The rich knowledge of the environment, reposing in human minds, libraries, and maps, had been totally excluded from consideration. My talk was on the proposal to undertake an ecological planning study of Japan. As an example I showed the ecological planning study of the Minneapolis-St. Paul metropolitan region.

The screen was by far the biggest I have ever seen. The projector lamp was brilliant. When the first slide was shown, the glass cracked; then a small burnt corner of the slide appeared with a puff of smoke. Quite regularly, every slide was cracked and burned. With an interpreter, one of my students, Harvey Shapiro, I embarked on a slideless exposition on ecological planning.

The following day I was required to make a presentation at the Tokyo Press Club, which was housed in an impressive building. There were some fifty or so journalists. I received a very lengthy introduction by Governor Hirata. Then he said, "Professor McHarg would be delighted to answer your questions."

There were no questions. I asked for a martini and got one. I lit a cigarette. Then I spoke. "If you do not have any questions, I do. Do you mind if I ask them?" No one demurred.

The first question was, "Why should a country with a superb history of consciousness of nature, embodied in language, poetry, painting, temples, and, most important, in the creation of gardens, abandon this tradition and embrace the inferior designs and materials, methods, and construction practices of the West?"

The short answer was that "MacArthur told us to abandon the feudal orient and embrace the democratic West"—but they had thrown out the baby with the bathwater.

Why would a country with a millennium of thoughtful land use and planning abandon all this? We can see how it was done in painting and scrolls, the forms of farms and temples, walls and paths—all were linked to nature in a marvellous vernacular. Why did they abandon this? It was believed that Western military and industrial supremacy reposed in Western materials and forms, and it was for this reason that the Japanese traditions were rejected.

I asked several more questions in the same vein. No response came from the audience until I finished. Then two young men approached me. "We represent the largest newspaper in Japan. We have taped your comments. Should you permit us to publish this, we will pay you $5,000 U. S."

The next day was my last. The culminating experience was with the minister of the environment, who was also deputy prime minister, Takeo Mikki. I arrived at his house at dinnertime. There was no alcohol, no food, only tea and a hot towel.

Mikki had an interpreter, a young Japanese Ph.D. from the Department of Regional Science at Pennsylvania. Econometrics were not pro-ecological. I could not assume a sympathetic translation. The meeting began with Mikki enumerating his responsibilities. He was charged with protecting endangered plants and animals. I retorted that perhaps the most endangered species in Tanaka's plan were the Japanese people. I recommended that as minister of the environment he undertake an ecological planning study, that, in concert with the existing socioeconomic studies and plan, would include understanding and sympathetic treatment of the environment. "This is not my province, I have no mandate to perform such a study," he replied. I continued to try to persuade him, without success. It was now 10:00 P. M., in a few hours I would fly home. I was tired, frustrated, and, indeed, felt that I had been used. It appeared that the Japanese government was quite willing to sacrifice the Japanese environment and people to achieve economic supremacy. It would not be deterred by my recommendations.

So it was time to conclude. I stood up. "Well, Mr. Mikki, if you do not undertake an ecological study from which to affect the Tanaka plan, there is only one thing left to do." I saw the question in Mikki's eye. He understood English very well; the interpreter was only a device allowing him to prepare answers. "What?" he asked. "Pull the plug." "The plug?" he questioned. "Like in the bath," I said. "If you do not undertake an ecological study, pull the plug and let the whole bloody archipelago sink under the waves. But before you do so, send Ryoan-ji to the Smithsonian, Ise to the Louvre, Saiho-ji to the Metropolitan in New York, Daisenin to the Rijksmuseum. These are testaments to a unity of man and nature expressed in the highest art, disdained by Japan, but they are too precious to be lost to the world."

WMRT Becomes WRT

I suppose that my parting with Wallace, McHarg, Roberts and Todd must be discussed. After all, this is an autobiography, and the separation was a very important event, certainly in my professional life.

There may have been circumstances that did not please my partners. Certainly I was receiving the bulk of attention, and this was unkind, particularly to David Wallace. Whereas my partners worked all day every day and traveled frequently, which made for an exhausting experience, my office time was limited to one day a week during the academic year. Of course, I worked full time at WMRT during university vacations. As I was paid by the hour, I had no particular reason to work eight-hour days. I think that it also rankled that I obtained more income from speeches than I did from my office work. Whatever the reasons for my departure, I must have generated some rancor.

The event that precipitated the separation resulted from the fall of the shah of Iran in 1979. The largest project in the office at that time was Pardisan, a commission from the shah with a budget of $1.8 billion. This might well have been the largest commission awarded to any landscape architect.

Pardisan 1973–1975

Pardis are those places where all the good things from God repose. Archimenian princes, it is thought, found idyllic sites, presumably in the savanna—forest edge of the Zagros Mountains in Iran, with clear, cool streams, copses of trees in the grasslands, abundant game, and a genial climate, and named them *pardis*, from which developed the English word *paradise*.

My experience in Iran began with the visit of an American-trained Iranian architect, Jahangir Sedaghalfar, who was scouring the United States to select a consultant to plan an environmental park in Teheran. He was acting as agent for Iran's minister of the environment, Mr. Eskandar Firouz.

I was selected and went to Teheran to learn of the project, which was ambitious. The initiative came from Firouz. He was grandson to the shah of the former royal family, his father had been an ambassador, and his wife was the daughter of the prime minister. He had studied in the United States at a prep school in Princeton and thereafter at Yale, where he obtained a degree in civil engineering, but, surprisingly, he had encountered and become fascinated with ecology.

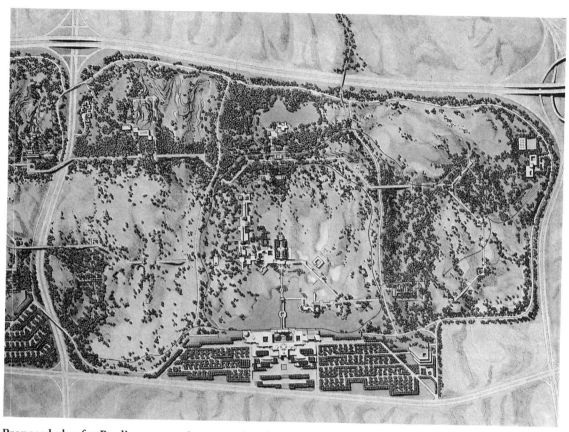

Proposed plan for Pardisan, an environmental park in Iran. I was responsible for the plan, with William Roberts, Narendra Juneja, W. Robinson Fisher, Anne Spirn, and others making important contributions. Juneja supervised the development of the master plan drawing. (The Mandala Collaborative/Wallace, McHarg, Roberts and Todd, 1975, "Pardisan: Plan for an Environmental Park in Tehran.")

Returning to Iran, he first became a member of parliament, then deputy minister of agriculture, and thereafter the first minister of the environment.

Firouz was a most impressive man, of medium size, slender, immaculately dressed, autocratic, extremely well informed, and powerful. His basic assumption was that very little was known of the Iranian environment: the Caspian Sea, the Elburz and Zagros Mountains, the full range of deserts, the Persian Gulf and coastal environments. Exotic wildlife included the Siberian tiger and the oryx, but, of course, the greatest wildlife consisted of the vast herds of onagers, camels,

A picnic in Pardisan, painted by the Office of Glen Fleck. (The Mandala Collaborative/Wallace, McHarg, Roberts and Todd, 1975, "Pardisan: Plan for an Environmental Park in Tehran.")

Great Sandy Desert exhibit. (The Mandala Collaborative/Wallace, McHarg, Roberts and Todd, 1975, "Pardisan: Plan for an Environmental Park in Tehran"; drawn by Colin Franklin.)

Moat

Horizontal Barriers — Uncomfortable Terrain

Slippery Slope

Display features for the Pardisan environmental park in Teheran, Iran. These drawings are from a 1973 feasibility study for Pardisan. William Roberts was the responsible partner for the initial feasibility study, with important contributions from Colin Franklin, Leslie Sauer, Richard Nalbandian, Dennis McGlade, Jack McCormick, Brian Spooner, Buckminster Fuller, and me. After Bill Roberts completed the feasibility study, I directed the rest of the planning, which included the master plan, a film about Pardisan, and stage one development. (Wallace, McHarg, Roberts and Todd, 1973, "Pardisan: A Feasibility Study for an Environmental Park in Tehran, Iran, for the Imperial Government of Iran.")

horses, cattle, sheep, and goats of the nomadic pastoralists. The country's ethnographic history revealed many people with different languages, religions, histories, and vernacular architecture: Bakhtiari, Baluchi, Fars, Turkomen, Kurds, and many more. When all regions had been identified and located, a process of synthesis was undertaken to locate the major physiological-social areas. Each of these would be replicated in Pardisan.

Prince Firouz at the Dardanelles

I engaged in planning an environmental park in Iran for the minister of the environment, Eskandar Firouz. During one of my many visits to that country he invited me to a party at his summer home, fifty miles from Teheran. The occasion was a reception for the American ambassador, Richard Helms. He and the CIA and the State Department are forever condemned for their failure to predict and avert the Iranian revolution. The house was old, handsome, and cold. I gravitated to the fire, where stood a small, elegant, and rather old gentleman, perhaps in his late eighties. He said, "Do I know you?" "No, you do not. I am a friend of Eskandar, my name is Ian McHarg." "So," he said, "you have not heard my stories. Sit down. May I get you a drink? My name is Prince Firouz, my father was the shah and I am a prince, not of Iran, but of Russia; Eskandar is my son. As a young boy I was dispatched to the court of the czar, where I became a page. Many Balkan princelings were similarly hostage in those days. I was tutored by Rasputin, a wise and powerful man; I was the darling of the czarina. In due time I became a member of the Household Cavalry and went on my first campaign in the Zagros Mountains to suppress insurgence by the Kurds. They were starving and mutinous, inspired, no doubt, by the painful constipation induced by eating bread made from acorn flour! But my most memorable recollection is when, as an aide to the czar, I accompanied him to the Bosphorus in 1913 for a historic meeting. The three reigning monarchs, all nephews of Queen Victoria —George V, Kaiser Wilhelm, and the czar— converged on Constantinople each in his own battleship, each in the uniform of a British admiral. They met. The meeting concerned the prospect of war. It was the kaiser who was attacked by his cousins. George said, 'Willi, we understand your withered hand, but you are far too bellicose. You are accumulating ordnance and dreadnoughts in a most provocative and threatening way. We are aware of your infirmity, but it gives you no license to behave so belligerently. Take care, you could provoke war and this could well be the end of our order.' And it was."

In the initial feasibility study it was ascertained that a one thousand acre site should be sought, located in the Teheran metropolitan region. A transect north-south through Teheran offered a wide variety of environments from deserts to the foothills of the mountains with Mount Damavand conspicuous in the view. The next step was an investigation of the selected elements of geology, hydrology, soils, vegetation, wildlife, and ethnographic history that should be included in each area.

The central purpose of the project was to undertake a comparative examination of adaptation to specific environments. Regions of the world were scrutinized to discern examples paralleling those found in Iran. An examination of the various rocks, water, soils, plants, animals, and people was conducted. The desert is crucial in Iran, but there are comparable deserts in Africa, Russia, the United States, and Australia, in much of which different plants, animals, micro-organisms, and people have achieved adaptive successes. These and other ecosystems would be documented.

The formal structure was first presented as a matrix with a hierarchy of bioclimatic zones related to water utilization, and these were arrayed against the continents. Iran was placed in the center, its constituent regions arrayed, and the analogues in each of the other continents located, faithful to geography. This was the organizing structure for the master plan of Pardisan.

The work had proceeded over several years; first a feasibility study, next a comprehensive plan, including a published report, a 16-mm movie by Charles Eames and Glen Fleck, and an elaborate model. The next step consisted of designs, working drawings, and specifications for Phase I. The project had engaged splendid consultants and maintained a staff of a dozen or more. An office was opened in Teheran to undertake the work, and a contract was let for construction of the sixteen-foot-high perimeter wall, several miles in length.

There were hints of forthcoming difficulty. The bank that handled our funds, the Anglo Iranian Bank, was burned. There was frequent gunfire in the streets of Teheran and the Persian administration was atrophied by fear. Yet, weeks before the collapse, Richard Helms, the U. S. ambassador, insisted that Iran would not fall. The United States was behind the shah. On the advice of our resident partner, Narendra Juneja, we decided to evacuate. This was relatively simple for the American employees but difficult for Juneja, who was Indian. However, everyone was evacuated and soon thereafter the shah's empire fell. We contemplated the situation: a very important job had ended, a major source of employment, and, not least, the government of Iran owed WMRT $300,000. We had made strenuous efforts to secure payment without success. Eskandar Firouz had been removed and replaced by one Manichour Feili, who was much less friendly and terrified at the prospect of being accused of being pro-American and making payment to us. We were very near to success, which would have prevented financial embarrassment, but it was not to be. So I had an unhappy meeting with my partners. I have no written record, but I believe that I can paraphrase the discussion, as I recall it. Perhaps my former partners would have remembered the conversation differently, but my recollection is as follows.

"Ian, you obtained the contract?"

"Yes."

"You were partner in charge?"

"Yes."

"Ian, while we had doubts and reservation, you recommended that we proceed. This being so we believe that the loss of $300,000 should be identified as your personal loss. We have determined to seize your assets to the value of $125,000. In addition, we will allocate the residual debt of $175,000 to your account. We would like your resignation."

I urged that the matter not be concluded, that efforts be made to obtain payment from Iran. Moreover, while I conceded that mine was the principal responsibility, I proposed that the loss be shared.

There were meetings and discussions to no avail. The parties asked for my resignation. I do not recall writing such a statement, but it was accomplished de facto. One day I returned to find that the lock to my office had been changed. I was excluded from my records, maps, slides, reprints, indeed, the product of twenty years of work with WMRT.

But the story did not end there. The United States impounded all Iranian assets to be held against claims by American enterprises. The cases involving less than one million dollars would be prosecuted by the U. S. State Department. Because we were included in this category, some splendid State Department lawyers assembled the evidence and, in due time, presented our case to the International Court at The Hague.

While a visiting professor at Berkeley, living in San Francisco in 1986–1987, I received a call from Arlen Specter, U. S. senator from Pennsylvania, who informed me that the International Court had approved our request and had awarded not only the original $300,000, but, with penalties, the sum of $700,000.

My partners, who had decided that the loss should be my single responsibility, now concluded that this payment should be allocated in four equal amounts. I insisted upon the return of my assets to the value of $125,000 and a quarter share, $175,000.

Of course, my major loss was my role in WMRT with a wonderful staff who had worked with me for decades. These people were among my closest friends, allies, and colleagues. Together we had developed and applied ecological planning. My separation ended that wonderful association. Narendra died; Jon Sutton and Michael Clarke left. WRT never assembled a comparable corps to undertake and develop ecological planning, nor was I able to. As a debtor I was in no position to borrow to create a new entity. Not only did I lose, but I believe that ecological planning itself lost its leading practitioner. Therein remains my continuing regret.

Chapter 8

A New Life

Pauline was dead. It was all over, a twelve-year fight, a testimony to enormous courage. "Grotehert," great heart, was dead. Two days ago she had come out of coma. "What day is it?" "Sunday." "What time is it?" "Two in the afternoon." "Why aren't you watching the Eagles?" Only the day before, a doctor had been inexpertly inserting an intravenous needle. The veins were flat, poor pricked veins; he tried, tried, and tried again. Then she bit him. Well done, I thought, her spirit will not die. But it did, finally.

It had been a long fight. It had began innocently when, one day, she said, "Ian, I have a small lump in my breast, I have arranged to have it removed. The operation is short, and I will be out by lunch." So we drove to Chestnut Hill Hospital. She went into the surgery. I waited for one hour, two hours. It was summer, a pretty day; the trees outside shaded the building. The noises were all benign and familiar, voices of greeting, a car starting from the parking lot, laughter. Then two doctors approached me. No ceremony. No introduction. "Your wife has acute lymphatic leukemia. She will be dead very soon. It is only a matter of weeks, perhaps a month." There was more. "We are having other blood tests conducted. She can leave in an hour."

I walked out of the hospital, down the hill to the Morris Arboretum, down the path to the Rose Garden. I knelt and prayed, "God, save this great woman, God save her, God, save her."

She was not to be told the news. The lump had been benign. It was the blood test that had disclosed her condition. Superficially, there was only a small cut and a Band-Aid. I would have to behave normally. I returned to the hospital, met Pauline, laughed at her fears, and we drove home. A lovely summer day.

There were secret phone calls; first, to my friend, a great doctor and cardiologist, Larry Meltzer. He was dumfounded. He would go to the hospital that very night, collect the slides of the blood samples, and have them tested by his colleagues. We arranged to telephone during the day, but only at our offices. Then I phoned Pauline's father, Daniel Crena de Iongh, director and treasurer of the World Bank and International Monetary Fund. I recalled that he was very susceptible to infection, which he revealed in swollen glands. This was suspicious. I advised Larry Meltzer of my father-in-law's condition and the name of his doctor in New York, a very famous physician. Yes, indeed, Crena de Iongh had lymphocytosis; he had had it since 1945, a white cell imbalance with manifestations similar to leukemia. Did Pauline have lymphocytosis? Was this a reprieve? Meltzer's colleagues had examined the blood tests. The results were ambivalent. There was a threat here, but the evidence of her father's long survival with a similar malady was heartening. All of the participants met in Meltzer's office at Presbyterian Hospital. We would say nothing, do nothing, but Pauline would be advised by the hematologists at Chestnut Hill Hospital that she should have regular examinations. One of the hematologists, Dr. McGehee, would assume responsibility for her supervision.

So it went, for some years without any problems. With each examination there would follow secret discussions as to the white blood count, and I looked closely for any evidence of swollen glands. As the years passed, the similarity in condition of daughter and father was admitted into conversation, and Pauline came to learn that she had lymphocytosis. She took this news without distress. She was strong, a powerful tennis player; she took canoe trips in northern Ontario year after year without fatigue. She had never made any concessions to illness in her life. She was a large, laughing woman, the picture of health. But there were changes. She began to suffer anemia. First she was given medicine and then, on one occasion, she required a blood transfusion. At this point a new figure was brought in. Dr. Frank Gardner had been appointed head of hematology at Presbyterian Hospital. Larry Meltzer thought that Pauline's condition now merited serious attention. Chemotherapy was necessary. Leukeran, nitrogen mustard, was the cell killer—what a ghastly weapon. So began the seesaw. White cells begin to proliferate, leukeran kills white cells—but also red cells. Anemia results from the death of red cells, cell formation is stimulated with cortisone. Cortisone produces swollen jaws and other unhappy side effects. Cortisone is discontinued. White cells accumulate, Leukeran is again employed. A delicate balance is necessary, but the tools employed are heavy-handed, they have no fine resolution.

At first, error resulted in anemia treated with blood transfusion. Later error or, rather, inability to control, resulted in coma. So in the final years there evolved a cycle of episodes: remission—illusion of normal life—then crisis, anemia, transfusion, remission, coma, recovery, remission, and so on. It became inexorable. Sometimes the remission was extended, sometimes alarmingly constricted. But the cycle became visible. Life had to accommodate to very important signals.

Meanwhile, two splendid boys were growing up. For my older son, Alistair, the episode began when he was thirteen, and for the next five years there were no visible manifestations of his mother's illness. He went off to Haverford College unconscious of her condition. His younger brother, Malcolm, was not so fortunate. He was six at the onset, and only eighteen when his mother died. He shared with me, very closely indeed, the final tragic years. He was severely tested. On one occasion he arrived home to find his mother in a coma. At other times he rode in a screaming ambulance to the hospital. How much time did he spend in visits to hospitals? Brave wee boy, he was asked to be a man much too early. But man he was, dependable, responsible, generous, uncomplaining, great. Surely it was this experience that impelled him to become a doctor.

This catalogue of events has omitted a whole procession of happy times: parties galore, many trips to Japan, Europe, South Africa, Brazil, and Australia; summers, winters, springs, and falls in the garden, planting trees, shrubs, ferns, and moss, moving large rocks, building ponds, little waterfalls. There are many photographs of smiling, laughing faces, but behind them all is the inexorable clock and the cycle of remissions and episodes. The photographs were all taken in times of remission; the episodes are recorded only in memory.

But now it is over. Pauline is dead. The body will be cremated, the ashes spread along the walk she took daily with Joan Coale, her closest friend, and Rusty, the shepherd dog. She walked downhill from the house, across a steep meadow into the shade of beeches with a carpet of partridgeberry, through the hemlocks and to the banks of the Cresheim, following it downstream to the confluence of the Wissahickon. This path I followed with an urn in hand, spreading ashes on the path.

There was a memorial. It began in the Germantown Friends Meeting. There were all our friends—how many there were. Emily Sunstein spoke of Pauline as a Roman matron, strong in character, in virtue, in laughter and courage, a joy and exemplar. Phillip Reiff spoke of the mark she had made on all of us. Ned Coale spoke of her love. We drove home, where a smaller group convened. Malcolm's choir from Germantown Friends School sang, on the balcony above the living room, Blake's lovely hymn, "A New Jerusalem." We went outside to the garden and stood around the pond. Narendra Juneja, my colleague and friend, passed out bowls of rose petals. As each person strewed a handful of petals on the water, it became a pond of rose petals. The next morning the petals lay on the bottom of the pond. I saw my face in the water—what a sad face, what a miserable, melancholy, haggard, bereft old man.

This was a threshold of my life: I had not expected such an event. For years my friends told me that I worked too hard. I had traveled incessantly, smoked and drank, took too little exercise, and my ancient tuberculosis had made me vulnerable. I would be the first to go. So my will, plans, and assumptions were all based on my predeceasing Pauline.

Immediately it became evident that the major justification for my activities had gone. To whom would I offer my efforts and passions, with whom would I share my plans and expectations? With no recipient, why then persist? There were, however, responsibilities: two young sons, colleagues and roles in the university, a group of marvelous friends, and those with whom I worked in my office. They could not be deserted, there were functions I must perform. Yet there is no doubt of the decline, the diminished commitment, the unfamiliar introversion, the tendency to look backward. My friends could not have been more solicitous. Many of them grieved with me, but the paradox was that their very presence and solicitude evoked Pauline powerfully, and I became racked with sobs, an embarrassment to my friends and myself. I had to separate to spare them and me, yet this act caused hurt, appearing to some as abandonment. It never was; admiration and affection persist to this day. I simply could not survive in the welter of recollections that their presence evoked. Nineteen seventy-five was a muted year.

Carol 1976

For most of us, life offers a succession of birth, adolescence, young adulthood, marriage, children, grandchildren, and death. I was following this common procession, but my wife's death suddenly changed everything. My own scenario, my will, the evidence of our respective family trees, were all based on longevity for my wife, an early demise for me. After all, her mother is alive at one hundred. Nor was I offended at this fate, for had I not survived the war and tuberculosis too? I had already had two remissions. I should not expect more. Yet I did receive very much more. Few people get such a second chance.

I was a melancholy widower, and lonely, but not because of any failure on the part of my friends. To the contrary: they were attentive and generous, yet to be in their company, the scene of so many earlier happier times, induced paroxysms of tears. I declined invitations; I could cry alone without causing embarrassment.

Then I devised a remedy. Unable to sleep, immersed in grief, I concluded that this was an insult to a life shared. Had we not laughed through millions of happy episodes? How dare I extinguish them, permitting the few dark late years to dominate memory and experiences? So, I devised a plan. When overcome by grief, I would defiantly exhume some splendid event—Philadelphia, Amsterdam, Roc Amadour, Temagami, Cape Town, Ravello, Christmas, Easter, Thanksgiving. These I would write, with great attention to detail. On occasion, I would select handfuls of slides and project sunlight and laughter onto the screen. It worked; I had a remedy at hand. If the abyss yawned, I had a pen and my slides. For every image of pain, hospital, indignity, fear, and despair, I had a counter. It took a year, but it worked.

One day I raised my head, looked around, and became more conscious of my surroundings, less preoccupied with past and inner self. Then I met Carol. It transpired that some years before, she had come to seek my advice on studying landscape architecture. At that time she was director of admissions for nurses at Methodist Hospital in South Philadelphia. I reviewed her transcript from Penn State, which supported her contention that college had been a social event rather more than an education. I recommended that she enroll in the College of General Studies and take courses in botany and plant geography, among others. If she received A's in these courses, she could anticipate being admitted to the program. Among the courses in which she enrolled was my own, "Man and Environment." There were more than two hundred students in that course, too many to know, but I discovered later that it was she who had received an A+ for an exemplary paper, "The Future of World Agriculture."

We met again in October of 1976. The occasion was Happy Hour in the Graduate School of Fine Arts, an institution I had originated to occur after classes each Friday night, when students would imbibe enough to inform my colleagues and me of the inadequacies of faculty and curriculum. It was early in the fall; I had not yet learned the names of all of the entering students. In a corner I saw a slender, dark-haired, brown-eyed, beautiful girl alone. I introduced myself, saying "This is a happy department, wonderful students and faculty, a marvelous course; come and join them."

I was much moved by her beauty, and her spirit. I learned of our earlier meeting and was reminded of her paper for "Man and Environment." She became a very powerful image in my field of experience. I sought her company. On one occasion, having returned from a speech at Harvard, I bore lobsters bought at Logan Airport. I went to her desk. "I have lobsters, would you care to have dinner with me and my sons, Alistair and Malcolm?" She was reticent. I left her with the burden of phoning to tell me she could not come. But unwilling to do so, she arrived. I cooked dinner and thought it a splendid occasion. Not long after, on my way to lunch, I met her in the corridor. "Do you have any plans for lunch? Will you join me?" We went to a charming restaurant only to find that our waitress was Hanna Coale, daughter of my closest friend. Our relationship would now become known to my friends, and I had to review the situation. The attraction was powerful and growing. Carol apparently liked me; she laughed at my stories. Yet I was the age of her father, a wrinkled old bastard. What could a man like me do for a beautiful young woman? And so I oscillated, attracted but recoiling in self-doubt, a yo-yo of irresolution. Yet the trend of these oscillations was forward. On one occasion Carol, her mother, and I lunched on a boat moored in the Delaware River. The waiter held a bottle of wine, served her mother and, standing poised beside Carol, said to me, "Does your daughter have wine?" On a later occasion a traveling companion confided, "It is seldom that one sees father and daughter traveling together." Their sense of timing was exact. Carol was half my age, twenty-eight to my fifty-six. She could well have been my daughter. Such comments only inflamed self-doubt. So I recoiled, causing great disappointment and anger. I was instructed to leave and not return until I had formed my resolve.

Shortly thereafter I went to Scotland, where I was still too cowardly to discuss my plan with my brother and sisters. To Joyce, I confided that I had a ladyfriend and together we bought her a sheepskin coat. This presented a clear threshold: either charge or retreat. I charged. We were in love. Yet advancing presented a predicament. I had made plans to spend the Christmas vacation in Martinique with Alistair and Malcolm. How could I leave Carol? I could not, so I arranged that we would all vacation together. It was not a wise decision. Alistair was almost the same age as Carol. Was his father having an affair with a young woman? Was his mother being replaced? I imagine the hurt would have been as great had he known but not been present. I had created the stereotypical drama of mother versus stepmother. The rules were clear, the actual persons did not matter: we had an old man, father; young woman, stepmother. Of course, there was anguish. Where did my loyalty lie? Any action leaning either to Carol or to my sons would hurt. I was an agent who could not possibly gratify all parties. It would certainly have been emotionally less stressful to all involved if I had remained a solitary, brooding widower, but now this was no longer an acceptable future. There was a marvelous, lively new life beckoning. It was real and possible, mostly because Carol had revealed that she might marry me.

Our first meeting had been in October, and despite episodes of tension, the December vacation in Martinique was blissful. Now, in March, I would meet her parents at the Philadelphia Flower Show. I was frightened. Would Bill Smyser bring a shotgun? Not at all. He was very friendly, as was his wife, Eleanor. Carol had long insisted that she would never marry, and they had concluded that whatever bond she would assume would be unusual, such as having an older man as a companion. Our meeting proved to be a warm encounter. Carol's brother Steve, editor of Rodale's *Organic Gardening*, knew of me and my work, so that my first visit to him, his wife, Margaret, and daughter, Carrie, was very pleasant indeed. However, Carrie looked at me solemnly for quite a time and then said, "You know what?" "No." "You are old, you have yellow teeth, and you are going to die." "Yes, that's true," I said, "but not yet."

During that summer, there were many parties for Carol and her friends, often at my swimming pool. Laughter, joy, and excitement filled my life, but I was still bedeviled by self-doubt. It was still two steps forward and one step back. I could not shed my reservations about myself as a swain. Young Lochinvar was gone; could there be a mid-fifties Lochinvar?

Then came another gigantic step. I was invited to visit Jedda in Saudi Arabia to contribute to curriculum design for King Abdulazziz University. I also had a massive project to design an environmental park, Pardisan, in Teheran. I planned a trip that would include Jedda, Teheran, and a Christmas vacation in Morocco. I invited Carol to join me. I concluded my consultation in Jedda and flew to Teheran, where Carol was to meet me, via a flight from Philadelphia to London and thence to Athens. But a number of flights were canceled, and I could not ascertain which one would bring her to Teheran. I identified all probable flights and planned to meet each one. The first disgorged its passengers into the hostile environment of Mehretrab Airport, with its severe police and immigration and custom officials. I saw her, uncertain in the crowd; she saw me and gleamed. My heart pounded. Carol. Carol. We met and hugged. It was my intention to propose immediately. I had made reservations in the finest restaurant in Teheran, but, as Burns said, "the best laid schemes o' mice and men gang aft a-gley," and so it was. The occasion was Ramadan. No alcoholic beverages could be served, the menu was severely curtailed, the chef was fasting. It was not a propitious time. The proposal was postponed.

We flew Air Maroc from Teheran to Athens and thence along the Mediterranean, following my wartime path in reverse: Sousse, Sfax, Mesaken, Hammamet, Carthage, Tunis, Bône, Constantine, Algiers, Oran. From there we went to Casablanca—no Bogart, no Sam, but exotic—a French-speaking Arab world. We traveled to Marakesh and then to Agadir, and it was there that I proposed, only to be rejected. However, on the following evening, Carol, who has an exquisite sense for fine restaurants, led me from the hotel along the shore, past an indoor swimming pool and a kitchen into a marvelous restaurant with wooden beams, low lights, fires, gleaming copper, and lovely music. Here was the time and place, here was a fitting circumstance. I proposed again and was accepted. We proceeded to Ourzazate in the Cedar Forest in the Ante Atlas Mountains, thence to Meknes, Fez, and back to Casablanca. Seeking the sun, we flew to Tenerife, only to find it crowded with noisy Germans fighting for chaise lounges. We learned of Dakar in Senegal, obtained reservations, and left on Air Afrique with a pilot bearing ceremonial scars on each cheek and a conspicuous gold front tooth.

The Hotel Meridien in Dakar provided a pleasant place, the sun shone, it was blissful. We were betrothed. We must return and transmit the good news.

I do not think my sons were enchanted; my sister certainly was not. "You are an old fool, you always wanted a daughter. This is not the proper way to have one." Carol's family, God bless them all, were generous with congratulations and good wishes.

During all of this time, Carol was a graduate student in the department of which I was chairman. Until that time when our names were connected, she was considered to be an exemplary student, receiving deserved approbation, but when it became clear that she and I were paired, nasty stories began to circulate, most describing a dirty old man. The faculty bent over backward to ensure that Carol would receive no preferential treatment, which meant that a larger burden was allocated to her. There were rumors that I was contributing to her work. Carol is too staunch an individual to tolerate that, but what had been a very happy student experience became less enchanting. And I, who had characteristically seen the faculty and students only through my first approximation, a roseate image, came to see warts, pimples, bile, and, I suppose, jealousy. It is a pity. I would have expected my transparent happiness to be a source of pleasure for my colleagues and students. There were those who did not wish us well, but certainly not enough to deter us.

Before graduation, Carol had rented a charming one-room schoolhouse in Eagle, in the eastern Chester Valley. There she moved from her collapsing apartment in West Philadelphia, its cast iron balcony sitting securely in the garden three floors below. For some time I traveled between Chestnut Hill and Eagle until we concluded that one house was enough and Chestnut Hill too saturated with old lives ever to be an acceptable habitat. This was a difficult decision for me, not because of artifacts alone, these could be moved, but because of the garden where I had worked joyously for almost two decades. There was a pond with minnows, sunfish, turtles, frogs, mallards, and even a resident bittern. There were great faces of Wissahickon schist, lifted perilously over the garage; waterfalls, trees, shrubs, and native herbs, brick terraces and steps. Few clients had ever required me to design a garden. For this one, I had been designer, client, and laborer. It was hard to leave the red foxes, deer, herons, red-tailed hawks, the yellow grosbeaks on the windowsill. Hard to go, but leave I must. If there was to be a new life, it must occur in another place. Carol and I were married at her family place in York, Pennsylvania, on May 28, 1977.

An Essay in Self Sufficiency

Carol's plan for my rescue, rehabilitation, and projected future included evacuation from a suburban location, immersion in a truly rural setting, and engagement in agricultural pursuits with an emphasis on animals. The implicit assumption was that clean air, our own water, good food, country folk, and animals (particularly their excrement) were requisites for my survival and our happiness.

We bought a small farm in Marshalton, Chester County. It contained a small but celebrated 1680 house, a tenant house, a barn, ancillary buildings, and fifty-five acres. Carol's family had been substantial and prosperous farmers for generations in York County, Pennsylvania. She knew the family farm and was inclined to rural life. I had no known agricultural connection, but I was willing to subscribe.

First we had to move. All of my furniture and belongings remained in the Philadelphia house, where my oldest son, Alistair, lived alone. Our shared goods and chattels were not formidable. We could rent a truck and move ourselves. As we did, the last load consisted of a few pieces of furniture, many house plants, and a bevy of chickens. I started out for Marshalton and in Downingtown came to a low bridge. The sign said "11'2" clearance." On the dashboard of the truck was a severe

Palm Coast, Florida

One day in Philadelphia I received a call from a Dr. Young of ITT. He had been the director of Levitt Brothers, which had been absorbed by ITT. He had a Ph.D. in psychology, in the pursuit of which he had studied the rat experiments of Jack Calhoun of NIMH and the work of endocrinologist Jack Christian, who had observed the effects of stress on deer and muskrats. Young had developed an aversion to high densities, employing Calhoun's term "pathological togetherness."

He intimated that ITT owned plus or minus thirty-five miles of Florida's eastern coast and planned to build a low-density new town there. His firm wanted me to plan it.

ITT had recently been involved in the CIA-led successful destruction of the democratically elected government in Chile. So I told Young that my reputation as a liberal Democrat would be jeopardized if I associated with ITT. "Come, come," he said. "At least come to New York to discuss the matter." I said that I would confer with my partners and advise him. They suggested that at least I investigate further, which I did. I asked my colleague Leslie Sauer if she would investigate Palm Coast for me. Then I discovered yet another source of information. Improbably, Penn's mens basketball team was in the NCAA quarter finals. During an intermission of the game in Memphis, a scantily dressed nymph, standing before a background of palms and ocean, asked the audience whether they would like a share of paradise: "For $500 down and $500 a month, buy a lot in Palm City, Florida."

Leslie returned. A large sales force was indeed at work, thousands of quarter-acre lots had been platted and sold on beach, dune, bay,

inlet, mangrove, swamp, and elsewhere. So I wrote to Dr. Young.

Dear Dr. Young,

With my partners, I am delighted to offer services to undertake a comprehensive plan for the new town of Palm Coast, Florida. We will perform this for $1 million in one year, but under the following conditions. I have learned that you have sold thousands of lots without benefit of any ecological understanding. Many of these are unsuitable for development. We therefore require you to repurchase these properties. Our ecological study will employ the most distinguished natural scientists of the region. We will be beholden to their interpretation. You will also be responsible to their and our determination as to suitability. If you concur, we will assist you in this endeavor. If you fail to respond to these environmental imperatives, we will join with the environmental movement to oppose your plan.

I received a phone call the next day. "Mr. McHarg, there is enough for both of us. We have a work force of five hundred salesmen. Let them continue to sell lots for a conventional development. You can have half the property, some eighteen miles, to employ your impeccable ecological planning."

"Sir," I said, "there is the problem of guilt by association. It is difficult for a lady to maintain an impeccable reputation if she is found in the company of whores. I would fear for my reputation. Thank you, but no thank you."

admonition: "This truck requires 10'6" clearance." Reassured, I proceeded under the bridge. There was the most horrifying noise. Had I been rammed, had a heart attack? What happened? The bridge sign was in error, there was not 11'2" clearance, as the removed roof of the truck testified. Moreover, the chicken coop had broken, there were chickens everywhere. But providentially, just then there were two police cars on the far side of the bridge, one manned by a state trooper, the other by a Downingtown policeman. "Gentlemen," I said, "Can you provide me with an affidavit? I would like you to testify that the ostensible clearance for the bridge is 11'2"; the requirement for the truck is 10'6"." They obliged. I collected the chickens, reloaded plants and furniture, and proceeded on my journey. Hoots, jeers, and cheers greeted me when I arrived, the roof a jaunty, jagged concertina.

We had made an earlier beginning with animals during our first year of marriage in the one-room schoolhouse in Eagle. Our commitment to animals began with Carol's dog, a pseudo-poodle called Algernon, who persisted for fifteen years at the center of an increasing array of animals. He was joined by Petunia, a stray cat who quickly multiplied. Algie was joined by a succession of three Scottish deerhounds and a Great Pyrenees, a black lab and Portuguese water dogs. Petunia was followed by a Himalayan, legitimate and barnyard progeny, a Maine coon cat, which sought existence inside walls, and sundry foundlings left on our doorstep. There was a time when we had eight cats. One of these we later transported to San Francisco and boarded in a Pacific Heights penthouse where animals were forbidden. Serious animal acquisition began with Carol's avowed intention to teach me to ride and the purchase of a beautiful mare, Mrs. Downey, from Edinboro, Washington, with impressive credentials—my birthday present. I reciprocated with John Grand for Carol, and we began riding.

At Eagle, pigs had made a brief entry into our lives. Carol responded to an advertisement stating that baby pigs were available in the nearby Amish country. The plan was for a suckling pig. Carol met the farmer's wife, who asked her how she proposed to transport the pig, revealing that not a carcass, but a lively piglet, was the purchase. It was placed in a cardboard box under the hood of a Volkswagen and later put into a shed in the garden. This excited Mrs. Downey and John Grand, who opened the shed door. Pursuit was to no avail. Either there is a feral pig roaming the environs of Eagle or someone had a free dinner. In Marshalton, Carol set out resolutely and returned with two young white York pigs named Melissa and Melinda, to which names they responded with amiable welcoming. Because their benign behavior induced confidence, I then joined in the effort with the purchase of two bred gilts, Durocs, covered with red hair and very pregnant. We named them Ruby and Rosy. One morning, viewing them in the barn, I concluded that delivery was imminent. So under instruction, I transported a circular table, chairs, linen tablecloth, crystal glasses, and a bottle of French champagne to the barn, and awaited the event. Ruby was first, and the beautifully packaged piglet emerged, ruptured its casing, stepped daintily around the umbilical cord, and found a ready nipple. So too did number two, and number three. After the birth of number ten there was a long pause. A call to the vet revealed the possibility of a backward exit as reason for delay. So Carol took my handkerchief, immersed hand and wrist, and emerged with the wrong-way piglet. It was followed by the rest, fifteen in all. We toasted with champagne and then observed Rosy, who proceeded to present eleven piglets without pause or problem—a magnificent delivery. But there were problems later. Large sows can asphyxiate their progeny, and ours did. We eventually bought birthing boxes, but the tragedy persisted.

Our population needed an adult male, and so back we went to Amish country, to a barn filled with boars. Boris was bought, the patriarch who fathered probably a hundred and fifty pigs, because, sell as many as we did, every three months, three weeks, and three days, the sows would deliver another litter. We could not control the numbers, so that when the entire consignment went to the butcher there were a hundred pigs. We ate magnificently of smoked bacon and sausage, scrapple, pork and suckling pig, but it might have been the most expensive food we ever ate. Our return covered the cost of feed but not of land, labor, or even the thought of profit.

We had made an initial try with hens at Eagle. We visited Zern's improbable emporium in Morgantown, where the contents of whole households were auctioned for single dollars and cents. Chickens were for sale; we examined cages and selected a bevy. The auctioneer was totally incomprehensible, so we hired an interpreter, identified our selection, and set off to examine other exhibits. On return we found a cage bearing our name, but not our selected chickens. It was, rather, the worst collection of culls ever seen, cross-beaked, bald-arsed, squinting, crippled.

At Marshalton we improved. Our first selection was Arucana hens, producing red and blue eggs, then a flock of Barred Plymouth Rock. Then followed deliveries by mail of day-old chicks and suddenly we had a barnyard flock. It expanded to include ducks, Peking and Muscovy, and then pheasants. Our problem was surfeit: How much mayonnaise can you use? How many deviled pheasant eggs can you eat?

Then came cattle. One day Carol revealed that she knew of a Scottish Highland bull and cow. Should we acquire them? We did. Sherman tanks with horns, they were, small, shaggy, and bulky. We named them Fergus and Fiona. We dreamed of calves, but it was not to be. Fergus lusted. At every paroxysm he would draw back his lips, and reveal his large square teeth in grimace. Some time would elapse between instinct and action, then he would cumbersomely wheel to Fiona and try to mount. With the least movement of her buttocks he would be undone. Minutes would elapse until the lustful grimace reappeared, then the slow pantechnicon move and another attempt, failed by Fiona's slight deflection. I would try to help, first with instruction, later by holding Fiona's head in a corner, pointing her bum to Fergus, but she could thwart him effortlessly. He never did beget a single calf. Ultimately, Fiona was joined by three Charolais cows, but to no avail. Fergus may have been impotent, but he was nonetheless a personage. He could jump a post-and-rail fence from a standing position. He would roam, his greatest antagonists the lower branches of some statuesque evergreens owned by our neighbor. He would attack these viciously, tearing off huge limbs. Our other neighbor, Devereux Farms, had a prize dairy herd and a very valuable bull. Fergus chose to attack. It took some effort to separate the combatants and imprison Fergus in a stone enclosure. His future was in peril—no calves, much trouble, the butcher was his fate. Steaks and hamburger went to the freezer, but upon Carol's decision, Fergus's head went to the taxidermist, and today he still looks over us.

We next acquired sheep. Black wool was in fashion, so black sheep we bought: one-third Karakul and wild, one-third Finn, and one-third Dorset, bred for blackness, twins, and wool. The ram was Randy, properly named. Had only Fergus been as proficient. Lambs came in abundance, but whoever had undertaken the selective breeding was unaware of the Pennsylvania calendar. For it was at Christmas and January that the lambs emerged. The ewes escaped from their warm environment and lambed in the snow. Many died, poor little black corpses.

In such an animal experiment there are always the runts, those rejected by their mothers, and the sick. They would end up in the kitchen, so it was not unusual to have baby pigs, baby lambs, and chickens in the kitchen and laundry room. Drenched chickens would be resuscitated with hair dryers; piglets and lambs would have their bottles. And there were incubators holding eggs. Every twenty-four hours the eggs had to be rotated; otherwise there would be smelly cherry bomb explosions.

It was a lot of work for a woman, a man, and a schoolboy who helped to feed the animals, particularly in bad weather. We had no tractor. Barrow, pitchfork, and shovel constituted our technology, but we ate wonderfully well.

We always had a large vegetable garden and eventually we began an orchard. Highland Orchards were nearby. I had an acquaintance who owned a Vermeer tree transplanter for 48-inch diameter balls, so an instant orchard was created of six-to-eight-inch caliper specimens of red and black cherries, red and yellow apples, peaches, pears, and nectarines, plums, and apricots. These were followed by soft fruit, black and red currants, blueberries, gooseberries, and raspberries.

We had achieved a considerable measure of self-sufficiency; our efforts supplied us with beef, mutton and lamb, pork in various forms, chicken, duck, pheasant, eggs, fruit galore, and a wide variety of vegetables. But it was not economical. The rewards were emotional and physiological.

When the food self-sufficiency program was in full swing, the idea of energy self-sufficiency arose, so plans were developed. The Broad Run was a hundred feet from the door. A dam would provide 15 feet of head; 2.5 cubic feet per second could power a turbine and produce all the electricity we needed. Plans were drawn and the cost calculated—$30,000. Manure from pigs, horses, cattle, and sheep was abundant, so we then considered a methane digester. Penn had a number of scientists working on this problem, and a plan developed. What of transportation fuel? I drove eighty miles each day to and from Penn and reproached myself for my prodigality with fuel, but five acres of corn and a still could provide all of the alcohol fuel for the mobility we required. And there was another option: We had a windswept ridge where a wind machine could be installed. All of these ideas seemed to cost the identical sum. Each appeared thoroughly economical, each could recover costs and provide profits. There were, however, no federal or state funds available, and no bank manager would provide a loan. Our efforts at conserving energy were limited to using wood fires. The stream flowed unchecked, the wind blew free, and the excrement ended up in the vegetable garden and the orchard.

It was a wonderful experiment, but with a negative conclusion. Such farming could provide a substantial degree of food self-sufficiency, but at very high cost in terms of both money and labor. I wish it had been otherwise. Wise and experienced farmers around us, even those engaged in high-technology agriculture, including the use of split embryo implants, managed only to maintain a way of life. Their land was their only asset, their incomes were minuscule.

We learned one day that our large neighbor, Devereux Farms, a philanthropy engaged in dairy farming with a work force of retarded young people, had determined to sell its land that was zoned for single-family houses at one unit per acre. The commute of forty miles to a vanished rural environment and a suburban sea had become intolerable, and we decided to sell as well. The Swedenborgian Church sought a retreat for its pastor and a small congregation of some thirty sexagenarians, and so, with constraints on the amount of building, we sold Old Mill Farm.

As our ownership came to an end, divestiture became necessary. We sold a hundred pigs to the butcher, and a flock of sheep to a buyer who concluded he did not want them all, so there were wild sheep on the property we sold. Mrs. Downey was sold into luxury. Her first foal, Skip Brick II, became a decent stud; her second, bred with Leonato, is Carissima, for long Carol's horse. John Grand aged, suffered with arthritis, and, with sadness, was put down. Every predator in Chester County came to resolve our chicken, duck, and pheasant surplus. I can see them now, chicken fat running down their chops, sitting in a sea of feathers.

During our time at the farm there were associated efforts at self-sufficiency. Carol made soap from animal fat, lye from wood ashes and herbs. She made candles, vinegars, and dried flower arrangements in addition to preserving fruits and vegetables, all of which were incorporated in her gourmet cooking.

There were lessons learned. Here we are now with thirty-five acres of beautiful land on which we have built. There will be animals, but fewer, selected more wisely, with possibilities of reasonable control and management.

The House

My lifetime accommodations have spanned the spectrum. I spent years of my army life living in holes in the ground, sleeping under trucks and the wings of planes and in abandoned structures. More permanent accommodations began with the two-story terrace in which I was born and spent my childhood, then ranged from Gosford House, a castle near Edinburgh, to an abandoned distillery in Burntisland, derelict weaving mills in Nottingham, horse stalls in Newmarket, to the beaches of East Anglia. In 1946 in Cambridge I began in a room in Harvard Street, then moved to a duplex near Fresh Pond. I lived in a basement apartment in eighteenth-century Edinburgh and then at Walcott Drive, Cherokee Apartments, in Chestnut Hill, Philadelphia. These accommodations were followed by a three-story Victorian house in West Mount Airy and, later, my first owned home, a modern house designed by Oscar Stonarov in the Cresheim Valley, part of Fairmount Park in Philadelphia. The next step was taken in my new life, the purchase of Old Mill Farm, fifty-five acres with the historical house built in 1680. It was small, with tiny rooms and windows and a great fireplace. It was thoroughly charming. A minor drawback was its tiny dimensions, probably an asset in Colonial days without central heating. But the greatest disadvantage to the house was its insatiable appetite for maintenance and restoration. It was indeed very old, and this was increasingly revealed in crucial repairs. When our neighbor decided to sell the land to development and we decided to sell, we had some time to plan our future, for I was to spend a year at Berkeley. It was at this time that Carol learned of the sale and purchase of the King Ranch, some five thousand acres in Chester County. Although most of the property existed in large farms, there were two properties, fields in fact,

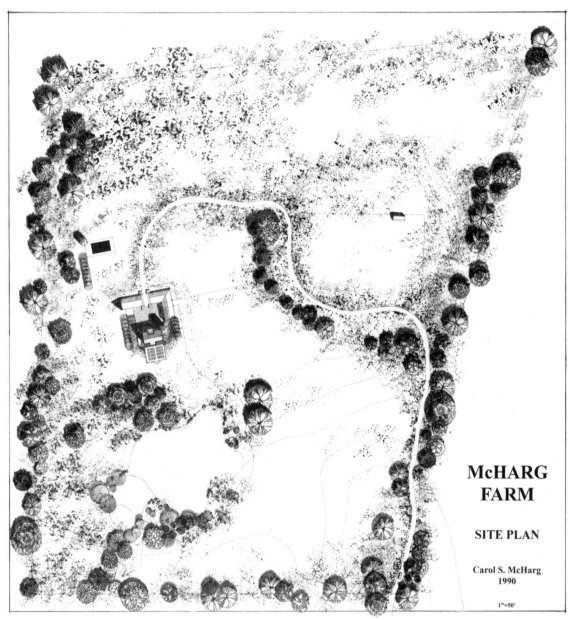

McHARG
FARM

SITE PLAN

Carol S. McHarg
1990

1"=50'

McHarg Farm Site Plan, Chester County, Pennsylvania. (1990, designed by Carol Smyser McHarg.)

each of thirty-five acres. One of these, which impinged on a six-hundred-acre forest preserve called the Laurels, most appropriately named, we bought. Through the insight, initiative and energy of Frolic Weymouth, the King Ranch was purchased and sold in intact parcels, the purchasers having donated the development rights of their properties to the Brandywine Conservancy, another of Weymouth's creations. So now we had land. We determined to build there.

The adjective *appropriate* deserves to be discussed. Carol and I are both landscape architects. My book, *Design with Nature*, and hers, *Nature's Design*, vaunted ecology, appropriate places fit for buildings, constructions fit for the environment. What was fit for our field in the heart of this pastoral landscape in the Chester Hunt?

We ascertained the geology. It was Wissahickon schist, at the southern boundary was the contact with Cockysville limestone, the geology of the Plan for the Valleys. The schist supported ridges; the limestone was associated with valleys. Jim Thorne, an ecologist at Penn, took soil samples. There were some soils unsuitable for septic tanks, but the remarkable aspect was that soils were compact, like concrete. Decades of grazing at one head per acre had induced this compaction. In a grazing regimen for cattle and horses woodlands were few and far between. Our woods were only a few acres, dominated by walnut, with Norway maples, and one tulip poplar—not very handsome or ecological. Save for a few ferns, the herbaceous layer was mostly Japanese honeysuckle and bittersweet. The hedgerow boundary was much better, with a rich punctuation of shadblow and native cherries. The site had a high point near the northern boundary and sloped steeply due south.

We investigated prospective house sites and discovered that there once had been a farmhouse and a barn on the property. An employee of the King Ranch remembered the house being dismantled and the masonry bulldozed into the basement. We found the rock pile.

We negotiated with members of the Brandywine Conservancy, who had obtained the development rights to the property. Stakes were hammered into the ground. The house site was well below the high point, partly shielded by the wood lot, squarely facing the cardinal points. The master bedroom would be facing east, the livingroom facing west, and the southern exposure protected by overhangs. There would be short views of the woodlot and long views of the horizon in all directions.

But upon our return from San Francisco, where I had gone for my 1986–1987 sabbatical, we needed a home. Carol found a house for rent, not far from our land. We also bought a small two story red brick house in nearby Unionville. It came with a one-story house and a large red barn. Carol prepared a plan for the land-owner on whose land sat our rented house and this lady sold our house from under us. We had to find a place to live. Rentals were scarce in Chester County, so we had no option but to move into our Unionville property. This was indeed a doll's house; it made Marshalton look like a castle. Yet we lived in these constricted quarters for more than a year, indeed, until our house was built.

Carol was familiar with her grandfather's farm in York County, inherited by her father. This farm had the ultimate cathedral of barns. It still stands, used for storing bags of dolomite. We considered building a barn on our land and investigated the Smyser barn. It was much too big to become a house, and, anyway, the owner would not sell.

Carol decided to investigate barns and quickly found a barn builder. We inspected his work and found it to be excellent but expensive. Carol concluded that an Amish barn builder would be as competent and much cheaper. We found Rueben Reihl—small, compact, Amish dressed, a walking stick. Yes, he took down barns; yes, he would try to find one for us. He found several, which we examined. The one we chose was destined to be destroyed. He would acquire it, dismantle it, mark the members, and move them to our land. We sought a construction loan for $300,000 and contracted with Rueben to build our house. We hired an architect but quickly found that his services were of small value and beyond our means. Adija Pal, an Indian architect, student of landscape architecture at Penn, was hired to produce working drawings. Carol was architect, supervisor, and general contractor. She gave a year of her life to the design and construction of the house. It was completed within a year—a masterly work.

The original barn was eighty-eight by forty-eight feet. It consisted of five bents enclosing four bays. We utilized only four of these and built a three-bay house, sixty by forty feet. The barn has a front with light on three sides. The ground floor, accessible at grade, contains the entry-dining room, which rises more than fifty feet to the ridge. The western bay holds the living room, with porches to the west and south. The eastern bay contains the kitchen, and over this bay are the master bedroom and bath. Children's bedrooms sit over the living room. The northern facade contains children's bathrooms, laundry, and stairs. Above the master bedroom is a guest bedroom, with a matching one over the children's bedrooms and playroom.

There is a marvelous intervisibility throughout the house. Light is crucial. Dawn appears dramatically through bedroom windows, sunset warms the living room. The house is a masterful exercise in design with light. The bent structures remain unchanged, and the original exterior boards are now the interior panels. Wherever the eye falls it finds delight—in wood beams, columns, joints, dowels, floor, and, above all, in the orchestration of light.

An old township road, unhappily named Tapeworm, follows a hedge into the property and rises along a hedgerow toward our house site. Little new road had to be built. The meadow, some thirty-five acres, comes to the base of the house. The only non-meadow is a gravel parking lot. Whatever horticulture we have grows in pots on decks and porches.

Between entrance and living room a large masonry wall has been built to accommodate four fireplaces: one in the basement, one for the dining room, another in the living room, and one more above in the children's playroom.

The materials are heartwarming. The floorboards, two and a half inches thick and eighteen inches wide, are of white oak, hemlock, and chestnut; the honey-toned paneling is from granary boards. The major structural timber is white oak in dimensions that no longer exist in the forests. The girts are eighteen by eighteen inches by forty feet.

The masons engaged in the project decided against using quarried stone, so they went into fields and collected weatherworn stones. Their technique involved "cheek masonry," whereby stones were bedded in cement but no cement showed in the joints, which were very tight. Such masonry is pure Zen.

Most of the workmen—barn builders, carpenters, masons, plasterers, and painters—were Amish. Because their religion prohibits the Amish from driving trucks or running a cement mixer, these jobs were performed by Mennonites. The prohibition does not apply to chain saws, power saws, power sanders, or staplers. The electricians and plumbers were not Amish but had chosen to work with Amish builders. It was not hard to understand their decision. This crew, headed by Rueben Reihl, including his second-in-command, Moses, together with Ephraim, Harold the driver-carpenter, and others were, without doubt, the most courteous, well-behaved, well-spoken people I have ever met. These were very skilled and industrious craftsmen; indeed, they never stopped working. Moreover, they were not expensive.

The most important aspect of this work force is that their labors gave an added luster to the house. They made it, they gave something of themselves to it. Their contribution seems palpable to this day.

Sir Kenneth Clarke and *Civilization*

Who cannot remember the visual orgy of *Civilization*? Out of the parade of trivial vulgarity and inconsequence that is commercial television, PBS brought that most suave, urbane, erudite, and assured upper-class Englishman, who with a magic wand enchanted us with the full panoply of art—neolithic to modern. Without a trace of doubt, with no hesitation, he marshalled art by time and attributed value. He located photographers of exemplary skill in improbable locations to record profoundly moving images, all accompanied by the commentary of established authority. I watched and listened in awe, not only of the creative genius of Western art, but the erudition and confident evaluations by the commentator. I was delighted, that is, until we reached the eighteenth-century English landscape tradition—Pope, Kent, Capability Brown, Sir Humphrey Repton, William Shenstone, Uvedale Price, and Payne Knight—that heroic tiny band who transformed England from a raddled medieval landscape into the fair land of today. To me, this was the greatest single act of art in the entire Western tradition, nothing less than the transformation of an entire nation into beauty and wealth. Not so, said Sir Kenneth, the eighteenth century is merely a Romantic aberration—a step at best sideways, perhaps backward—from the classic tradition through the Renaissance.

Now this was the only area of art history that I knew better than Sir Kenneth. He was wrong as to fact; he was in even greater error as to judgment. Poussin, Salvator Rosa, and Claude Lorraine all contributed to this great accomplishment, which, in terms of social value, exceeded all of the painting and sculpture of the period. I turned off the television and took my fury to bed, where in sleep I dreamed. I was in a hovel, probably in Flanders. A poor slattern wiped her hands on her apron, a man and some children were at the table eating potatoes, and an abject fellow sat on the floor, his back to the wall, disconsolate. It was that failed missionary and uncertain painter Vincent van Gogh. There was a knock on the door of the hovel, and the women opened it to see a magnificent figure—top hat, cloak, morning coat, gloves, tie—an impeccable upper-class Englishman. He said, "Madame, I wish to speak to Vincent." The dream dissolved, a new image appeared: a barge in Amsterdam, a man and woman sitting at a table. The woman, Saskia, reveals that she is pregnant, has syphilis, and is going to leave her companion. He sits with blood running down his jaw, his ear in his hand. There is a knock at the door, she opens it, there resplendent is a suave, elegant, upper-class Englishman in top hat and evening clothes. "My name is Kenneth Clarke. Could I speak to Vincent?"

No, he couldn't speak to Vincent, or for Vincent, or for the English eighteenth-century landscape tradition either.

At the onset the crew was skeptical. Barns are for cattle and hay, not for people. But as the construction proceeded their interest awakened. Rueben and Moses began to discuss how best to solve problems. The budget was established by the construction loan, and any modifications to the original plan required comparable eliminations. But costs never dominated discussion. Solution of the problems at hand was the basis for investigation. There were, in fact, some serious problems, notably with the stairs. These involved cantilevers, and rather complicated ones at that. Here Moses revealed a new talent, producing meticulous scaled working drawings, which he proceeded to realize. Some rather important architects, Sir Peter Shepheard, Laurie Olin, Bob Hanna, John Johansen, and others, have admired this work and concluded that they could not explain how it was done. But they were unanimous in their admiration. The house was built at a cost usually associated with a warehouse. The decision to build a barn proved to be appropriate and extraordinarily economical. Here, Carol and I would raise our two young sons, Ian William and Andrew.

Germantown Friends School

When Malcolm was about ten years old, attending the Germantown Friends School, he came under the direction of a magnificent teacher, Sally Satterthwaite. This particular year the students were addressing the topic of the Renaissance in Italy and France.

I usually took the boys to school, and on one such occasion the teacher asked me whether I would be willing to give a talk on the gardens of the Renaissance. I had visited and photographed all of the conspicuous works, so I assented.

I worked diligently, selecting the most dramatic images of Villa d'Este, Lante, Aldobrandini, Mondragone, Vaux-le-Vicomte, and Versailles. I prepared the lecture, carefully insisting that I must constrain my vocabulary to conform to the audience.

The lecture was to be given early one morning. I went to the classroom, checked the projector, the screen, the focus and awaited the audience. This was a new experience. The children came whooping into the room; there was pushing, shoving, and little effort being given to seating. One child seemed to be the instigator. I picked him up and held him at eye level. "Who are you?" "Stacy Mogul." "Oh, so you are Stacy Mogul. I have heard of you, noisy, quarrelsome, a pest. Now listen, when I put you down, you and all the others will sit silently." The treatment was successful. The audience sat quietly. I began. Great images of the Goblet Fountain appeared, the Walk of One Thousand Fountains, the main axis of d'Este, then Lante, and, finally, Vaux-le-Vicomte and Versailles in France. I spoke slowly, limiting myself to description of the projects. It was a beautiful show, and I was well pleased. When the students left, one remained. Her name was Joan Yarnall; I had known her since babyhood. I had bathed her on occasion, I had read her stories. She was blonde, blue-eyed, serious. She said, "Thank you, Mr. McHarg. You know what? I knew many of the words you used."

White House Task Force on Energy and Environment

Early in his administration President Carter convened a Mini Task Force on Energy and Environment. He sought the support of the environmental lobby for his energy proposals and brought some leading figures to Washington to review and recommend. There may have been twenty participants among them, including Eugene Odum, H. T. Odum, and George Woodwell. Eugene Odum had been a member of Carter's transitional government and was a confidante.

An undersecretary presented the energy plan and asked for comments. The scientists, one after another, expressed reservations about the commitment to nuclear power, the emphasis on the exploitation of U. S. western coal, and the concomitant problem of water scarcity. Most of all they were concerned about the puny commitment to the development of renewable resources and alternative energy sources—active and passive solar, wind and geothermal power, photovoltaic cells, mini- and micro-hydropower, biomass and tidal surge. H. T. Odum delivered an inspired commentary on oil shale exploitation and the gassification and liquifaction of coal, showing that the energy produced was exceeded by the energy employed. The measure of net energy was novel to the officers of the U. S. Department of Energy (DOE).

The scientists were clearly interested in each other's statements, but the audience was not. The undersecretaries of DOE and the senior bureaucrats did little to disguise their profound disinterest. No matter that President Carter wished to obtain the support of environmental groups for his program, members of the DOE did not share his interest; indeed their attitude was as to antagonists who inspired neither interest nor fear.

As the meeting drew to its close, Eugene sat beside me and whispered, "We are not getting these people's attention. You are here under your own name, without institutional affiliation. You are free to speak your mind. Please do. Speak plainly."

I spoke. "Gentlemen," I said, "presumably the purpose of this meeting is to secure the support of environmental groups for the president's energy plan. Many of us voted for Mr. Carter, we like him and would like to help. But there are serious obstructions. Not least the Department of Energy. After all, many of the faces we see today in this department are those we came to loathe as members of the Atomic Energy Commission, a group careless of the health of America's human population, unknowing and uncaring of the environment. Need we remind you of Operation Ploughshare, dedicated to the use of atomic bombs to construct a new Panama Canal and Alaskan ports, studies conducted without reference to epidemiology, health physics, plant and animal ecology, utterly oblivious to the effects upon not only the ecosystem, but also human health and well-being? You have not changed, you are still the big nuke men, you cannot be entrusted with the environment. If President Carter wishes the support of environmental groups, you should be replaced by persons more knowing of the environment and energy, sensitive to the health and welfare of the people and plants, animals, and microorganisms that populate this land. Indeed, this line of reasoning leads us to the secretary of this department, James Schlesinger, a man whose political life has included the U. S. Department of Defense, the Atomic Energy Commission, and now the Department of Energy.

"This department is thoroughly misnamed. Surely a more exact title would be the Department of Nuclear Weapons. The alliance between these departments is vivid. They comprise the biggest menace in the country, not only to the survival of man but to life. There is not a vestige, not a spicule of environmental sensibility, to be found in these agencies or James Schlesinger. Surely he, with you, must be replaced if we are to have confidence in Carter's plan and the trustworthiness of this agency to execute it."

Within two weeks Schlesinger was dismissed, certainly not because of me, but I had done my best.

Taiwan

In 1983 I received an invitation to Taiwan through the efforts of three former students: Lung Shung Chang, an Eisenhower fellow who had obtained a Ph.D. in city and regional planning, now administrator of the Taiwan EPA; Shu-li Huang, who had obtained a Ph.D. in ecological planning; and Monica Kuo, a talented landscape architect, who married Shu-li Huang. The invitation ostensibly was to advise the government on the creation of a system of national parks, particularly the Li-Wu River Gorge in the Taroko National Park. It transpired that there was a larger purpose, never made explicit, but revealed by the roles and audiences I would encounter. In fact, the major purpose of my visit was to support the small, emergent environmental movement in Taiwan, which had originated mainly with the

American-educated children of the country's leadership. They had parted from
their parents' undeviating pursuit of economic growth, deploring the human environments being created, notably in Taipei, and rejecting the lure of an increasing
plethora of consumer goods. Their goal was an improved living, working, and
recreational environment, and they were unwilling to sacrifice it for continued
economic growth. I was there as their spokesman. However, it was not enough to
assert this position; it must be seen to be relevant and effective. I must provide a
demonstration.

The choice of Taroko Gorge was an inspired one. A proposal had been made
to create a national park there. A massive formation of white marble runs across
Taiwan, ending in steep cliffs along the eastern ocean. The Li-Wu River has transected this and cut a steep gorge, a miniature Grand Canyon with the chasm
shrunken to a cleft. Taroko is located where the marble touches the sea, itself
bordered by a precarious road, clinging to the cliffs and frequently going through
tunnels. This means of access to the marble at Taroko explained its exploitation.
The mountain face at the entrance to the gorge was the site of intensive quarrying.
Explosive charges, placed at the toe of the mountain, produced massive talus slopes
of raw white marble. Pieces the size of boxcars were removed to nearby factories
and transmuted into elfs, dryads, and Chinese lions, and into smaller and smaller
sizes ending in white marble ashtrays. Surely this defilement was incompatible
with the entrance to a national park. I suggested to the minister of the Interior and
the prime minister that it would be wise to prohibit quarrying and substitute mining. Let the operators cut an entrance into this huge formation and remove material as required. The entrance could be judiciously located, as could transportation,
to eliminate any conflicting impression.

In addition to marble sculptures, there was a battery of other activities utiliz-
ing the white marble. It was being crushed into aggregates of differing sizes and,
ultimately, into powder for manufacture of PVC pipe and cement. Crushing produced clouds of dust, blasting created noise, and the entire process involved a
parade of trucks, all antithetical to a national park experience. I suggested that the
raw rock slides be revegetated with the use of hydraulic methods from land and air.
Mining was more appropriate for these activities than quarrying.

Another issue was that Tai Power, a government authority, had been instructed
to proceed with hydroelectric development for the drainage basin that culminated
in Taroko. This region is among the most active orogenic areas in the world. The
mountains rise from sea level to 14,000 feet in a few miles, looking like teeth pushing out of gums. Road construction in such a region is hazardous and inordinately

expensive. Moreover, the volume of water was modest. Indeed, capturing the entire hydroelectric potential of the watershed, putting all of the rivers and streams into pipes, would yield the power equivalent of half the standard coal- or oil-fueled thermal electric plants. Generating stations would have to be constructed underground and roads built on precipitous slopes.

The project was easy to ridicule, which I proceeded to do. Surely Taiwanese ingenuity could provide substitutes—geothermal, ocean surge, photovoltaic cells, biomass, or even the more prosaic coal. Taiwan was importing coal very cheaply from Indonesia. Was it really necessary to put every stream into pipe, to rob the landscape of the very water that had created a scene of international significance? I persuaded the minister of the Interior, Executive Yuan, and the prime minister to abandon the hydroelectric scheme and investigate alternatives.

The next problem was by far the greatest. The leading industrialist in Taiwan, with substantial interests abroad, was determined to build the biggest cement plant in Asia at the park entrance. This man could not be taken lightly; my contacts were impressed, afraid of his power and anger. It was stated that he had left school at fourteen, which somehow purported to explain his savagery!

This gentleman owned an extensive area of flat land in a small bay at the mouth of the gorge, on which he proposed to construct the cement plant. I suggested an alternative, by which the government would seek to identify a location, suitable for the purposes of crushing marble, manufacturing cement, and exporting it, mainly to Indonesia, combined with importing coal from that country. It would also assume responsibility for necessary highway or railroad construction and port expansion. The owner would be asked to consider employing the land at the park entrance for prestigious hotels, shopping, golf courses, and other appropriate recreational activities. At this time, by happenstance, the father of regional science, econometrics, Walter Isard, then of Pennsylvania, was in Taiwan. He might be retained to employ his Taiwan graduates to seek economically feasible alternatives.

So it was arranged that I would meet the great man in his sanctum sanctorum and present the idea. Would he investigate the possibility of using his site near the park for resort facilities if the government associated with him to locate and improve a site for cement manufacture export and coal importation?

I arrived in the room and sat down, joining the dozen or more people who accompanied me, all sitting on the edge of their seats. The great man and his sycophantic entourage entered. I stood, but there was no acknowledgment. He began a furious, bellowing tirade. "Taiwan does not need foreign environmentalists. We

Silver Belt Falls occurs at the contact area between the gneiss cliffs and mountains of the lower Li-Wu River Gorge and the marble cliffs and mountains of the central portion of the Taroko National Park. (Photograph from Hanna/Olin, Ltd., 1986, "Li-Wu River Gorge Study, Taroko National Park, Republic of China.")

The Tunnel of Nine Turns is one of the most spectacular areas of the Li-Wu River Gorge in the Taroko National Park. (Photograph from Hanna/Olin, Ltd., 1986, "Li-Wu River Gorge Study, Taroko National Park, Republic of China.")

have transformed a parochial province into a world industrial power. What does he know of Taiwan? Why should we listen to him? . . ." and so on, for hours it seemed. I became impatient; I blew my nose, coughed, turned my back. I did not know then what he was saying but I could see that my colleagues were frightened and cowed. He was certainly not being complimentary; indeed, he was being very rude. Enough. I stood up and walked out.

The developer called a press conference and recapitulated his statement. He never heard my offer, at least not from me. But the minister of Interior and the prime minister did, and they agreed with me. The owner would not be permitted to build the cement plant at the entrance to the national park. The environmentalists had achieved an important victory.

With this battle won it was possible to exploit our success, so my hosts arranged for me to give several addresses to natural scientists and conservationists. I presented a method for creating a system of national parks, an ecological planning method to be used and, finally, the utility of undertaking a national ecological inventory.

It is generally true that local successes do not necessarily persist, but in Taiwan there has continued to be slow but sure improvement. There was a price; I would be surprised if I were ever invited to return to Taiwan. However, a vast 94,800-hectare Taroko National Park was created. Subsequently, my colleagues Bob Hanna and Laurie Olin were invited to Taiwan, and their firm completed an admirable plan for the Taroko Gorge National Park.

Three Mile Island Health Fund

Mr. David Berger, Philadelphia attorney, led the class action suit against General Public Utilities (GPU), operators of Three Mile Island (TMI), Reactor 2. A settlement was agreed to among the parties, which recognized $25 million in damages as a result of the TMI accident and set up the Three Mile Island Public Health Fund. The U. S. District Court approved the settlement. U. S. District Judge Sylvia H. Rambo retained continuing jurisdiction of the fund. Judge Rambo approved all expenditures and actions of the fund. At its inception, the fund consisted of $5 million, which grew to more than $10 million with interest earned. Pursuant to court authorization, it has been used for the following purposes:

1. Research into the specific effects of the TMI accident on the health of persons living in and around the facility;
2. Research into the long-term effects of ionizing radiation on human health;
3. Planning for nuclear power plant emergencies in the future at TMI;
4. Monitoring the ionizing radiation released by the TMI facility reactors under normal operations and during emergencies.

A son of David Berger, Jonathan Berger is a regional planner and was a member of the Penn faculty of Landscape Architecture and Regional Planning for a decade.

Jon serves as the executive secretary of the Three Mile Island Public Health Fund to this day. It was he who introduced incoming students to ecological planning and helped pioneer the application of concepts from human ecology to planning.

David Berger knew of my habit of assembling teams of scientists to undertake planning studies. He asked me to advise him regarding members of the contemplated scientific advisory board that would review research proposals to be supported by the fund. I was delighted to do this, but it proved to be more difficult than I had imagined. Radiation was a highly charged subject. Moreover, any scientist who wished to do research on ionizing radiation had to supplicate the old Atomic Energy Commission (AEC) or its successor, the Nuclear Regulatory Commission (NRC). These agencies did not brook disputation, far less contradiction. Success required unquestioning subservience. Those few who disputed current assumptions on the effects of low-level ionization were denied support and persecuted.

I learned from Rusell Train, administrator of EPA, that it would be difficult to find a group of objective and distinguished scientists to compose the advisory committee. Train had sought to require an environmental assessment of nuclear facilities, but he could not find objective voices. He searched in Britain and in Europe, but nuclear scientists everywhere were beholden to the AEC and NRC.

However, we succeeded in inviting Karl Z. Morgan, legendary health physicist, to chair the advisory committee. He had given evidence during the trial. Morgan, in turn, brought in Thomas Cochran from the Natural Resources Defense Council and Dean Abrahamson, physicist and doctor. I recruited George Woodwell, the great ecologist, founder of radio ecology, and Jack Geiger, epidemiologist. John Cobb and Edward Radford were also enlisted. I served on the advisory committee too. This was a superb committee; its members have served since 1979 and have performed very well indeed.

Of course, the problem was extremely difficult. The country was polarized. There were those who viewed the Department of Defense and the Atomic Energy Commission as bulwarks of our defense, protection from communism. More commonly, however, these agencies were seen as careless of public health in the episodes at TMI, Hanford, "the down winders," Marshall Islands, and Chernobyl, which fueled antinuclear passions. In the TMI region, citizen groups resolutely rejected all statements made by the nuclear lobby. Even our group, viewed as antinuclear by the establishment, was viewed with suspicion by the citizens' advocacy organization TMI Alert.

Objective statements would be difficult to find; they would require strict and expensive research. The results would not only be scrutinized by the courts but would also be viewed with suspicion by the protagonists.

It was in this light that research began and proposals were solicited, reviewed and then forwarded to Judge Rambo. After approval, work would begin. Research in progress would be reviewed.

Most of our work occurred during a seven-year period in the 1980s. I participated in this board composed of brilliant members. For most of this time we would meet roughly once each month, dine at a splendid restaurant, and spend the following day together.

The examination was exhaustive. Research proposals were solicited to address each problem. Jan Beyea resolved the discrepancies in descriptions of the TMI event. He invented meteorological models to simulate the radioactive plume. Ruth Patrick, among others, addressed the subject of monitoring. She proffered unique insights into the utility of biological monitoring. The subject of emergency planning was addressed by Roger Kasperson and his colleagues in geography at Clark University. The health study, investigating the incidence of cancer, was pursued by Drs. Maureen Hach and Mervyn Susser of Columbia University. Excess incidence and mortality for several cancers were reported, and the findings indicated some possibility of a connection with the accident. Further study is required to assess the nexus of causation and followup through the year 2000 has been funded. The largest single contract was awarded to Alice Stewart, the formidable British epidemiologist. All of the records of exposure to radiation by employees of the national nuclear facilities were forwarded to Birmingham for her analysis and review.

The final major contribution by the board was the discovery and acquisition of highly accurate and economical radiation monitors. These were distributed to citizens' groups whose ongoing task was to monitor ionizing radiation.

Of course, my interest in radiation had a long and intense history. I had encountered Grand Junction, Colorado, the uranium capital of the country, in 1949. I learned that uranium mining was being undertaken by subcontractors of the Atomic Energy Commission, who felt no need to warn employees of the perils of radiation. Moreover, the tailings were available free to anyone and were being incorporated into concrete cinder block and, thence, into buildings—churches, schools, and homes. Decades later a high incidence of radiation pathology and morbidity led to the discovery of high radiation levels in many of these buildings, which were then destroyed. There was also the Rulison, Colorado, case: A nuclear bomb was exploded below ground to compress natural gas. The site was found to be highly radioactive, and the well was capped.

My personal engagement with this subject began with the discovery that Pauline had chronic lymphatic leukemia, and part of my mind then focused on cancer and cancer research. In 1982, Carol was diagnosed as having cancer, which amplified my preoccupation with cancer and its treatment. So immersion in the Three Mile Island scientific advisory board was an expansion of a long-term pre-occupation in which my professional interests coincided with personal ones.

My involvement with the Three Mile Island Public Health Fund immersed me in the greatest environmental crisis of all time. We could survive Styrofoam cups, litter, and perhaps even the devastation of rain forests, but the resolution of a superpower confrontation by nuclear weapons would be terminal. When the nuclear winter investigators completed their analysis, they concluded that the only refugia to escape nuclear radiation would be the tip of Patagonia and the southern island of New Zealand. Was it God's plan to repopulate the world with marsupials, Maoris, and Scots?

TMI, of course, was focused on low-level ionizing radiation, but advocates in the Atomic Energy Commission, the Department of Energy, and the Nuclear Regulatory Commission were concerned with nuclear problems at all levels. While our investigation concentrated on the actual TMI event and its effects, our role was viewed as hostile by the establishment. There was deep antagonism. Over the seven-year period of our intense work, this antipathy grew and, with it, the con-viction that DOE was actively disinterested in illuminating the health effects of low-level ionizing radiation. It took Herculean efforts by attorney Danny Berger of Berger and Montague to "persuade" DOE to release the medical histories of all persons who had worked for the nuclear establishment and worn badges to measure the radiation they received. The medical histories of more than 600,000 such persons were transmitted to Alice Stewart at Birmingham University. The conclusion of her studies, employing the largest sample ever, will reveal the best information on the medical effects of ionizing radiation and close an important chapter. These findings will more than justify the efforts of the scientific advisory board. Of course, the greatest change in the nuclear threat was effected by Mikhail Gorbachev—may he be venerated henceforth.

The fund is still in existence, but its resources are being depleted, as planned. Consequently, the scientific advisory board now meets infrequently. As of 1995, the fund has spent more than $10 million on independent assessments of cancer risk and adverse pregnancy outcomes at TMI; improved emergency planning for the TMI region; the design and construction of a citizen-run real-time, on-line envi-ronmental radiation monitoring system; and studies on the effects of low doses of ionizing radiation on the health of human populations. The most notable of these studies has been the Department of Energy cohort of more than 600,000 workers by Alice Stewart.

Chapter 9

Retrospect and Prospect

I have undertaken more than one hundred ecological planning and landscape design projects. It would be as tedious to read them all as to write about them. There should be an alternative. Can they be grouped into subjects and seen as contributing to the evolution of the human ecological planning method? My roles have varied from partner to inspirator, colleague to critic, but it is fair to say that my professional practice emphasized multidisciplinary teams and depended strongly on collaboration. My role, most often, was as leader of the orchestra and, sometimes, as part of a small band or as a soloist. There were, however, discrete subject fields with distinct problems. I have chosen this device to structure the following presentation: river basins, metropolitan regions, transportation, new towns, waterfront improvements, and other projects.

The origins of the ecological planning method were simple indeed when we embarked on the Metropolitan Open Space Study and Plan for the Valleys in the late 1950s and early 1960s. The tools employed were rudimentary geology and hydrology—little information on either soils or vegetation, but rich data on land use. Indeed, I was unaware of Nevin M. Fenneman of the University of Cincinnati, who had published *Physiography of the Western United States* in 1931 and *Physiography of the Eastern United States* in 1938, and of Charles B. Hunt and his *Physiography of the United States* (1967) and the conception of physiographic regions. When studies from the Plan for the Valleys were later published in *Design with Nature*, they required serious augmentation and revision. Yet even with the modesty of the data and perception at that stage in development, the first professional application of the method in Plan for the Valleys was an instant success. This is more an indictment of prevailing planning than a paean to ecological perceptions.

327

When in the 1960s a faculty of natural scientists was appointed at Penn, there was an immediate and significant increase in our understanding of natural systems. The study of Route I-95 between the Delaware and Raritan Rivers utilized Jack McCormick and Nicholas Muhlenburg as critics, if not participants. It is salutory to recall that this project took all of six weeks. It may have been the first major demonstration of the evaluation of natural factors as either propitious, neutral, or detrimental to the highway alignment. To the best of my knowledge, this was the first expression of the statement that, although natural factors could be described objectively, it was necessary to observe that personal attitudes toward these factors could be expected to vary systematically between individuals and groups.

Another merit of this demonstration was that it shared the characteristics of a scientific experiment. Data used were overt and explicit, as was the method employed. Therefore, any other person using the same data set and method would reach the same conclusion. When it was recognized that different groups, with different values, were likely to occupy any planning region, it became necessary to recognize that, given agreed-upon data, the value system of the problem solver would generate the solution. Such solutions would vary with groups having distinct values. The opinions of persons or key informants, therefore, expressing opinions about, for instance, flood plains or hurricane zones, would provide information quite as objective as the scientists' descriptions of rocks, soils, plants, and animals.

River Basins

I first encountered the subject of river basins in a course in government at Harvard given by Arthur Maas. It primarily addressed the TVA but also investigated the then-current proposal for a similar compact for the Columbia River. The major burden of the course was the philosophical basis of the project, as presented by David Lilienthal, the first TVA director, in an inspirational book entitled *Democracy on the March* and in an excellent critique by Sir Julian Huxley entitled *TVA*.

Although a determination of the hydroelectric potential of the Tennessee River basin required specific knowledge of climate, geology, physiography, and soils, at the least, these were conspicuously absent in the published reports. Certainly such data would have been indispensable for the location and design of dams, but this same inventory could have been employed for other objectives of TVA—improved agriculture and forestry, recreation, housing, and, most important, industry induced by abundant cheap electricity.

So when, in 1967, I decided to function as a professional staff member for the Udall Task Force on the Potomac, there were no precedents known to me. It would have been helpful to learn of Charles Eliot's study and plan for the Boston metropolitan region. This was a much smaller region, but it was the first ecological planning study ever performed. Unfortunately, neither the members of the task force nor the faculty at Penn were aware of this most original study. So, perforce, we had to reinvent the wheel.

Our first problem was scale. My largest studies had included 3,000 acres in the Philadelphia metropolitan region. The Potomac basin is almost 14,700 square miles and covers parts of four states and the District of Columbia. The appropriate scale was no longer 1:24,000, but a tenfold increase—1:250,000. This produced maps six feet long, three feet wide. We concluded that the study should first consider basinwide factors, thereafter address the physiographic regions, and, finally, examine prototype sites, the last at a scale of 1:24,000. As a unifying device, we embarked on a chronological recapitulation of the past to explain the present.

We learned that the physiographic regions of the Potomac were shared by the James, the Susquehanna, and the Delaware. We soon found that geological history defined not only physiographic regions, but also the rocks and their specific features. In this inquiry we were investigating the geological history of the eastern seaboard and learning of the phenomena and processes constituting the regions and the basin. This produced an enormous increase in the knowledge of processes and materials. The development of a study method was a challenging intellectual exercise for students, faculty, and task force alike. We were most fortunate to have M. Gordon Wolman, hydrologist, as a member of the task force, as well as John T. Hack, a senior geologist and expert on the Alleghenies in the U. S. Geological Survey (USGS).

So we mapped geology, defined geological features, assembled and constructed sections. We located weather stations and associated statistical data; we mapped physiographic regions—the Allegheny province, ridge, and valley, the Great Valley, the Blue Ridge, the Crystalline Piedmont (including the Triassic basins), and the Inner and Outer Coastal Plains.

Geological data were excellent at the scale of 1:250,000, but no finer resolution existed. Contour intervals from the USGS, at 1:24,000 were more than adequate; soils data were available in county soil surveys at 1:15,000—much too fine for the river basin but excellent for site examinations. Soil associations were employed. We studied surficial and groundwater hydrology. The Great Valley and the Coastal Plain were areas of abundance, the other regions less well endowed. A cumulative profile of the Potomac and its tributaries was developed, relating water quality to geologies and land uses.

Of course, the physiographic regions were dramatically unique. The borders between any two regions were astonishing: the Allegheny Plateau, the front and the valley and ridges; the corrugations of this region with the flat Great Valley; the contrast with the Crystalline Piedmont and, finally, the fall zone and the Coastal Plain. It became clear that the geological history of each of these explained their development history and their resources, as is true to this day. The forested plateau with clean streams was ideal for recreation. The ridge and valley had been dominated by coal mining. The Great Valley was a vast and invaluable agricultural resource. The Crystalline Piedmont was more variegated, with agriculture and forest land, but mainly urbanized. Finally, the Coastal Plain was a vast reservoir, substantially forested, a great recreational resource.

We had no specifics on vegetation, the only information on plants being the green areas on the USGS 1:24,000-scale maps, signifying "cover for troops." It was necessary to map vegetation from air photographs, for which we had expert advice from Nicholas Muhlenberg. Jack McCormick was particularly knowledgeable about the vegetation of the Coastal Plain.

Wildlife data were scarce, restricted to information for hunting and fishing licenses, and so we were limited to identifying vegetation, elevation, slope, and aspect as constituting particular habitats.

Land use data were available from published maps and from air photography. The first phase in developing a model consisted of displaying these data on mylar transparencies; meteorology, geology, hydrology, soils, vegetation, wildlife, and land use. This was the first formal development of the "layer cake model" in which chronology was employed as the unifying device.

From this first review I invented "intrinsic suitability," a device to identify and array both propitious and detrimental factors for all land uses. Angus Hills in Ontario had conceived of "carrying capacity," a measure to determine suitable factors, notably for agriculture and forestry. He was an inspired soils scientist. My objectives, however, were different. I was interested in developing a method to locate the "most fit" environments for all prospective land uses.

I believe that this was the first demonstration of a device to establish fitness for prospective land uses, and it has held up well. It can be used as a first approximation using gross data, and it is as amenable to handling high-resolution data.

Essentially, the method consisted of describing factors objectively within all categories and then identifying the degree to which they were suitable for various land uses. Climate factors, including length of growing season, first and last frost, precipitation, soil attributes, soil drainage, elevation, slope, aspect, and vegetation cover were clearly linked to agricultural suitability. Moreover, each category—such as slope or soil type—had a range in value so that a composite array of weighted factors could be computed. A parallel set of detrimental factors could also be identified, weighted, and arrayed. In this scheme, hydric soils, very steep slopes, exposed bedrock, short growing season, and susceptibility to fire, among others, fell into the detrimental category. The resolution required identification of these regions where all or most propitious factors existed, and where none or few detrimental ones did. The process was repeated for each of the physiographic regions, and the last examination was of the Washington metropolitan region.

I suppose the most important conclusion drawn from the study was that nature is systematic, and, therefore, that the presence of opportunities and constraints for all prospective uses is systematic too. This means that the planning process can become overt, explicit, replicable, having the characteristics of a scientific experiment.

The next greatest benefit from the exercise was the mammoth amount of knowledge accumulated, assimilated, and employed. It set standards that would be used subsequently in a decade of river basin studies for the Delaware.

There was a general conclusion that geomorphology was the integrative device for physical processes and ecology was the culminating integrator for the biophysical. These contributed to understanding process, meaning, and form.

The project occupied an academic year. On completion it was photographed with a Hasselblad camera by Charles Meyers, one of the students involved. Maps and a slide show were presented in Washington to Secretary Udall; Russell Train, then of the Conservation Foundation; sundry functionaries from Interior, USGS, Fish and Wildlife Service, the Soil Conservation Service, the Forest Service, the National Park Service; and to various political figures, among whom was a conspicuous opponent, Senator Robert Byrd of West Virginia. He deeply resented a federal intrusion into his bailiwick and, with his fellow West Virginia senator, successfully opposed the proposal. The presentation was widely applauded and led to the employment of WMRT to produce the book *Potomac*, published by the Government Printing Office in 1967.

During the next year I was on sabbatical, but I planned to undertake a comparable study of the Delaware River basin. My colleague William Roberts became chairman during my absence and directed the study. I retained John V. Phillips, the legendary South African ecologist, to join the department and contribute scientific insights to the enterprise. In 1969 the first investigation addressed the entire river basin.

In the following year, when I returned, I determined to continue the Delaware River basin study by examining each of the physiographic regions. This involved a monumental amount of mapping and induced a mutiny among students in the department. The students were correct, the prodigious task of coloring massive maps was substituting physical labor for learning. I thought better of this approach and concluded that examining sample sites at a scale of 1:24,000 was a more appropriate method for learning about physiographic regions.

The study continued for a decade, a marvelous example of the accumulation of increasingly richer data, an expansion of perceptions, a significant improvement to planning capability. It is probably true to say that the ecological planning method experienced its evolution in the Potomac and the Delaware basin studies at Pennsylvania.

During this period I was ignorant of the ethnographic method that the NIMH grant would later produce. We assumed that multistate administration of both the Potomac and the Delaware would employ new federal and state powers. In truth, the Delaware compact gave great power to the River Basin Commission, which it resolutely avoided using. Similarly, because the Potomac River Basin Compact included the governors of the states comprising the basin and the secretary of the Interior, the Compact could have undertaken comprehensive planning for the maintenance and enhancement of water quality. However, the Compact refused to engage in planning and limited itself to adjudication of water allocation in the area.

Unfortunately, the marvelous accumulation of perceptions embedded in faculty intellect, maps, reports, and student exercises never did have any effect on the Delaware River Basin Commission. When the Compact was created it was staffed with engineers and economists, so that when I went to Trenton to offer our vast compendium there was no one on the staff who could read, far less understand, the material. To this day the Delaware River Basin Commission has not yet undertaken an ecological inventory like that done, year after year, at Penn. However, many Penn graduates who participated in these studies, notably Glenn Eugster and Cecily Kihn, later worked for the U. S. Department of the Interior in Philadelphia. There, they pioneered greenway planning during the late 1970s and through the 1980s in numerous river corridors throughout the Northeast, including several in the Delaware basin.

Recovery from Insult or Assault

I have always been enamored with the definition of health as the ability to recover from assault or insult. There have been a number of such events in my life, and there will be more. How have I responded? Bereavement, illness, divorce, unemployment, firing, disability—I have had my share.

I lost my maternal grandmother when I was thirteen. This was my first encounter with death, first funeral. It occurred on Friday the 13th, 1933. I am not superstitious, but I still walk warily on this anniversary. The defeat at Dunkirk in 1940 was the next massive insult. The pride of the British Empire was reduced to a disorganized rabble, dropping weapons, fleeing to the west of France to be evacuated by the brave navy, merchant marine, and private sailors. The sinking of the *Abdiel* in 1943 was next; several hundred sailors and as many parachutists died. I swam for hours through the burning sea and emerged with nothing more than barnacle etchings on buttocks and back.

I recall the time in the winter of 1943, when I opened a letter to learn that my mother had died. Death in the Sangro Valley was common that winter, but the news of my mother's death convulsed me.

I suppose the greatest insult to my body and psyche was the onset of tuberculosis in 1950. It robbed me of energy, mobility, pride and imposed a stigma, a badge of shame. This feeling persisted for years but with time receded, so that today it is a memory more than four decades old.

The largest blow to my life was leukemia, suffered by Pauline, which lasted for twelve years and ended painfully. This deprivation has been muted but not eradicated.

And the experience has been duplicated. Carol has survived four episodes, which she has surmounted without complaint, with remarkable courage. I cannot fail, given this example.

The remaining insults are less serious, but cumulative. The forced resignation from Wallace, McHarg, Roberts and Todd robbed me of a fascinating practice that I have been unable to resurrect. Age pursued me. At sixty-five I was deemed incapable to continue as chairman of the department I had founded. It fell into other hands and began a marked change, a slow decline. Five more years brought me to age seventy and mandatory retirement, with the result that I have become emeritus, have lost my status as a member of the standing faculty, and have been denied the right to participate in the selection of a new dean, a new chairman, my successor.

How have I adapted? If I cannot teach at Penn, I can teach—and have taught—elsewhere, at Harvard, Penn State, Arizona State in Tempe, the University of Oklahoma, Ball State, and the University of Oregon.

If I no longer have an enterprise like WMRT, I must perform differently. I have created a small office with not more than one staff member and have undertaken studies for the Girl Scouts, Riverdale, Blue Heron, Colusa County, and The Settlement in Ann Arbor and have produced "A Prototype Database for a National Ecological Inventory for EPA." Meanwhile *Design with Nature* has been translated and published in French, Italian, and Japanese. It has been reprinted in both paperback and softback. And I have written this autobiography.

With the loss of my practice I turned my attention to other problems, focused on the national environment, and then expanded this quest to include the entire earth.

In 1994, I had pain over the heart. Was it a heart attack? Fortunately, no. But some plaque was found, so I underwent an angioplasty. A balloon on a wire made its way to my heart and removed the plaque. I experienced a great surge of oxygen and energy. So many around me fell: Roberto Burle Marx died, Sir Peter Shepheard had a stroke, and the newsletters from the Second Parachute Squadron report a declining number of survivors.

I am still sought as a keynote speaker, I am beginning a new life as the director of a computer lab at the University of Oklahoma, and teaching invitations continue. Just three years ago, Carol and I built a marvelous house. In 1990 I received the National Medal of Art and in 1995 I received the Thomas Jefferson Medal at Monticello. Can I maintain dignity, act with generosity and perhaps with wisdom, continue to seek and solve problems, recover from assault and insult? I pray God.

Metropolitan Regions

My first encounter with metropolitan planning was with the open space study for the Philadelphia metropolitan region performed for the Urban Renewal Administration. The presentation I made to Alan Boyd, acting secretary of the Department of Transportation, came to the attention of Vice President Hubert Humphrey. He concluded that this method should be applied to the Twin Cities metropolitan region. He arranged for the Chicago HUD office to finance and supervise the exercise, which was published in 1969. The next metropolis to be studied was the Denver region, performed for the Regional Transportation District in 1972. An ecological study for the San Francisco region followed in 1974, employing new and elaborate geophysical data. The client was the Association of Bay Area Governments (ABAG). The final study, the first to include the application of the computer, was performed for the Toledo metropolitan region.

The most significant observation about these investigations was the recognition of the abundant and relevant data totally excluded from the planning process. This was brought to my attention at the onset of the Twin Cities study. I arranged an appointment with a professor of geology at the University of Minnesota and disclosed that I was about to undertake an ecological planning study of the region. I asked whether he could advise me of available data. Sadly, he took me to a room filled with flat map files. "This is my life work, here is substantially the sum of knowledge of the geomorphology of this region. Save for a few inquires from engineers, these data have not been used."

Of course, we seized upon this cornucopia, yet the volume of data and the fine resolution required aggregation. The cost of this process exceeded both our charge and the budget. Yet, clearly, this was an indispensable source of invaluable information for society.

Ground and surface water hydrology data were rich; fish censuses revealed not only fish and wildlife but water quality. Although the quality of data available varied from region to region, there was always a mother lode of vital but totally neglected information. Such oversight should have occasioned no surprise. Almost all city planning curricula assumed that the profession was an applied social science, so economics, statistics, government, demography, and environmental law occupied conspicuous roles in instruction. The natural sciences were all but universally absent; geography was the sole exception.

This criticism of the profession applied equally to planning agencies. The Twin Cities Metropolitan Council, Denver Regional Transportation District, Association of Bay Area Governments in San Francisco, and the Council of Governments in Toledo were uniformly innocent of natural science, which proved to be the weak link in the planning process. There could be no progress without planners competent in environmental science. Penn had introduced this into the curriculum in the 1960s.

The metropolitan regional studies contained significant lessons. This first was the recognition of the abundance of environmental data that were not being employed. Of course, the agencies generating data were limited by mandate; for instance, USGS was responsible for geological, physiographic, and hydrologic data. A review of this information, however, revealed severe disparities. Geological data were all but absent, save at the level of states; hydrology was spotty; topography and land use were generally very good. The Soil Conservation Service (now the Natural Resource Conservation Service) was and is conspicuously excellent in presentation and interpretation, and climatic data from the National Weather Service and the National Oceanic and Atmospheric Administration are uniformly excellent. Neither the Forest Service nor the National Park Service has provided useful information on vegetation. The U. S. Fish and Wildlife Service and similar state agencies provide rich data, notably of hunted creatures. So, while there are abundant data, largely disdained by the planning process, these vary in respect to resolution, quantity, and, above all, consistency.

The next lesson learned was that neither clients, professional staff, nor consultants could predict which data would prove to be crucial at the onset of a study. The response to this predicament was to undertake comprehensive inventories at a general scale, which were to disclose the most important subjects to be pursued.

In the Twin Cities metropolitan region, geomorphology was shown to be critical, in particular as to the proportions of clay in soils. Soils rich in clay did not present the hazards of contamination to groundwater. In contrast, glacial drift and till, sands and gravels, and overlying aquifers represented serious constraints.

The Woodlands study presented a different problem. The presence or absence of a fragipan was crucial, and the depth of a fragipan determined the depth to the seasonal high water table and water storage capacity. These last, in turn, determined vegetation species and value.

In Medford the site contained representatives of both the Inner and Outer Coastal Plains. These regions exhibited quite different characteristics of soil properties, depth to water table, and vegetation. In Denver the major divisions were the front range, the hogbacks, and the prairie. Aquifer recharge and soil properties required intensive investigation. In San Francisco the most vital concern was seismic susceptibility, and with it, the threat of landslides. The other significant factor here was the incidence of wildfires.

Our experience confirmed the premise that distinct regions contained specific constraints, each of which deserved detailed investigation.

The last observation was limited to a study for the Toledo Council of Government. This was the only computerized metropolitan regional study undertaken during my tenure at WMRT: Here the availability of data in digital form became important. Since the time of that project, a great amount of environmental data have become available in digital form, and this prospect is improving rapidly.

Transportation Planning

It is extremely fortunate that I had the opportunity to enter the field of highway route selection in the 1960s, so early in my career. While landscape architects had invented the field in 1926 and achieved marvelous accomplishments (the Bronx River Parkway, the Westchester County Highway System, and the Blue Ridge Parkway), their numbers were too small to absorb the phenomenal expansion and they were simply displaced by highway engineers. This group revealed no comparable sensitivity to the landscape and no aesthetic sensibilities whatsoever. As traffic volumes increased, so did design speed. Highway design and construction, employing even larger and more powerful equipment, remorselessly gouged the landscapes and dissected cities. The Highway Fund was enormous; growth accelerated to the point that predictions could be made to justify construction of expressways in almost all urban locations. The combination of limitless money and enormous technological power led to arrogance, carelessness, and, often, stupidity. It was assumed that highway engineers could build anything anywhere. It was not necessary to understand the characteristics of an environment and equally unnecessary to elicit the attitudes of the populations to be impacted. In fairness, it should be stated that while the original landscape architects were inordinately sensitive to the visual qualities of landscape and vegetation, they were also largely innocent of environmental science. However, the engineers brought no sensitivity whatsoever, only massive power.

My first encounter occurred at the peak of this situation. Given the prevailing ignorance, it was not difficult to reveal omissions and recommend improvements, which I proceeded to do.

The study of I-95 began with an address to the Institute for Advanced Studies in Princeton and led to the formation of the I-95, Delaware to Raritan Committee, and my first commission in highway route selection. (Wallace, McHarg, Roberts and Todd published the final report in 1965.)

The method to be employed was invented by me with the assistance of Narendra Juneja and Lindsay Robertson. It was the essence of simplicity. Surely every aspect of the environment could be evaluated as either propitious, neutral, or detrimental for a highway. We would examine climate, rocks, soils, water, vegetation, and wildlife on these terms—which were propitious, which were not. Many evaluations were relative, others quantitative. Igneous and metamorphic rocks require blasting and are expensive to remove. Sedimentary rocks are easier and cheaper. Sand and gravel are not only cheap but valuable, and prices were available. Tributaries can be spanned by culverts, rivers by expensive bridges; certain soils have high compressive strength, but not peat or muck. Forests may be beautiful, but to fell, grub, and clear costs money. Wildlife is valuable, even if the benefits are limited to revenue from deer and duck licenses. Fog, snowdrifts, icing, floods, hurricanes, intense storms—all have environmental consequences, and it is possible to evaluate risks and costs they represent.

So the method proceeded, with a simple-minded evaluation of environmental factors and a gradient of values. These were superimposed, revealing the darkest areas of highest cost and, thank God, a clear alignment, spanning the area, largely white, where social costs were either absent or minor. The highway did not violate Princeton or any other community, it avoided historical buildings and sites, agricultural land, the Stoneybrook-Millstone watershed, and everything near and dear to the community. Moreover, it cost many times less than the New Jersey State Highway "Cost-Estimate Alignment."

This method's distinction from traditional engineering lay in its dependence on natural science factors, arrayed as a layer cake, and their evaluation. It was, I believe, the first environmental impact analysis; it permitted an evaluation of the impact of any proposed alignment. Certainly, it was the first ecological study for a highway alignment. The accomplishments of the study, of course, were not entirely due to its merits. It was the involvement and political power of Lady Bird Johnson that ensured its success.

There was a rudimentary attempt to incorporate social values into the evaluation. Each of the distinct constituencies that comprised the 600-square-mile region had the opportunity to weigh all of the factors employed. They could exclude factors or give multiple weights to selected factors. This role was performed by the constituencies, not by the consultant. It was precursory to a much improved method developed later. Fortunately, there was a substantial unanimity of view among the impacted populations. Even though they covered a large region and exhibited a considerable spectrum of economic status, the approach worked.

The next enterprise was almost identical. It was initiated by a proposal, supported by Robert Moses and Governor Nelson Rockefeller, to build a scenic highway transecting the Staten Island Greenbelt. I had been employed by the New York City Parks Department to evaluate and advise on the disposition of a massive piece of public property on the Island, largely acquired by tax delinquency proceedings. In the middle of this I received an urgent call from August Hecksher, advising me of the highway plan and requesting a study to discern an ecologically sensitive alternative. The I-95 study had been published in *Highway Research Record.* Now the method was no longer novel, and success in the Staten Island highway study would depend on the merits of the evidence. The method was replicated, perhaps with better evidence than for the I-95 study, but the evaluation system remained unchanged. Hecksher presented the evidence, and Moses and Rockefeller presented their plan. Douglas Carroll of the Tri-State Transportation Agency adjudicated and decided against power and for ecology. This was my second win in two tries. (The Wallace, McHarg, Roberts and Todd Staten Island report was published in 1968.)

The third of the sequence of transportation planning projects involved the State Highway Department of Delaware (undertaken by Wallace, McHarg, Roberts and Todd, 1973). This surprised me. I had made many uncomplimentary remarks about the Department of Transportation, Bureau of Public Roads, state highway departments, and highway engineers. Why would the state of Delaware ask for my assistance? No other contractors were invited, and I came to learn the reason. The United States Department of Transportation had observed that much of the traffic in Wilmington had neither origin nor destination there. They determined that it should be deflected to reduce urban traffic volumes. An outer beltway was necessary, and I was asked to ascertain such a route. When I looked at the map, the issue became clear. Wilmington, bordering the Delaware, is a half circle. The city occupies the center, and the surrounding pastoral landscape is peppered with Du Ponts in chateaus of varying magnificence. An outer beltway would inevitably bisect and despoil much of this landscape and offend its most powerful citizens. Surely, then, a noted environmentalist should undertake a meticulous environmental analysis to support this contentious proposal. He would never participate in destruction of the landscape. So I was going to be screwed. How much better to screw the screwer. I informed the department that I was willing to participate, but with one condition. I would not locate the outer beltway but would design a process to do so and develop the necessary data. The department agreed. This was my initiation into computerized ecological planning. E. Bruce MacDougall, later a dean at the University of Massachusetts, was the computer scientist, aided by Lewis Hopkins. A very rich data set was assembled and digitized in one-acre cells. These included meteorology, geology, hydrology, soils, vegetation, wildlife, historical buildings and places—and Du Pont properties.

When completed, a list of all factors from the entire data set was plotted and distributed to the four senior highway engineers. They were required to identify each factor as propitious, neutral, or detrimental for the proposed highway. They were also required to weight each factor either 0-3, 0-10 or 0-100. All values would be normalized. The resulting selection and weighting then produced four distinct alignments. Clearly, the engineers had not colluded. The costs to be incurred in each, which were quite significant, were compiled. I was then asked to select the preferred alignment, but I declined, indicating that I had no contractual agreement to do so. I was required only to design the method. The four senior highway engineers must choose the factors and weight them without my selection and endorsement. To this day they have been unwilling to proffer an alignment with such high environmental costs, and so the proposal has been aborted.

The lesson learned was powerful: given an agreed-upon data set objectively describing a region, these data will be variously evaluated depending on the value system of problem solver. Each set of values will produce a discrete solution. Here, with four highway engineers, the range was small—how much greater it would be in a region with very distinct value systems and many constituencies, among them conservationists and developers.

The last in the procession of route selection problems was located in Washington, D. C. Wallace, McHarg, Roberts and Todd was required to undertake the route selection process for the rail system of the Washington Metropolitan Transit Authority (WMTA). This was a laborious and expensive project. Environmental assessments, which I had earlier initiated, were now the law of the land and held little challenge. In succession, each partner assumed the role of supervising one alignment. A, B, C, D, and E Routes were done. I was required to supervise F Route (now called the Green Line).

A problem with the process arose. The retired general who directed the enterprise did ensure that consultants developed the appropriate objective data, conforming to the "layer cake" simulation that had been used earlier. Thereafter, however, he and his colleagues selected and weighted factors according to their own lights. Here a covert value system was being utilized in conjunction with an overt ecological inventory.

To attack this problem, we would proceed to undertake the ecological inventory as had been performed heretofore, but this would be augmented with selected socioeconomic data: workplaces of the population in the corridor, income, car ownership, age (including too young and too old or infirm to drive). This work was performed entirely by David Hamme.

The Washington Metropolitan Transit Authority mandate contained several discrete objectives. The first was provision for transit-dependent persons (in practice, mostly poor and black), the second was the provision of alternatives to move persons from automobiles to a transit system (mostly lower-middle-class white), and the third was the reduction of takings. The transit authority had belatedly become very sensitive to the political consequences of destroying buildings and transecting neighborhoods for transit facilities.

The corridor followed the Anacostia River to Prince George's County. Alternatives were quite obvious. We would develop and present alternatives based on each of the mandated objectives.

Given a hypothetical alignment, with station intervals, it was simple to describe radii of walking distance to each station and count the transit-dependent people within the circumscribed areas. The alignment could be moved to capture the maximum number. It was so moved and, at least hypothetically, captured more than ninety percent of those dependent on a transit system.

The next objective was to diminish automobile travel. Here the relevant factors were automobile ownership and home and work locations, and alignments were developed to connect them. Two quite different routes emerged. The first was selected for the black poor, the second for the white middle class.

The third objective, to diminish takings, was analyzed. This was simple. An alignment could be found that selected open spaces, public and private, or moved underground, if the construction of tunnels involved no destruction or takings.

All alternatives were constrained by the same budget, and three distinct alignments were revealed, clearly the most vivid evidence that it is the value system of the problem solver that generates the solution.

Now, by this process we had avoided the covert evaluation that the general's staff at WMTA had employed to manipulate the objective environmental factors. The process was overt, explicit, and replicable, just like a scientific experiment. Three distinct values and their objectives produced three distinct solutions. The first helped to solve problems of the black poor, the second improved travel for the middle-class whites, and the third resolved social problems at the expense of the environment.

The general saw that he had been placed on a cleft stick. He must use explicit values; unwilling to do so, he resigned. The resolution of the alignment is still pending.

Now the process of highway route selection had become balanced. The original preoccupations with environmental data had been augmented to include elicited values, and these were employed in the formation of solutions directly consequential to constituent values.

The next step in the evolution of theory addressing transportation problems occurred at the metropolitan level. My involvement began at a meeting with the first secretary of Transportation, Alan Boyd. I recommended to him that the process of selecting major new transportation facilities should first include a comprehensive ecological inventory and evaluation, from which propitious and detrimental factors should be identified and employed. During the conversation I also recommended that alignments should be evaluated, not only in terms of destroying or degrading the environment, but also for their ability to induce development into propitious environments and for explicit social ends.

Metropolitan studies with an emphasis on transportation were undertaken for the Denver Regional Transportation District, where the initial objective was achieved—a thorough ecological inventory—much aided by the U. S. Geological Survey (USGS) in Denver and faculty of Colorado State University, and the importance of inducing development into propitious areas was recognized and accepted. (The report was published by Development Research Associates and Wallace, McHarg, Roberts and Todd in 1972.)

A subsequent study for the San Francisco metropolitan region absorbed a massive data set, mainly geological and hydrologic, from the USGS at Menlo Park. (The Wallace, McHarg, Roberts and Todd report was printed in 1974.) Under the direction of David Wallace, an extensive socioeconomic inventory was also developed in order to give specificity to inducing highways into locations propitious for social reasons. The recipient was ABAG, whose staff were then ignorant of environmental factors and exercised little power in affecting social programs. The data were used by counties and by some municipalities, but, to the best of my knowledge, little work was performed.

Yet the issue survived. Under President Ford, the secretary of Transportation was William Coleman, a Philadelphia lawyer and old friend. He was apalled at his staff and their ignorance of the environment and asked for my aid. He convened a meeting and introduced me in somewhat the following way: "There are perhaps only two people in this audience who are innocent of despoiling the American landscape and its cities, Ian McHarg and I. He has some advice that you should hear and learn. We cannot have this department as an enemy of this land and its people."

However, it was the oil embargo, the rise in gasoline prices, and the shrinking of the Highway Fund that were more efficacious.

New Towns

During my period as a student, 1946 to 1950, the subject of new towns was central to planning. The Ministry of Town and Country Planning resolved to build some seventeen new towns in Great Britain. The first of these was Stevenage, for which the planner was Peter Shepheard, later a member of the Pennsylvania faculty for twenty years and the dean for five. Harlow, Crawley, Hemel Hempstead, and Basildon would ring London. The anticipated population was 30,000, the area 15,000 acres. In the north of England, Peterlee was planned, in Scotland, East Kilbride and Glenrothes. The ideal plan had been developed by Sir Patrick Abercromebie. Sir William Holford, Gordon Stevenson, and Peter Shepheard were all disciples of Abercromebie and the leading lights of the enterprise. I was throughly familiar with the literature of this proposal. I had read the Scott, Uthwatt, and Barlow reports. Indeed, I was offered the post of planner for the town center of East Kilbride by the planner, an American-trained Canadian, now emeritus professor of architecture in Berkeley, Donald Reay.

It was when asked in 1953 to investigate the location of another new town, a satellite of Glasgow, that I had my first professional encounter with the subject. I had already voiced my displeasure at the standards of municipal housing, first in an article in *The Scotsman* ("Municipal architecture is a travesty and shame . . ."), then in an article entitled "Open Space and Housing," published in the 1955 *Architects' Year Book*, in the "Courthouse Concept," published in the 1957 edition of the *Year Book*, and in "Can We Afford Open Space? A Survey of Landscape Costs" published in a 1956 issue of *Architects' Journal*.

In response to the insights of James Marston Fitch on microclimatology in *American Building* and a new book by Rudolph Geiger, *Climate Near the Ground*, I sought to find an "ideal site" in terms established by Vitruvius and honored by a succession of historical architects. This I found, west of Glasgow, on the steep slopes over the Old Kilpatrick Hills, overlooking the Firth of Clyde. The conventional dogma of terrace housing, used in the new towns, was anathema and, more important, totally inappropriate here. The site was quite steep, facing due south-southwest, overlooking the Renfrewshire Hills. Save for the ribbon of urbanization bordering the Clyde, both the site and the prospect were totally rural—hills, heather and bracken trees, and valleys. I had encountered an example of successful adaptation to steep slopes in a development in Zurich called Neubuhl by the architects Haefli and Moser. In this arrangement of stepped housing, the roof of the lower house became balcony, terrace, and garden for its upper neighbor. The scheme was four houses deep. Each had the characteristic of being an attached single-family home with a private entrance and private open space. I obtained advice and criticism from my colleague, Blanco White, and proceeded to design a site plan based on modular units—rectangles, L's, and T's—with slopes corresponding to house depths and floor-roof dimensions. Each house and garden was designed to guarantee views and privacy. That is, you could see middle and long distance, but could not look down on your neighbor's garden. On the summits were located high-rise apartments for singles and childless families overlooking the community, which from their vantage was a sea of roof gardens.

I still think it is a marvelous idea. It would have been improved with a funicular railway, perhaps with covered escalators. And, of course, it could have benefited from larger-scale investigations. However, it was, if you recall, rejected by the undersecretary of the Department of Health for Scotland on the grounds that the experiment could not be undertaken "for it has not ever been undertaken in England yet." This immediately led to my departure for the United States.

When I recounted this story to an upper-middle-class audience in the auditorium of the Royal College of Physicians in 1990, nearly forty years later, there was
a groan.

In the preceding description of my approach to the "ideal site," there is a clear
omission: there is no discussion of community or social process. Yet I was not disinterested in this subject. In 1953, I submitted an article entitled "The Measure of
the Site Plan" to the *Architectural Review*. It was accepted for publication; indeed,
I received a very flattering letter from the editor, J. M. Richards. I was even asked
to give an address on the subject for the third program of the BBC, but the article
was never published.

The burden of the article was that the value of open space in housing should
be measured by the degree to which plans provided both private and public open
space, the latter to induce and facilitate social intercourse. Supporting evidence for
the hypothesis was derived from G. Scott Williamson of the Peckham experiment,
a Leo Kuyper, sociologist from Manchester, and Henry Wright. It included examples from the Netherlands, Frankendaal in Amsterdam by Merkelbach and Elling,
the Neubuhl in Zurich by Haefli and Moser, housing at Wrexham in Wales by
Gordon Stephenson, plus a number of Scandinavian "footpath" plans. These
studies represented the leadership in the design of open-space systems for
housing.

This interest in spatial organization of open space and housing as an inducement to social intercourse did not find fertile ground at Pennsylvania, in spite of
the extraordinary concentration of social science planners there. Dominant was
Herb Gans, author of *The Levittowners* and an arch critic of the dogmas of modern architecture. Martin Meyerson, Jack Dyckman, Chester Rapkin, and Charles
Abrams were concerned with social policy at larger scales and not remotely interested in the project scale of architecture and landscape architecture.

I have referred to the West Philadelphia study conducted in 1959 by Steen Eiler
Rasmussen, Robert Geddes, David Crane, and me, in which my disillusion with the
dogmas of modern city planning crystalized. The thirty-story towers and slabs
interspersed among two- and four-story terrace housing, located without thought,
for either the natural environment or the needs, desires, preferences and aversions
of the population, caused a profound rejection. This mode of total demolition followed by shoe box reconstruction was applied to Trenton in New Jersey the following year. It confirmed my resolution to investigate environmental processes and
their implications for development and, simultaneously, to pursue the incorporation of environmental values into planning and design. This focus employed my

entire energies, and it was not until the Woodlands project that my attention turned again to the subject of new towns.

It is important to recognize that I was not entrusted with the charge of designing this new town. No, my role was limited to investigating the natural processes comprising the site and their implications for development. Of course, it quickly became clear that this realm was overwhelmingly the most important subject to be investigated, and therein lay most of the constraints and opportunities afforded by the environment. But in the eyes of George Mitchell, owner and developer, and his planner, Bob Hartsfield, there were others equally important. William Gladstone and Associates of Washington was entrusted with the subject of market analysis, which was performed brilliantly. William Pereira, the Los Angeles architect, was given responsibility of urban design and architecture; Espey and Sons were the engineers. As the study proceeded, the dominance of the environment became increasingly apparent; geology, hydrology, and ecology were clearly superior to civil engineering, while the urban design–architect role dwindled to producing perspectives.

I made a serious attempt to expand the ecological model to include human ecology. I designed a mini-conference and invited a number of distinguished social scientists to contemplate the problem of selecting the future population, eliciting from these citizens their attitudes and preferences to the environment, and using these consciously as tools in planning and design. The conference was a great success, but it was belittled by a misbegotten economist who proclaimed, "We don't need to know what people want, we only need their money." He was fired for his excesses. I met him later in the Dallas airport, threadbare and derelict. It could not have happened to a better man.

This stratagem was rejected for the Woodlands, but I decided to use the idea for an advanced studio at Penn. Again I had a brilliant class, including my successor as chairman, Anne Spirn. We placed an advertisement in the Philadelphia newspapers, requesting past or future inhabitants of Houston to participate in an interview. A wide social range responded and their observations were remarkable. People from the Northeast going to Texas, Southerners, Californians, and other groups revealed distinct preferences for environment. First-time visitors to Houston emphasized horses, boots, Stetsons, and riding; southern blacks avoided yards and preferred condominiums with manicured open space; native Houstonians preferred conspicuous facades and the display of automobiles. This constricted account appears to deal in stereotypes, but the experiment did reveal specific social groups with distinct preferences and aversions, knowledge of which could certainly have improved the marketing process. Of course, the single decision that has had the largest effect was to preserve and nurture the woodlands themselves, which has been done most effectively.

Waterfront Improvements

Always alert to finding significant problems that society was ignoring, I decided to do a reconnaissance of the twenty-two mile waterfront on the Delaware within the Philadelphia city limits. Now, twenty-two miles is a serious dimension; it is half the distance across Scotland at its narrowest point. The examination was difficult, impeded by gates, walls, barbed wire fences, dogs, and uniform dereliction. Once there had been a hundred and sixty finger piers. Old prints show boats moored, some at dock, others moving in the bustling channel. No more—there were only three working piers in the entire length we surveyed. The remaining piers and pier-head buildings were in profound disrepair. It was clear that they had no future. Moreover, the attitude of the city toward its waterfront could not have been more cynical; it was home to a municipal incinerator, two thermal electric plants, a police academy, Graterford Prison, and the one appropriate installation, the Torresdale Treatment Plant. These facilities occupied only a trivial amount of the available space, the rest was in various conditions of abandonment and deterioration. Still, it was easy to see what the Delaware waterfront had once been. Just across the Neshaminy Creek lay Andalusia, the beautiful Biddle property, with riverfront beaches, bluffs, marginal wetland vegetation, and woodlands. Moreover, the view across the river to New Jersey was quite attractive.

We decided to embark on a study. Of course, the Delaware River basin had been extensively analyzed earlier but here the resolution would have to be much finer and more intensive.

A sliver of coastal plain occupied the western banks of the Delaware before encountering the Wissahickon schist of the Crystalline Piedmont. The fall zone was expressed at the waterworks on the Schuykill, on the Frankford, the Pennypack, and Neshaminy Creeks. The last two streams occupied wooded corridors.

Water quality in the Delaware was abysmal. A gauging station located under the Ben Franklin Bridge for decades had never shown any dissolved oxygen. The surfeit of Philadelphia sewage was consuming it all. It was not until after President Lyndon Johnson's 209 program for increased sewage treatment that oxygen appeared, and almost immediately so did the shad run. And now in the 1990s the sturgeon are returning. The coastal plain segment of the riverfront was coterminous with the 100-year flood plain. Tinicum Marsh contained a relic of what must have been a very extensive marsh environment; vegetation and wildlife were typical and abundant. The land use history was dominated by shipping, piers, warehouses, ship handlers, and associated industry, which included major shipbuilding facilities that had survived through World War II.

There was virtually no evidence of a working port. Ore ships sailed to and from Fairless Steel in Levittown, oil carriers delivered to the many refineries, mostly downstream from Philadelphia, there was a small marina in Essington, and these constituted the total water use.

At this point I was invited by Marciarose Shestack to participate with her in producing an hour-long television program. We obtained the use of the governor's boat, a helicopter, and a film crew and proceeded to survey the entire length of the river. The program was entitled "Dream for a Neglected River." It had an effect, for I was invited by the city planning commission, over the strenuous objections of Ed Bacon, to undertake a planning study of the waterfront.

In the course of the earlier Penn student project, an important stratagem emerged. The major opportunity for a connected facility throughout the length of the river lay in that area between the bulkhead and pierhead. The bulkhead was the land edge, the pierhead was the limit that piers could occupy. Let us propose filling between bulkhead and pierhead to create a new continuous edge, from 300 to 600 feet wide. We would use this as the lever to create humane and viable prospective land uses. This wide ribbon could connect to the riverfront and give structure to the many abandoned and vacant sites.

It so happened that the wildest and most beautiful lands were on the New Jersey side of the river. Many occupied small, remote, and lovely watersheds—Raccoon Creek, Mingus Creek and, of course, the Rancocas. It became clear that there was an extraordinary opportunity for a new national park serving the metropolitan region. Stewart Udall was quite excited about the project. He and Lady Bird Johnson revealed that, should Philadelphia adopt the plan, there would be substantial sums of Accelerated Public Works Funds to aid the endeavor. But the planning commission concluded that a massive concentration on the Delaware would detract from the primary objective of central city development: Penn Center, Market East, and Society Hill. The opportunity was not pursued in Philadelphia. Of course, the idea was later incorporated into the Lower Manhattan Plan, which included filling out to the pierhead lines, thus rescuing the Hudson waterfront and supporting Battery Park and the esplanade.

A Scot in America

It has not been a disadvantage to be a Scot in the United States; it might even be an asset. There are no antidefamation leagues for Scots. Indeed, while Germans, Irish, Jews, Poles, Italians, Mexicans, Cubans, and even the English, have generated localized antipathy, the Scots seem to have avoided this. They are often viewed as cute—"I love your brogue" (Scots have an accent, the Irish a brogue), "I just loved Scotland." Of course, there is the perennial inquiry as to what do Scotsmen wear under the kilt, to which the best answer was given by a drum major at the Highland Games. Drum majors are selected for their manly beauty, and this one was a paragon, dressed like a peacock in full kilted regalia, preening for the populace. A beautiful American tourist approached and, with guilty ingratiation, asked the question? "What is worn under a kilt?" "Worn, madame? Worn, indeed," he said, head back, stomach in, chest out. "Nothing worn," he said. "Nothing whatso-ever. Everything is in perfect working order."

Now, Scotsmen in bulk in their native land are not benign. There must be some explanation for their favorable reception in the United States. There is one ability, well developed in every Scotsman, that may clarify the matter. I assure you that every Scotsman can sponta-neously discern the basic inferiority of any other, and every Scotsman knows of this ability. I utter a few words and I am identified and minimized as a Glasgow keelie. Such a capacity does not induce gregarious behavior, and Scots tend not to associate. Indeed, with the exception of forced migrations, after the first and second Jacobite Rebellion in 1715 and 1745, when whole clans left for Canada, North Carolina, New Zealand, and elsewhere, migration of Scots was usually by individuals and small families. Fortunately, other

nationals do not share this ethnic capability, and abroad we move freely knowing that we escape the revealing perceptions of our fellow nationals.

In addition, the environments initially selected by the Scots did not engender envy. What other people, driven from an inhospitable climate, islands and mountains, would have cho-sen Nova Scotia for a new native land? What other people in American history marched res-olutely through the rich coastal plains, the Piedmont with its wide, fertile valleys, the Great Valley in the Hudson, Delaware, Susquehanna, Potomac, and James, ever more fertile, and then climbed into the steep ridges and narrow valleys to the Allegheny Mountains and the Smokies to settle on thin, poor soils, there to find familiar poverty and adversity in a new land?

In Scotland, where it is necessary to work hard in order to stay warm, there was, in the last century and early in this century, a strong reli-gious virtue ascribed to work and duty. Long committed to education as the essential ingredi-ent in social mobility, serious, even dour, and hardworking, the people of this land prospered.

Their natural resentment of authority and their egalitarianism were consonant with the democratic aspirations of the new Americans. While the colonists had only to contend with George III, not a notably brutal monarch, the Scots had fifteen hundred years' experience with the English—all bad—and recent memory included General Wade, the duke of Cum-berland, the bloody massacres of Killiekrankie and Culloden, and the forced dispossession of the Clearings.

Moreover, the Scots had no history of the serfdom that characterized English history. Their social organization was the clan and the chief. While the position of chief was hereditary, as they were all one family, there were ample opportunities for leadership; it did not necessarily proceed from father to son.

Such resistance to authority was incorporated in that Scottish invention, the Presbyterian church. The Roman Catholic and the Anglican churches were hierarchical, the former seen as requiring layers of intermediates to address God. The Presbyterians concluded that because any man or woman could pray directly to God without intercession, no Virgin, pope, cardinal, bishop, or priest was necessary. Furthermore, their church organization was strictly democratic. A congregation formed and elected elders. The elders chose the minister and assumed responsibility for his instruction.

Woe betide any Scot who puts on airs, who behaves pridefully or arrogantly. "Cut him down to size," they would say, "Cut the legs af'n him." Underlying this was the view encapsulated by Burns: "We are a' Jock Tamson's bairns." We are all of common stock, meaning shared and commonplace, but there is still virtue and dignity there, for "A man's a man for a'that."

The Scots' resistance to congregation can be exemplified by their participation in the functions of the Saint Andrew's Society of Philadelphia. Two celebrations occur each year, Saint Andrew's Day and the Burns Supper. Some hundreds of Scots, severed by several generations from their ancestral home, converge. Most are accoutered in full kilted regalia. There is a speech, a splendid dinner, and abundant alcohol—free. As the evening wears on, singing begins, revealing a familiarity with Scottish songs rarely exceeding the first two lines. The second occasion draws a much smaller group. The attraction of a free dinner and drinks is insufficient to lure them back into the company of their kin.

Another attribute of the Scots was exemplified in my early days in America. When I arrived in Philadelphia, I was invited to become a member of the Society. I was advised that it had been established in the 1800s to assist indigent Scots. Apparently, there had been remarkably few appeals, indeed none in this century, and the resources of the Society had been prudently invested. It was rich. I had a remedy for this failure of philanthropy. I recommended that the Society sponsor a dozen Scottish students to attend the University of Pennsylvania annually. A committee was established to investigate the proposal, but its members arrived at a more economical solution. As tuition at Pennsylvania was exorbitant and was cheap at Edinburgh, Glasgow, and Saint Andrew's universities, surely it was much better to send American students of Scottish descent to the Scottish universities, which they did. However, it must be said that later they did support Scottish students in the United States.

I sometimes speak with Americans who have traveled to Scotland and find that I have become a device allowing them to recount the pleasures there, a very amicable role indeed. They tell of luxury hotels, salmon fishing, grouse shooting, castles—a Scotland I never knew.

But not only am I a stranger to the world of wealth in Scotland, I am an anachronism there. Unlike Scots of my own age, I have been separated from the country for well nigh forty years. My memories are of historical time and have not been amended by recent history. I am immediately distinguishable. In Scotland, I have been called a Yank, but not because my accent is American. A Scottish accent is like a hare lip, a cleft palate, a stigma; it cannot be removed. No, it is my idiom that marks me as a Scots American. No better fate could have befallen me.

President and Mrs. Bush awarding me the National Medal of Art on September 10,
1990. I was the first landscape architect or planner to receive the award. (Photograph
courtesy of the Bush Presidential Materials Project.)

Other Projects

Several other projects deserve mention but not extended treatment here. I hope
they may be the focus of future scholarly studies. Certainly they merit scrutiny and
critical analysis. These other projects range in scale. The location of the new
national capital, Abuja, for Nigeria, is perhaps the largest. An example of regional
scale is the study of 30,000 acres in Colusa County in California for Gerard
Blakeley. This study included, among other things, the impoundment of the
Sacramento River to create a lake of the dimensions of Loch Lomond in Scotland.
It also included several sites for institutions looking for a new home. The Toronto
waterfront study, also of regional scale, comprised a rich data set, a discriminating
suitability analysis, and a handsome report. Another regional example involved
identifying and protecting the Niagara escarpment in Ontario. In the field of ecological analysis, leading to a program of restoration, was the Twin Rivers Ranch in

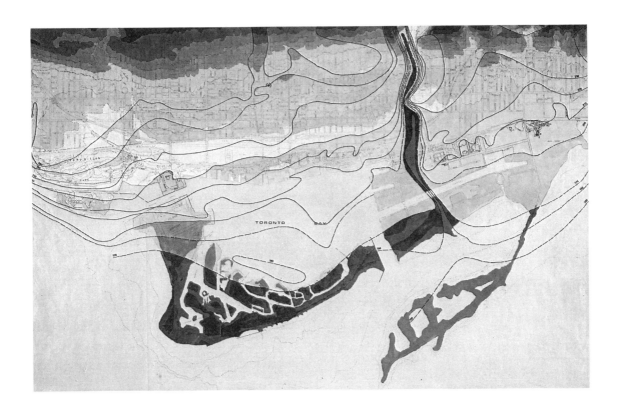

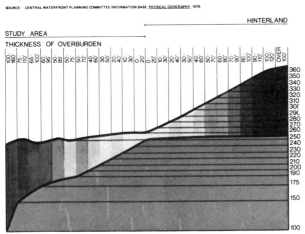

LAND
SURFICIAL MATERIAL: THICKNESS

SOURCE: CENTRAL WATERFRONT PLANNING COMMITTEE INFORMATION BASE, PHYSICAL GEOGRAPHY, 1976.

Analysis of land features of the Toronto Central Waterfront. Narendra Juneja played a leadership role in the development of an environmental plan for the Toronto, Ontario, Canada, waterfront. Anne Spirn also made a major contribution. Others contributing to the ecological inventory were Carol Reifsnyder, Arthur Johnson, and William Robinson. (Wallace, McHarg, Roberts and Todd, 1976, "Environmental Resources of the Toronto Central Waterfront"; drawn by Narendra Juneja.)

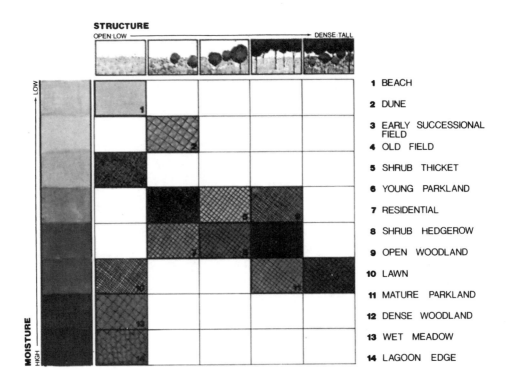

STRUCTURE

OPEN·LOW ──────────────→ DENSE·TALL

MOISTURE (LOW → HIGH)

1 BEACH
2 DUNE
3 EARLY SUCCESSIONAL FIELD
4 OLD FIELD
5 SHRUB THICKET
6 YOUNG PARKLAND
7 RESIDENTIAL
8 SHRUB HEDGEROW
9 OPEN WOODLAND
10 LAWN
11 MATURE PARKLAND
12 DENSE WOODLAND
13 WET MEADOW
14 LAGOON EDGE

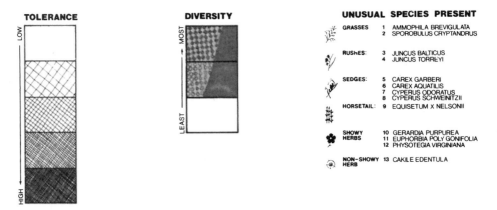

TOLERANCE (LOW → HIGH)

DIVERSITY (LEAST → MOST)

UNUSUAL SPECIES PRESENT

GRASSES
1 AMMOPHILA BREVIGULATA
2 SPOROBULUS CRYPTANDRUS

RUSHES:
3 JUNCUS BALTICUS
4 JUNCUS TORREYI

SEDGES:
5 CAREX GARBERI
6 CAREX AQUATILIS
7 CYPERUS ODORATUS
8 CYPERUS SCHWEINITZII

HORSETAIL:
9 EQUISETUM X NELSONII

SHOWY HERBS
10 GERARDIA PURPUREA
11 EUPHORBIA POLY GONIFOLIA
12 PHYSOTEGIA VIRGINIANA

NON-SHOWY HERB
13 CAKILE EDENTULA

Analysis of vegetation features of the Toronto Central Waterfront. Narendra Juneja and I were responsible for the ecological inventory, with Anne Spirn, Carol Reifsnyder, Arthur Johnson, and William Robinson making important contributions. (Wallace, McHarg, Roberts and Todd, 1976, "Environmental Resources of the Toronto Central Waterfront"; drawn by Narendra Juneja.)

Tampa, Florida, a remarkable example of successful regeneration of a degraded landscape by Robert and Bob Thomas. The search for conservation-minded custodians to buy properties in the Evans Ranch in Colorado and to give the development rights to the Colorado Land Trust, was another ecological strategy.

The 1972 study for Wilmington and Dover in Vermont for the Windham Regional Planning and Development as well as the Vermont State Planning Office was distinguished by the fact that all data were generated by residents. A retired geologist, a forester awaiting military duty, a soils scientist, a hydrologist—and intelligent and energetic integrator—Helen Reese, developed a rich inventory. Michael Clarke was in charge of the operation. The product was outline ordinances, which were incorporated into Act 250 and early state conservation laws in Vermont. Vermont, in turn, influenced subsequent state planning and growth management laws and policies.

In the realm of development, the project in Breckenridge, Colorado, conducted with Russell Moore and Design Studio West, is an example of successful ecological planning and design. For this project, I obtained a serendipitous reward. The owners asked me to sell their property. I intimated its availability to prospective buyers, and one of those nominated bought it. I received a one percent seller's fee of $17,000 which arrived on the day when I received a notice from IRS requesting the same amount. Amelia Island, Lake Austin, and Sanibel have been mentioned as examples of ecological planning studies developed to write ordinances. Indeed, these were successful, but the ensuing development also deserves recognition. Finally, Cascade Valley Park in Ohio is the largest urban park constructed in this century. Jonathan Sutton, himself from Ohio, worked with me on this project which compares in scale and significance to Fairmount Park in Philadelphia.

During the 1980s, I undertook an ecological inventory and completed a landscape design for the Edith Macy National Training Center for the Girl Scouts of America in Chappaqua, New York. I also directed plans for Riverdale and Blue Heron parks in New York City. These designs and plans involved marvelous teams of post WMRT colleagues—mostly more recent Penn graduates and Penn faculty: Robert Giegengack, Art Johnson, Rob Turner, Barbara Seymour, Jorge Sanchez-Flores, Ed Hollander, Jim Thorne, Jon Berger, John Radke, Kim Sorvig, Kate Deregibus, Reza Ghezelbach, Dorothy Wurman, and Michael Skaller, among others. While interesting experiments, the Chappaqua, Riverdale, and Blue Heron plans were not implemented as was recommended.

In 1959, I had taught a studio which focused on West Philadelphia. Since that time there have been many changes. In the late 1980s and early 1990s, West

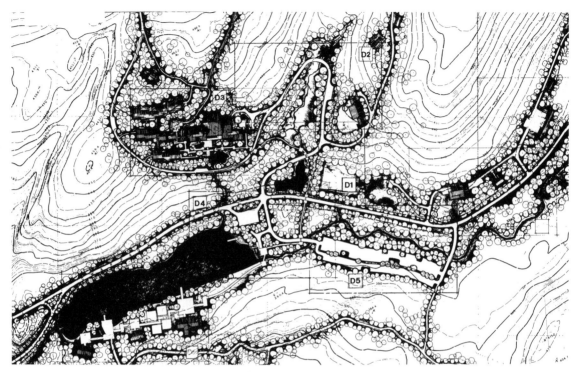

The comprehensive plan of the Edith Macy National Training Center in Chappaqua, New York, for the Girl Scouts of America, designed under my direction in 1981 and 1982. Illustrative Master Plan; D1 through D5 on the plan illustrate specific elements of the design. (Ian L. McHarg, "Comprehensive Plan, Edith Macy National Training Center.")

Philadelphia was again a subject for student examination and became the focus of a research project, "The Greening Study," directed by Anne Spirn, then chairman of landscape architecture and regional planning at Penn, and employing faculty and graduate students.

The direction of this project is entirely different from that of the early example. In the 1950s a massive redevelopment was envisioned in which existing buildings would be demolished and the area transformed with 30-story towers and slabs, two-, three-, and four-story townhouses, an abstract arrangement of bland boxes with no reference to the environment, no concern for the displaced population, and no attention to the needs and desires of the new occupants.

The focus of Anne Spirn's work was totally inverted. The point of departure now involves recognition of small-scale groups whose energies created community

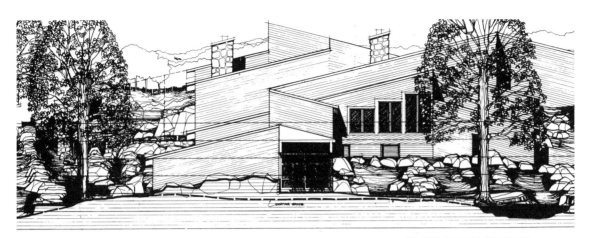

NORTH-SOUTH SECTION

EAST-WEST SECTION

East court of the Edith Macy National Training Center. (Ian L. McHarg, "Comprehensive Plan, Edith Macy National Training Center"; drawn by Jorge G. Sanchez-Flores.)

gardens, which organized community involvement and expanded into many other realms; security, jobs, the quality of municipal services, rehabilitation, and restoration. Now that there are community organizations that have identified issues in their neighborhoods and mobilized their resources to resolve them, there are no significant public funds available. Financial support must be obtained from philanthropic organizations.

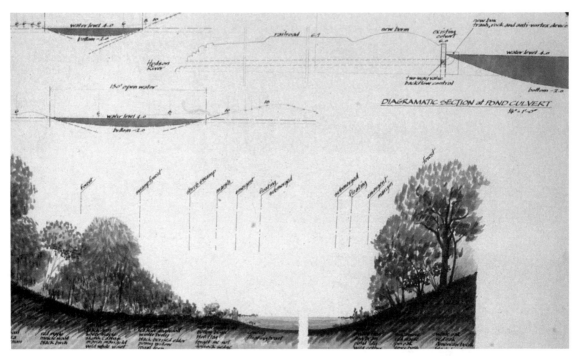

From 1984 to 1989, I led a team of landscape architects and ecologists, which included
Carol Smyser McHarg, James Thorne, Dorothy Wurman, and Kim Sorvig, to develop a
plan for Riverdale Park in New York City. This is a cross-section of the plan completed
for the New York Department of Parks and Recreation. (Drawn by Dorothy Wurman.)

A second inversion involves the environment, totally ignored thirty years ago
but now recognized as a critical issue. This is not merely an academic issue: Streams
that were earlier culverted have subsided, as have the houses built on them; there
are low areas that do not drain; air pollution and the presence of lead, asbestos,
PCBs, and dioxins are conspicuous problems. Most important of all is the need for
nature's presence in the city. Community gardens, small parks, playgrounds, street
trees, all take high priority. This approach, generated by small-scale popular action,
reveals the needs and desires of neighborhood populations. Indeed, here are examples of a new urban form derived from popular perceptions.

Thirty years ago, federal policy richly funded large-scale redevelopment projects that were based on architectural dogma, oblivious to the needs of occupants
and the environment. Now that these needs are recognized, no public funds are
available. A pessimist would regret this public failure; an optimist would conclude
that we are no longer funding execrable projects and there is now a more basic and
humane understanding of the problems and the elements of solution.

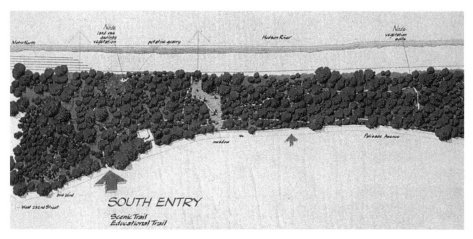

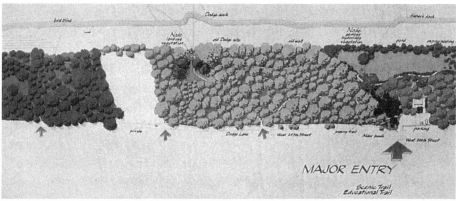

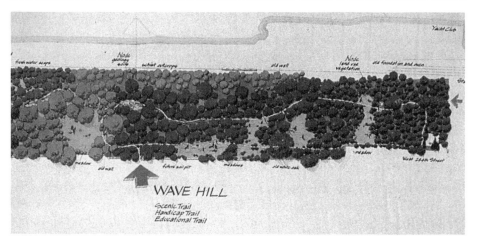

Environmental Analysis and Schematic Design, Riverdale Park (1984–1989, New York
Department of Parks and Recreation.)

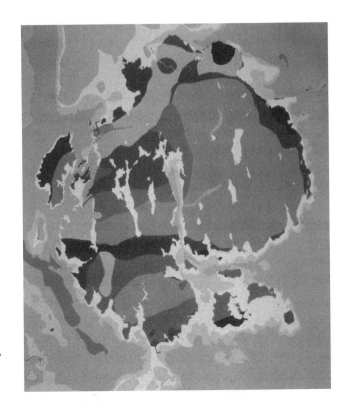

In the spring of 1994, I returned to Harvard University as a visiting professor. I taught a geographic-information-systems based studio using Mount Desert Island, including Acadia National Park, in Maine.

Bedrock Geology Map of Mount Desert Island, Maine. (1994, Ian McHarg, Cristian Basso, Elke Bilda, Ho-Shu Chou, Buzz Constable, Paul Cote, Iram Farooq, Karen Mans, Sarah Peskin, Girish Ramachandran, and Joel Young, Graduate School of Design, Harvard University.)

Mount Desert Island

I was invited by Michael Van Valkenburgh to teach at Harvard during the spring semester of 1994. This was quite a surprise. I had received many invitations to teach—at Berkeley; Pennsylvania State University; Auckland, New Zealand; and, later, as Bruce Goff Professor at the University of Oklahoma, but while I had received innumerable invitations to give speeches at Harvard, I had never, in almost forty years, been invited to teach there.

There was a reason. For decades, there were two discernible poles in landscape architectural education. Harvard, with a strong design emphasis was one; Hideo Sasaki, Chuck Harris, Peter Walker, Laurie Olin, Linda Jewell, and Michael Van Valkenburgh all reflected this focus. The major competitor was Penn, with its ecological emphasis, its strong composition of environmental sciences and, can one say, its assumption of primacy both nationally and internationally. This attitude was much resented in Cambridge. And there was more.

Charles Eliot, innovator, inventor of what we would now call ecological planning, was destined to become the major figure in the field of the environment in

Digital Terrain Model of Mount Desert Island, Maine. (1994, Ian McHarg, Cristian Basso, Elke Bilda, Ho-Shu Chou, Buzz Constable, Paul Cote, Iram Farooq, Karen Mans, Sarah Peskin, Girish Ramachandran, and Joel Young, Graduate School of Design, Harvard University.)

the United States. He had, however, one flaw: he died prematurely of spinal meningitis at the age of thirty-seven.

This paragon was born in 1857. He attended Harvard as an undergraduate. His father was president there. In 1880 he determined to spend the summer at the family's favorite vacation spot on Mount Desert Island, Maine, and invited some friends, including a professor of geology. He decided to undertake an inventory of the island. His companions selected or were allocated subjects—geology, oceanography, hydrology, marine biology, meteorology, plants, animals, and people. Photography was an important inclusion. This group assumed the name Champlain Society, after the famous explorer. Their study persisted for six years.

This inventory was the first ecological study undertaken, ever, anywhere. It was remarkable for its comprehensiveness. It was also remarkable that, in contrast to the separatism and reductionism of science, then as now, this environmental study used the landscape as the integrative device and, in its final innovation, not only were rocks, clouds, plants, and animals included, but the original inhabitants were also studied.

Moreover in 1880 Eliot conceived of a plan for metropolitan Boston and pro-

ceeded with the first metropolitan ecological study ever undertaken. It has not yet
been equaled, let alone exceeded.

I had spent perhaps a decade trying to develop ecological planning before I
heard of Eliot. My focus was not on the history of landscape architecture, which
would have brought Eliot to my attention. In contrast, my total pursuit was in the
physical and biological sciences, particularly ecology. I have not been able to identify the moment when I first came upon Eliot, but I suspect that the first serious
encounter, beyond anecdote, was a presentation by Professor Lynn Miller of
Pennsylvania State University, who had studied Olmsted, Eliot, Copeland, and
Codman. Imagine my chagrin on learning of this great man who had preceded me
by some sixty years and had built a towering edifice, which should have been
embraced by twentieth-century America, and of which I was ignorant.

I became a strong advocate of ecological planning and of Eliot. Here was the
founding father, without honor, not only in his own country, but in his own university. For my message suffered disdain as did Eliot's. Thus it was with particular
pleasure that I accepted the invitation to teach at Harvard. I chose to examine
Mount Desert Island a century after Eliot had undertaken his landmark study. My
wish was that Eliot would receive a belated honor he had long deserved. I expressed
the hope that a bronze statue of Eliot be cast and placed in the foyer of Gund Hall
in the Graduate School of Design, representing his primacy in the environmental
movement. This has not been done, but without doubt the massive ecological
planning study of Mount Desert Island, employing very rich and accurate data and
the most powerful computers and plotters, did much to bring Eliot's contribution
to serious consideration by faculty and student alike.

The subject of ecological planning became increasingly central in my addresses
from the sixties, whenever I gave them, and certainly during visits to Harvard. There
I bemoaned the fact that during four years of graduate study I had not been introduced to Eliot, indeed, scarcely informed about F. L. Olmsted or his sons. They were
not favorites of the École des Beaux Arts faculty, nor was I. Thus, not only was Eliot
rejected, but so too were my message and I. I was receiving too much public attention,
indeed honor, to be disdained, but Harvard resisted accepting the ecological view.

No longer. After an introduction by Frederick Smith, the distinguished ecologist Richard Forman succeeded in generating an ecological framework and added
Michael Binford to establish a significant ecological presence at Harvard. Will Eliot
be formally exhumed and honored?

Here is a paradox. The massive concentration of environmental scientists at
Penn, integrated by the ecological view, the supreme example of multi- and interdisciplinary education in the United States (at least, according to *Science*) is today

being dismantled, perhaps for reasons of economy, change, or novelty, or because of a convinced preference for design as the crucial component in the curriculum. For whatever reason, ecological planning and design is in decline at Penn but growing elsewhere, notably at Harvard and at the University of Virginia, where there is a schoolwide interest in sustainable design and environmental ethics.

When I received the invitation to teach at Harvard I leapt at the opportunity of reviewing, in 1993, the Mount Desert Island that Eliot had begun to address in the late nineteenth century. The original study had two major products: the first was the *Geology of Mount Desert Island*, the other was the *Vegetation of Mount Desert Island*. In addition, previously, I had undertaken a computerized ecological study with a group of regional planners at Pennsylvania who had assembled a very rich data set.

The class at Harvard was quite small, six master's candidates, two Loeb fellows and a fellow from MIT. In addition, the Graduate School of Design hired a young man, Paul Cote, as a computer specialist familiar with Sun workstations and Arc/Info software.

At Penn the project had been limited by available hardware and high costs. Although the data digitized were very rich, our ability to plot out maps was restricted to the use of a black-and-white line printer. Maps were colored by hand. Not so at Harvard. Through the efforts of Carl Steinitz and others, Harvard had state-of-the-art landscape planning computing facilities. The HP ink-jet plotter permitted the production of astonishingly beautiful maps. New software facilitated the employment of many automatic procedures. In particular, an elaborate Digital Terrain Model was employed to display geology and physiography in three dimensions, on which we draped rivers, soils, vegetation, wildlife habitats, and land use. Suitability analysis included draping all selected factors on the Digital Terrain Model.

Planning at Harvard did not emphasize data from the natural sciences. Indeed, for many decades, the landscape architecture curriculum did not require students to study any natural science.

The data for all of the subjects in the Mount Desert Island Study were of incomparable quality. Indeed, the Digital Terrain Model was produced by ESRI in Redlands, California. Information on vegetation was developed from satellite imagery by the National Park Service in Denver. The data on ecology, soils, wildlife, and land use were of a quality not yet achieved in any professional office or governmental department.

The final review of the work at Harvard enthralled the jury, which included officials from the National Park Service, Acadia National Park, the communities of

Mount Desert Island, and a large proportion of the faculty and students of the Graduate School of Design. They applauded warmly. The dean and chairman both described the project as an incandescent success.

A Prototype Database for a National Ecological Inventory 1992

In 1972–1973, I produced a study entitled "Towards a Comprehensive Plan for Environmental Quality." This was initiated by the U. S. Environmental Protection Agency (EPA) who contracted with the American Institute of Planners (AIP) who, in turn, subcontracted me. The report concluded that an ecological inventory should be conducted to identify the ecosystems that comprised the nation, their conditions, and their trends, for which I recommended the creation of a national ecological laboratory in Washington and forty similar laboratories, one for each of the forty physiographic regions in the nation. Each would be staffed with the appropriate scientists who would monitor, inventory, and advise on environmental policy. Administrator Russell Train was very pleased with the report, but he did not think that this role should be performed by EPA, as it would involve a conflict of interests between scientific inventory and regulation. However, neither USGS, NASA, nor the U. S. Department of Agriculture was willing to undertake the task. The major reason was that available computer compatibility was inadequate for the task.

With the presidency of George Bush, Bill Reilly, protégé of Russell Train, became administrator of the EPA. He exhumed my 1974 report and asked whether the subject should be reexamined. Had computer capability improved in the interim? I received a contract from EPA and spent two years of my life with colleagues Jonathan Berger, John Radke, and Kathleen Wallace. We were partners in an enterprise named Expert Information Systems, and operated an excellent computer lab. We produced a document entitled "A Prototype Database for a National Ecological Inventory," which was submitted to the leadership of the Environmental Mapping and Protection (EMAP) section of EPA in January 1993. At that time Bill Reilly was no longer administrator, which meant that the chief source of the concept was gone—a great pity, for the study was a call to arms and it needed a strong advocate.

The report first observed that EPA, in effect, had no scientific capability and recommended that distinguished persons, representing all of the disciplines of the environment, be constituted into an executive committee to advise the administrator on the conduct of the inventory. A list of appropriately distinguished candidates was included.

It should be noted that it was during our study that EMAP had been created. This entity, in addition to a small headquarters in Washington, had a branch in Corvallis, Oregon, devoted to biostatistics, another in Las Vegas, Nevada, preoccupied with remotely sensed imagery, mainly satellites, and a group at Warrenton, Virginia, concerned with air photography and landscape ecology. EPA also had a research capability, invested in the Research Triangle in North Carolina.

These groups had agreed on a method for the inventory. They proposed covering the nation with a forty-square-kilometer hexagonal lattice and undertaking 6 percent sample inventories. We reviewed this proposal and concluded that it was inadequate. A 6 percent sample would take sixteen years to cover the nation. The commitment to forty-square-kilometer samples was too restrictive and myopic. We suggested a three-part inventory, a national scale, including the United States and its neighbors (Canada, Mexico, the Caribbean, the Atlantic, and Pacific), studied at the scale of 1:1 million. We next recommended the undertaking of a higher-resolution inventory, appropriate to the regional scale, at 1:250,000. Finally, in this context, we accepted the EMAP proposal for forty-square-kilometer hexagons at 1:24,000.

We recommended a new title for the enterprise. Among those preferred was "The State of the Nation, the Health of the Environment." We also observed that the commitment to undertake a national inventory could be the single most important environmental decision in the nation's history.

EMAP is unknown to the public, scorned by the environmental fraternity. If our proposal is accepted, a full range of environmental disciplines at a high level of distinction will be appointed to an executive committee. And when this group has designated the necessary staff and developed a plan for the national inventory, we recommended a large scale publicity campaign to obtain popular and scientific participation and support.

The report examines existing data at the three scales—national, regional, and local—evaluates these and, most important, identifies available data in digital form. It was proposed that an extensive data set be included in the inventory: physical oceanography (where applicable), geology, geomorphology, physiography, hydrology, soils, vegetation, limnology, marine biology, wildlife, and land use. We urged the employment of chronology as the unifying rubric.

We observed that the greatest problem lies not with data, but with integration. A test forty-square-kilometer hexagon was selected and employed to provide a demonstration. This sample used Washington Crossing, straddling the Delaware, in Pennsylvania and New Jersey. This allowed the examination of edge conditions between states and counties, and variation in nomenclature as well as variations in the quality of data.

The resulting inventory, it was suggested, was appropriately extensive and should be considered as the basic minimum. The subsequent labor on the inventory should, of course, provide topical data, and these should be enriched.

I have performed inventories in Minneapolis-St. Paul, San Francisco, Denver, Toledo, and other metropolitan regions. I found that there were vast repositories of data on each of these regions reposing in the minds of scientists, their libraries, bibliographies, and maps. We proposed, for data collection and monitoring for the national ecological inventory, that this function be devolved to regional institutions. Clearly, there must be an integrative function, which should be assigned to the EPA in Washington.

While Bill Reilly was administrator, the Database Prototype Study had enthusiastic support. When President Bush was not reelected, the interest and support of Bill Reilly was not continued by the new administration. The resolve to undertake a National Biological Survey has now consumed the interest of Interior, while EMAP has receded in importance.

The National Academy of Science Committee in Science of the National Park Service recommended that an inventory of the vegetation of the national parks be undertaken. Congress funded this activity, but it too, has been halted, pending a resolution of the National Biological Survey.

In spite of the unequaled concentration of intelligence on the environment, represented by Vice President Al Gore, Secretary Bruce Babbitt of Interior, Carol Browner administrator of EPA, Tim Wirth of the State Department, and M. Gordon Wolman and Peter Raven in key positions within National Academy of Sciences committees, the entire environmental movement has atrophied. This is both unexpected and tragic.

The Global Environmental Inventory

The experience of seeing the entire earth, viewed from space, was like the discovery of a magic mirror. We could see ourselves whole, at last, an extended family photograph: clouds, mountains, oceans, rivers, forests, cities of people, all visible. Where were we in the picture? Of course, the most moving response to this novel image, was voiced for us all by Lewis Thomas: "The earth is alive."

For all of history, life has been local and parochial. Only tiny portions of the earth could be directly experienced. But looking into the night sky, we saw planets, stars, galaxies, and the moon, all coherent in black space. The silvery moon as orb and crescents revealed her wholeness. Now, in a total reverse, the earth can be viewed from space and from the moon. Today many satellites scan the face of the earth, some capable of discerning details as small as a clenched fist, so at last we can see the globe, record what we see, diagnose, and, most important, regulate our behavior accordingly.

From which I devised my mantra: this small rotating orb, the earth our home, blue-green from oceans and verdure, a green celestial fruit, a little sphere half washed by sunlight, is the arena of billions of years of silent evolution, that great yearning whereby our antecedents sought their destiny, made their bequests, proffered their legacy for our custody and the fulfillment of our aspirations, gave gifts beyond expectation, measure, or price.

The view of the earth from the moon had a profound effect on me. I had gravitated in scale from local projects to metropolitan regions, river basins, and, finally, the continent, but now it became apparent that I must begin to address the environment of the earth. Uncertain of what I could do, it would be enough to reserve a compartment in the mind identified with the entire earth.

I had been introduced to the national environment in 1972 when Russell Train, then administrator of the EPA, asked me to advise him on a national ecological inventory. He was distressed that he was unable to speak with assurance of the environments which comprised the nation, their health or their tendencies. A national ecological inventory should permit him to report to the president, Congress, and the American people of these environments, their history, and current health, and to promulgate policies to maintain and enhance them.

In 1972–1973, as subcontractor to the American Institute of Planners, I wrote "Towards a Comprehensive Plan for Environmental Quality." It was long, but its salient recommendations were short. The country contains forty homogeneous zones, physiographic provinces, and regions. Each of these has characteristic geological histories and, thus, all have similar physiography, hydrology, soils, vegetation, wildlife, and resources. In each zone should be created a national ecological laboratory staffed with the appropriate range of scientists required to undertake inventories and monitoring and to engage in modeling. One lab would be located in Washington, charged with synthesizing national data and promulgating policies.

Train and his staff were pleased but did not feel competent to undertake this task, so I was charged to introduce the concept to various agencies. My first visit was to USGS in Menlo Park, California. This group contained a rich assembly of natural scientists, notably geologists, hydrologists, and soils scientists. They approved of the idea but resisted the proposal that the agency should be renamed the United States Ecological and Geological Survey and empowered to undertake the inventory. Their position was simple. Should they perform this role, they would multiply their power and inevitably become subject to great political presssure. They had long sought to be apolitical and so rejected the idea.

I next traveled to NASA at Ames, California, home of satellite imagery and remote sensing, with massive computer capability. I received an attentive hearing. The response, however, was humorous. "While the inventory should be performed, we at Ames are not interested in the earth. We think of it as a rather dull planet."

So the proposal died, but not my interest. Later that year, I was invited to give an address to the Australian and New Zealand Academy of Science in Auckland. Among my remarks I observed that island ecosystems are among the easiest to inventory and model and recommended that New Zealand do so. To my delight, the idea was warmly accepted. I have returned twice since. On the last occasion, I organized a seminar attended by the majority of environmental scientists in the country to review progress and recommended future development. In 1988 a digital cadastral survey had been completed and plans were being developed to undertake the environmental inventory.

In 1980, several years after my presentation in Auckland, I addressed the Australian Institute of Architects on the occasion of their centennial. Again I recommended an ecological inventory. While there was strong support for the proposal from the national research agency, CSIRO, it was concluded that such an initiative must stem from the states, as it did. New South Wales, Victoria, and Western Australia followed the New Zealand example by first digitizing cadastral surveys. However, in Western Australia an extraordinary inventory is underway, linked to a most impressive skill and computer capability.

The next presentation was also to an island ecosystem, this time Taiwan's. Once more I recommended a national ecological inventory. The idea was accepted, but progress has been slow. Apparently, however, there is a determination to proceed, and it appears that I may be invited to assist and, I hope, participate. Indeed almost half of the island has been inventoried and mapped.

The conception of large-scale ecological inventories has always been dependent on computer capability. In 1974 data were digitized in cells rather than polygons and thus contained a significant and fundamental error. Cells had only one attribute: it was all or nothing. Fifty-one percent became 100 percent, 49 percent became zero, and boundaries became saw-toothed. There were also limits as to the size of data banks, retrieval, and speed.

A decade later there developed magical improvements. The first was the capability to digitize in polygons using exact boundaries of attributes; output reflected polygons, and no error was introduced. Next it became possible to superimpose multiple factors, to engage in analysis and undertake suitability searches; that is, to locate those regions where all or most propitious attributes were located with no or few detrimental factors. Memory and speed expanded, cost declined, and it became possible for universities to acquire minicomputer capability, as they did in my department at Penn in 1985. At that point, I hired the brilliant, volatile, noisy enthusiast John Radke, geographer and geographic information systems specialist from the University of British Columbia, Vancouver, who engaged with great success in developing computerized ecological planning. Unfortunately, this paragon was little appreciated by Penn, and he was seduced to Berkeley and given appropriate salary, status, and lab.

I had an agendum, and upon his arrival I gave Radke a series of objectives. The ecological planning I undertook was expensive, prohibitive for many towns and even for some counties. I believed that the remedy to reduce costs could be provided by the computer and the possibility of creating automatic procedures. The objective was to do such planning with greater accuracy, to include more complex data, and to achieve better analysis, thus producing superior products, faster and cheaper than possible by manual methods. All but the last have been accomplished, but the prospect of significant economy while not yet uniformly demonstrable, is a certain prospect in the near future.

The sum of this experience is that it can be asserted that current computer capability can undertake elaborate ecological inventories, perform analysis, fulfill all of the traditional interpretations heretofore done manually, and perform functions that were impossible by manual methods.

All of which leads to my sabbatical in Berkeley in 1986. My sixty-fifth birthday fell on 20 November 1985, at which point I received a letter from my dean (a one-time student), observing that at sixty-five I must resign my role as chairman. I had founded the department in 1955 and had been its chairman for thirty-two years. None of my colleagues had been interested in the position. The reason was simple: It paid no salary, did not permit any reduction in teaching, and was simply an added burden. However, I saw the role as the instrument for leading growth and development; it was not a chore, rather, my life's work. But it must end. The dean's letter continued, "We must appoint a successor and I am sure that it would make life simpler if you were not around during the initial year. Why don't you take a sabbatical?" I had had one sabbatical during the thirty-two years, during which I wrote *Design with Nature*.

Shortly after receipt of that letter I was in Berkeley to give a speech. I had dinner with friends who, having learned of my sabbatical, asked what I proposed to do. "Oh, I'll probably stay at home and write a book." "Would you like to come to Berkeley, we would love to have you?" I phoned Carol and asked, "How would you like to spend a year in San Francisco?" "I would ask for a houseboat in Sausalito," she said, "and if they accede, accept." So I wrote a letter of contract. It transpired that houseboats came in two forms: squalor, which I could have afforded but rejected, and sumptuous luxury, which I could not possibly afford. So instead we went to a penthouse in Pacific Heights, among the yuppies, with a view of the Golden Gate Bridge, Presidio, Sausalito. The lights of the marina and the lighthouse at Alcatraz winked at us as we lay to sleep.

As I was on sabbatical from Penn, my responsibility to Berkeley was only half-time, which translated into two courses, one in each semester. The first, in the fall, was on theory. It offered me an opportunity to read and discuss the works of those scientists who had contributed to our understanding of the environment. We explored Charles Darwin, Lawrence J. Henderson, Gregory Bateson, James Lovelock, Loren Eiseley, Marston Bates, Lewis Thomas, Lynn Margulis, Frank Fraser Darling, the Odums and the conservationist tradition, George Perkins Marsh, John Muir, Gifford Pinchot, Aldo Leopold, Rachel Carson, and contemporary ecology. The reading was rich, the insights magical; it was a delicious course.

In the spring, I was asked to replicate the course that I had given for decades at Penn, "Man and Environment." But here at Berkeley there were marvelous new opportunities. With few exceptions, the eastern Ivy League colleges had scorned the environment; not so in the west. Berkeley has massive power in environmental science, but so too do Davis, Humbolt, Stanford, and Pitzer. There was in this region an august figure associated with each of the environmental sciences, and so I assembled a formidable array of speakers. The course was organized ecologically and used chronology as its organizing mode. Alvarez presented geology; Harold Robinson, the atmosphere; Luna Leopold, the hydrosphere; Gepsner, soils; Litiger, the evolution of plants; Otto Schultz, the evolution of animals; Johanssen, the evolution of the human species. Kenneth Watt spoke to the biosphere, Paul Shepard addressed Gaia. Nuclear war was explored by Holdren, nuclear winter by Harte, population by Paul Ehrlich, epidemiology by Leonard Duhl, and remotely sensed imagery by John Colwell, father of the field.

I arranged for the course to be given from two to three o'clock, which meant that I could take the great men to lunch. During these occasions, my guests marveled at my freedom, in that I delivered so few lectures myself. "What else are you doing?" "Well, I have begun to write a book" (this work, in fact). "But you have discretionary time." "Indeed." "You know, there is one useful thing you might do; there are lots of people collecting global environmental data. Would you like to pursue this matter?" The question was, clearly, what data do we already have? What can we do with it? So I asked for and received permission to make many expensive telephone calls, and then embarked on the quest to ascertain what global environmental data had been and were being collected. I spent six months concentrated on this effort and have pursued it sporadically ever since. It so happens that a skeletal inventory does exist. Clearly, there is no shared objective, no plan, no coordination. Independent agencies and scientists are pursuing their own research objectives, but the sum is valuable and significant. Yet I am one of a small number of persons who are aware of these resources.

The National Oceanographic and Atmospheric Administration and the UN Meteorological Office employ a vast network from around the world and, with their satellite capability, have an infinitude of data, perceptions, and predictive capability for weather systems developed to unimaginable capability. This network is now invaluable for the investigation of the world warming hypothesis.

Geology, regrettably, has few digital resources. Global tectonic plates do exist in digital form, and a program has been developed to portray the history of tectonic plate movements, but the necessary data, which are abundant worldwide, exist only as paper maps. The CIA-produced Data Bank II, which contains continents, islands, rivers, and political boundaries, is the only source of digital surficial hydrology. No global groundwater data have been digitized. Digital elevations are available worldwide, with varying degrees of resolution. The capability exists to place a laser altimeter in a shuttle and produce global elevations with one-meter resolution. Soils have been digitized by UNEP and FAO including not only descriptions, but attributes. Vegetation data are available in time series form, derived from weather satellites by Choudhery and Tucker of NASA, Goddard, and the Defense Mapping Agency is engaged in preparing a global land use map using 1:1,000,000 operational and navigational charts. There are other data—on evaporation from the oceans, ozone attenuation, and much more.

When I came to learn of this resource, I sought funds from foundations to bring all of the participating scientists to one location, to reveal their data to each other, to determine the value of these data and the functions they could perform, and to ascertain what more was needed, to be provided by whom, where, at what cost, and so on. I was unsuccessful.

Meanwhile, I was also investigating what the UNEP was doing. Near Nairobi, in limbo, were forty scientists, all estimable. They were constrained by the fact that half of them were on loan, their computer capability was less than that which I commanded personally, and they could not be assured of electricity for more than half the time. This, constituting the world's formal commitment to understanding and managing the global environment, was totally inadequate. What were the alternatives?

The solution to the problem came in a flash. Who knew most about space, the atmosphere, the oceans? Who placed seismographs on the ocean floor? Who could discern the numbers on a registration plate from space? Who has unparalleled capability with satellites and computers? Why, the defense establishment—the National Security Administration, Defense Military Intelligence, the Defense Mapping Agency, the National Aeronautics and Space Administration, the United States Army Corps of Engineers, and the United States Geological Survey. Moreover, they have time series data dating from the beginning of satellites. And, of some significance, they are faced with imminent unemployment. Gorbachev's unilateral initiatives de-escalated the prospect of nuclear war, and for the most part the Eastern European satellites have rejected communism and marched resolutely westward. Targets and missiles, so carefully monitored, are now nonexistent or neutralized. Only atomic submarines require careful scrutiny. Can those whose infamous life's work involved destroying the earth be given responsibility for its protection? Can the United States establish an arm of UNEP employing the incomparable data it has compiled, its unequaled capability in satellites, sensors, and computers, to inventory and model the earth? Should the United States choose to do so, so would the Russians with their massive capability. Many nation-states would also seek to share in this venture and participate.

During the period of my life, we have occupied three distinct positions. The first, the Western view, was license to plunder the earth for profit. Although this was wasteful, prodigal, and ultimately threatening, it continued. The apex of this anthropocentric view, the second period of my life, was the assumption that our rights included employing the nuclear cataclysm to solve arguments, which, with nuclear winter, would have seriously depleted the life-stock and created a thoroughly life-inhibiting physical environment.

There is another option: Come to learn the way the world works. This is the third period: the ecological era. See this as the most important challenge to education and society. Devise rules of conduct and behavior responsive to this world; employ the intrinsic opportunities, recognize the inherent constraints, engage in ecological planning and design. Surely, that should be the way of the world, the pathway of humankind, the creative enzyme in the biosphere.

Conclusion

As this autobiography neared a conclusion, its terminus continued to elude me. There was always another citation, an incident for the chronology, an award or anecdote to add. In my imagination, I recorded a very dramatic but purely fictitious end: With a too emphatic impress of the final period to the final sentence, the author slumps over the typewriter in a fatal paroxysm. But surely this would not do for me, with two young children (Andrew, age eight, and Ian William, thirteen) and a young wife, Carol.

Indeed, reality mirrors art. On the afternoon of Thursday, August 17, 1995, I returned home on the hottest day of a heat wave. I planned to shower and change. From the bathroom I could see Carol and the boys helping buyers persuade our mare to enter an unfamiliar horse box. In vain, she would not be persuaded. I began dressing and had stooped to tie my shoe laces when a blinding pain engulfed my lower back and the insides of my legs. I tried to rise, but my legs failed me. I was put into Carol's car and taken to Chester County Hospital, where an aneurysm was diagnosed. Immediate surgery was recommended and undertaken.

So here, indeed, is terminus for the book, but not for life. The quest continues.

History has provided my conclusion for me, my wildest dreams have been realized. The future never looked better for the environment, and my fondest hopes and aspirations hold a degree of probability unimaginable only a few years ago.

Totally unpredicted by our public sages, begotten by two modest words, *peristroika* and *glasnost*, restructuring and openness—an unlikely theory to reject the communist manisfesto—a total transformation of the world has taken place. And the instrument is even more unexpected; a Russian agnostic and economist, Mikhail Gorbachev, never associated with the environment, totally unknown to the world until recently. In his time, he has resolved the greatest threat to humankind, life, and the environment. Nuclear Armageddon was incontrovertibly the most diabolic threat to the entire earth ever conceived. Apparently, it is abating, the implacable enmity of Russia and the United States has diminished, and, indeed, there is evidence of cooperation, even cordiality. Yet each was ready and capable of annihilating the other, both were poised to retaliate, national treasuries were continually robbed to maintain and expand this obscene, satanic capacity to threaten the survival of life and the human species.

All but gone.

There must have been an event, a few years ago, when the realization struck that extinction, at least for all plants, animals, and microorganisms of the world, was no longer inevitable, that life expectancy might well revert to a preatomic probability. There must then have been a shuddering sigh of relief, a great exhalation. The sword of Damocles had been sheathed. Life would endure—that extraordinary process whereby matter is ordered, infused with vitality, processes, form, capabilities, roles, purpose, and meaning—propelled by some unknown, blind yearning recorded in evolutionary history, impelled forward. This process would again assume primacy. It would not be necessary to contemplate strategies to adapt to the evolutionary retrogression of nuclear war.

I am continually astonished at the imperturbability of the world's population to this monumental event. Yet it is like a thick black line demarking crucial phases of history, preatomic and postatomic. It is of geological and biological dimensions, like the ice sheets of the Pleistocene. And given the prospect of nuclear winter, this is a very apt simile.

Nuclear war and winter would have had profoundly deleterious effects on atmosphere, oceans, life, and people. Who knows what unimagineable amount of time it would have taken to adapt to the nuclear cataclysm? Indeed, would life and man ever have been able to retrieve the preatomic past?

Yet there has been no celebration. The world's greatest sporting events, each in their own time, produce joyous celebration. How much greater is the gift of life and survival for the earth. Should there not be a worldwide celebration? It would not be too difficult to write the scenario. First, let us identify missile sites and targets. These include the major cities in the United States, Europe, and Russia. Celebration should be in tandem. Select a Russian missile site and its American target. Invite the American population to witness the dismantling of the missiles and throw a party, with music, dancing, eating, drinking, theater, oratory, *glasnost*. Marriages should occur, Russo-American babies should be conceived. Reciprocally, the citizens of a Russian target city fly to the United States to celebrate the dismantling of their angel of death, with instant, popular verification and celebration. So too in Europe, parties are convened at the sites of NATO and Warsaw Pact missiles and targets. Aggressors and victims, relinquishing their tragic and diabolical roles, celebrate their survival and rediscovered humanity.

Yet it may be premature to announce victory when terrestrial missiles are dismantled and atomic artillery and tactical weapons disarmed, for there remains an ominous spectre, the armadas of nuclear submarines lurking under ice sheets, in oceanic abysses, and imperceptible in steep thermal gradients. These alone could undertake a full-scale nuclear war. It will be necessary to bring them to home ports and disarm them. Then there can be celebrations.

Who will be absent? Certainly the Generals Overkill, the Dr. Strangloves, the arms contractors who fattened on their satanic productions. There will be sadness on the part of those made unemployed by the cessation of arms manufacture, and the merchants who benefited from them. Their numbers, however, will be small; the benefactors include the majority of creatures—men, plants, animals—and indeed the futures of them all. It would be a very good bargain.

In a sense this would be a victory celebration without a war. Yet it should rival and exceed the celebrations for victory in Europe and victory in Japan—for the victory is the world's.

The Cold War has ended, the Berlin Wall is not only breached but has been dismantled, the Warsaw Pact nations are marching westward, Poland, Czechoslovakia, Romania, Bulgaria, and the Germanies unite; only Albania persists as an encysted monument to archaic communism. Who would have believed in 1991 that communism would be dethroned as the obligatory theology of Russia? Who would have believed that there would be a serious quest for voluntary federation in that empire?

Yet what has this to do with the environment? Nothing begins to compare with nuclear war as an agent of environmental devastation. Unhappy as we may be with litter, Styrofoam cups, landfills, toxic dumps, and even massive deforestation, they are as a dandruff compared with the effects of nuclear war and nuclear winter, a devastated world with only tiny refugia in Patagonia and New Zealand, challenged to repopulate the world, an irradiated graveyard.

So it appears that the greatest single factor in the environmental quest has been resolved. We can address the mutilations that have occurred rather than the vulcan effects of nuclear war. And there is an additional benefit. Given the recession of the nuclear nightmare, the state of the world's environment has risen in public recognition so now is an opportunity for the global environment to assume primacy in the world's agenda.

This is *volte face*, a complete reversal of values. At one moment the superpowers were intent on spraying the earth with atomic weapons, inducing massive death, mutilation, enduring radiation, nuclear winter, a cindered planet with a shrunken population of creatures. Within the shortest span, we have gained a reprieve in which this depraved intention can be replaced by a resolve to protect and sustain the earth. Thank God.

At last, and not before time.

Now there are three dominant requirements: to understand the way the world works, to consider the consequences of contemplated actions, and to link power to prediction and intelligence. Clearly, our power, mechanical, electronic, and nuclear, exceeds our brains.

We need an inventory, anecdotal stories and isolated examples are not enough. We need an objective, extensive inventory of the world's population and ecosystems—plant, animal, and human. We also require a baseline for examination of historical conditions and identification of trends. It should be located in time prior to the Industrial Revolution, when the composition of atmospheric gases was in dynamic equilibrium, modulated by the oceans and microorganisms, when human activities were isolated pockmarks on the global epidermis, no more significant to the world's health than pimples, when the enormous biodiversity of ecosystems worldwide was unimpaired.

The establishment of a baseline is most important, as it has proven extremely difficult for scientists to allocate the constituent roles in the carbon dioxide cycle. It may finally be impossible. Microorganisms are all but invisible, and their activities have not been studied extensively or understood, yet it is they who have the major role in the world's metabolism. However, empericism may be simpler. It is possible to reconstruct the biosphere at some earlier time of dynamic equilibrium and use this model as a basis for reconstruction.

Next, we must initiate massive global ecological inventories and both invent and install sensors to provide a continuous monitoring process. From baseline to present, we must observe changes and the operation of constituent processes, particularly biogeochemical cycles. This permits predictions based on the extension of current practices and a management plan linked to objectives for global environmental quality. I can think of no human activity of greater importance. It should be seen as the primary consequence of recognizing the global environment as the principal objective in the world's agenda. It identifies the most important purpose of the world's population for now and all time.

We must come to know this world, to understand how it works, and to regulate our behavior to maintain and enhance the biosphere. We must identify the welts, lesions, wounds, and suppurations on the global epidermis. We must learn to green the earth, to restore the earth, to heal the earth. I long to live to see it.

Still, if one has to find a fitting conclusion for a life devoted to the environment, here is one: I can rest happy if indeed the world concurs on the primacy of the global environment. I will receive a gift beyond my wildest expectation if inventories are inaugurated and monitoring undertaken, if responsive global environmental management ensues, and, best of all, if we can complete inventories by early in the twenty-first century and devote the next 100 years to restoring the earth. It took 250 years to devastate the world, to reconstitute it in a century will be a serious challenge.

Can it be done? Of course it can; the history of the earth is a demonstration of an evolutionary process that has included many catastrophic events—the transformation from an anaerobic to aerobic world, possibly the greatest, the creation of an atmosphere to minimize ultraviolet radiation and permit life to occupy the oceanic photic zone and colonize the land, the great ice ages, the profound climatic changes that punctuate life history, the periods of massive extinctions—but adaptation proceeded. The earth was aflower before the advent of people and, indeed, until the recent development of Western technology. The sum of all pernicious human actions is trivial to the biosphere, important only because of its inhibition to man.

Remove all people from the earth, except a few lonely observers, and watch it recover. This process may be too slow and we are, fortunately, no longer resolved to extirpate humankind. Indeed, a better solution would not only engage people in healing the earth, but provide constructive employment for the largest human population in history. Perhaps, in fulfilling the objective of restoring the earth, there is justification for this inordinate human population of five billion, a vast multiplication of human regenerating cells, lymphocytes inducing infectious health, restoring, greening, and healing this miraculous orb, the earth our home.

I would love to be here when this process is apace. In my mind's eye I see myself with a group of scientists, looking at the earth from space, viewing the shrinking deserts, the burgeoning forests, the clear atmosphere, the virgin oceans, smiling at the recovery, anticipating the day when a successor will announce, "the earth is healed, the earth is well."

On September 10, 1990, I received the National Medal of Art from President Bush. Included in his remarks was an astonishing and totally unexpected statement: "Let us hope that in the next century the finest accomplishment of art will be the restoration of the land."

The ecological view and the skills of landscape architecture and ecological planning must contribute leadership for this restoration—it is, indeed, a quest for life.

A Poem to the World's Children

Dearest children,
   Do you know
   that we have inherited
   a miracle?

   All matter—
   the heavens, sun, the earth itself—
   is made
   from the ashes of stars,
   cycled by volcanoes,
   in sea and air,
   clouds, rain, rivers, rocks, and soils;
   matter permeates us all,
   creatures infused with life,
   animated,
   including you
   playing, smiling children
   now.

   Exult in this
   prodigious
   unexpected world,
   birdsong and butterflies,
   puppies and pandas,
   foals and flowers,
   dappled trout,
   time,
   the seasons,
   music, joy, laughter,
   you and me,
   joined in this improbable
   universe.

   Recoil from the loathsome
   mutilated and scabbed land,
   foul seas, rivers, air,
   squalid slums,
   wastes,
   diseased tissues on the
living earth—
repudiate them.

Resolve to protect the earth;
it is our home;
all creatures are kin,
brethren,
gifted with life,
aching for fulfillment,
doomed to die;
but
our breath will fuel flowers;
our tears will join the magic cycle;
our carbon will find other homes;
our wastes will replenish;
in this sense we are immortal,
as is the world.

We are transients,
but we can be guardians;
we can protect and restore;
it needs resolve,
commitment, energy and art.

So you must aim to protect
all that is wild and wondrous,
to heal mutilation,
salve wounds,
restore the earth.

Then bequeath a better legacy,
a finer future
for the earth and
its creatures,
for all children
now and forevermore;
make it a quest for life
in God's name,

                                    Amen

Chronology

November 20, 1920	Born, Clydebank, Scotland
1925–1931	Radnor Park Elementary School
1932–1936	Clydebank High School
1934	Copy boy, Associated Scottish Newspapers
1935	Editor's boy, Associated Scottish Newspapers
1936	Withdrew from high school, became pupil-apprentice to Donald A. Wintersgill, landscape architect for Austin and McAslan Ltd., Glasgow
	Enrolled in West of Scotland Agricultural College
	Enrolled in Glasgow College of Art
1937	"Boy" racing editor, Associated Scottish Newspapers
May 1938	Enlisted in British Army
September 2, 1939	Mobilized into the regular army at the onset of World War II
1940	Sailed to Saint-Malo in France with Second British Expeditionary Force
	Promoted to lance corporal and corporal
March 20 & 21, 1940	Clydebank bombed
1942	Sent to Officer Training School
	Commissioned second lieutenant
	Posted to Second Parachute Squadron
	Embarked to Oran for North African Campaign
	Trained for parachute invasion of Sicily (Augusta) canceled
September 1943	Participated in invasion of Italy
September 9, 1943	HMS *Abdiel* sinks
Mid-September, 1943	Acquedotto Pugliese reconstruction, Italy
November 1943	News of my mother's death

April 1944	Promoted to captain
August 1944	Participated in invasion of South of France
September 1944	Led invasion of Greece (Megara)
1945	Won competition to design British military cemetery in Athens
April 1946	Promoted to major
August 1946	Met Pauline Crena de Iongh
September 1946	Demobilized at the rank of major
	Entered Harvard Graduate School of Design
August 1947	Married to Pauline
1949	Bachelor of Landscape Architecture, Harvard University
May 8, 1949	Alistair born
1950	Master of Landscape Architecture, Harvard University
	Returned to Scotland
September 1950	Admitted Southfield Colony for Consumptives, Edinburgh
1951	Master of City Planning, Harvard University
May 1951	Went to Hotel Belvedere, Leysin, Switzerland
September 1951	Discharged
Fall 1951	Returned to Edinburgh, planning officer, Department of Health for Scotland
	Offered lecture course in landscape architecture to Edinburgh College of Art, followed by Glasgow College of Art in 1952
1954	Appointed assistant professor of landscape architecture and city planning at the University of Pennsylvania
Summer 1955	Pauline and Alistair arrived in Hoboken
1955	University of Pennsylvania Department of Landscape Architecture created

December 10, 1956	Malcolm born
1957	Promoted to associate professor, University of Pennsylvania
1958	Karl Linn joined faculty
	Received grant from Rockefeller Foundation
September 1959	"Man and Environment" course first introduced
1960–1961	Produced television series *The House We Live In* for CBS
1961	Promoted to professor, University of Pennsylvania
1962	Co-founded Wallace-McHarg Associates
	Plan for the Valleys
1965	Wallace, McHarg, Roberts and Todd (WMRT) formed
1965–1967	American Institute of Architects Potomac Planning Task Force
1966	Received Grant from Ford Foundation
	Sabbatical, wrote *Design with Nature*
	White House Task Force on Conservation and Natural Beauty
June 1967	Completed *Design with Nature*
	Appointed member Philadelphia Art Commission
1968	Filmed *Multiply and Subdue the Earth*
January 1969	*Multiply and Subdue the Earth* shown on PBS
1969	Profiled in articles in *Time* and *Life*
	ABC, New York, moon landing show with Marshall McLuhan, Howard K. Smith, Bill Moyers
	Mike Wallace television show
	Today show
	My father died
	Design with Nature published

	Horace Albright Lecture
	Ecological Study of Twin Cities
April 1970	Earth Week
May 12, 1970	Royal Institute of British Architects discourse, London
May 15, 1970	Edinburgh University address
1971	White House Task Force on Children and Youth
	Australian Institute of Architecture Centennial Convention
September 21, 1971	*Progressive Architecture* Jury
1972	Four Seasons, New York: Fortune 500 speech
	Hazleton Human Ecological Study
1972–1973	"Towards a Comprehensive Plan for Environmental Quality" for the U.S. Environmental Protection Agency
1973	Received grant from National Institutes of Mental Health
1974	Pauline died
	Medford report published
	Nigerian National Capital Site Selection, Abuja
May 1974	Presentation of Pardisan Comprehensive Plan—report, movie, and model, in Teheran, Iran
1975	Met Carol Smyser
1976	Kennett Square Human Ecological Study
1977	Profiled in *Science* article
May 1977	Married to Carol
1979	Resigned from WMRT
1981	Comprehensive Plan, Edith Macy National Training Center Girl Scouts of America, Chappaqua, New York

	Ecological Planning of Metropolitan Regions, Mexico City Mega City Conference
1982	Smithsonian Conference
August 27, 1982	Ian born
1984	Taroko National Park, Taiwan
1986	Consultation, Government of New Zealand
	Foundation professor, University of Auckland
	Consultation, New South Wales, Victoria; West Australia, Northern Territories
1986–1987	University of California at Berkeley, senior visiting professor
1987	Consultation, State of Hawaii
	Profiled in *Pennsylvania Gazette* article
November 19, 1987	Andrew born
1988	Keynote address, Geographic Information Systems Conference, San Francisco
1989	Medford Plan Review
	Established computer mapping laboratory with Jon Berger and John Radke
September 10, 1990	Received National Medal of Art
1991	EMAP—A Prototype Database for a National Ecological Inventory
	Soil and Water Conservation Society Address, Lexington, Kentucky
June 28, 1991	Three Mile Island Conference
	Taipei—National Ecological Inventory for Taiwan
	TV episode for *Leakey Journal*
	Benjamin Franklin Honors Seminar
	American Institute of Architects Jury, Boston

August 7, 1992	Stopped smoking, Caron Clinic
	A Prototype Database for a National Ecological Inventory, with J. Radke, J. Berger, and K. Wallace
	EMAP Presentation to EPA
1993	To Japan—Shebunsha arrangement to translate *Design with Nature* into Japanese
April 1993	Arizona State University Landscape Architecture: Ecology and Design and Planning Conference
	Mazatlan, Mexico, Ecotourism Conference
1994	Visiting professor, Graduate School of Design, Harvard University
	Wrote introduction for the Japanese edition of *Design with Nature*
February 3, 1994	*Multiply and Subdue the Earth* on video, and donation from Environmental Systems Research Institute
Fall 1994	Bruce Goff Professor, University of Oklahoma
October 17, 1994	In Japan to launch Japanese edition of *Design with Nature*
November 8, 1994	Spanish translation of *Design with Nature* sent by Carlos Ayallah
February–March, 1995	Ball State University, Muncie, Indiana, Sustainability Seminar

Awards

Brookhaven Distinguished Scientist
Bradford Williams, 1968
Honorary Doctorate, Amherst College, 1970
Honorary Doctorate, Lewis & Clark College, 1970
B.Y. Morrison Award, 1971
Danz Award, 1971
Brown & Haley Lecture, 1972
Creative Arts Award, Brandeis, 1972
American Institute of Architects Medal for Allied Professions, 1972
Cecil and Ida Green Lecture, 1974
Art Alliance Medal, 1975
Neutra Medal, 1975
Centennial Professor, University of Texas, 1976
Honorary HHD, Bates College, 1978
Bradford Williams Medal, 1979
Fellow, Royal Society of Art, 1980
Distinguished Professor, Texas A & M University, 1983
Bracken Memorial Medal, 1983
Connoisseur Award, 1984
Mitchell Award, 1984
American Society of Landscape Architects Medal, 1984
René Dubos Regeneration Award, 1987
National Endowment for the Arts Award, 1987
National Medal of Art, 1990
Neutra Medal, 1992
Council of Educators in Landscape Architecture Distinguished Educator, 1992
Honorary Degree Heriot-Watt University, 1992 (Scotland)
Lifetime Achievement, Harvard University, 1992
Bruce Goff Professorship, University of Oklahoma, 1994
Geographic Information Systems World, Lifetime Achievement, 1995
Thomas Jefferson Medal in Architecture, University of Virginia, 1995

Bibliography

PUBLICATIONS

Book

Design with Nature. Garden City, N.Y.: Natural History Press, 1969. Natural History Press/Doubleday, 1970. Reprint. Second edition. New York: John Wiley & Sons, 1994. National Book Award finalist. Translated into French (*Composer avec la nature,* with original French contribution, edited by Max Falque, Cahiers de L'IAURIF, vols. 58–59, 1980), Italian (*Progetto con la natura,* Franco Muzzio, editore, 1989, Padova, Italy), Japanese, German (forthcoming), and Chinese (forthcoming).

Chapters in Books

"Ecology and Design." In *Ecological Design and Planning* edited by George F. Thompson and Frederick R. Steiner. New York: John Wiley & Sons, 1996.

"Introduction." In *The Built Environment,* edited by Tom J. Bartuska and Gerald L. Young, pages ix–xi. Menlo Park, Cal.: Crisp Publications, 1994.

"Nature Is More Than a Garden." In *The Meaning of Gardens,* edited by Mark Francis and Randolph T. Hester, Jr., pages 34–37. Cambridge, Mass.: MIT Press, 1990.

"Natural and Cultural Heritage Resources in Your Community." In *Taproots, Stewardship Through Heritage Discovery: Description of a Program for Secondary Schools and Proceedings of the Conference "Knowing Home,"* edited by Toby Tourbier, pages 113–118. Newark: Water Resources Center, University of Delaware, 1985.

"Ecological Planning." In *Onshore Impacts of Offshore Oil,* edited by William J. Cairns and Patrick M. Rogers, pages 139–143. London: Applied Science Publishers, 1981.

"Three Essays on Urban Space." In *Urban Encounters,* edited by ICA staff, pages 21–24. Philadelphia: Institute of Contemporary Art, 1981.

"Appropriate Stormwater Management." In *Stormwater Management Alternatives,* edited by J. Toby Tourbier and Richard Westmacott, pages 23–30. Newark: Water Resources Center, University of Delaware, 1980.

With Arthur H. Johnson and Jonathan Berger. "A Case Study in Ecological Planning: The Woodlands, Texas." In *Planning the Uses and Management of Land,* edited by Marvin T. Beatty, Gary W. Petersen, and Lester D. Swindale, pages 935–955. Madison, Wis.: American Society of Agronomy, Crop Science Society of America, and Soil Science Society of America, 1979.

"Ecological Planning: The Planner as Catalyst." In *Planning Theory in the 1980s,* edited by Robert W. Burchell and George Sternlieb, pages 13–15. New Brunswick, N.J.: Center for Urban Policy Research, 1978 (2d ed. 1982).

"Biological Alternatives to Water Pollution." In *Biological Control of Water Pollution*, edited by Joachim Tourbier and Robert W. Pierson, Jr., pages 7–12. Philadelphia: Center for Ecological Design and Planning, University of Pennsylvania, 1976.

"Il Bacino del Fiume." In *Risorse del Territorio e Politica di Piano*, edited by Guido Ferrara, pages 77–78. Venezia, Italy: Marsilo, 1976.

"Must We Sacrifice the West?" In *Growth Alternatives for the Rocky Mountain West*, edited by Terrell J. Minger and Sherry D. Oaks, pages 203–211. Boulder, Col.: Westview Press, 1975.

"The Place of Nature in the City of Man." In *Urban Areas*, edited by D.R. Coates, pages 30–41. Stroudsburg, Pa.: Dowden, Hutchinson & Ross, 1974.

With Michael G. Clarke. "Skippack Watershed and the Evansburg Project: A Case Study for Water Resources Planning." In *Environmental Quality and Water Development*, edited by Charles R. Goodman, James McEroy III, and Peter J. Richerson, pages 299–330. San Francisco: W.H. Freeman and Company, 1973.

"Architecture in an Ecological View of the World." In *Environmental Solutions*, edited by Nicholas Pole, pages 83–92. Cambridge, England: Cambridge University Conservation Society Eco-Publications, 1972.

"Values, Process and Form." In *Economic Growth vs. the Environment*, edited by W.A. Johnson and J. Hardesty, pages 19–25. Belmont, Calif.: Wadsworth Publishing Company, 1971.

"Ecological Planning for Evolutionary Success." In *Master Planning the Aviation Environment*, edited by Angelo J. Cerchione, Victor E. Rothe, and James Vercellino, pages 7–10. Tucson: The University of Arizona Press, 1970.

"The Place of Nature in the City of Man." In *Challenge for Survival: Land, Air, and Water for Man in Megalopolis*, edited by Pierre Dansereau and Virginia A. Weadock, pages 37–54. New York: Columbia University Press, 1970.

"Open Space from Natural Processes." In *Metropolitan Open Space and Natural Process*, edited by David A. Wallace, pages 10–52. Philadelphia: University of Pennsylvania Press, 1970.

"Man's Debt to Nature: Ecology and the Goals of Urban Development." *The Urban Industrial Frontier: Essays on Social Trends and Institutional Goals in Modern Communities*, edited by David Popenoe, pages 141–156. New Brunswick, N.J.: Rutgers University Press, 1969.

"Values, Process and Form." In *The Fitness of Man's Environment*, edited by Smithsonian Institution Staff, pages 207–227. New York: Harper & Row, 1968. (Paperback edition. New York: Harper Colophon, 1970).

"The Place of Man in Nature and Nature in the Environment of Man." *Taming Megalopolis*, edited by Wentworth Eldrege, pages 540–547, 1967.

"Ecological Determinism." In *The Future Environments of North America*, edited by Frank Fraser Darling and John P. Milton, pages 526–538. Garden City, N.Y.: Natural History Press, 1966.

"Man and Environment." In *The Urban Condition*, edited by Leonard J. Duhl and John Powell, pages 44–58. New York: Basic Books, 1963.

"Regional Landscape Planning." In *Resources, The Metropolis, and the Land-Grant University* (Proceedings of the Conference on Natural Resources, No. 410), edited by A.J.W. Scheffey, pages 31–35. Amherst: University of Massachusetts, 1963. (Comments by others on McHarg's remarks continue through page 37.)

Articles

"Green the Earth, Heal the Earth." *Journal of Soil and Water Conservation* 47, no. 1 (1992):39–41.

"The House We Live In: Remembering a Meeting of Minds." *1991–1992 Almanac* (The Annual of the International Council of National Academy of Television Arts and Sciences) (1992):47–50.

"The American Landscape into the 21st Century." *Renewable Resources Journal* (Summer 1989):17–18.

"Human Ecological Planning at Pennsylvania." *Landscape Planning* 8 (1981):109–120.

"The Garden as a Metaphysical Symbol" (The Riding Reflection Lecture 1979). *Journal of Royal Society* 128 (February 1980):132–143.

"Human Ecological Planning." *Proceedings of Australian and New Zealand Academies of Science* (January 1979).

With Jonathan Sutton. "Ecological Plumbing for the Texas Coastal Plain." *Landscape Architecture* 65, no. 1 (January 1975):78–89.

"Design with Nature" and "The Garden as a Metaphysical Symbol." *Ontario Naturalist* 13, no. 1 (March 1973):20–39.

"Values, Process and Form." *Options Meditéranéenes* 13 (June 1972):19–25.

"Best Shore Protection: Nature's Own Dunes." *Civil Engineering/ASCE* 42 (September 1972):66–70.

"Man, Planetary Disease." *Vital Speeches of the Day* (August 1971):634–640.

"Man and Nature—A Space Odyssey." *Consulting Engineer* 36 (March 1971):79–82.

"Architecture: an Ecological View of the World." *The Structuralist* 11 (August 1971):83–89.

"Ecological Values and Regional Planning." *Civil Engineering/ASCE* 40 (August 1970):40–44.

"Is Man a Planetary Disease?" (Annual Discourse: Ian McHarg). *RIBA Journal* 77 (July 1970):303–308.

"Design and Nature." *Cities 70* (Architecture and Engineering Forum). Los Angeles: Southern California Extension Company and Los Angeles Department of Water and Power, 1970. Section III, 30 pages.

"Architecture in an Ecological View of the World." *AIA Journal* 54 (5 November 1970):47–51.

"What Would You Do With, Say, Staten Island?" *Natural History* 78, no. 4 (April 1969):27–37; with an introduction by Frances Low on page 26.

"A Comprehensive Highway Route-Section Method." *Highway Research Record* 246 (1968):1–15.

"Ecology, for the Evolution of Planning and Design." *Via* 1 (1968):44–66.

"Where Should Highways Go?" *Landscape Architecture* 57, no. 3 (1967):179–181.

"An Ecological Method for Landscape Architecture." *Landscape Architecture* 57, no. 2 (1967):105–107.

"Blight or a Noble City?" *Audubon Magazine* 68, no. 1 (February 1966):47–52.

"Architecture, Ecology and Form." *Perspective* (published by the Students' Architectural Society, University of Manitoba) (1966):50–59.

With David A. Wallace. "Plan for the Valleys vs. Spectre of Uncontrolled Growth." *Landscape Architecture* 55, no. 3 (March 1965):179–181.

"School News: A New Role for Landscape Architects." *Landscape Architecture* 54, no. 3 (April 1964):227–228.

"The Place of Nature in the City of Man." *The Annals of the American Academy of Political and Social Sciences* (Urban Revival: Goals and Standards) 352 (March 1964):1–12.

"The Ecology of the City." *Journal of Architectural Education* 17, no. 2 (November 1962):101–103.

"The Ecology of the City." *AIA Journal* 38, no. 5 (November 1962):101–103.

"The Humane City: Must the Man of Distinction Always Move to the Suburbs?" *Landscape Architecture* 48 (January 1958):103–107.

"The Courthouse Concept." *Architects' Year Book* 8 (1957):74–102.

"The Court House Concept." *Architectural Record* 122 (September 1957):193–200.

"The Return to the City." *The General Magazine and Historical Chronicle* 59 (Spring 1957):1–6.

"Can We Afford Open Space? A Survey of Landscape Costs." *Architects' Journal* 123 (March 1956):260–273.

"Landscape Architecture." *Pennsylvania Triangle* 41, no.7 (April 1955):36,42.

"Open Space and Housing." *Architects' Year Book* 6 (1955):75–82.

"Architecture in the Netherlands." *Quarterly Journal of the Royal Incorporation of Architects in Scotland* 94 (1953):41–46.

Reviews, Essays, and Published Symposia and Proceedings

"Ian McHarg, FASLA, Keynote Address." In *Renewing the American City,* Proceedings of the 1995 Annual Meeting and Expo. edited by Karen L. Niles, page 15. Washington, D.C.: American Society of Landscape Architects, 1995.

"This Bug's for You." *New York Times Book Review,* 6 June 1993, 45–46.

"On Finding the Earth." *GSD News,* pages 31. Cambridge, Mass.: Graduate School of Design, Harvard University, 1993.

"An Ecological Basis for Human Settlement." In *International Symposium on City Planning in Harmony with the Human Environment*, pages 7–25. Japan: Ministry of Construction, 1992.

With James F. Thorne, Jon Berger, and D. Andrew Pitz. "Issues for Landscape Ecology in Urban Park Planning." In *Proceedings from Selected Educational Sessions of the 1990 American Society of Landscape Architects' Annual Meeting, Landscape Land Use Planning Committee.* edited by Julius Fabos and Jack Ahern, pages 56–78. San Diego, California, October 27–30, 1990.

"Cities 2000: Transportation and Urban Design." edited by Anil Verna. Los Angeles: University of California Los Angeles, 1989.

"The Legislative Landscape, A Quarterly Update—Summer 1989." *Landscape Architecture News Digest* 30, no. 7 (1989):7–8.

"A Model for Unity." *Penn in Ink* (Fall 1983): 2.

"Ecological Planning of Metropolitan Regions." A paper presented at Primer Congreso Internacional de Planificación de Grandes Ciudades (First congress of planning of major cities), pages 248–249. Mexico City: Departamento del Distrito Federal, Programa de Intercambio Científico y Capacitación Técnica del Departamento del Distrito Federal, 1981.

"Design with Nature." In *On Human Dimensions* (excerpts from papers presented May 20, 1975, at the John Walley Commemoration Design Conference), pages 37–44. Champaign, Ill.: Trustees of the University of Illinois, 1976.

"The Preconditions for Effective Comprehensive Planning for Environmental Quality." In *Proceedings of the Conference on Landuse Planning: Implications for Citizens and State and Local Governments*, pages 19–50. March 26–27, Columbus, Ohio, 1974.

"Planning Procedures and Techniques for Environmental Conservation in the Natural Landscape." In *Planning for Environment Conberiata* (International Symposium). Pretoria, South Africa: Department of Planning and the Environment, Institute of Lands Architecture, 1973.

"The Consequences of Today." A record of papers given at the Royal Australian Institute of Architects Centenary Convention, May 22–28, 1971, Wentworth Hotel, Sydney. Supplement to *Architecture in Australia* (August 1971):638–646.

"Man: Planetary Disease" (The 1971 B. Y. Morrison Memorial Lecture). Washington, D.C.: U.S. Department of Agriculture, Agricultural Research Service, 1971.

"The Plight." *Ecosphere, A News Bulletin of the International Ecology University* 1, no. 1 (November 1970):10–16.

"The Metropolitan View." In *Transcript of the Proceedings of the Planning Seminar for Water Resources Development.* New York: Department of the Army Corps of Engineers (February 1969).

"And in Leisure Time" (manuscript). *Urban American Conference Proceedings* (September 11–13, 1966), pages 59–71. Washington, D.C.: Urban America, Inc., 1966.

"Landscape Action Program" (extract). In *Beauty for America, Proceedings of the White House Conference on Natural Beauty*, May 24–25, 1965, pages 481–484. Washington, D.C.: U.S. Government Printing Office, 1965.

"Natural Sciences and the Planning Process." Conference on Natural Resources, the Ford Foundation Discussion Papers. February 27, 28, 29, March 1, 1964.

"Ecology of the City: A Plea for Environmental Consciousness." In *The Architect and the City* (papers from the AIA-ACSA Teacher Seminar, Cranbrook Academy of Art, June 11–12 1962), edited by Marcus Whiffen, pages 43–58. Washington, D.C.: AIA Department of Education, 1962.

PROFESSIONAL REPORTS, PLANS, AND DESIGNS

University of Pennsylvania Projects (1963–1992)

With John Radke, Jonathan Berger, and Kathleen Wallace. "A Prototype Database for a National Ecological Inventory." Washington, D.C.: U.S. Environmental Protection Agency, 1992.

Center for Ecological Research in Planning and Design. "Guidelines for Land Resource and Analysis for Planning." Philadelphia: Department of Landscape Architecture and Regional Planning, University of Pennsylvania, and Harrisburg: Department of Environmental Resources, Commonwealth of Pennsylvania, 1975.
The report was written by Ian L. McHarg, Narendra Juneja, E. Bruce MacDougall, and Jonathan Berger.

Narendra Juneja. "Medford: Performance Requirements for the Maintenance of Social Values Represented by the Natural Environment of Medford Township New Jersey." Philadelphia: Center for Ecological Research in Planning and Design, Department of Landscape Architecture and Regional Planning, University of Pennsylvania, 1974.
Ian L. McHarg, principal investigator; Narendra Juneja, deputy principal investigator and report author; Arthur Sullivan, deputy principal investigator; W. Robinson Fisher, project director; Robert Giegengack; Ronald Hanawalt; Michael Levin; Seymour Subitsky; Ruth Patrick; Thomas Lloyd; Robert Snyder; Victor Yannacone; Arthur Palmer; and University of Pennsylvania graduate students.

University of Pennsylvania. "Metropolitan Open Space from Natural Processes." Philadelphia: Urban Renewal Administration and the States of Pennsylvania and New Jersey, 1963.
Ian L. McHarg, principal investigator; David A. Wallace, project director; Ann Louise Strong; William Grigsby; Anthony Tomazinis; Nohad Toulan; William H. Roberts; Donald Phimister; and Frank Shaw.

Department of Landscape Architecture. "Sea, Storm, and Survival: A Study of the New Jersey Shore." Philadelphia, Pennsylvania: University of Pennsylvania, 1963.
Ian L. McHarg, Roger D. Clemence, Ayre M. Dvir, Geoffrey A. Collins, Michael Laurie, William J. Oliphant, and Peter Ker Walker.

Post Wallace, McHarg, Roberts and Todd Projects (1981–1994)

With Cristian Basso, Elke Bilda, Ho-Shu Chou, Buzz Constable, Paul Cote, Iram Farooa, Karen Mans, Sarah Peskin, Girish Remachandran, and Joel Young. "Mount Desert Island, Maine." Cambridge, Massachusetts: Landscape Architecture Studio, Graduate School of Design, Harvard University, 1984.

With John Radke and Jonathan Berger. " The Settlement Plan." Ann Arbor, Michigan: Domino Farms, 1989.

With Jonathan Berger. "A Re-Examination of the Medford Master Plan." Medford, New Jersey, 1989.

With James Thorne, Jonathan Berger, John Radke, and Kate Deregibus. "Blue Heron Lake Park Plan." New York: Department of Parks and Recreation, 1987–1990.

With Joseph McBride, James Thorne, Steven Stiz, and Lan Shing Huang. "White Oak Ranch Plan." Colusa County, California: Gerald Blakeley, 1986.

With Carol A. Smyser, James Thorne, Dorthy Wurman, and Kim Sorvig. "Riverdale Park Plan." New York: Department of Parks and Recreation, 1984–1989.

"Report of Taroko Gorge: Planning a National Parks System for Taiwan." Taipei, Taiwan: Government of the Republic of China, 1984.

"A Proposal to Undertake an Ecological Planning Study for Sedona, Arizona." Philadelphia, 1983.

"Comprehensive Plan, Edith Macy National Training Center, Chappaqua, New York." Washington, D.C.: Girl Scouts of America National Council, 1981.
    Ian McHarg, project director; Jorge G. Sanchez-Flores; Robert Turner; Edward Hollander; Barbara Seymour; Robert Giegengack, geomorphologist; William Johnson, biochemist; and Michael Skaller, ecologist.

With M. Paul Friedberg. "Gateway National Park Plan." New York: U.S. National Park Service, 1981.

With Marty Zeller, Don Walker, Russell Moore, and Michael Skaller. "Stewards of the Valley Plan, Evans Ranch." Denver: Colorado Open Land Trust, 1981.

Wallace, McHarg, Roberts and Todd Projects (1965–1980)

"Environmental Assessment and Planning Strategies for Indian River Shores, Vero Beach, Florida." Amherst, Massachusetts: Otto Paparazzo, 1980.
    Ian L. McHarg, partner-in-charge, and John Keene. Additional planning and architecture by Callister Payne & Bischoff of Tiburon, California. The project was partially completed.

International Planning Associates. "The Master Plan for Abuja, the New Federal Capital of Nigeria." Lagos, Nigeria: The Federal Capital Development Authority, 1979.
    Archisystems, Planning Research Corporation, Wallace McHarg Roberts and Todd. Abraam Krushkhov, project director; Walter G. Hansen, associate project director; Thomas A. Todd, partner-in-charge for Wallace, McHarg, Roberts and Todd planning and design; Ian L. McHarg supervised the ecological study, and others contributed.

International Planning Associates. "A New Federal Capital for Nigeria" (Report No. 2. Site Evaluation and Site Selection). Lagos, Nigeria, 1978.
    Archisystems, Planning Research Corporation, Wallace, McHarg, Roberts and Todd. Abraam Krushkov, project director; Walter G. Hansen, associate project director; Thomas A. Todd, partner-in-charge for Wallace, McHarg, Roberts and Todd planning and design; Ian L. McHarg, technical review; and others.

In association with Economic Research Associates and Alan M. Voorhees Associates, Inc. "Denver Metropolitan Areawide Environmental Impact Statement." Denver: Regional VIII, U.S. Department of Housing and Urban Development, 1978.
Ian L. McHarg, George Toop, John Beckman, and Anne Spirn.

"Ecological Study for Northwestern Colorado Council of Governments." Frisco, Colorado: Northwestern Colorado Council of Governments, 1978.
Ian L. McHarg, partner-in-charge; Michael Clarke, associate partner; Robert Geigengack; Arthur Johnson; and Richard Nalbandian.

"'208' Study for Detroit Metropolitan Area." Detroit, Michigan: Southwest Michigan Council of Governments, 1978.
Ian L. McHarg, partner-in-charge; Michael Clarke; David Hamme; and Ronald Walters.

"Laguna Creek Study." Sacramento, California: Laguna Creek, circa 1977.
Ian L. McHarg, partner-in-charge; Michael Clarke; and Robert Grunewald.

"'208' Study for Toledo, Ohio." Toledo, Ohio: Toledo Metropolitan Area Council of Governments, 1977.
Ian L. McHarg, partner-in-charge; and Michael Clarke.

"Washington Metropolitan Transit Authority F Route Environmental Impact Study." Washington, D.C.: Washington Metropolitan Transit Authority, 1977.
Ian L. McHarg, partner-in-charge; David Hamme, associate; and Richard Nalbandian. The F Route is now known as the Green Line of the Washington D.C. Metro.

Ian L. McHarg. "Regional Goals for Planned Growth." Prepared for the Toledo Metropolitan Area Council for Governments. Philadelphia: Wallace, McHarg, Roberts and Todd, 1976.
Ian L. McHarg, Michael Clarke, and others.

Ian L. McHarg. "Evaluation of Major 208 Facility Plans." Prepared for the Toledo Metropolitan Area Council of Governments. Philadelphia: Wallace, McHarg, Roberts and Todd, 1976.
Ian L. McHarg, Michael Clarke, and others.

"Environmental Resources of the Toronto Central Waterfront." Prepared for the Central Waterfront Planning Committee, City of Toronto. Philadelphia: Winchell Press, 1976.
Ian McHarg, partner-in-charge; Narendra Juneja, senior associate partner; Anne Spirn, project director; Carol Reifsnyder; Clive Goodwin; Arthur Johnson; Marta Griffiths; Roger Smith; Beth Kitchen; William Robinson; John Czarnowski; Jane Laughlin; Margaret Dewey; John Purkess; and Rodney Robinson. Narendra Juneja was the project leader, with Anne Spirn playing a major role.

"Lake Austin Growth Management Plan." Austin, Texas: City of Austin, Department of Planning, 1976.
William H. Roberts, partner-in-charge; Ian L. McHarg, partner; Michael G. Clarke, senior associate partner/project director; Narendra Juneja, senior associate partner; Susan Drew; Beth Kitchen; Anne Whiston Spirn; Mukund Lokhande; Carol Reifsnyder; Richard Nalbandian; Jane Laughlin; Espey, Huston and Associates, Incorporated, hydrologic studies; and Richard Lillie, director, Department of Planning, City of Austin.

The Mandala Collaborative/Wallace, McHarg, Roberts and Todd. "Pardisan: Plan for an Environmental Park in Tehran." Prepared for the Department of Environment, Imperial Government of Iran. Philadelphia: Winchell Press, 1975. The report was written by Ian L. McHarg, assisted by W. Robinson Fisher, Anne Spirn, and Narendra Juneja. Eskandar Firouz and Jahangir Sedaghatfar were responded from the Iran Department of the Environment. Nadar Ardalan and others from the Mandala Collaborative of Tehran were involved in the planning. Many Wallace, McHarg, Roberts and Tood staff were involved, including William Roberts; Colin Franklin, project director; Tom Atkins; Rob Turner; Richard Collier; Tim Van Epp; Carol Franklin; Leslie Sauer; Rolf Sauer; Ed Boyer; and Siddartha Thakar; in addition to those who assisted in writing the report and others. Several Wallace, McHarg, Roberts and Todd project staff, including Neal Belanger and Vicki Steiger, lived and worked in Iran for periods of the project. Key consultants included Yehudi Cohen, Charles Eames, R. Buckminster Fuller, Glen Fleck, David R. Goddard, David Hancocks, Brian Spooner, Solomon Katz, Jones and Jones (especially Jon Coe of their staff), and Sven Svendsen. Hosein Nasr was an advisor to the project.

"San Francisco Metropolitan Regional Environmental Impact Procedure Study, California." San Francisco: Bay Area Council of Governments, 1974. David Wallace, partner-in-charge; Ian L. McHarg, consulting partner; Richard Nalbandian; Ed Boyer; Carol Reifsnyder; Leslie Sauer; John Rogers; Frits Golden; Robert Pierson; and others.

"Owl Creek: A Feasibility Study for Future Development." Houston, Texas: Mitchell Development Corporation of the Southwest, 1974. Ian McHarg, supervising partner; Narendra Juneja, senior associate partner; David C. Hamme, senior associate partner; Colin Franklin, project director; Mukund Lokhande; Faye Brandon; Hans Harald Grote; Carol Reifsnyder; Jane Laughlin; A. Allen Dyer and others from Colorado State University; Thomas Prather; F. Robert McGregor; Kenneth R. Wright; and Charles Wolcott.

"Woodlands New Community: An Ecological Plan." Houston, Texas: The Woodlands Development Corporation, 1974. Ian L. McHarg, partner-in-charge; Jonathan S. Sutton; Narendra Juneja; Richard Nalbandian; Dennis McGlade; Doris Zorensky Cheng; Mukund Lokhande; Anne Whiston Spirn; Colin Franklin; Leslie Sauer; William P. Lowry; and others.

"Woodlands New Community: An Ecological Inventory." Houston, Texas; The Woodlands Development Corporation, 1974. Ian L. McHarg, partner-in-charge; Narendra Juneja, associate-in-charge; James Veltman, project manager; Richard Nalbandian; Dennis McGlade; Doris Zorensky Cheng; Jonathan Sutton; Colin Franklin; Leslie Sauer; and others.

"Woodlands New Community, Phase One: Land Planning and Design Principles." Houston, Texas: The Woodlands Development Corporation, 1974. Ian L. McHarg, partner-in-charge; Jonathan S. Sutton; Narendra Juneja; Richard Nalbandian; Dennis McGlade; Anne Whiston Spirn; Doris Zorensky Cheng; Mukund Lokhande; Colin Franklin; Leslie Sauer; William P. Lowry; and others.

"Woodlands New Community: Guidelines for Site Planning." Houston, Texas: The Woodlands Development Corporation, 1973. Ian L. McHarg, partner-in-charge; Jonathan Sutton, associate partner-in-charge; Richard Nalbandian; Anne Whiston Spirn, project director; and others.

"Pardisan: A Feasibility Study for an Environmental Park in Tehran, Iran." Prepared for the Imperial Government of
    Iran. Philadelphia: Wallace, McHarg, Roberts and Todd, 1973.
    William H. Roberts, partner-in-charge; Ian L. McHarg, participating partner; Colin Franklin, project captain; Leslie
    Sauer; Ross Bateup; Charles Fleisher; Richard Nalbandian; William Becker; Dennis McGlade; Sven Svendsen; Nader
    Ardalan; Jack McCormick; Theodore Reed; Brian Spooner; R. Buckminster Fuller; and others.

"Progress Report: Evolution of Land Planning and Design Guidelines for Eaton's Neck Point, Asherochen, Long Island,
    New York." Amherst Fields, Amherst, Massachusetts: Otto Paparazzo, 1973.
    Ian L. McHarg, partner-in-charge; Jonathan S. Sutton, project director; Leslie Jones Sauer; Oscar R. Martinez-
    Conill; Mihran R. Nalbandian; Edward Boyer; Mark Weglarz; Charles Watson; Anne Spirn; Carol Reifsnyder;
    Charles Barnett; Orville Terry; and John Burger. In collaboration with Callister Payne & Bishoff of Tiburon,
    California, master planners and architects. The project was not completed.

In association with Tippetts Abbett, McCarthy, Stratton and Gladstone Associates. "Ponchartrain New-Town-in-Town,
    New Orleans, Louisiana." Dallas, Texas; Murchison Brothers, Pontchartrain Land Corporation, 1973.
    David A. Wallace, managing partner; Ian L. McHarg, partner; William H. Roberts, partner; Thomas A. Todd, part-
    ner; Richard W. Huffman; Narendra Juneja; Donald H. Brackenbush; David C. Hamme; Michael G. Clarke; Robert
    Gladstone; Dennis McGlade; and others.

"Hugh Moore Parkway." Easton, Pennsylvania: The Hugh Moore Parkway Commission, 1973.
    Ian L. McHarg, partner-in-charge; Thomas Todd, contributing partner; Michael Clarke, associate partner-in-
    charge; Narendra Juneja, contributing associate partner; Doris Cheng; Colin Franklin; Dennis McGlade; Carolyn
    Jones; Leslie Sauer; Edward Boyer; Margaret Dewey; Caren Glotfelty; Carol Reifsnyder; Donald Phoenix; Frank Gill
    and Rick Mullen of the Academy of Natural Sciences; J.C. Fisher Motz; Carol Franklin; Liz Colley; and James Reilly,
    executive director, Hugh Moore Parkway.

"Outer Wilmington Beltway Corridor Study." Dover: Delaware Department of Highways and Transportation, Division
    of Highways, 1973.
    Ian L. McHarg, partner-in-charge; Narendra Juneja; David Hamme; E. Bruce MacDougall; Lewis D. Hopkins; Ed
    Boyer; Meir Gross; and Dennis McGlade.

"Towards a Comprehensive Plan for Environmental Quality." Washington, D.C.: American Institute of Planners for the
    U.S. Environmental Protection Agency, 1973.
    Ian L. McHarg, partner-in-charge; Gerald R. Mylroie was the American Institute Planners (AIP) project director.
    An AIP advisory group was formed, which included Robert C. Einsweiler, chairman; Alan Kreditor; James C. Park;
    Robert Paternoster; E. Jack Schoop; Paul H. Sedway; and Harold F. Wise.

"Study of the Integrity of Chesapeake Bay." Annapolis: Maryland Department of State Planning and Chesapeake Bay
    Interagency Planning Committee, 1972.
    David Wallace, partner-in-charge (Ian McHarg had a minor consulting role).

"An Ecological Planning Study for Wilmington and Dover, Vermont." Brattleboro, Vermont: Windham Regional Planning
    and Development Commission and the Vermont State Planning Office, 1972.
    Ian McHarg, project director; Michael Clarke, project manager; David Hamme; Narendra Juneja; and others.

"Comprehensive Planning Study of the Piedmont District, New Castle County, Delaware." Circa 1972.
    Ian L. McHarg, partner-in-charge; David C. Hamme, project director; and others.

With Development Research Associates. "Ecology: Natural Suitabilities for Regional Growth." Denver: Regional Trans-
    portation District, 1972.
    William H. Roberts, partner-in-charge; Ian L. McHarg, consulting partner; Ross Whaley, reconnaissance coordina-
    tor, and others from Colorado State University; F.A. Branson; R.F. Miller; R.S. Aro; Dennis McGlade; Ed Boyer; and
    others.

With Development Research Associates. "Regional Growth 1971–2000." Denver: Regional Transportation District, 1972.
    William H. Roberts, partner-in-charge; Ian L. McHarg, consulting partner; Dennis McGlade; Ed Boyer; and others.

With Development Research Associates. "Ecological Studies of the Regional Transportation District, Denver, Colorado"
    (Interim Technical Memorandum, Task 5 of the Joint Venture). Denver: Regional Transportation District, 1971.
    William H. Roberts, partner-in-charge; Ian L. McHarg, consulting partner; Ross Whaley, reconnaissance coordina-
    tor; William Marlatt; Stanley Schumm; Robert Longenbaugh; Robert Heil; Dale Romine; William Moir; and Harold
    Steinhoff.

"Amelia Island, Florida: A Report on the Master Planning Process for a Recreational New Community." Hilton Head
    Island, South Carolina: The Sea Pines Company, 1971.
    William H. Roberts, partner-in-charge; Jonathan Sutton, project director; Ian L. McHarg, consultant partner; Jack
    McCormick, vegetation studies and coordinator of the work of natural scientists; Dennis McGlade; and others.

"Ecological Planning Study for the New Community." Houston, Texas: George Mitchell Development Corporation, 1971.
    Ian L. McHarg, partner-in-charge.

"Skippack Creek Ecological Study, Montgomery County, Pennsylvania." Norristown, Pennsylvania: Commissioners of
    Montgomery County and the Supervisor of Lower Providence Township, 1970.
    Ian L. McHarg, partner-in-charge; Michael Clarke; Ruth Patrick; and others.

"Ecological Study for Twin Cities Metropolitan Region, Minnesota." Prepared for Metropolitan Council of the Twin
    Cities Area. Philadelphia: U.S. Department of Commerce, National Technical Information Series, 1969.
    Ian L. McHarg, partner-in-charge; Narendra Juneja; Ravindra Bhan; Charles Meyers; Derik Sutphin; James
    Veltman; Michael Clarke; Thomas Dickert; Robert Drummond; Keith Grey; Anthony Neville; Richard Ragan; and
    Mark Turnbull.

"Sunstein Garden." Philadelphia, Pennsylvania: Lee and Emily Sunstein, late 1960s.
    Ian L. McHarg, landscape architect.

"An Ecological Study for the Future Public Improvement of the Borough of Richmond [Staten Island]." New York: City of
    New York Office of Staten Island Development, Borough President of Richmond, and Park, Recreation and Cultural
    Affairs Administration, 1969.
    Ian L. McHarg, partner-in-charge; Narendra Juneja; Charles Meyers; Derik Sutphin; Robert Drummond; Richard
    Ragan; Ravindra Bhan; Archibald Reid; and Howard M. Higbee.

"Least Social Cost Corridor Study for Richmond Parkway, New York City." New York: New York City Department of Parks and Recreation, 1968.
Ian L. McHarg, partner-in-charge; Narendra Juneja, project supervisor; Derik Sutphin; Lindsay Robertson; and Charles Meyers.

"Toward a Comprehensive Landscape Plan for Washington, D.C." Prepared for the National Capital Planning Commission. Washington, D.C.: U.S. Government Printing Office, 1967.
Ian L. McHarg, partner-in-charge; Narendra Juneja; Derik Sutphin; Charles R. Meyers, Jr.; Karen Meyers; Lindsay Robertson; and Robert Drummond.

"The Lower Manhattan Plan." New York: New York City Planning Commission, 1966.
David Wallace, partner-in-charge, and Ian L. McHarg, William Roberts, and Thomas Todd, consulting partners.

"The Lower Manhattan Plan, Summary Report." New York: New York City Planning Commission, 1966.
David Wallace, partner-in-charge, and Ian L. McHarg, William Roberts, and Thomas Todd, consulting partners.

"Red Clay Creek Reservation Study, New Castle County, Delaware." Red Clay Creek Association, mid-1960s.
Ian L. McHarg, partner-in-charge.

"West Point Area Study, Hudson River Valley, New York." Tarrytown, New York: Hudson River Valley Commission, mid-1960s.
Ian L. McHarg, partner-in-charge.

With American Institute of Architects Task Force on the Potomac and the University of Pennsylvania. "The Potomac." Washington, D.C.: U.S. Government Printing Office, 1965–1966.
David Wallace, partner-in-charge; Ian McHarg; Narendra Juneja; Nicholas Muhlenberg; D. Bradford; S. Manwell Bradford; John Chitty; Barry Christie; Marjorie Dawson; Gary Felgemaker; Richard Galantowicz; Louise Kao Leach; Charles Meyers; John Murphy; William Rosenberg; James Sinatra; Griet Terpstra; Joachim Tourbier; Richard Westmacott; and Mary Wolfe.

"A Comprehensive Highway Route Selection Method Applied to I-95 between the Delaware and Raritan Rivers." Princeton, New Jersey: Princeton Committee on I-95, 1965.
Ian L. McHarg, partner-in-charge; Narendra Juneja; and Lindsay Robertson.

Wallace-McHarg Associates Projects (1963–1964)

"Inner Harbor Master Plan." Baltimore, Maryland: City of Baltimore, 1964.
David Wallace, partner-in-charge; Ian McHarg, consulting partner with Thomas Todd, William Roberts, Narendra Juneja, and Lindsay Robertson.

"Plan for the Valleys." Towson, Maryland: Green Spring and Worthington Valley Planning Council, 1964.
David A. Wallace, Ian L. McHarg, Thomas A. Todd, William H. Roberts, Ann Louise Strong, William G. Grigsby, Nohad Toulan, Anthony Tomazinas, and others.

"May's Chapel Village, Greenspring Valley, Maryland." Baltimore County, Maryland: Keelty Realty Corporation, 1963.
Ian L. McHarg, partner-in-charge, and William Roberts, project director.

"Lauer Farm." Wyomissing, Pennsylvania: Wyomissing Foundation, 1963.
    Ian L. McHarg, partner-in-charge; William Roberts; and Nicholas Muhlenberg.

As Ian L. McHarg, Landscape Architect (1945–1962)
Landscape Plans and Designs

Parks and Plazas

Southwest Washington Town Center Park, Washington, D.C.

Delaware River Park, Philadelphia, Pennsylvania

Farragut Square, Washington, D.C.

York Memorial Park, York, Pennsylvania

Fables Memorial Park, Cranford, New Jersey

Maple Shade Park, Maple Shade, New Jersey

Springfield Township, Philadelphia, Pennsylvania

Swiss Pines, Phoenixville, Pennsylvania

Pennsylvania State Office Building, Philadelphia, Pennsylvania (1955)

Universities, Schools, and Colleges

Germantown Friends School, Philadelphia, Pennsylvania (with Anthony J. Walmsley and Michael Langlay-Smith,
    1960–1961)

Medical Research Building, University of Pennsylvania, Philadelphia, Pennsylvania (Louis I. Kahn, Architect, with
    Anthony J. Walmsley, 1960)

Botany Building, University of Pennsylvania, Philadelphia, Pennsylvania (with Anthony Walmsley, 1960)

Campus, University of Pennsylvania, Philadelphia, Pennsylvania (with Anthony J. Walmsley, 1959–1960)

Woodland Avenue Gardens, University of Pennsylvania, Philadelphia, Pennsylvania (1955)

Plattsburg Junior College, Plattsburg, New York

Stamford Nursery School, Stamford, Connecticut

Housing

Southwark Public Housing, Society Hill, Philadelphia, Pennsylvania (Oscar Stonarov and Frank Haws, architects, 1959)

Red Rock Heights, San Francisco, California

Jenkintown Apartments, Jenkintown, Pennsylvania

Eastwick New House Study, Philadelphia, Pennsylvania

Eastwick, Area #1, Philadelphia, Pennsylvania

Henry Meigs Development, Philadelphia, Pennsylvania

Shopping and Town Centers

Cheltenham Shopping Center, Philadelphia, Pennsylvania (Solomon Kaplan, architect, and with contributions by Anthony J. Walmsley and Michael Langlay-Smith 1959–1960)

Newtongrange Town Center, Newtongrange, Scotland

Gardens

Mrs. Albert M. Greenfield, Philadelphia, Pennsylvania (with Anthony J. Walmsley, 1959–1960)

Lloyd Wells, Whitemarsh, Pennsylvania

Miller House, Norristown, Pennsylvania

Lawrence K. Meltzer, Philadelphia, Pennsylvania

Cemetery

Design of Cemetery for British Soldiers Killed in Action in Greece. British Army War Graves Commission, Athens, Greece (1945).

Miscellaneous Professional Report

Lieutenant Ian L. McHarg, editor and collator, and Major McNeil, translator. *Report on Destruction and Repairs to Apulian Aqueduct.* Bari, Italy: Allied Army Command (September–October 1943).

FILMS, TELEVISION, AND VIDEO

Chris Zelov, producer. *Ecological Design: Inventing the Future.* Cape May, New Jersey: Ecological Design Project, 1994.
   Ian McHarg appears in this film about design and planning projects influenced by R. Buckminster Fuller.

Joan Saffa, producer. *Lawrence and Anna Halprin: Inner Landscapes.* San Francisco: KQED-TV, 1991.
   Ian McHarg appeared in the documentary.

Frederick Steiner, Bob Curry, and Bill Wagner. *The Only Essential Industry: Farmlands Preservation in Whitman County, Washington.* Pullman, Washington: KWSU-TV Film Documentary, 1979.
   Ian McHarg was interviewed in the documentary.

Glen Fleck, producer. *Pardisan.* Venice, California: Charles Eames Studio, 1977.

Austin Hoyt, producer; Ian McHarg, organizer and on-screen host. *Multiply and Subdue the Earth.* Boston: WGBH, 1969.

Ian L. McHarg. *The House We Live In* (TV series). New York: CBS; Philadelphia: WCAU-TV, 1960–1961. Guests included Harlow Shapley, David Goddard, Carleton Coon, Margaret Mead, Abraham Heschel, Gustave Weigel, Paul Tillich, Swami Nikhilananda, Alan Watts, Erich Fromm, Julian Huxley, Loren Eiseley, Lewis Mumford, Arnold Toynbee, Alexander Leighton, Kenneth Rexroth, Frank Frazer Darling, Luna Leopold, and others.

PROFILES AND CRITICAL REVIEWS

David Salvesen. "The Woodlands, Special Award, The 1994 ULI Awards for Excellence." *Urban Land* 53, no.12 (1994):24.

Cynthia L. Girling. "The Marketing of Recreation and Nature: The Woodlands, Texas Revisited." In *CELA 1993 Public Lands/scapes Proceedings of the 1993 Conference of the Council of Educators in Landscape Architecture*, edited by Robert G. Ribe, Robert Z. Melnick, and Kerry Ken Cairn, pages 43–56. Washington, D.C.: Landscape Architecture Foundation, 1994.

Richard Ingersoll. "L'Orizzonte perduto delle città nuove: The Woodlands e Almere nella vastità megalopolitana" (The lost horizon of new towns: The Woodlands and Almere in the megalopolitan sprawl). *Casabella* 614 (1994): 22–35 (English summary pages 70–71).

Amedeo Petrilli. "Design with Nature [by] Ian L. McHarg [book review]." *Spazio e Societa* 16, no. 64 (October–December 1993):127–128.

Daniel S. Smith. "The Woodlands, Texas." In *Ecology of Greenways*, edited by Daniel S. Smith and Paul Cawood Hellmund, pages 196–202. Minneapolis: University of Minnesota Press, 1993.

William Thompson. "A Natural Legacy: Ian McHarg and His Followers." *Planning* 57, no. 11 (1991):14–19.

Laura Biondi. "Progettare con la Natura." *Casabella* 54, no. 574 (December 1990):29.

Heidi Landecker. "In Search of an Arbiter." *Landscape Architecture* 80, no. 1 (1990):86–90.

John Gilbert Widrick. "Ian McHarg." In *The Book of the School,* edited by Ann L. Strong and George E. Thomas, pages 178–179. Philadelphia: Graduate School of Fine Arts, University of Pennsylvania, 1990.

Marshall Ledger. "On Getting the Lay of the Land." *The Pennsylvania Gazette* 85, no. 4 (1987):30–36.

Joseph C. Dunstan. "Design with Nature, 14 Years Later." *Landscape Architecture* 73, no. 1 (January 1983): 59, 61.

Keith Croes. "Profile: Ian McHarg." *County Lines* (June 1982):18–25.

B.J. Lee. "An Ecological Comparison of the McHarg Method with Other Planning Initiatives in the Great Lakes Basin." *Landscape Planning* 9 (1982):147–169.

Harvey Shapiro. "The Introduction of the McHargian Method to Japan." *Landscape Architecture* 69, no. 6 (November 1979): 575–577.

Constance Holden. "Ian McHarg: Champion for Design with Nature." *Science* 195 (28 January 1977):379–382.

———. "Ian McHarg: Champion for Design with Nature." *Landscape Architecture* 67, no. 2 (March 1977): 154–156, 180.

Lewis D. Hopkins. "Methods for Generating Land Suitability Maps: A Comparative Evaluation." *Journal of the American Institute of Planners* 43, no. 4 (1977): 386–400.

Yukihisa Isobe and Harvey A. Shapiro. "Ecological Planning: Its Method and Application. Part II, The Implications of Ecological Planning Regions for Land Use Policy Making and Planning in Japan" (special issue). *Kenchiku Bunka* 32, no. 367 (May 1977): 29–152 (in Japanese).

Yukihisa Isobe, Harvey A. Shapiro, and Teiji Ito. "Ecological Planning: Its Method and Application. Part I" (special issue). *Kenchiku Bunka* 30, no. 344 (June 1975):47–136 (in Japanese).

Andrew J. Gold. "Design With Nature: A Critique." *Journal of the American Institute of Planners* 40, no. 4 (1974):284–286.

———. "Planner McHarg on Cities, Cars and Chicken Dung." *People Weekly* (April 1974):48–51.

Dennis Farney. "Land Politics." *The Atlantic Monthly* 233, no. 1 (January 1974):10–17.

David Streatfield. "Ideas into Landscape: Leaders Do Not Wait to Be Called." *Landscape Architecture*, no. 2 (1972): 148–151.

Jean-Paul Viguiar. "L'évaluation d'impact des décisions sur l'environnement: Trois approaches Américaines." *Urbanisme: Revue Française* 41, no. 129 (1972):11–14.

Irene Kiefer. "An Angry Advocate for Nature's Plans." *Smithsonian* 2, no. 10 (January 1972):54–57.

Michael Laurie. "Notes on Professor Ian McHarg." *Edinburgh Architectural Association Yearbook* 15 (1971):97–103.

Dennis Farney. "Father Nature." *Wall Street Journal* 178, no. 42 (August 1971):1.

R. Burton Litton, Jr., and Martin Kieieger. "Design with Nature." *Journal of the American Institute of Planners* 37, no. 1 (1971):50-52.

Y. Isobe. "Leaders for Tomorrow's America: V=Ian L. McHarg, Design with Nature." *Kenchiku Bunka* 26, no. 291 (January 1971):149–166 (in Japanese).

Max Ways. "How to Think About the Environment." *Fortune* 81, no. 2 (1970):98.

Roger Barnard. "Man in Nature: On Ian McHarg." *Journal of the Royal Institute of Architects* 77 (May 1970):211–212.

Ursula Cliff. "Ian McHarg: The Designer as Ecologist." *Design and Environment* 1, no. 2 (1970):28–32, 65.

———. "Environment—The Land: How to Design with Nature." *Time*, 10 October 1969, 70–71.

———. "Ian McHarg vs. Us Anthropocentric Clods." *Life*, 15 August 1969, 48B–48D.

———. "Ian L. McHarg." *Parks & Recreation*, 7 (July 1969):27–29.

Raymond K. Belknap and John G. Furtado. "The Natural Land Unit as a Planning Base." *Landscape Architecture* 58, no. 2 (1968):145–147.

———. *Three Approaches to Environmental Resource Analysis*. Washington, D.C.: The Conservation Foundation, 1967.

Edward J. Milne. "Providence Tomorrow?" *The Rhode Islander Magazine* (*Providence Sunday Journal*), 11 June 1950, 1–6. (A Review of Harvard graduate student plan for downtown Providence, Rhode Island. The team included Robert L. Geddes, William J. Conklin, Ian L. McHarg, and Marvin Sevely.)

PUBLISHED INTERVIEWS
AND PANEL DISCUSSIONS

GIS World Interview. "Ian McHarg Reflects on the Past, Present and Future of GIS: 1995 GIS World Lifetime Achievement Award Winner." *GIS World* (October 1995):46–48.

Louise Mozingo. "Ecologically Informed Designers: An Interview with Ian McHarg." *On the Ground* 1, no. 2 (1995):1–4.

E. Lynn Miller and Sidónio Pardal. *The Classic McHarg: An Interview.* Lisbon, Portugal: CESUR, Technical University of Lisbon, 1992.

Michael Leccese. "At the Beginning, Looking Back." *Landscape Architecture* 80, no. 10 (October 1990):92–97.

Cliff Ellis, editor. "Ian McHarg on City Planning." *Berkeley Planning Journal* 3, no. 2 (1987–1988):34–35.

Larry Paul Fuller, editor. "The Land: America the Beautiful" (panel discussion including Ian McHarg). In *The Land, the City and the Human Spirit*, pages 18–20. Austin, Texas: University of Texas, 1985.

Ed Hollander, editor. "An Interview with Ian McHarg." *Penn in Ink* (Spring 1982):41–43.

Charles Blessing, Edmund N. Bacon, Oscar Newman, Ian McHarg, and George Ramsey. "Five Experts Describe their Concept of the Ideal City." *Planning* 44, no. 11 (December 1978):30–33.

MY (pseudonym, author's full name unknown). *What Do We Use for Lifeboats When the Ship Goes Down? Conversations with Robert Reiner, John Todd, Ian McHarg, Paoli Soleri, and Richard Saul Wurman.* New York: Harper Colophone, 1976. Copyright held by "Observations from the Treadmill, RFD 1, Union, Maine 04862." Interview with McHarg is referred to as Lifeboat 3, pages 99–120.

Urban Design Jury (Charles A. Blessing, M. Paul Friedberg, and Ian L. McHarg). "No Awards, No Citations." *Progressive Architecture* 53 (January 1972):102–109.

James Nathan Miller. "A Sensible Plan for Future Development." *Reader's Digest* 97, no. 580 (1970):77–81. Translated into Italian: "Evitiamo che il progresso distrugga l'ambiente." *Selezione del Reader's Digest* (Ottobre 1970):35–39.

Ian McHarg and Athelstan Spilhaus. "Two Views of the Environmental-Ecological Problems" (Excepts from talks at the Sixth Annual Architects and Engineers Forum in Los Angeles, April 14, 1970, on "Cities in the 70s"). *Environmental Design: West* 1, no. 4 (August–September 1970).

———. *Proceedings of the National Conference on Instruction in Landscape Architecture.* Asilomar, Pacific Grove, California, July 5–7, 1957.

MISCELLANEOUS

Russell Clive Claus. "The Woodlands, Texas: A Retrospective Critique of the Principles and Implementation of an Ecological Planned Development" (master's thesis). Cambridge, Mass.: Department of Urban Studies and Planning, Massachusetts Institute of Technology, 1994.

Peter Walker and Melanie Simo. *Invisible Gardens: The Search for Modernism in the American Landscape.* Cambridge, Mass.: MIT Press, 1994. (The authors include a chapter, "The Environment: Science Overshadows Art," in which McHarg's work is featured and contributions by other leading landscape architects are briefly mentioned.)

Cynthia L. Girling and Kenneth I. Helphand. *Yard–Street–Park.* New York: John Wiley & Sons, 1994 (The authors describe the planning of the Woodlands and its contributions to new community design.)

James Bischoff. "From Barn to Royal Cottage: The Planning of Old Farms Forest—Devonwood, USA." *Ekistics* 58, nos. 346–347 (1991):97–109.

Ann L. Strong and George E. Thomas. *The Book of the School: 100 Years.* Philadelphia: Graduate School of Fine Arts, University of Pennsylvania, 1990.

Frederick Steiner, Gerald Young, and Ervin Zube. "Ecological Planning: Retrospect and Prospect." *Landscape Journal* 7, no. 1 (1988):31–39.

Nao Hauser. "New Year's Dinner from a Country Kitchen." *Bon Appetit* 32, no. 1 (1987):76-84.

George T. Morgan, Jr., and John O. King. *The Woodlands: New Community Development, 1964–1983.* College Station: Texas A & M Press, 1987.

Philip Bedient, Alejandro Flores, Steven Johnson, and Plato Pappas. "Floodplain Storage and Land Use Analysis at the Woodlands, Texas." *Water Resources Bulletin* 21, no. 4 (1985):543–551.

Department of Landscape Architecture and Regional Planning. "501 Course Primer." Philadelphia, University of Pennsylvania, 1985.

Monica Pidgeon. *Ian McHarg, Ecological Planning.* London, England: Pidgeon Audio Visual, 1984. Slide-tape presentation.

Thomas Todd. "The Master Plan for Abuja: The New Federal Capital of Nigeria." In *Land Conservation and Development: Examples of Land-Use Planning Projects and Programs,* edited by F. R. Steiner and H.N. van Lier, pages 115–144. Amsterdam: Elsevier, 1984.

Anne Whiston Spirn. *The Granite Garden: Urban Nature and Human Design.* New York: Basic Books, 1984. (Professor Spirn includes discussion about the Woodlands New Town. She was a participant in the planning and design of the Woodlands.)

Grady Clay. "On Baltimore's Inner Harbor." *Landscape Architecture* 72, no. 6 (November–December 1982):48–53.

Simpson Lawson. "Baltimore Re-Examined." *AIA Journal* 71, no. 13 (November 1982):56–63.

Arthur E. Palmer. *Toward Eden.* Winterville, N.C.: Creative Resource Systems, Inc., 1981.

Narendra Juneja and James Veltman. "Natural Drainage in the Woodlands." In *Stormwater Management Alternatives,* edited by J. Toby Tourbier and Richard Westmacott, pages 143–157. Newark: Water Resources Center, University of Delaware, 1980.

Thomas A Todd. "Nigeria Plans Its New Capital." *Urban Design International* 1, no. 2 (January–February 1980):12–17.

Noel Moffett. "Abuja—The Pros and Cons." *West African Technical Review* (July 1980):94–99.

———. "Abuja: The City of the Future." *West African Technical Review* (June 1980):68–69.

———. "Abuja: The City Plan." *West African Technical Review* (May 1980):76–78.

———. "Abuja: The Regional Plan." *West African Technical Review* (March 1980):116–120.

Ajose-Adedgun and Abubakar Koko. "Nigeria Builds Abuja in the Shadow of Aso Hill." *Architectural Record* 165 (June 1979):37.

Noel Moffett. "The Federal Capital City, Part Two." *West African Technical Review* (May 1978):107–111.

———. "Nigeria's New Federal Capital City." *West African Technical Review* (April 1978):109–113.

Boyd Gibbons. *Wye Island.* Baltimore: Johns Hopkins University Press, 1977. (Boyd Gibbons describes the planning process for a new community on Wye Island, Maryland. The Wallace, McHarg, Roberts and Todd physical plan was directed by William Roberts for James Rouse.)

John Clark. *The Sanibel Report: Formulation of a Comprehensive Plan Based on Natural Systems.* Washington, D.C.: The Conservation Foundation, 1976. (John Clark describes the planning process for the Wallace, McHarg, Roberts and Todd plan directed by William Roberts.)

Grady Clay. "Radicalism Revisited in Wilmington and Dover, Vermont." *Landscape Architecture* 64, no. 3 (April 1974):132.

Philip Morris. "The Southern Seacoast—Keeping Its Balance." *Southern Living* (March 1973):76–83, 103–104.

William H. Roberts and Jonathan Sutton. "Seeking the Right Environmental Fit for a New Resort Community at Amelia Island, Florida." *Landscape Architecture* 63, no. 3 (April 1973):239–250.

Paul Beaver and Bernard L. Krause, composers. *In a Wild Sanctuary* (1970 album dedicated to Ian McHarg and others). Warner Brothers Records. W.B. 1850.

David A. Wallace, editor. *Metropolitan Open Space and Natural Process.* Philadelphia, University of Pennsylvania Press, 1970.

Department of Landscape Architecture and Regional Planning. "An Ecological Approach to Regional Planning." Philadelphia: Graduate School of Fine Arts, University of Pennsylvania, 1968.

William H. Whyte. *The Last Landscape.* Garden City, N.Y.: Doubleday, 1968.

P/A Staff. "Ecology: Man Shapes His Environment." *P/A News Report* (September 1967):51–55.

G. Holmes Perkins. *University of Pennsylvania, Graduate School of Fine Arts* (exhibition catalog of work of the School on the occasion of the American Institute of Architects' 1960 Convention in Philadelphia). Philadelphia: University of Pennsylvania, 1960.

John D. Black and Ayers Brinser. *Planning One Town, Petersham, a Hill Town in Massachusetts.* Cambridge, Mass.: Harvard University Press, 1952. (Based on a Harvard student studio project by Robert Barre, William Barton, Sanford Farness, Roscoe Jones, Donald Kimmel, George Kolinsky, Charles Lettek, Blanche Lemco, Ian McHarg, Vincent Oredson, Harold Taubin, Caleb Warner, and J. E. Zemanek.)

Index

Page numbers in italic refer to illustrations or captions.